Articulation and Voice

ARTICULATION AND VOICE

Improving Oral Communication

Robert G. King

Bronx Community College of the City University of New York

Eleanor M. DiMichael

Board of Education, New York City Bureau for Speech Improvement

Macmillan Publishing Co., Inc.
New York

Collier Macmillan Publishers
London

Copyright © 1978, Macmillan Publishing Co., Inc.

PRINTED IN THE UNITED STATES OF AMERICA

All rights reserved. No part of this book may be reproduced or transmitted in any form or by any means, electronic or mechanical, including photocopying, recording, or any information storage and retrieval system, without permission in writing from the Publisher.

A portion of this material has been reprinted from *Improving Articulation and Voice*, by Robert C. King and Eleanor M. DiMichael, copyright © 1966 by Macmillan Publishing Co., Inc.

Macmillan Publishing Co., Inc.
866 Third Avenue, New York, New York 10022
Collier Macmillan Canada, Ltd.

Library of Congress Cataloging in Publication Data

King, Robert G
    Articulation and voice.

    Bibliography: p.
    Includes index.
    1 Voice culture. 2. English language—Phonetics. I. DiMichael, Eleanor M., joint author.
II. Title.
PN4162.K46   808.5   76–24464
ISBN 0–02–364250–5

Printing: 1 2 3 4 5 6 7 8   Year: 8 9 0 1 2 3

To Four Master Teachers—
Johnnye Akin, Rena Calhoun,
Magdalene Kramer, Claude M. Wise

Preface

FOR a second time, we two have collaborated and the result is this textbook, *Articulation and Voice*. This volume is not a revision of our first book, *Improving Articulation and Voice*, but we have used a few paragraphs and exercises from it. Although this entire book is a product of genuine co-labor, Robert King is primarily responsible for the section on articulation, and Eleanor DiMichael is primarily responsible for the section on voice.

In both parts of this book we begin with a chapter on basic principles, grounded in sound communication theory and linguistics. We are writing for general students, and we have tried to make these chapters as clear and concise as possible. We have tried to limit ourselves to providing only the information students really *need* to know. We hope you will find us frank and honest, but not insensitive; our style clear and comprehensible, but not condescending.

Unlike most other books in the field, this book begins with articulation rather than voice. This order is not accidental; our years of teaching experience have led us to conclude that this approach is more effective. We believe that a sound program of articulation improvement provides a good basis for voice improvement. Noticeable changes will take place in the sound of your voice when you learn to produce sounds clearly and precisely. Improved articulation is basic and necessary to a successful program of voice improvement.

We have attempted to organize the material in a step-by-step approach. In Part I, we deal first with the sounds of the American English language, then with sounds in context and in combinations, next with whole words, and finally with the elements of rhythm and melody. When treating sounds, we first explain how the sound is produced. We then discuss each of its major variations (allophones) and each of the common problems or deviations related to the sound. Finally, we give exercises designed to help students overcome problems in producing that sound. We have attempted to make the exercises specific, useful, and fun. We do not believe in tongue-twisters, but rather think the exercises should help prepare you for improved everyday speech.

In Part II, we have organized the material around the four elements or aspects of voice: quality, loudness, pitch, and rate. The part on voice begins with what we believe are the basic components of good voice production: relaxation, respiration, and resonance. We have provided the theories you need to know and understand for your program of voice improvement. This is not a book on speech pathology for pathologists. We think speech pathologists would find our explanations accurate, but elementary. We have tried to be as specific as possible with regard to voice problems, and we have provided you with practical, usable, and effective voice improvement exercises. These exercises have come out of years of experience in classroom teaching and private practice in speech improvement.

From our students and our colleagues over the years, we have learned much, and we acknowledge that debt. We have been exposed to master teachers of Phonetics and Voice and Diction, who would recognize many of the concepts and some of the techniques. To Lloyd Chilton, executive editor at Macmillan, who has encouraged and assisted us in the preparation of this manuscript, we are especially grateful.

R. G. K.

E. M. D.

Contents

I
Articulation

Articulation Glossary

Abutting consonants: Two different, adjacent consonants; one ends (terminates) the first syllable and the other starts (initiates) the following syllable.

Addition: An articulation error, in which a sound is added or inserted that does not belong.

Affricate: A single consonant phoneme produced by combining the articulations for a stop and a fricative.

Allomorph: A variation (variant form) of a morpheme.

Allophone: A variant form of a phoneme; there are two kinds of allophones of a phoneme: those that can be used interchangeably without affecting meaning and those that appear only in certain contexts.

Alphabet: A set of written letters that tries to represent the phonemes (the speech sounds) of the language; the English alphabet has twenty-six letters to represent forty-two phonemes.

Alveolar ridge: The gum ridge behind the upper front teeth.

Articulation: Obstruction (either partial or complete) of the outgoing air stream by the lips, teeth, tongue, palate, and velum.

Aspiration: Release of a sound with a puff of air.

Assimilation: A change in a sound caused by the influence of a neighboring sound.

Bilabial: Articulated by the two lips.

Centralizing (centering): Centralization is a distortion of a sound caused by raising the tongue in the center of the mouth instead of the front or the back.

Cognate: One of a pair of sounds, articulated in the same place and released in the same manner, but distinguished from each other by the presence or absence of vocal fold vibration.

Compound consonant: A group of two or more consonants that serve to initiate or terminate a syllable.

Consonant: A speech sound characterized by obstruction, either partial or complete, of the outgoing air stream.

Continuant: A consonant on which the air stream is impeded, but not completely stopped; a sustainable consonant; a consonant that can be continued (held on to).

Contour: The pitch pattern (melody) of a phrase; each contour contains at least two pitch levels and a phrase terminal.

Dentalization: Distortion of a sound by placing the tongue on the teeth.

Devoicing: Weakening of vocal vibration on a voiced consonant because of the influence of a neighboring voiceless sound or of the pause following the sound.

Diacritical marks: Modifying marks used by dictionaries, in combination with letters of the alphabet, to represent pronunciation.

Dialect: A variation of a language spoken by a regional or social group.

Digraph: A combination of two written letters representing one speech sound: for example, *th* in *thing*, *ph* in *phony*, and *ng* in *ring*.

Diphthong: A blend of two vowels, the first of which is fairly strong and the second of which is relatively weak.

Dissimilation: A sound change in which one of two similar or repeated sounds is altered to become less like the other one.

Distortion: An articulation error, in which a sound is changed by being produced in an unusual way.

Enunciation: How clear and understandable speech is; how precise the articulation is.

Etymology: The study of the derivation of words; etymology is a division of lexicology.

Foot: A rhythmic group made up of a single strongly stressed syllable alone or a few syllables grouped around a single strongly stressed syllable.

Form words: Words that do not usually carry main ideas, but are necessary for the form (grammar) of our sentences; form words have a strongly stressed form and a weakly stressed form (the more commonly used of the two forms).

Fricative: A consonant on which the air stream is emitted with audible friction because the air is forced out between two articulators.

Fronting: Distortion of a sound by arching the tongue near the front of the mouth rather than at the back or center of the mouth.

Functional varieties: Those varieties of an idiolect that differ in degree of formality or informality.

Glide: A consonant on which the articulators move from one position to another.

Glottal stop: A stop sound made at the glottis.

Glottis: The space between the vocal folds.

Grammar: The study (descriptive, not prescriptive) of the patterns used in forming words and sentences.

Haplology: Omission, in speech, of one or two repeated consecutive sounds or syllables.

Homonym: A word written like and pronounced like another word of the same language, but different in meaning.

Homophone: A word pronounced like another word of the same language, but different in spelling and meaning.

Homorganic sounds: Sounds articulated at the same place; for example, /t/ and /l/ are homorganic because both are articulated by the tongue tip on the alveolar ridge.

Idiolect: An individual's personal variety of a language.

International Phonetic Alphabet (IPA): A symbol system devised by the International Phonetic Association to represent the sounds of the principal languages of the world; each symbol represents one sound—no matter what the language.

Interpersonal: Between persons; person to person.

Intonation: Melodies that result from pitch changes and pitch differences in phrases.

Intrapersonal: Inside a person; within one human being.

Labiodental: Articulated by the lips and teeth.

Lateral: The consonant on which the air is emitted over the sides of the tongue.

Lexicology: The study of words as the expressions of ideas.

Lingua-alveolar: Articulated by the tongue and the alveolar (upper gum) ridge.

Lingua-dental: Articulated by the tongue and teeth.

Lingua-palatal: Articulated by the tongue and the palate.

Lingua-postalveolar: Articulated by the tongue and the area just behind the alveolar ridge.

Lingua-velar: Articulated by the tongue and the velum.

Melody: The "tune" of a phrase, created by the varying pitches used in its utterance.

Metathesis: Reversal of sounds.

Morpheme: The smallest meaningful unit in a language; a meaning unit from which words are made; a root, a prefix, or a suffix.

Morphology: The study of word formation.

Nasalization: A distortion caused by nasal resonance on non-nasal sounds.

Nasals: Consonants on which the air is emitted through and resonated in the nose.

Nonphonemic diphthong: Blend of two vowels, each of which retains its phonemic identity.

Nonstandard dialects: Varieties of a language that differ from the variety spoken by those in positions of power and prestige.

Nonverbal: Without words; not in words.

Occlusion: The bringing of the edges of the inner surfaces of the upper front teeth and the edges of the outer surfaces of the lower front teeth together.

Omission: An articulation error, in which a sound is left out (omitted) in the pronunciation of a word.

Oral: Made by, or related to, the mouth.

Phonation: The vibratory process by which sound is produced at the vocal folds.

Phone: A speech sound.

Phoneme: A significant sound; a sound that may distinguish one word from another word; a group of phonetically related or similar sounds (phones) that function as one sound in a given language; a minimum unit of distinctive sound features; the smallest significant sound class; a family of sounds (phones) that are phonetically similar and that may be used interchangeably without affecting the meaning.

Phonemic diphthong: A blend of two vowels that functions in the language as a single sound; a blend of two inseparable vowels that have lost their separate phonemic identity—the blend itself functioning as a distinctive phoneme.

Phonemics: The study of the significantly different sounds (phonemes) of a language.

Phonetics: The study of sounds (phones).

Phrase: A thought group, a sense group, a unified idea that can hang together; a succession of syllables uttered on one stream of outgoing breath; a breath group.

Phrase terminal: The use of rising, falling, or level pitch at the ends of phrases.

Pitch levels: Four significant, relative pitch ranges used in American English intonation.

Prestige Dialect: The variety of a language spoken by the people in positions of power or prestige. (Also called Status Dialect and Standard Dialect).

Pronunciation: The uttering of words; pronunciation involves selecting sounds and syllabic stress.

Raising: Distortion of a sound by elevating (raising) the tongue from the usual position for forming the sound.

Resonation: The process by which sound generated at the vocal folds is amplified in the cavities of the head and chest.

Respiration: The process of breathing, which forms the motor force of speech; we speak on the exhaled air stream.

Retracting: Distortion of a sound by placing the tongue in back of the usual position for forming the sound.

Rhythm: The pattern of pulses or beats created by variations in duration and intensity of syllables.

Semantics: The study of the meaning of words.

Sibilants: The high-frequency sounds characterized by hissing: /s/, /z/, /ʃ/ (sh), /ʒ/ (zh), /tʃ/ (ch), and /dʒ/ (j); the *s* family of sounds.

Simple consonant: A single consonant that serves to initiate (start) or terminate (end) a syllable.

Standard dialect: See Prestige Dialect.

Status dialect: See Prestige Dialect.

Stop: A consonant on which the air stream is completely obstructed (stopped).

Stress: Various degrees of prominence given to a syllable, usually by varying duration, intensity (force or volume), and pitch.

Substitution: An articulation error in which one sound is replaced by another.

Syllable: A sound or group of sounds uttered on one chest pulse, a pulse of air created by slight contraction of the intercostal muscles of the chest.

Syntax: The study of sentence formation.

Unvoicing: Distortion of a voiced consonant by turning it into its voiceless cognate.

Velum: The soft palate.

Verbal: Related to, or using, words.

Vocal: Related to, or produced by, the human voice.

Voiced consonant: A consonant on which the vocal folds vibrate.

Voiceless consonant: A consonant on which the vocal folds do not vibrate.

Vowel: A speech sound on which the air stream is emitted with relatively little obstruction and that is formed by modifying resonance in the mouth.

1

Basic Principles

"VOICE and diction!" we hear you saying. "Voice and diction! They've got me taking voice and diction!" And one of your more cynical fellow students chimes in, "Yeah, voice and diction. Sounds like an old-time vaudeville team. Can't you just hear the M.C. saying, 'And now, ladeez and gentlemen, for your pleasure and edification, we bring you the amazing team of Voice and Diction!' " Then joining in, you say, "No, it sounds to me more like a shyster law firm. 'Got a traffic ticket that needs a fixin'? See the crackerjack law firm of Voice and Diction!' "

Voice and Diction—or maybe the course you have started is called Voice and Articulation. Either way, you have a right to know what you have gotten yourself into. *Voice* is a common word, so you know what it means. A course in voice and diction, or a program of voice improvement (or therapy), will help you overcome any problems you may have with your speaking voice. *Diction* is not a common word; it means speaking clearly, speaking distinctly. Articulation means producing speech sounds. In a program of articulation improvement (diction), you would learn to make all the sounds of a language correctly and clearly. Whether the course is called Diction or Articulation, it will focus on helping you make speech sounds clearly and distinctly—for your own *and* your listeners' sakes.

Of course, the goal of any (speaking) voice program is not just a "beautiful" voice, and the goal of any articulation program is not just making the clear, isolated sounds of a language. The goal is to help you communicate better with other human beings. This book, then, is about *communication*. It is about human communication—communication in and between human beings.

This book is about oral communication, messages spoken and heard, instead of written and read. Other teachers and other books may concentrate on helping you to improve your writing or reading skills. But, important as those skills are, they are outside the scope of this book. We have written this book to help you improve your oral (spoken) communication skills. And we think that is just as important—if not more so!

Of course, improving the way you speak is not easy, but it is certainly possible. You already can speak, sending messages out loud. Maybe you can speak more than one language. But we will work on your oral communication in just one language: American English. And we will concentrate on one dialect (variety) of American English: the dialect spoken by business and professional people in the United States. Sometimes that dialect is called "the Status Dialect"; sometimes it is called "the Standard Dialect." We will talk more about that dialect later, but you should know that, of all the dialects spoken in the United States, it is the one given the greatest prestige.

If you do not now speak "the Status Dialect" of American English, you may want to learn to speak it all the time. Or, you may want to learn it to add to the dialect or dialects you already speak, to be used when you need it. Either way, the choice is yours. But we do want you to know, right from the start, that that is the dialect we are focusing on (teaching), and we assume that it is the dialect you want to learn to speak. Whether you decide to speak it on all occasions or only on certain occasions is up to you.

You already know a lot about communication. We hope to ADD to what you know. You already have ways of speaking. We hope to ADD new or different ways to the ways you already talk, so you will have more *options* (choices) about how you speak. If you have more choices, you gain flexibility over your communication in American English. The more ways of speaking you have to choose from, the more control you have over your communication.

Almost all authorities on communication agree that you learned to speak the way you do now. You can learn to speak in other ways too. Of course, that task is not an easy one, but it is certainly possible! If you learned to speak in the first place, then you can learn new patterns now. Naturally it will take some training and some effort. It took time and effort to develop your present speech patterns (although you probably have forgotten how much effort it was); it will require some time, some motivation, and considerable practice to develop new speech patterns to add to or replace the old ones.

How You Learned: Why You Speak as You Do

Maybe you are saying, "The way I talk is natural to me. If I talked any other way, it would be phony." Then we have to remind you that your speech is not *natural*. It did not just happen. It was learned! You learned to talk as you do now. Maybe it was a long time ago, and you have forgotten all about it, but you acquired your speech patterns.

Of course you were born with certain abilities. But how you developed those abilities and what speech habits you learned with those abilities are the result of accidental influences, over which you had very little control.

The way you talk now may *seem* natural to you, because you are used to it. But it really isn't based on your nature nearly so much as on a collection of accidents.

Why do you talk the way you do? Because of your heredity and your environment. Those two factors shaped your speech—as they did so many other things about you.

Your *heredity* gave you your body; that body provided the structure—the mechanism—that you use when you speak. None of us has any control over his or her genes. We can't change many of the body characteristics we inherited from our ancestors. Of course we can modify and develop the body we inherit, but those modifications are limited. And we can learn to use our bodies in different ways, but there are limits imposed by our bodies there too. For example, you have vocal folds (some people have called them vocal "cords," but that describes them poorly). Those vocal folds are a certain length, width, and thickness. They come with your body. Neither we nor you can change them. However (and that "however" leads us to the second factor) there is environment.

Your *environment* (everything surrounding you) influenced the ways you learned to use the speech mechanism of your body. And the environment factor is pure chance. What country were you born in? What part of the world did you grow up in? What language or languages did your parents speak? What language or languages did your friends and playmates speak? What section of the country did you grow up in? Have you lived in other parts of the country? What schools did you attend? If you grew up in a city, in what area of the city did you live? What was the economic status of your parents? What kind of education did your parents have? What kind of social status did your family have while you were growing up? What ethnic groups did you belong to or associate with? What other organizations or groups did you belong to and associate with? How much did you listen to the radio and watch television as a young child, and what stations and programs did you listen to most? Who did you admire most while you were very young? What kind of image did you have of yourself, and how much did you like that image (self-esteem) when you were a child? What kinds of relationships did you establish with your family and friends? What kinds of speech patterns did you hear or relate to most—and, therefore, adopt as models to be imitated?

The answers to all these questions are important because these aspects of your environment played a part in shaping your speech habits. The language you speak, the variety of that language (dialect) that you speak, the way you produce the sounds of the language, the way you pronounce words, the words you choose to say what you mean, and your own patterns of rhythm and melody (see Chapter 7) when you talk, all are results of your environment and your reaction to that environment.

All of these are acquired; they are not dictated by your body (heredity).

The influences of your environment, your sensitivity to those influences, and the ways you received and reacted to those influences largely determined what communication patterns you learned.

How You May Resist New Learning: Obstacles to Be Overcome

"The way I speak now seems natural to me. Why should I learn another way of talking?" As teachers of voice and articulation we face this question all the time. We have already given you half of the answer. There is no such thing as "natural" speech patterns. You didn't get your speech patterns automatically. You learned them. But the question, "Why should I learn another way of talking?" must be answered. Unfortunately (or fortunately), *you* are the only one who can really answer that question.

First, you have to take a good, honest, critical, analytical look at the way you talk now. You may have taken your speech patterns so much for granted you have never analyzed them at all. You must, if you are going to answer the "Why?" question.

After you have taken this good hard look at your speech patterns (and you may have to use a tape recorder or get a speech teacher or therapist to help you with the analysis), you have to discover whether those patterns suit your purposes and needs well. Of course you have to think through what your purposes and needs are. What kind of job, business, or profession do you want to go into? What kind of social status do you want for yourself and your family? What kind of people will you be socializing with, working with, working for? What people will you be trying to influence? How do those people speak, and what kind of speech patterns do they respect?

Once you know what kind of speech patterns you now have, you need to decide whether those patterns will help you achieve your long-range goals in your personal life and in your career. If you don't know what kind of speech patterns are needed for those purposes, find out. Consult people in those positions and in those fields. It may be that the speech patterns you now have will serve your purposes well. If they suit *all* of your purposes, goals, and needs and if they will *always* suit your purposes, goals, and needs, then there is no reason to learn any new ones. *But,* if your present speech patterns will *not* suit all the communication situations you will face socially and professionally, then you do need to learn new ones.

The decision on whether you should learn new ways of speaking is your own. No one else can make it for you. Unless you are motivated and willing to put out the effort needed, you will probably not learn new speech patterns anyway. But before you decide the question, let us share some of our experiences.

The inability to speak the Status Dialect, or the Standard Dialect, can be a serious handicap to your career plans. A student we know graduated in Accounting with an excellent academic record. He was well trained; he was intelligent; he was ambitious; and he was eager to work. He went to the personnel office of United Parcel Service in New York City to apply for a position in their accounting department. When he asked at the personnel office for an application and an interview, he was told, "They're hiring truck drivers down the hall." The problem was not the color of his skin or the way he was dressed (he was quite neat in jacket and tie), but in the way he spoke. He said only a couple of sentences, but those few sentences impressed the personnel representative as the speech of a truck driver, not that of an accountant. That's a prejudice, you say. Indeed it is. Speech prejudice is very much alive. And it is easier to teach you the speech patterns expected at IBM, UPS, ITT, ATT, and GE than it is to change the attitudes of the people who do the hiring for those companies. There have been all sorts of power movements in this country—Black power and Red power—but Green power is where power "is at" in the United States. And *green* power is what we are talking about. We've heard that "money talks." Maybe so, but if it talks, it talks in the Standard Dialect! And if you want to be cut in on your share of the green power, you will have to be able to talk in that dialect too. If you don't have the ability to speak in that dialect now whenever you want to or need to, then maybe you have found the answer to "Why should I learn another way of talking?"

Some writers have called the Standard Dialect of American English "the national language" to contrast it with those varieties spoken by out-of-the-mainstream, or out-of-power, groups. The inability to speak the Standard Dialect can be a handicap to your "social mobility." One of our students a number of years ago was a bright young man from Brooklyn. He entered Columbia College, the Ivy League college of Columbia University, as a premed student. We remember him most vividly because of his distinctive speech patterns. He had lived all his life in a very small neighborhood in Brooklyn and had associated only with people who lived within a few blocks of his home. He went to a private school in that neighborhood. Indeed, he had hardly ventured out of that tiny neighborhood world until he came to live in the dorm at Columbia as a freshman. He had never listened to radio or TV much because he spent most of his time reading and studying. He spoke the dialect characteristic of his tiny Williamsburg, Brooklyn, New York, neighborhood. A number of the sounds were different from the way most Americans would produce them. And the rhythms and melodies of his sentences would strike most Americans as "foreign!" Almost no one else at Columbia spoke the way this young man did. Everyone who met him and heard him speak noticed his "strange" patterns; most people found his speech patterns distracting, and some found them annoying. After this young man discovered that his speech patterns were interfering with his interpersonal communication (communication with other human beings) in his new social environment, he had to decide whether to learn new patterns. The decision was difficult for him. Everyone he had known and loved all his life spoke in the familiar patterns. But he decided to learn the "national language" because he was not certain he would live the rest of his life in the small community he had come from. He decided that learning to fit in with, and speak like, the larger society did not necessarily mean rejecting the smaller society or unlearning its dialect. He decided there were reasons—social reasons—for learning another way of speaking. Would you have come to the same conclusion?

Some of you, of course, are saying, "But what do *you* think? You're supposed to be the experts. What do you say? *Should* I learn new speech patterns?" If forced to answer, we would say yes on two conditions: (1) that the communication skills you now have are not the most effective possible or are not the patterns used in the Standard American English Dialect; and (2) that your present communication skills will be a handicap to you—personally, socially, or professionally (economically).

If your *real* question is, "*Can* I learn new speech patterns to use when I need them?" the answer is yes—if you want to and are willing to work at it. We have had many students over the years who *have* learned new patterns. It *can* be done.

How You Can Learn New Patterns: A Plan

Of course, it is true that you have been practicing your old speech habits for a long time. Those patterns have been reinforced by repetition. Whether you want to replace the present habits or merely add to them, you will have to work at the process. If you see the need for learning new patterns, If you really want to learn the new patterns, and if you are willing to put out the effort to learn the new patterns, you *can* overcome the obstacles.

To establish a new speech habit requires three steps: (1) awareness of the problem (or difficulty), (2) development of new skills, and (3) transfer of the new skills into everyday use. In this book we try to make you aware of specific problems you may need to work on, to tell you simply and clearly how to develop the new skill, and to give you interesting, realistic practice materials. Through the use of these practice materials, you should be able to establish the new habits and transfer them into your daily speech.

We will work on two different kinds of problems, so the book is divided into two parts. Unlike most books on the subject, this book takes up articulation before it deals with voice. That is no accident; we have done it deliberately. We believe that this order creates a more logical and systematic program of speech communication improvement.

In Part I, "Articulation," you will work on the process of producing the sounds of the language. Our goal is to help you make each of those sounds in the customary way (in the United States) and in a clear and distinct way. To do that, we will have to work to get good oral (mouth cavity), pharyngeal (throat cavity), and nasal (nose cavity) resonance (amplification) on those sounds. All of this work on sound production will affect your voice; it should improve the balance of resonance in your voice.

In Part II, "Voice," we build on the work you have already started in your program of articulation improvement. We take advantage of the skills you have already acquired, or at least begun acquiring, in Part I.

Basic Definitions

Before we begin your program of speech improvement, we must make clear what we mean by some basic words. You will find these words throughout this book, so it is very important that we agree at the very beginning on their definitions. Unless you know and understand the vocabulary we are using, you will not be able to use this book and its program of speech improvement. We will not use technical words that you do not need, but an understanding of the following terms is essential to our study: communication, speech, verbal and nonverbal communication, language, dialect, status dialect, nonstandard dialects, idiolect, and functional varieties.

COMMUNICATION

You hear the words *communicate* or *communication* every day. "The reason I like Toni so much is that we are able to communicate." "Of course Professor Gross talks, but he doesn't seem to try to communicate!" "What we see here," said Cool Hand Luke, "is a failure to communicate." Communication, although a common word, is a technical word. And we are using the word *communication* in a very specific sense.

In its broadest sense, the word *communication* refers to a process in which a response is evoked (elicited or induced) by a message sent and received. In that sense, flipping a switch to turn on a lamp, pushing a button to ring a bell, and the thermostat turning on a furnace are all examples of communication. A message was sent; a message was received; the receiver reacted to the message. Communication occurred.

Some animals can communicate. Bees do a kind of dance, and the other bees know where to find the food supply. Mama pigs can tell the difference between baby pigs' squeals for "I'm hurt" and "I'm hungry." The messages may be simple, but there are messages sent, received, and responded to. It is clearly communication in the broadest sense of the word.

Human communication, a narrower term, refers to communication in which a human being is involved as a sender, a receiver, or both. Some writers have noted that human beings are transceivers (combination transmitters and receivers), and they are right. If you see a picture and respond, human communication has occurred. If you hear a song and respond, human communication has occurred. If you yell at your cat Anathema and she runs to her favorite hiding place, human communication has occurred. If you grip my hand and I understand your feelings, human communication has occurred. In all of these instances, a human being is involved in the communication process. But some of these instances, although part of human communication, are outside the concern of this book.

We are concerned with communication within and between human beings. We are limiting our attention here to human communication where the message sender and the message receiver are *both* human. That is only one aspect of human communication, but it is the only aspect we will deal with in this book. You must keep in mind that if the communication is within one human being (*intra*personal communication), the *same* human being is both sender and receiver of the message. On the other hand, if the communication is between human beings (*inter*personal), one person will be the message sender and the other the message receiver.

Before explaining more about intrapersonal and interpersonal communication (both are very important concepts), we should point out one important characteristic of our definition of communication: it is *receiver*-oriented. For communication to take place, as we have defined it, something or someone must receive a message and react to it. No matter how much transmitting goes on, if the message is not received and reacted to, communication does not occur. Put on the human level: no matter how much talking you do, if nobody listens and responds, there has been no communication. The implications of this receiver-oriented definition of communication are staggering. We are reminded that talking is not a synonym for communication, that a speaker must speak so that his or her listener can and will listen and will respond as the speaker intends, and that a speaker must consider the listener's attitudes and beliefs and adjust to them to get the proper response. This receiver-oriented definition of communication reminds us that the cliché "Do your own thing" is a poor formula for successful interpersonal communication. Some other implications that we need to keep in mind are that the sender may be unaware of what message the receiver got, that the message received may not be the message intended by the sender, that an unintended receiver may pick up the message unknown to the sender, and that the receiver's reaction may be very different from the one the sender wanted to elicit.

We said earlier that we are concerned in this book with communication that occurs within and between human beings. Communication that occurs *inside* a human being is called intrapersonal communication. When we humans think to ourselves, we are both message sender and receiver-responder. When our brain sends messages to parts of our body, and our body responds, intrapersonal communication is happening. Intrapersonal communication is very important in speech production, as we will see later. (See pp. 350–351.)

Communication *between* human beings is called interpersonal communication. To be *inter*personal (*inter* means "between"), the communication must involve a give and take; the participants must be transceivers —both transmitting and receiving messages; and there must be at least two human beings involved. Most writers agree that interpersonal communication takes place in a face-to-face setting, so the participants are aware of each other and can receive impressions (messages) from the other person or persons present, through all the senses. Even if one person does all the talking, all the participants are both sending and receiving messages. We send messages in ways other than just through talking. And we receive messages from other people even when they are not speaking. (See the material on verbal and nonverbal communication on pp. 22–23 .) The speaker picks up messages from the listener(s) while speaking, and listeners send messages back to a speaker without saying a word. Don't be deceived into thinking such a communication situation is one-way communication. It isn't. It is interpersonal, because there is real give-and-take going on.

In interpersonal communication, we strive for *efficient* and *effective* communication. That means that (1) we want the communication process to work so the receiver *understands* the sender's message accurately (*efficiency*), and (2) the sender wants the communication process to work so the receiver will react as the sender intended (*effectiveness*). These basic goals are important to our study.

Interpersonal communication succeeds (is efficient) only if the receiver receives the message the sender intended to send. That should be obvious on the face of it. So the sender (the person talking) must send (talk) in such a way that the receiver can understand the message. That should be obvious too. But doesn't it logically follow, then, that anything in the sender's speech patterns that interferes with the listener's understanding of the intended message must be faced, overcome, and (if possible) eliminated? That principle of interpersonal communication has serious implications for the student of articulation and voice. Are you an efficient interpersonal communicator? If not, what barriers to efficient communication do your speech patterns present? How is the way you speak hindering you from getting across the messages you want to transmit? The articulation and voice improvement program presented in this book is geared to helping you overcome the barriers to efficient interpersonal communication your present speech patterns may impose.

No one sends a message unless that person has a purpose, a goal to achieve. We send messages in order to get particular reactions and responses. A message in interpersonal communication is said to be *effective* when the sender gets the reaction or response that sender wanted. To do that, a speaker must adapt the message to the beliefs, attitudes, expectations, purposes, and background of the listener(s). Again, these interpersonal communication principles contain important implications for us and our study.

Just as you faced potential barriers to efficiency in your transmission, so you must face potential barriers to effectiveness in the way you speak. If there are any aspects of your speech patterns that interfere with your getting the responses you want from listeners, you should face those problems and undertake a systematic program to overcome them so far as possible.

In our discussion of communication we defined it as a process involving the sending of, receiving of, and responding to a message. We noted that human communication requires a human being as sender, receiver, or both. But we narrowed our focus further because we give attention in this book only to two aspects of human communication: intrapersonal and interpersonal. We pointed out that the principles of interpersonal communication have important implications for students of articulation and voice. The goals of efficient and effective interpersonal communication, especially, raise important questions that you must answer in your own mind. If you discover that there *are* barriers to efficient and effective interpersonal communication in your speech patterns, then you should undertake a systematic program of voice and articulation improvement.

SPEECH

We have used the words *speech* and *speak* many times in this book already. Both are everyday words. We all have seen persons bending over someone who is unconscious and saying, "Speak to me!" Or we have heard the comment, "When she's mad at me, she simply refuses to speak." Maybe you have said about someone you know, "I find his (or her) speech unpleasant. The way he (or she) speaks turns me off." But what do the words *speech* and *speak* mean?

One way of defining these words is to give synonyms for them; just give other words that mean the same thing, or at least something similar. If we take that approach, we would tell you that *to speak* is *to talk* and that a person's speech is his or her way of talking. Another way of discovering the meaning of words is to search through dictionaries. One dictionary defines speech as "vocal utterance" ("spoken sounds that mean something"); another dictionary says that speech is "making communicative sounds"; and still another says that to speak is "to utter words with the human voice."

Back in the Dark Ages, when we were majoring in "Speech" at college, we had to memorize a definition of "Speech." The prescribed definition was "Speech is social adaptation and reciprocal stimulation through voice and visible action." That definition focuses on two human uses (functions) for speech: (1) in adapting or adjusting ourselves to the people around us, and (2) in stimulating or influencing the people around us in an effort to make them adjust themselves to us. The definition took note of two elements comprising speech: (1) the use of voice to communicate, and (2) the use of body activity to communicate. As useful as that definition may have been, it has some weaknesses. It omits one of the three major uses, or functions (as we see them), and it combines two of the three elements of speech (as we see them) under the single heading of "voice."

We agree with Frank E. X. Dance[1] that there are three *functions* of speech communication: (1) the development of a person's mental processes, (2) a person's adjustment to his or her environment, and (3) a person's manipulation of (attempts to influence) his or her environment.

We believe there are three distinct *elements* in speech communication: (1) vocal—the use of the human voice, (2) verbal—representing abstractions by a spoken symbol, and (3) physical (physical from the point of view of the sender; visible from the point of view of the receiver)— the use of the entire body, including posture, movement, and facial expression.

All the definitions of the words *speak* and *speech* make it clear that speaking is something that people *do*. It is an action; it is an activity. That action involves something our bodies do (so there is a physiological factor) and something produced that can be heard (so there is an acoustic factor) and seen (so there is a visible factor).[2] R. H. Stetson, in his book *Motor Phonetics: A Study of Speech Movements in Action*, defined speech as "a series of [body] movements made audible"[3] [or hear-able].

[1] (See his essay "Toward a Theory of Human Communication" in his book *Human Communication Theory* (New York: Holt, Rinehart and Winston, 1967), pp. 301–303.)

[2] In his excellent book, *Articulation Testing and Treatment: A Sensory-Motor Approach*, Eugene T. McDonald observes that many textbooks do not offer a clear definition of the word *speech* and confuse the term with *language*, on the one hand, and with the processes by which speech is produced, on the other. If you want his logical, but very technical treatment, see pp. 71 ff. of his book.

[3] R. H. Stetson, *Motor Phonetics: A Study of Speech Movements in Action* (Amsterdam: North Holland Publishing Company, 1958).

Although Stetson did not note the visible component of the end product of speech, his definition does remind us that speech is a communicative *act* involving body processes.

When we human beings speak, we turn our bodies into transmitters. We send out communicative signals by activating, monitoring, and controlling certain movements in the body. There are four related, but separate, processes involved in the transmission of speech communication: respiration, phonation, resonation, and articulation. Later in this book, we will deal with each of these processes in more depth. For now, it is enough to explain each of them briefly.

All sound-making instruments or devices must contain two parts: (1) something that will vibrate, which we call the *vibrator*, and (2) some source of energy or power, which we call the *motor*. Because sound *is* vibration, you can see that it is necessary to have something that will vibrate and something that will set the vibration to going. These two parts are the absolute minimum. But most sound-making instruments also have a third part: something that will amplify, or reinforce, or resonate, the vibration. We call this the *resonator*.

In a guitar, the strings are the vibrator, the fingers of some human being are the motor, and the curvaceous box is the resonator. In a clarinet, the mouthpiece has a reed that serves as vibrator, the player's breath stream is the motor, and the entire tube of the instrument itself is the resonator.

We said earlier that we human beings use our bodies as transmitters. We are sound-making instruments. And our bodies have all the necessary ingredients: the vocal folds in the larynx are the vibrator, the exhaled breath stream is the motor, and the cavities of the throat and head are the main resonators. In addition, we have articulators, which we will explain soon.

There are, then, four processes involved in speech production. Let's look at each of these processes briefly:

1. *Respiration*. The source of power for speech is the stream of air coming from the lungs as we exhale. Of course we have to breathe to stay alive. But breathing for speech is slightly different from breathing for life. In breathing for speech, we must *control* the exhaled breath—deliberately and voluntarily—so it will fit our speech communication needs. Respiration is explained in detail, with directions for developing control over it, on pp. 352–358.

2. *Phonation*. Usually, while we are breathing for life, the air stream in and out makes no noticeable sound. To make sound, we set the air stream into rapid vibration. Sometimes we do this unintentionally, as when we snore. To produce speech, we deliberately set the air stream into vibration. The exhaled breath passes through the larynx (commonly called the voice box). The stream of air passes between the vocal folds

(which are contained within the larynx), and the vocal folds begin to vibrate. The vocal folds generate a complex pattern of vibrations, consisting of a fundamental tone and several overtones (harmonics) when voiced sounds are produced. These vibrations set up sound waves (a tiny buzz, really) that pass outward through the vocal tract. This vibratory process of creating sound waves in the larynx is called phonation. We explain this process in more detail on pp. 360–366.

3. *Resonation*. The tones generated by the vocal folds are tiny and weak. They must be enlarged and strengthened, reinforced, amplified—resonated. The word *resonation* means "the process of sounding again": re+son+ation. And that is exactly what happens in this process. The tones produced by the vocal folds are selectively echoed in the pharynx (the chamber in back of the nose and mouth and above the larynx), the mouth, and the nose. We can modify these cavities (changing the echoing chambers) and thus modify the resonance. We can make the cavities longer or shorter, wider or narrower. We can make their walls softer or harder. We can even shut off cavities, making it possible to resonate sounds in one, two, or all three of the cavities. This process of resonation takes the tiny tones produced in the larynx and, by sympathetic vibration in the pharynx, mouth, and nose, amplifies and enriches the sound. For a more detailed explanation of this process, see pp. 366–370.

4. *Articulation*. Articulation is the process by which the outgoing air stream is divided into distinguishable speech sounds. The word *articulation* comes from a Latin word for *joint*. A joint, as you know, is a place where two things come together. In the process of articulation, we "joint" the outgoing air stream to make individual, recognizable speech sounds. When we articulate, we bring two things together (either completely or partially) to modify the expelled breath. The articulators we use are the lips, teeth, tongue, hard palate, and soft palate. These articulators chop the air stream up into individual speech sounds.

In our discussion of the meaning of the term *speech*, we have defined it as the act of producing audible, visible, and verbal signals. All three elements are important parts of the product: speech communication. Receivers get messages from the voice of the speaker, apart from the words the speaker uses; receivers get messages from the body cues coming from the speaker; and receivers get messages from the words (verbal symbols) used by the speaker. All three elements are included in the term *speech*.

After discussing the meaning of the word *speech*, we turned our attention to the four processes by which speech is produced. We found that (1) air expelled from the lungs provides the energy for speech production (the respiration process); (2) the vocal folds in the larynx can be set into vibration to produce tone (the phonation process); (3) the tone produced in the larynx can be amplified and enriched by sympathetic vibration in the cavities of the throat and head (the resonation process);

(4) and the outgoing air stream can be modified ("jointed") into individual speech sounds (the articulation process).

VERBAL AND NONVERBAL COMMUNICATION

We human beings take in information (receive messages) through the five senses: sight, hearing, smell, taste, and touch. If we receive messages and respond to them, communication has taken place. You can see instantly, then, that lots of the messages you get are not packaged in language at all. This communication without words has been labeled nonverbal communication.

It may seem awkward to divide all communications human beings receive into the two categories of verbal (word messages) and nonverbal (not-word messages). But the division does remind us that words are not the only means of human communication and that any study of speech communication is incomplete without attention to nonverbal elements.

Linguistics, the systematic study of language, is several centuries old. The systematic study of nonverbal communication was begun much more recently. As you would expect, the basic principles of linguistics have been more clearly formulated than the concepts related to nonverbal communication. Experts do not yet agree on the categories that "nonverbal communication" ought to cover. Abne Eisenberg and Ralph Smith list three major types of nonverbal communication, whereas Larry Barker and Nancy Collins list eighteen. In spite of the differences among writers in the field, they agree on some principles important to our study.

We are concerned with nonverbal cues transmitted by human beings and received by human beings. Other elements of nonverbal communication are outside the scope of this book. Speech (the act of transmitting oral messages) includes verbal as well as nonverbal elements. When a person speaks, that person utters words (made out of individual speech sounds). But a person's voice can vary in many ways and still be saying the same word. If you and I have a conversation, will somebody who was not present know what was really expressed by the two of us if that person is dependent on reading a typed transcript of the words of the conversation? Of course not, you say. There might be ambiguities. And besides, tones and feelings are not conveyed in a transcript. You're right. We get part of the meaning—maybe *much* of the meaning—from hearing the voices of people as they speak words. So having an audio tape recording would be much better than having a written transcript. It would add the *vocal* element to the *verbal* element. But even with the audio tape recording, would that third person get *all* the meanings transmitted by the two of us in our conversation? The answer is no, again. There is still an element missing. But give that person a videotape of our conversation, and the missing element is added: the visual component of speech communication. But note: Two of the three elements of speech communication (transmission) are nonverbal.

The implications are clear. Any program of speech improvement worthy of the name must give attention to nonverbal as well as verbal elements of speech communication. True enough, the words will carry the more abstract and intellectual content. But the nonverbal elements will carry most of the emotional content: feelings, attitudes, and physical state. Eisenberg and Smith note: "Broadly, nonverbal messages have three overlapping functions: (1) to clarify, confirm, or deny verbal messages: (2) to reveal the attitudes, emotions, and physical state of the sender; and (3) to define the individual's social identity."[4]

We began this discussion of verbal and nonverbal communication by noting that the five senses are the avenues by which we get messages. Oral verbal messages come to us through only one of those avenues: we only hear them. But nonverbal communication can be received through many different senses. We can, therefore, receive (and respond to) several different nonverbal messages at the same time. Doesn't that help pile up nonverbal messages and make them all the more influential?

LANGUAGES

As important as nonverbal messages are, words carry the heaviest freight of meaning. The two nonverbal elements of human speech communication (the speaker's use of voice and the speaker's use of body) do convey messages about the speaker's emotions. But *idea* messages— abstract concepts—are carried by the verbal element of human speech communication: language.

Words are verbal symbols. When we talk about the verbal symbols of the human race collectively, we call that abstract collection *language*. Language is an abstraction in the same way that law, medicine, and painting are abstractions. Law refers to that area of knowledge dealing with rules governing human conduct; medicine refers to the art or science of preserving or restoring health; painting refers to the art of those who make visual representations (paintings). Like the other three words, language refers to a concept. Language refers to the use of words to stand for things, actions, relationships, and ideas. But that is "language" in the collective sense.

We can talk not only about language in the abstract sense, we can talk about *languages* in a very specific sense. We can talk about languages—just as we can talk about laws, medicines, and paintings. Laws are specific regulations; medicines are specific remedies; paintings are specific products of a painter's skill. *A language* is a specific verbal code.

[4] Abne M. Eisenberg and Ralph R. Smith, Jr., *Nonverbal Communication* (Washington, D.C.: The Bobbs-Merrill Co., Inc., 1971), p. 35.

A code, as you know, is a system of signs or symbols. A language is a code because it is a collection of symbols that stand for ideas. Some writers define a language as "a set of conventional [based on customs] signs."

Our definition is a little more complicated than that, but give us a chance to explain it. We think every word in the definition is necessary. We define a language as "a conventionalized system of arbitrary vocal signs." There are five key words in that definition; each of those words reminds us of some important aspect we need to understand about languages.

First of all, a language is a *system*. It is a code. It has a pattern. It is not just a random collection of words. It is organized; it has structure. There is order to it. That means, then, that a language can be analyzed and that it is predictable. A language has a system.

To the person who does not know the system, a language is a secret code. But to one who has broken the code—figured out the patterns and how they work—it is not secret or mysterious at all. In this book, we are dealing with the system (code) of American English. If that is a foreign language to you, we will try to make the system clear to you—so you can use the code to communicate effectively. If American English is your native language, we hope to increase your understanding of the patterns, so you will be more efficient and effective communicators in that language.

We have noted that a language is a system. That system is made out of *signs*. Signs is another word for symbols. A sign, or symbol, is something that stands for something else. Languages are codes made out of words— verbal symbols. Each language system has its own set of words (or signs). Those words represent meanings in the minds of the people who use the language. Words do not convey (carry) meanings; rather, they stir up meanings (in the minds of the listeners) and stand for meanings (in the minds of the speakers and listeners). It is important to keep in mind that meanings are not in the words themselves, but in the people who use the words. If the meanings were carried in the words themselves, each of us would be able to understand all the languages of the world. The spoken word (no matter what language it was in) would bring the meaning to us—if the meaning were *in* the word. But words are *signs:* they stand for meanings; they are the representatives of our ideas, not the ideas themselves. The word *signs* in our definition of "a language" reminds us that each language system is constructed of verbal symbols that are used to stand for ideas.

We used two words in our definition to limit the word *signs*. We limited the symbols of a language to *vocal* ones. That means we believe a language is made up of *spoken* symbols. A language does not need a written form to be complete. There are still many languages in the world today with no written form. The written form is not the language. The written form is an attempt to *represent* the language. The language itself is made up of words spoken and heard; these *vocal* signs stand for the ideas. When we talk about language throughout this book, we are talking about vocal signs, oral symbols.

Notice that the definition describes those vocal signs (that languages are made out of) as arbitrary. That concept is important. The word *arbitrary* means "not logically supported," "not reasonable," or "random and unpredictable." How does the word *arbitrary* apply to the spoken symbols, or words, of a language? Well, it reminds us that there is no logical connection between the word (the sign-symbol) and whatever it represents (the meaning). The names of things are arbitrary names, chosen at random for no apparent reason. One name for a thing makes just as much sense as another. Is there any sensible reason to call the thing we call a table a "table"? Isn't it just as logical to call that object MEES or TISH or MEHsah or traPEHzee as to call it TAYbul? The other names for the object are from the Parsi, German, Spanish, and Greek languages—spelled so you can pronounce them approximately in those languages. But the thing itself is the same. And the Parsi name for it is no better or worse, no more sensible or less, than the German, the Spanish, the Greek, or the English names for that same object. Which of these is the *right* name for the object? Which is the *logical* name for the object? Those are foolish questions, because the spoken symbols of a language are *arbitrary*.

So far we have discussed four of the five key words in our definition of a language. We have observed that a language is a *system* (code) made of *arbitrary vocal signs*. There is one more factor to be noted. The system is a *conventionalized* system. The word *conventional* means customary, of course. So the word *conventionalized* in our definition reminds us that the structure of a language is based on the customary usage of some group of people. Each language developed among some group of people; each group developed its own set of customary patterns. Those patterns are neither right nor wrong, good nor bad; they are just customary, or conventionalized.

In summary, then, a language is a conventionalized system of arbitrary vocal signs. A language is a structured code, based on the customs of some group of people, made up of spoken symbols chosen at random.

All languages—no matter how complicated (such as Navajo) or how simple (such as English)—have three basic elements:

1. A set of sounds, called phonemes.
2. Regular patterns, called grammar.
3. A collection of words, called vocabulary.

We must look at each of these three elements in more detail, if we are to understand the nature of a language.

1. *Phonemes.* Every language uses a set of sounds. American English has about forty-two such sounds. But different languages use different sounds. Spanish uses approximately thirty-two phonemes. We have some sounds in English that the Spanish language does not have—the vowel sounds in the words sh*u*t and b*oo*k, for example. And Spanish has some sounds we do not have in English—the trilled sound of *rr* in such words as *perro,* for example. One of your authors has had great difficulty trying to master two phonemes in Greek, because the two sounds are very different from any sounds we have in English.

Each language uses a given number of speech sounds, out of which words in that language are made. These basic sounds are called *phonemes.* At the risk of confusing you, we must contrast the words *phone* and *phoneme.* A phone is a sound—any sound; a phoneme is a significant sound. A phoneme, then, is not just a sound; it is a sound that can change the meaning of a word. A phoneme is a sound that may distinguish one word from another word. The *i* in *hill* and the *e* in *hell* are different phonemes in English; they cannot be substituted for each other without changing the meaning of words. In order to master any language, you must learn the phonemes of that language and learn to produce them in the conventional ways. But many phonemes have several differing varieties (called *allophones,* based on the Greek words for *other* and *sound*). Let us prove it to you. Check to see if the *t* sound you make in the words *top, stop, pot, city,* and "*fight* the good fight" are all exactly the same. If you are in doubt, put a candle about four inches away from your mouth and say the first three words again. Do all three *t* sounds have the same amount of explosion when you pronounce the words?

Even though we think of /t/ as one sound—and it is one phoneme (sound family)—it has several differing variations (*allophones*). To master a language fully, you must master not only all the phonemes of the language, you must learn the allophones of each phoneme and which variation to use when.

2. *Grammar.* All languages have regular patterns. Those patterns in a language are called its grammar. Grammar, then, is a description of the structure of a language. It is not a prescription of what ought to be; it is a description of what is. Every language has its own patterns. You can call those patterns rules if you think of rules as presently accepted customs rather than rigid, unchanging laws.

A friend of ours (who learned four other languages before learning English) recently said, "English is so simple; it has no grammar at all!" Of course he was joking. All languages, including English, have grammar; they have predictable patterns. Our friend simply meant that English grammar is much simpler than the grammar of the other languages he knows. Don't you imagine that the simpler patterns of English have helped make it "a world language"?

We can hear some of you saying, "I wish that were true, but English is a very difficult language." Remember, whenever we talk about the language, we are talking about the *spoken* language. The written language, we agree, is a mess; our spelling is not phonetic and is very difficult to learn. But the grammar of the (spoken) language *is* relatively easy. If Spanish was your first language, just compare it with English for a moment. To learn a verb in Spanish, you must learn six times as many forms as you must learn for that verb in English. Look at the future tense of the verb speak, for example:

ENGLISH	SPANISH
I will speak.	*Yo hablaré.*
You will speak.	*Tu hablarás.*
He (she) will speak.	*El (ella) hablará.*
We will speak.	*Nosotros hablaremos.*
You will speak.	*Vosotros hablaréis.*
They will speak.	*Ellos hablarán.*

In English, we use the same form of the verb all the way through the tense. In Spanish, there are six different forms of the verb in that one tense! Every language has its own patterns. Grammar is the study of the patterns used in forming words and sentences in a language. You can guess, then, that grammar has two subdivisions: (1) the study of patterns for making words, called *morphology*, and (2) the study of patterns for making sentences, called *syntax*.

Morphology, the study of word formation, gets its name from the word *morpheme*. Morphemes are the meaning-units that words are made out of. Sounds (phonemes) do not mean anything, you remember; they can *change* meaning, but they do not *have* meaning. Morphemes are units that do *have* meaning. They are the building blocks we put together to form words. You may think of them as roots, prefixes, and suffixes. The word *previewer* is made up of three meaning units or building blocks: *pre* (which means "before"), *view* (which means "to look at"), and *er* (which means "one who"). A previewer, then, is "one who looks at [something] before." The root is *view; pre* is a prefix (because it is put in front of roots), and *er* is a suffix (because it is attached after roots).

You have to know patterns to construct words. If you know that *-er* means "one who" and that it can be attached after any verb (the pattern), you can make up words you have never heard before. If you know the verb *work*, you can build the word *worker*—whether you have been taught that particular word or not.

However, you must be careful. Remember that morphemes have to do with meaning—not with spelling. An *actor* is "one who acts," even though the *-er* is spelled with an *o*. And note that the word *singer* is made up of two morphemes (sing + er), but *finger* is made up of only one morpheme. The word finger is indivisible; a *finger* is not "one who fings." The word *finger* was not constructed of *fing* + *er*. Fing does not mean anything, so it is not a morpheme. Or, put another way, the *er* in finger is a completely different *er* from the one in *singer*.

A morpheme, then, is the smallest unit in a language that has meaning. But, just as phonemes had variations called allophones, morphemes have variations called allomorphs. And you must learn all the variations (*allomorphs*) and which one to use in what instance. An example should make this point clear. Pronounce the word *robes* out loud. If you pronounced the word in the conventional way, the last sound in the word was /z/. The difference between the singular robe and the plural robes is the /z/ sound at the end of the plural word. Now pronounce the word *ropes* out loud. You should notice that the last sound this time is not [z] but /s/. But they both mean the same thing: they both indicate "more than one." There must be at least two allomorphs of the plural morpheme in English. There are. In fact, our little experiment-example is not finished. Now pronounce the word *roses* out loud. What do you add to the word *rose* to show that the word is plural? If you are not sure, say the word *rose* by itself first and then say the word *roses*. In roses, the plural allomorph is different from both of the other two. This time the plural ending was /ɪz/. So there are at least three allomorphs of the plural morpheme in English. Can you figure out the pattern of which variation (allomorph) to use when?

To construct words, you must know word patterns, morphemes, and allomorphs.

Syntax, the second subdivision of grammar, is the study of sentence formation. The word comes from a Greek word that means "to put together in order" or "to draw [soldiers] up in line in battle order." Syntax refers to the patterns for making sentences in a particular language. English has certain patterns for sentences. Other languages may have completely different patterns. One sentence pattern in English, for example, is "I told her." In Spanish, however, you would say, "*Yo le dije.*" (I her told.) You cannot necessarily transfer a pattern from one language to another. Recently, I heard someone say, "Where he went?" That person spoke standard Spanish and understood the customary patterns for sentence construction in Spanish. Unfortunately, the person did not know that the English pattern for such questions is quite different. To express that idea, we use the pattern "Where did he go?"

To construct sentences, you must know syntax, the patterns for making sentences.

3. *Vocabulary.* Words are spoken symbols. They stand for ideas. Every language has a collection of words. The name for that total stock of words in a given language is *lexicon;* it comes from the Greek word for "word."

Lexicology is the study of words as expressions of ideas. The people who compile dictionaries are called lexicographers. There are two divisions to the study we call lexicology: (1) etymology, which is the study of the origin and history of words, and (2) semantics, which is the study of the meaning of words. Etymology traces the evolution of words; semantics studies definitions. Both are outside the scope of this book.

DIALECT

A language is spoken by some group of people, but you know that not all speakers of a language talk alike. There are variations of languages spoken by subgroups. These variations are called dialects. Dialects differ enough from each other to be noticeable, but they do not differ enough from each other to be called different languages.

The distinction between a different dialect and a different language is not always clear; sometimes the distinction is as much based on political and national considerations as on more linguistic and scientific ones. Are Danish and Swedish different languages or merely different dialects of the same language? Well, a Dane could talk to a Swede, each using his own language, and they would probably understand each other's meaning. But, with nationalistic fervor, each would assure you he was speaking a separate and distinct language: citizens of Denmark speak Danish, and citizens of Sweden speak Swedish! But the languages may be separated less by sounds, grammar, and vocabulary than by national boundaries.

In general, though, if a speaker and listener notice differences but can still understand each other, the differences are dialectal. If the differences are so great the speaker and listener cannot understand each other, they are speaking different languages.

All languages, you remember, have three basic elements: (1) a set of sounds, called phonemes; (2) regular patterns for making words and sentences, called grammar; and (3) a collection of words, called vocabulary. Dialects may vary from each other, therefore, in three ways: (1) they may use different sounds; (2) they may use different grammatical patterns; and (3) they may use different words for the same things.

Listen to the Vitalis commercials on TV. Did the person in the commercial talk about "greasy kid stuff," pronouncing the word *greasy* to rhyme with *fleecy?* If so, the person is probably from north of the Mason-Dixon line in the United States. Or did the person pronounce greasy to rhyme with easy? If so, the person is probably a Southerner. That dialectal difference, of course, is a *sound* difference. Can you think of other such examples?

Suppose you asked another student in one of your classes whether the instructor takes attendance in every class, and the other student answered, "Yes, she sure do!" You would understand the other student, but you would probably notice that the word *do* was used where most speakers of American English would use the word *does*. That dialectical difference is a *grammatical* difference.

What do you call drinks like Pepsi, Coke, Seven-Up, and Dr. Pepper? If you are a New Yorker, you call them soda. If you are a Southerner, you call them soft drinks (to distinguish them from hard liquor, no doubt). Or you may call them tonic or pop. These dialectical differences are *vocabulary* differences.

Dialect differences may cause confusion. Sound differences, grammar differences, and vocabulary differences all can present barriers to understanding. But, if we speak the same *language*, we can ask questions and clear up the misunderstandings.

People from the northern portion of the United States may pronounce the words *hoarse* and *horse* alike; people from the South make a clear distinction by pronouncing the word *hoarse* with a long O vowel. If a Southerner thought a Northerner said, "I'm a little horse today," he could saddle the fellow with clarifying questions. In the same way, if a New Yorker stopped in a Georgia grocery store, asked for soda and received a box of bicarbonate of soda, the New Yorker could hand it back and patiently explain that sodas are things you drink. Sooner or later, the Yankee would get the refreshment he wanted.

People who associate together develop common customs. People who associate together develop language customs in common also. These customs, peculiar to the subgroup, are the basis of a language's dialects. People who live in the same region of the country, people who come from the same ethnic group, or people who belong to the same social or economic group may tend to associate together and, therefore, develop a distinctive language variety. A dialect, then, is a variety of the same language spoken by a regional or social group.

STATUS DIALECT, PRESTIGE DIALECT, OR STANDARD DIALECT

One language is as good as another, of course. A language is a tool used for communicating. If both speaker and listener know, understand, and react to a language in an essentially similar manner, that language works for them. In the same way, one dialect is as good as another if it works to accomplish the purposes of the speaker and the listener.

It is equally true, however, that not all dialects have the same status or prestige. There is a dialect of American English (sometimes called the "Standard Dialect") that is accorded more status or prestige than the other dialects. This dialect gets more respect, as comedian Rodney Dangerfield would probably tell you, because it is spoken by the people with the greatest status and prestige in American society. This dialect is spoken by the upper-middle and upper classes. For that reason, it has been called the Business and Professional Dialect. More recently, it has been called the Career Dialect or Career Speech.

Other languages have standard dialects also. If you were a French student studying the pronunciation of French in France, you could check your own pronunciation of the language against the standards set by the French Academy. Spain also has an Academy of scholars to define and describe the standard dialect for Spanish pronunciation. In Great Britain, there is also a preferred standard of pronunciation, but it is not laid down by any official agency or organization of scholars. Rather, it is the dialect that distinguishes the elite, educated class from the lower social classes. This dialect is called "Received British Pronunciation" because it is the kind of language spoken by the people received (entertained) in the homes of those in the highest social stratum.

There is no official agency in the United States to prescribe what is "standard" and what is not in the pronunciation of American English. Nor is there *one* nationally uniform standard ("received") dialect taught in the influential schools and universities of this country. (The "Received British" wipes out regional patterns and sets a nationally uniform pattern for the upper class. See a production of G. B. Shaw's play *Pygmalion* or of the musical *My Fair Lady* for an enjoyable comment on Received British.) However, even *without* an official standardizing agency or Academy and with acceptable regional variations in pronunciation, we can talk about a standard dialect of American English.

"Standard" speech patterns, like good manners in general and table manners in particular, are not prescribed by law, codified in any statute, or decreed by any binding authority. Rather, they consist of socially accepted (and respected) customs, established by the practice of the social leaders of our communities. These social leaders set the styles and fashions for most of our practices; their practice sets up the criteria for what is in "good taste."

There is nothing in the Status Dialect (or Standard Dialect) itself—the sounds, grammatical patterns, or words used in it—that makes it better than any other dialect of American English. The fact that it is the dialect spoken by the people in power—the style setters, the fashion leaders, and the taste makers—gives this dialect its status and prestige. If the people in power spoke a different way, that way would be "standard."

Whether the Status Dialect is *better* than other dialects of the language is really irrelevant. Because this dialect is spoken by those in status positions, the dialect itself is given respect. And, in turn, those people who can speak the Status Dialect are given more respect than those who cannot. Perhaps that should not be true, but is *is* true, and we must deal with reality. The Status (or Standard) Dialect is the dialect used—and expected—in education, business, and the professions. It is the dialect we will teach you in this book.

We mentioned that there are acceptable regional variations of the

Standard Dialect in the United States. You should know, however, that those variations are quite minor and the regional variations are diminishing. The mass media of communication (television, especially) have reduced regional differences and will doubtless continue to do so.

Too, we Americans move around the country a great deal. At least one family in five will move this year. Our constant mobility is helping to melt the regional variations. An executive of IBM told us a few years ago that IBM stands for "I'll be moved!" His company had stationed him in many parts of the United States, but his speech patterns were standard and would be recognized as the Status Dialect whether he was in Atlanta, Boston, New York, Cleveland, Houston, or San Francisco.

NONSTANDARD DIALECTS

Nonstandard dialects are those that differ noticeably from the Standard Dialect. Who would notice? Speakers of the Standard Dialect. And what would they notice? Major differences in the three elements of a language: sounds, grammar, and vocabulary.

Speakers of Standard American English would notice if someone said "Git out!" instead of "Get out!" or described Racquel Welch as "purty" (pretty). They certainly would be aware of the differences if someone said, "Dese are de once" for "These are the ones," or "axed" for "asked," or "She kep' it up" for "She kept it up," or "oncet" for "once." These *sound* differences would be recognized—anywhere in the United States—as nonstandard.

Arthur Bronstein and Beatrice Jacoby prefer the labels "cultivated and educated forms" and "uncultivated and uneducated forms"[5] to the terms *standard* and *nonstandard*. But the principle remains the same. They agree that "cultivated, educated speakers" would look askance if someone said, "We don't never do it" or "I ain't got it." All over the United States, these *grammatical* differences would be recognized as nonstandard.

There are vocabulary differences, too, between the Status Dialect and nonstatus (or nonstandard) dialects. Words that are taboo in the Standard Dialect may be commonly used in some nonstandard dialects of American English. Many of the taboo words are very old, and everyone knows them. But they are simply not uttered by "cultivated, educated speakers"—at least in polite society! The acceptable words for many body parts and body functions are Latin-root words, such as anus and defecate; the Anglo-Saxon (English) words for the same things are taboo—unacceptable. And any speaker of the Standard Dialect will certainly notice if someone violates these *word*, or *vocabulary*, taboos.

Of course any language is constantly changing. The only languages

[5] Arthur J. Bronstein and Beatrice F. Jacoby, *Your Speech and Voice* (New York: Random House, 1967).

that are not undergoing change are the ones no longer spoken. A language is a social custom, and all social customs change over a period of time. We cannot tell you what will be standard or nonstandard fifty or a hundred years from now. Our job is to describe accurately what is standard and nonstandard now.

IDIOLECT

Everyone who speaks American English speaks a dialect (regional or social variety) of that language. But everyone also has distinctive speech patterns all his or her own. We call those individual varieties idiolects. The word *idiolect* may be new to you, but you have seen *idio-* before. *Idio*syncrasies are mannerisms characteristic of one person. An *idiom* is a way of saying something peculiar to one language. An *idiolect*, then, is one person's individual variety of a language.

Many different influences have helped shape the way each of us speaks. Each of us has put those elements together in a unique and personal way. You will become more conscious of your own idiolect; you will have to analyze it; you will want to evaluate it; and you may want to modify it or add to it.

FUNCTIONAL VARIETIES OF AN IDIOLECT

Even a person who always speaks in the Standard or Status Dialect will not always speak in exactly the same way. That person will adjust his or her speech style to the formality of the situation and to his or her relationship to the listeners. We speak in many different kinds of social situations, and we must adapt our speaking style accordingly.

Surely you do not speak the same way at a party with your close friends as you do in the classroom. And we doubt that you speak the same way in the classroom that you would in a formal public speech. If you speak with the same degree of informality at a job interview you use at home, you may not get the job.

It is important to keep in mind that formal is not a synonym for standard, and informal is not the same as nonstandard. These functional (or situational) varieties exist within the Standard Dialect. "Cultivated, educated speakers" vary their speaking styles between two extremes: careful, precise formal forms and casual, simple, informal forms. The speaker fits the speech to the situation: public, formal, and impersonal at one extreme and private, informal, and intimate at the other. Any given situation may fall somewhere between the two extremes, and the functional variety of speech chosen will fall somewhere between the two extremes as well.

The most formal variety (within the Standard Dialect) is marked by careful control: precision in the production of sounds, care in the construction of sentences (few, if any contractions such as I'll or can't, for example), and caution in the choice of words (avoiding slang and colloquial expressions). When using this variety, a speaker also demonstrates greater control of his or her voice—avoiding extremes of pitch, loudness, rate, and quality.

The most informal variety (within the Standard Dialect) is casual and relaxed. Although articulation of the sounds is clear, it is less perniciously precise than in the most formal variety; sentence structure includes contractions and more informal, popular constructions (even Winston Churchill said, "It's me," on informal occasions); and, although outright taboo words are still avoided, slang and colloquial expressions are included. (In the formal variety, you would call him your "fiancé," but in the informal variety, you might refer to him as "the guy I'm going with"). When using the informal variety, a speaker will be more relaxed and "natural" in the use of his or her voice—letting the variations in pitch, volume, rate, and quality express attitudes and emotions more openly.

As we have said, informal varieties are not necessarily nonstandard. But you must learn which informal varieties are within the Standard/ Status Dialect and which ones *are* nonstandard. And you must develop enough sensitivity to be able to select the appropriate functional variety for each situation you are in.

Representation of Sounds

Phonetics is the study of the sounds of spoken language. Earlier in this chapter, we distinguished between a phone (a sound) and a phoneme (a significant sound). Phonetics is the study of phones, all the sounds heard in a language; and phonemics studies phonemes, the basic sounds of a language that can change the meaning of a word.

We will use the phonetic approach in this book, as we classify sounds, describe their production, and analyze their reception. We will organize our material around the phonemes of the language, but we will note the variations of the sounds (allophones and dialectal variations).

The language is what we speak: what we write is an attempt to represent the language (what we speak). The little flecks and specks of ink on this page are not words; they stand for words because words are *spoken* symbols. But we need to look at our writing system and the problems it presents and decide on some satisfactory way of representing the sounds of our language. If we are going to help you work on your production of sounds, we must have some consistent method of symbolizing those sounds on paper.

There are three kinds of writing systems in use to represent languages: (1) ideographic writing, (2) syllabic writing, and (3) alphabetic writing. The Chinese and Japanese still use ideographic symbols in their writing;

each symbol (sign) stands for a whole idea or word, without reference to the sounds in the word. Highway and traffic signs around the world are being changed from alphabetic to ideographic because no matter what language you speak, the sign will mean something to you. If the sign has a curved arrow pointing to the right with a straight line across the arrow, the idea is "No Right Turn," no matter what language you think those words in or what sounds you use to stand for those ideas. Syllabic writing uses written characters that represent spoken syllables rather than separate sounds. Alphabetic writing uses letters (written symbols) to represent sounds of the language.

About three thousand years ago, some folks—probably the Phoenicians—developed the first true alphabet, with individual letters representing sounds. But that alphabet was incomplete; it had symbols for the consonants, but none for vowels. The reader had to guess the vowels to complete the word; it was a kind of ancient form of Speed Writing. The Hebrews developed their alphabet some time after the Phoenicians, but they too devised letters only for the consonants. (It was many centuries later before scholars invented a system for indicating vowels in Hebrew script.) When the Greeks took over the Phoenician alphabet, they made a significant change. The Greek language had fewer consonant sounds than the Phoenician language, so the Greeks had some Phoenician symbols left over. These extra symbols they used to represent their vowels. When the Romans came along, they took from both the Greek and Phoenician alphabets to make their own. And the Pax Romana (and, later, Roman missionaries) spread the Roman alphabet throughout Western Europe.

HOW ENGLISH SPELLING GOT THAT WAY

English is basically a Germanic language. The Angles, Saxons, and Jutes invaded and took control of the British Isles in the fifth century A.D.; they were Germanic tribes that brought their dialects of German with them. The alphabet we use is the Roman alphabet! In the sixth century, Christian missionaries from Rome arrived, bringing the Latin language and alphabet. The sounds of Old English (Anglo-Saxon) were different from the sounds of Latin, so the sounds (phonemes) of English and the Roman alphabet never did match up perfectly. From the beginning, the alphabet we have used in English has not been completely phonetic.

Later developments gave our poor alphabet even more problems. In 1066 William the Conqueror, Duke of Normandy, invaded and conquered the British Isles. After his victory, William brought Normans from the continent to settle in Britain. The Normans, a French people, spoke Norman French, which became the language of the upper class—the nobility and businessmen. The masses continued to speak English, but many French words were incorporated into the language. In a couple of centuries, the use of French declined, but French had made an indelible mark on the English language.

In more modern times English "borrowed" words from many other languages. Usually the borrowed words kept their original spellings; some of the borrowed words changed in pronunciation from that of the original language, and some did not. Because each of the languages we borrowed from had different phonemic systems (and different writing systems to represent the sounds), spelling in English became even more inconsistent.

Well, there it is in brief: Take a basically Germanic language and add some Latin; add a lot of French (at least twenty-five per cent); add large pinches of Greek, Italian, Spanish, and assorted other languages; and then represent the mixture with a Latin (Roman) alphabet. Stir in the fact that pronunciations tend to change while spelling vigorously resists change, and you have a recipe for our inconsistent spelling system in English.

PROBLEMS WITH ENGLISH SPELLING

Anyone who has tried to learn to read and write English knows that there are irritating obstacles in our spelling system. We might as well face the problems and learn to cope with them; English has successfully resisted almost all efforts to simplify and regularize its erratic spelling. And there are no signs of relief on the way.

If our spelling were phonetic, each symbol would represent one sound consistently. Of course that is not the case. We have some forty-two phonemes in American English (give or take a couple, depending on your dialect), and we have an alphabet with twenty-six letters. Already we are in trouble. It is impossible to match one letter with one sound and come out even. But the problem is even worse: three of the twenty-six letters are useless, duplicating tasks already taken. (1) C is either a K or an S. Look at the word *accent*. The first C is pronounced like a K, and the second C is pronounced like an S. (2) X is either a KS or a GZ. In the word *extra*, the X is pronounced as KS; in the word *exact*, the X is pronounced as GZ. (3) Q is pronounced as KW; notice how Q is pronounced in the words *quiet, quick,* and *queen.* So we really have only twenty-three letters to represent forty-two sounds. And four basic problems result: (1) one spelling may represent more than one sound; (2) more than one spelling may represent the same sound; (3) two or more letters may represent one sound; and (4) some letters are "silent" and represent no sound in the word.

Let's look at each of the problems with English spelling.

1. *One spelling may represent more than one sound.* We will give you a list of examples, but the list will be far from complete. It is just to give you an idea of the scope of the problem. In the left-hand column,

we have placed a letter or letters of the alphabet. In the right-hand column, beside those letters, we have listed words in which the same letter (or letters) is pronounced a different way *in each word*. Try the lists out loud; you will see what we mean. If you are not sure of the pronunciation of a word, look it up in your dictionary.

SPELLING	DIFFERENT SOUND REPRESENTED
a	fate, fat, calm, walk
e	beg, sergeant, tête-à-tête
i	sight, fit, elite
o	no, hot, hog, woman, women, come
u	cup, full, rule, bury, busy
ai	laid, said, plaid
ea	meal, steak, breakfast, hearth
ei	veil, deceive, heifer
oa	road, broad
oe	doe, does
ou	troupe, out, fought, couple, curious
ough	though, through, thorough, rough, cough, bough
ow	row (a line), row (a fight)
s	bus, his, sugar
th	then, thin, thyme
wh	which, who

This brief list should give you an idea of spelling problem number 1: the same letter or letters can stand for several different sounds.

2. Problem number 2 is nearly the reverse of problem number 1: *More than one spelling may represent the same sound.* Here we want to list the basic sounds of the language (and throw in one common sound combination for good measure) and show you the various spellings for each sound (with a word to illustrate each spelling variation). But it is difficult to make such a list for you because we have not yet discussed the individual sounds of the language and have not yet taught a consistent writing system to represent the sounds. Nevertheless, to prove our point about English spelling, we are going ahead. We will list forty-two sounds and one common sound combination. In the left-hand column is the sound's symbol from the International Phonetic Alphabet (IPA), which will be discussed later; in the next column is the symbol for the sound (diacritical marks) found in the paperback edition of the American Heritage Dictionary (with slight modifications); in the third column from the left are the various ways of spelling that sound; and in the fourth column are word examples to illustrate each of the spelling variations. Remember that we are trying to prove that we spell the same sound in several different ways.

IPA	DICTIONARY	SPELLING	WORD-EXAMPLE
1. p	p	p, pp	pet, stopped
2. b	b	b, bb	ball, ribbon
3. t	t	t, tt, th	touch, bottom, thyme
		ed, ght	passed, right
4. d	d	d, dd, ed	do, ruddy, paused
5. k	k	c, cc, cch	cord, accord, Bacchus
		ch	chorus
		ck, cq, cu	sack, acquire, biscuit
		k, qu, que	kiss, liquor, antique
6. g	g	g, gg, gu, gue	go, egg, guard, travelogue
		gh	ghoul
7. h	h	h, wh	he, who
8. f	f	f, ff, gh, ph	foe, off, cough, physician
9. v	v	v, vv, f, ph	vest, savvy, of, Stephen
10. θ	th	th	thin
11. ð	*th*	th, the	then, breathe
12. s	s	s, sc, sch, ss	see, scene, schism, miss
		c, ce	cite, price
13. z	z	z, zz, s, sc	zoo, dizzy, his, discern
		ss, x	scissors, xylophone
14. ʃ	s͜h	ce, ch, ci	ocean, Chicago, species
		s	sugar
		sch, sci, se, sh	Schick, conscious, show
		si, ss, ssi	tension, issue, mission
		ti	nation
		psh	pshaw!
15. ʒ	z͜h	g, s, si	mirage, pleasure, vision
		z, zi	azure, brazier
16. tʃ	c͜h	ch, tch, te	chew, match, righteous
		ti	question
		tu	actual
17. dʒ	j	g, gg, d	logic, exaggerate, gradual
		dg	judgment
		dge, di	lodge, soldier
18. m	m	m, mm, gm	me, summer, phlegm
		lm, mb	calm, dumb
		mn	solemn
19. n	n	n, nn, gn, kn	no, runner, gnaw, know
		pn	pneumatic

20. ŋ	n͡g	n, ng, ngue	sink, sing, tongue
21. l	l	l, ll	let, tell
22. r	r	r, rr, rh, wr	rank, curry, rhyme, wring
23. j	y	i, j, y g	union, hallelujah, yes, monsignor
24. ʍ	h͡w	wh	which
25. w	w	w, o, u	wail, choir, quietly
26. i	e	e, ee, ea, ae ie, ei, eo oe i, ey, uay	be, bee, sea, Caesar piece, deceive, people subpoena machine, key, quay
27. ɪ	ĭ	e, ee, i, ie o, u, ui y	English, been, hit, sieve women, busy, built hysterical
28. e and eɪ	ā	a, ai, ao, au ay, ea, eh, ei ey	ate, straight, gaol, gauge pay, break, Eh!, weigh obey
29. ɛ	ĕ	a, ae, ai, ay e, ea, ei eo, ie, oe, u	many, aesthetic, said, says bed, leather, heifer leopard friend, Oedipus, bury
30. æ	ă	a, ai	glad, plaid
31. ɑ	ä, ŏ	a, e, ea, o	alms, sergeant, heart, box
32. ɔ	ô	a, ah, au, aw o, oa, ou	call, Utah, laud, raw orgy, broad, ought
33. o and oʊ	ō	o, oa, oe, oh oo, ou, ow, au eau, eo, ew	obey, so, road, doe, Oh! brooch, soul, grow, haute beau, yeoman, sew
34. ʊ	o͞o	o, oo, ou, u	wolf, took, could, pull
35. u	o͝o	eu, ew, o, oe oo, ou, u, ue ui	leucite, grew, move, canoe taboo, coupon, rule, sue fruit
36. ʌ	ŭ	o, oe, oo, ou u	done, does, flood, double but
37. ə	ə	a, aa, ae ai, au, e ea, eo eou i, ia ie, io, iou o, oi, ou u, y	above, Canaan, Michael captain, authority, listen sergeant, dungeon gorgeous beautiful, parliament conscience, region, vicious bishop, porpoise, furious cranium, analysis

38. ɝ	ûr	ear, er, ir	heard, herd, third
		or, our, ur, yr	worm, courage, turn, myrrh
39. ɚ	ər	ar, er, ir, or	liar, mother, nadir, actor
		our, ur	favour (British), femur
		yr	martyr
40. ɑɪ	ī	ai, ay, ei, ey	aisle, bayou, sleight, eye
		i, ie, uy, y, ye	nice, pie, buy, sky, dye
41. ɑʊ	ou	ou, ough, ow	rout, bough, town
42. ɔɪ	oi	oi, oy	toil, joy
bonus			
43. ju	yōo	eau, eu	beauty, feud
		eue, ew	queue (British), few
		ieu, iew, u, ue	adieu, view, unite, hue
		yew, you, yu	yew, you, Yule

In all forty-three cases, the list in the "spelling" column is of the various ways to represent *one* sound; the word list gives examples of each spelling variation. Surely we have established problem number 2: the same sound can be spelled several different ways.

3. *Two or more letters may represent just one sound.* It is obvious that, if you have forty or so phonemes and only twenty-three useful letters in your alphabet, you are going to have to double up in some way. Some letters will have to be used more than once if all the sounds are going to be represented. Add to that the needlessly doubled letters and some other inconsistencies, and you have spelling problem number 3. Here is a brief, suggestive list just to illustrate the problem. In the left-hand column are letters, each group representing only one sound; a sample word appears in the right-hand column.

pp	puppy
bb	hubby
dd	madder
tt	matter
cc	account
ch	chorus
gg	egg
ff	muffler
sch	schism
sch	Schick
zz	muzzle
tch	watch
dge	bridge

ng	hang
ngue	tongue
ll	tall
mm	slimmer
nn	thinner
th	ether
th	either
ea	steal
aw	saw
oo	food
oo	foot

Clearly, our spelling system in English is not a matter of one symbol per sound. More than one letter can stand for a single sound.

4. *Some letters are "silent" and represent no sound in the word at all.* The silent letters in our words would test the patience of Job! The problem is that these "silent" letters are not always silent; sometimes they represent sounds and sometimes they do not. You just have to learn the spellings of the words containing the useless letters. And you must be careful not to be tricked by the spelling into adding sounds when you pronounce these words.

We will list some of these troublesome words to illustrate the point. In the left-hand column are listed the silent letters; in the right-hand column are some of the words containing that letter in their spelling. Try the words out loud. Are you tempted at times to put in a sound just because the letter is there?

SILENT LETTER(s)	SAMPLE WORDS
b	lamb, climb, dumb, limb, numb, thumb, plumb, plumber, debt, subtle, doubt, subpeona
ch	yacht
e	dime, sake, rode, done
g	design, reign, phlegm, diaphragm, gnarl, gnash, gnat, gnaw, gnome, Gnostic, gnu
gh	night, light, right, weight, caught
h	rhythm, ghost, heir, honest, honor, hour
k	knee, knew, knife, knight, knock, knot, know, knowledge, knuckle
l	palm, calm, psalm, half, calf, talk, chalk, walk, almond, Lincoln
n	column, hymn, kiln
p	pneumatic, pneumonia, pshaw! (Maybe someone still says it!), ptomaine, receipt, cupboard
ps	corps

t	often, soften, hasten, listen, moisten, whistle
th	clothes
w	wrench, wrist, writ, write, wrong, wrestle, wretch, sword

This list ought to be enough to remind you, if indeed you needed reminding, that some letters appear in the spelling of our English words that represent no sound at all in the word.

All right, we hear you saying. We know the problem. What's the solution? And your question leads us to a brief discussion of the IPA (the International Phonetic Alphabet) and then into a brief discussion on the diacritical marking systems used in our dictionaries.

TWO WAYS TO REPRESENT THE SOUNDS OF AMERICAN ENGLISH

When somebody asks you about a word, do you think of the written "word" first? If we should ask you how many sounds there are in the word *though,* would you think first of the letters in the written "word"? Well, check yourself. How many sounds does that word have? We hope you answered "Two." If not, were you thrown off by the six letters we use to spell the word?

Do you find it difficult to think in terms of *sounds* in words, rather than *letters?* That is natural, because your teachers have emphasized the written form for so many years. But we want you to begin your program of speech improvement by closing your eyes to the letters used in spelling and opening your ears to the *sounds* spoken in words. At first, you will have to concentrate to think in terms of sounds, but with practice it should come more easily. Surely we have proved to you that the spelling is unreliable as a guide to pronunciation! Your ears—once trained—will be a much more dependable guide.

Let's test your ears for a moment. Say the word *many* and then the word *penny.* As you say them, you can hear four sounds for both words. The first sound in the word *many* is an /m/, and the first sound in the word penny is a /p/. But are the second sounds—the vowels—in each word the same sound or different sounds? Try the words out loud again just to be sure. Were you thrown off by the spelling? The second sound in both words is the same sound—although we spell one with *a* and one with *e.* Test your ears again. Are the first sounds in the words *honest* and *home* the same sounds? Or are the first sounds in the words *one* and *only* the same sounds? If you said yes to either of these questions, your ears need more training.

When we discuss the sounds of American English with you in this book, or when you concentrate on various sounds of the language in your class, a clear and consistent system for representing the sounds in writing is needed. We need a symbol system that will identify each sound precisely to avoid ambiguity and confusion. To accomplish this goal, we need a writing system that has one symbol for each sound and only one sound for each symbol.

In 1888 an international group of scholars designed such an alphabet for the sounds of English, and the International Phonetic Alphabet was born. In the years since, the International Phonetic Association has expanded and modified the International Phonetic Alphabet into a system with enough different characters to represent the sounds of the world's principal languages. This sound representation system has three advantages: (1) Each IPA symbol stands for one sound; that symbol always stands for the same sound—regardless of regular spelling of the word; and that sound is never represented by a different symbol. (2) Because IPA symbols represent sounds, they can be used to accurately record how a speaker actually pronounces a word or phrase. The IPA makes it possible to represent differences in pronunciation of words or phrases. (3) Each IPA symbol stands for the same sound—no matter what the language. In this book, we will use only the symbols for the sounds heard in American English, but with these symbols and others of the IPA you could pronounce words from other languages; IPA symbols are the same for all languages. The IPA could help you in learning to pronounce any language correctly.

We will use IPA in this book as a means of identifying sounds. You will probably use IPA in your class for this purpose also. It is a useful tool. Of course, learning the IPA symbols for sounds is not an end in itself; it is a means to an end. But your instructor will probably have you learn the IPA symbols as soon as possible to aid you in your program of speech improvement.

The only dictionary of American English words that uses the IPA symbols is Kenyon and Knott's *Pronouncing Dictionary of American English,* published by Merriam-Webster. This dictionary does not give definitions for words, only pronunciations. Although it needs to be updated, it is still a very useful reference guide.

All other dictionaries use a system called diacritical markings to represent sounds. Diacritical marks are a code of dots and lines; dictionary editors use them to indicate pronunciation. For the most part, these marks are added to letters used in regular spelling. There are three major problems associated with diacritical markings: (1) Different dictionaries use different markings to represent the same sounds. So it is necessary to study the explanation each dictionary provides for its marking system, if you are to use it intelligently. (2) The diacritical marks are added to regular letters of the alphabet, and it is easy to get confused by similar symbols. (3) Some dictionaries use more than one symbol for the same sound—primarily the result of an attempt to stay as close as possible to the original spelling of the word. This duplication can be confusing also.

Of course there are some advantages to becoming familiar with and learning to use diacritical markings. The dictionaries that are the most widely available and the most widely used indicate pronunciations in diacritics. Also, you should be familiar with diacritics from your past experience using dictionaries, so you already have that tool for identifying sounds. Because using diacritics builds on what you already know and prepares you for future everyday pronunciation checking, many teachers prefer to use a system of diacritical markings in teaching articulation and voice.

In this book, therefore, we will include both systems for representing the sounds of American English. When identifying a sound in this book, we will use both the IPA symbol and the diacritic symbol for the sound.

In American English, there are forty-two phonemes (as we count them): twenty-five consonants, fourteen vowels, and three phonemic diphthongs. They are presented here with a key word containing the sound, the IPA symbol, and the symbol from the *American Heritage Dictionary of the English Language:*

KEY WORD	IPA SYMBOL	*American Heritage Dictionary* SYMBOL
Consonants:		
1. pill	p	p
2. box	b	b
3. tool	t	t
4. do	d	d
5. king	k	k
6. good	g	g
7. whee	ʌ	hw̆
8. feel	f	f
9. veal	v	v
10. thigh	θ	th
11. thy	ð	*th*
12. sue	s	s
13. zoo	z	z
14. show	ʃ	sh̆
15. mira*ge*	ʒ	zh̆
16. chick	tʃ	ch̆
17. jerk	dʒ	j
18. hand	h	h
19. let	l	l
20. me	m	m
21. not	n	n
22. si*ng*	ŋ	n͡g
23. we	w	w
24. right	r	r
25. young	j	y

Vowels:

1. each	i	ē
2. itch	ɪ	ĭ
3. age	e	ā
4. edge	ɛ	ĕ
5. add, am	æ	ă
6. odd, alms	ɑ	ŏ, ä
7. awe	ɔ	ô
8. owe	o	ō
9. full	ʊ	oŏ
10. fool	u	ōō
11. up	ʌ	ŭ
12. *a*bout	ə	ə
13. *ea*rn	ɝ	ûr
14. moth*er*	ɚ	ər

Phonemic
  Diphthongs:

1. ice	ɑɪ	ī
2. out	ɑʊ	ou
3. oink	ɔɪ	oi

Looking over this chart of symbols, you may have the impression that they are weird and that learning them will be difficult. Actually, the IPA symbols are not as new and strange as they appear at first glance. You already know sixteen of the twenty-five consonant symbols. Check it out: count up the ones you are already used to using. They add up to sixteen of the twenty-five symbols. Granted, in regular spelling we use them to stand for several different sounds, and the IPA uses them to stand for only one sound each, but you do know the symbols. The other nine IPA symbols for consonants are not so difficult either. Number 25 is a familiar letter used in a slightly new way. In IPA, the /j/ stands for what we think of as the y sound. Maybe you can remember that it is the j from the word "hallelu*j*ah" used consistently. Or pretend that you are German; Germans pronounce the *j* as y, don't they? Numbers 10 and 11 are not totally new to you. If you have studied much math, you have used the Greek letter *theta* (θ); the name of the letter starts with the /θ/ sound. Number 11 is an Old English letter named "ethe." You have seen it before. Does it look more familiar to you in these contexts?

We ðe People   ðe Olde Taverne

The "ethe" (ð) is not a *y* and never was; it is the symbol for the voiced "th." Number 7, as you see, is simply the *w* letter turned upside down; it represents the sound many Americans still say (your authors included) as the first sound of such words as *whee, why,* and *what.* Otherwise, those words sound like *we, Y,* and *Watt.* Speakers of Standard American English who do not use the /ʍ/ sound, of course, have only twenty-four consonant phonemes in their idiolects.

It is not as easy to make associations with the IPA symbols for the vowels and phonemic diphthongs. (Diphthongs are blends of two vowels. We have other diphthongs in the language, but these three functions as single sounds—hence, as phonemes. All but two of the other diphthongs are simply combinations of two vowel phomemes. Those two are [oʊ] and [eɪ], which are allophones—variations—of the phonemes /o/ and /e/.) You will find it difficult to associate the IPA vowel symbols with regular spelling, because our spelling is so inconsistent. The simplest thing to do is just memorize the seventeen vowel and phonemic dipthong symbols by writing each of them over and over as you pronounce the sound out loud. It should not take long to master all of them.

We should point out to you that some authors omit the symbols /ʌ/ and /ɝ/ from their list of vowel phonemes. They argue that the only difference between /ʌ/ and /ə/ and also between /ɝ/ and /ɚ/ is duration (or length, or stress); this difference, they say, is insignificant. If there is no significant contrast, they argue, /ʌ/ and /ə/ and also /ɝ/ and /ɚ/ are not separate phonemes, but allophones of the same sound. They use the /ə/ symbol for both /ʌ/ and /ə/; they use the /ɚ/ symbol for both /ɝ/ and /ɚ/. The issue is not settled. Until it is, we will follow the IPA custom and use separate symbols and list them as separate sounds.

We have listed for you the significant sounds of American English, and we have given you two alternative ways of representing those sounds. Your instructor will tell you which of the systems (or both) you will be using in your class. Learn the symbol system(s) right away. It will facilitate communication between your instructor and you, your classmates and you, and these writers and you when discussing sounds.

2
The Sounds of American English: Consonants

IN THIS chapter and the next we are going to focus on the forty-two phonemes of American English. We will discuss these sounds as separate entities in connected speech. When you say a phrase or sentence, you do not speak a sound at a time, one after another. You speak in a continuous flow of movements from the beginning to the end of each phrase. In that continuous flow, each sound is modified by the sounds around it.

Each sound, then, in daily speech, undergoes a wide variety of modifications or changes. Different people will produce the same sound in many different ways in differing contexts. But we *can* talk about individual sounds because each sound has a group of distinctive features (characteristics that mark that sound off from all the other sounds of the language). However much a sound may vary, each sound has a number of basic characteristics (distinctive features or components) by which it is identified.

Do you have difficulty producing some of the sounds of American English? Or have you been told that your production of some sound is nonstandard? Then you have a problem with some of the distinctive features of those sounds. Perhaps there is a problem related to only one of the distinctive features of that sound. However, it is necessary for you to learn the basic characteristics of the sounds, how they are produced and how they sound.

Speech sounds are divided into two groups: consonants and vowels. These two groups of sounds differ in two ways: (1) how they are produced, and (2) how they are used.

You can check out the first difference between consonants and vowels by looking in a mirror and making a few sounds. While looking in the mirror, say the sounds (not the names of the letters, but the *sounds* themselves): /t/, /k/, /f/ on a continuous breath—if you can. Then, while still looking in the mirror, say "Ah, oh, aye," on a continuous breath. Did you notice that the first set of sounds had the air stream checked, or impeded, on the way out? Did you also notice that your mouth was

47

partly open and the air came out without much interference on the second set of sounds? That is a major difference between consonants and vowels: To produce consonants, the outgoing stream is either completely stopped or is markedly impeded (constricted). To produce vowels, the outgoing air stream is relatively unobstructed. In consonants, the air flow is partly or completely blocked. Vowels are relatively "open" sounds, produced by modifying the resonance in the mouth.

Another major distinction between consonants and vowels is that they serve two different functions in our syllables. (A syllable is a sound or group of sounds uttered on one chest pulse. "Don't" is a one-syllable word, uttered on one pulse; "worry" is a two-syllable word, uttered on two pulses—the first is stronger, or stressed, and the second is weaker, or unstressed.) Consonants serve the function, generally, of starting and stopping our syllables. Another way of saying the same thing is to say that consonants either initiate (or release) a syllable or terminate (or arrest) a syllable. Vowels, on the other hand, provide a specific quality or form the nucleus (or peak) of a syllable.

Let's try some syllables to see if we can make the separate functions of consonants and vowels clearer. Out loud, say the word, *oh*. That syllable has a peak, a nucleus: that is, a vowel. (A syllable is somewhat like a cell: it has a nucleus and, maybe, a cell wall. The nucleus around which a syllable centers is the vowel; the cell wall—front and/or back—is made up of consonants.) The vowel provides the carrying power for the syllable; the vowel is the peak of sonority in the syllable. The syllable *oh* contains only a vowel. If you pronounce the word *ho*, however, you will see that your syllable is started by a sound *before* the vowel. Pronounce the word *oak*; this syllable does not have a consonant to start it (the open /o/ vowel is the beginning again), but it does have a consonant to close (or terminate) the syllable. Now pronounce the word *Coke*. That syllable contains the same vowel (peak/-nucleus), but it has a consonant to initiate it and terminate it. Consonants serve to start or arrest syllables. Of course there may be more than one consonant at the beginning or end of a syllable. The words *gloat* and *gold* are good examples. Hopefully, you can see that vowels and consonants serve different functions in our syllables.

Distinctive Features: Classification of Consonants

Every sound in our language can be identified (set off from all the other sounds of the language) on the basis of a group of distinctive characteristics (or features or components). Consonants are distinguished from each other on the basis of three classes of features: (1) the presence or absence of voicing (vibration of the vocal folds); (2) the place of articulation; and (3) the manner in which the sound is emitted. If you note all three of these features about a consonant, you have identified it and separated it from all the other consonants of the language.

For example, to identify the consonant at the beginning of the word *be,* you would note its distinctive features: /b/ is (1) voiced, because it is made with the vocal folds vibrating; (2) bilabial, because it is articulated by bringing the two lips together; and (3) a stop, because the air stream is stopped completely in its emission. Therefore, /b/ is a voiced bilabial stop. These three descriptions (or features) classify the /b/ consonant in American English.

Let us look at each of these classes of features of consonants separately.

VOICING

Of the twenty-five consonants of American English, fifteen are made with the vocal folds vibrating. These fifteen consonants are classified as *voiced* consonants. These sounds are the first consonants in the following words:

Word	IPA Symbol	Dictionary Symbol
bare	b	b
dare	d	d
get	g	g
vet	v	v
then	ð	*th*
Zen	z	z
azure	ʒ	ẓh
meal	m	m
kneel	n	n
angle	ŋ	n̂g
low	l	l
woe	w	w
rue	r	r
you	j	y
June	dʒ	j

There are ten consonants not made with vocal vibration. These ten consonants are classified as *voiceless* consonants. These consonants are the initial sounds in the following words:

pie	p	p
tie	t	t
kite	k	k
why	ʍ	ḫw

fie	f	f
thigh	θ	th
sigh	s	s
shy	ʃ	s̮h
high	h	h
chide	tʃ	c̮h

Some of the consonants can be grouped into pairs called cognates. Each of the two sounds in the pair is articulated in the same place and released in essentially the same manner; they differ in that one is voiced and the other is voiceless. (Another difference, although not nearly as important, is that a voiceless consonant tends to have greater aspiration—that is, more breath released—in its emission than its voiced cognate does.) Note these cognates (pairs of sounds), illustrated by the first consonant in the following words:

	VOICELESS			VOICED	
WORD	IPA	DICTIONARY	WORD	IPA	DICTIONARY
peer	p	p	beer	b	b
toe	t	t	dough	d	d
kill	k	k	gill	g	g
whee	ʍ	hw̮	we	w	w
fear	f	f	veer	v	v
thigh	θ	th	thy	ð	*th*
sue	s	s	zoo	z	z
assure	ʃ	s̮h	azure	ӡ	z̮h
chin	tʃ	c̮h	gin	dӡ	j

On the consonant chart (see p. 53), when two phonemic symbols are side by side in the same block, the symbol on the left is a voiceless consonant and the symbol on the right is its voiced cognate.

PLACE OF ARTICULATION

To form consonants, the outgoing airstream is obstructed at some point along the route by the articulators—the lips, teeth, tongue, hard palate, and velum (soft palate). The closure (obstruction) may either be complete or partial. To impede the exhaled air column and, thus, articulate a sound, you may bring together your two lips, the lips and teeth, the tongue and teeth, the tongue and gum ridge, the tongue and hard palate, or the tongue and velum. One sound, the /h/, is made by squeezing the air through the vocal folds.

You remember we said earlier in the book that articulation means making a joint (bringing two things together) to hinder the outgoing air. One distinctive feature of every consonant in American English is *where*

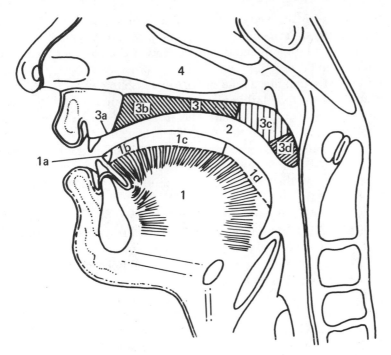

FIGURE 2–1. *The oral cavity and its articulators. 1: Tongue. 1a: Tongue tip. 1b: Blade of tongue. 1d: Back of tongue. 2: Mouth (oral cavity). 3: Palate. 3b: Hard Palate. 3c: Soft palate. 3d: Uvula. 4: Nasal cavity.*

the articulation takes place—that is, what articulators are brought together to obstruct the breath stream.[1]

MANNER OF EMISSION

Another characteristic feature of every consonant is how it sounds (its acoustic properties) or how the air comes out.

Pronounce the word *pot* and check on the way the /p/ comes out. Did you notice that for an instant, while the two lips are completely closed, the air stream is blocked and *nothing* comes out at all? And then did you notice that when the lips are opened to release the sound there is a little explosion of air? Try the word *sin* out loud and notice how the /n/ sound

[1] Some recent research has convinced Drs. Raymond H. Colton and Gerald N. McCall of the SUNY Upstate Medical Center that the larynx (voice box) itself acts as an articulator. Even if this is so, the places of articulation mentioned here are sufficient to identify or classify the consonants of American English, to establish the consonants' distinctive features, and to assist you in your program of speech improvement.

is emitted. The air is blocked off by the tongue up on the gum ridge and is hummed up through the nose. Now pronounce the word *live* and hold on to the last sound for a moment or two. How is the /v/ sound emitted? How does it sound? Is it different from the other two we have looked at so far? Does it sound like a kind of friction noise to you?

Next say the word *toll*, and hold on to the last sound for a little while. Where is the tongue on that sound? Has it blocked the air from coming out of the middle of the mouth? Yes, that's right, it has. And the air is coming out on both sides of the tongue—that is, out of the two sides of the mouth. Finally, look in the mirror as you say the word *will*. Do your lips move as you say the /w/? Does the sound change as you make it— that is, as the lips are moving?

The way the air is emitted on a consonant is one of a consonant's distinctive features. The manner of emission is a distinguishing mark of a consonant. Based on this characteristic, consonants are divided into six classes: (1) stops (sounds on which the air is stopped completely), (2) fricatives (friction noises with the air squeezed between two articulators), (3) affricates (combinations of a stop and fricative into single sounds), (4) nasals (sounds emitted with nasal resonance), (5) lateral (a sound emitted with the air coming out over the sides of the tongue), (6) and glides (sounds on which there is continuous movement of the articulators from one position to another).

The stop consonants are sometimes called plosives or stop plosives, because they often are released in a little plosion (or explosive puff of air). In the production of these sounds, the air stream is *always* completely stopped, but it is not always exploded on release. Therefore, it has seemed best to us to call these sounds stops, rather than plosives. The other consonants are sometimes all grouped into a division called continuants because, unlike stops, they can be continued—or their release extended. The designation *continuant* is of no real use in describing distinctive features because the narrower terms—fricatives, affricates, nasals, lateral, and glides—must be used to distinguish individual consonants from each other.

The consonant chart that follows clarifies the way in which the use of the three classes of distinctive features can classify or identify any consonant of American English.

The Twenty-Five Consonant Phonemes

We will now look at each of the twenty-five consonant phonemes in detail. For each sound we will explain the correct (customary) production of the sound, discuss the various allophones of the phoneme, give specific warnings (on spelling, for example) if they are necessary, list and describe common deviations (errors, problems, or dangers) in the articu-

Consonant Chart

MANNER OF EMISSION

	Stops	Frictives	Affricates	Nasals	Lateral	Glides
Two Lips (bilabial)	p b	ʍ (hw̯)		m		w
Lip-Teeth (labio-dental)		f v				
Tongue-Teeth (lingua-dental)		θ ð (th) (t̯h)				
Tongue-tip- Gum Ridge (lingua-alveolar)	t d	s z		n	l	
Tongue-blade- Back of Gum Ridge (lingua-post alveolar)		ʃ z (s̯h) (z̯h)	tʃ dz (c̯h) (j)			r
Tongue-blade- Hard Palate (lingua-palatal)						j (y)
Tongue-back- Soft Palate (lingua-velar)	k g			ŋ (n̯g)		
Glottis (glottal)		h				

PLACE OF ARTICULATION

lation of the sound, and provide exercises to use in improving your production of the sound.

STOPS

Stops are consonants produced by momentarily blocking the outgoing air stream completely. Often, in the production of these sounds, the air stream is completely blocked, air pressure is built up at the point of obstruction, and then the built-up breath is released in a little explosion. (For that reason, as we have said, these stop sounds are also called plosives.) There are six stops in American English (three pairs of cognates): /p/ and /b/; /t/ and /d/; /k/ and /g/. The first of each pair is voiceless and the second is voiced.

There are some characteristics common to all stops. First and most important, they are characterized by firm contact of the articulators (complete closure) so the outgoing air is totally blocked. Without firm, complete closure, stops are not stops.

Another common characteristic is that the voiceless stops are aspirated more. That is, more breath is released; they are "breathier" than their voiced cognate partners. Also, even in the same phoneme, the amount of aspiration (breath released) will vary, depending on the position of the stop in the syllable and on the neighboring sounds. (We will explain this characteristic in more detail when discussing the allophones of each stop consonant.) Generally, a stop will be more explosive at the beginning of a syllable and will not be exploded at all (imploded) at the end of a word or phrase. If a word ends with a plosive and the next word in the phrase begins with a vowel, the words are hooked together (linked; elision takes place) by making the stop sound the first sound in the next syllable. (Say the words, *look out,* as you ordinarily do, in one phrase. You will note that you do not say one word at a time, but blend (link) the two words. The syllables do not divide at the word divisions, but as *loo-kout.* The /k/, then, is at the beginning of a syllable rather than at the end of a syllable. That is the reason it is exploded rather than imploded. On the other hand, say the word look as you ordinarily would. You do not explode the /k/ stop, do you? It is imploded at the end of the word or phrase. But it did stop completely.

There are some other characteristics common to stops also. If a stop is doubled (doubled in sounds, not just in spelling), we do not make the stop twice. We do not block the air, build up the pressure, release it, then block the air again, build up pressure, and release it again. Instead, we make the stop once and indicate the doubling by holding the closure longer than usual before the release. The closure for the /t/ in the word *lasting* should be only half as long as the closure for the /t/ in *last time,* which must represent the final /t/ in *last* and the initial /t/ in *time.* In the same way, if two different stop sounds come together in the same word or in consecutive words, the first stop sound is stopped, but not exploded; the second is stopped *and* exploded. If you ask for a *hot dog,* you do not explode both the /t/ and /d/ stops, do you? The /t/ must stop—firmly closed—but it is the /d/ only that explodes. Try the word out loud to be sure; then, as a double check, say bac*k d*own. Doesn't the same thing occur? Both stops stop, but only the second is released in an explosion.

One other aspect of stops should be noted. Sometimes they are followed by the /l/ sound or by a nasal sound. Pronounce the word *bottle* out loud. The second syllable is /tl/, a stop and the /l/. When a stop is followed by /l/ in the same syllable, the stop is firmly closed, but the explosion-release is over the sides of the tongue. Try the word out loud again, and see if, indeed, this is exactly what happens. Something similar occurs when a stop is followed by a nasal sound. The stop is formed, but the explosion-release is through the nose. Pronounce the word *button* and observe what happens. The second syllable is /tn/, a stop and the nasal sound /n/. The tongue closes off the air completely for the /t/, but the plosive release occurs nasally.

Let us analyze the three pairs of stop cognates.

/p/ and /b/

Production of the Stops /p/ and /b/

If you raise the velum (soft palate) so no air can escape up through the nose, close the two lips firmly to block the outgoing breath stream completely, build up air pressure by holding the lips closed for a moment, and then release the compressed air by quickly opening the two lips, you will produce a bilabial (two lips) stop. There are two bilabial stops in English. One is voiceless (it is produced without the vocal folds vibrating) and is represented in both IPA and the dictionaries by /p/. The other bilabial stop is voiced (there is vibration of the vocal folds) and is represented in both IPA and the dictionaries by /b/.

Allophones of the Stops /p/ and /b/

There are three allophones (variations) of the /p/ phoneme. They vary in the amount of breath released (the degree of aspiration) when the sound is produced. Each of the allophones can be represented in IPA. The strongly aspirated allophone is [pʰ]; the weakly aspirated allophone is [pᶜ]; the unaspirated allophone is [p⁼].

/p/ is strongly aspirated if the /p/ initiates a stressed syllable. Note that there is a strong puff of breath when you release the /p/ in these words:

pear	compare
peer	appear
pose	suppose
port	report
Hop in.	Help out.

/p/ is weakly aspirated after /s/ in the same syllable. Note the difference in aspiration when /s/ precedes the /p/:

pie	spy	aspire
peel	spiel	bespeak
pair	spare	despair
pot	spot	despot
Whip her.		Whisper.
clapper		Clasp her.

This sound is also weakly aspirated if the /p/ initiates an unstressed syllable. Note that there is not such a strong puff of breath when you release the /p/ in these words:

potato	(Compare the stressed syllable: Poe.)
vapor	(Compare the stressed syllable: poor.)
happy	(Compare the stressed syllable: P.)
pathetic	(Compare the stressed syllable: path.)

/p/ is usually unaspirated when final in a word or phrase. Say these words and phrases as you usually do and you will discover that there is no puff of air on the release of the /p/:

tape
rap
bump
Call a cop!
Send for help!

Also, there is usually no aspiration of /p/ if the next sound is a consonant. Pronounce these examples:

cupcake
topmost
capful
Hop down.
It's a crap game.

There are four allophones of the /b/ phoneme. Because the /b/ is a voiced phoneme, it is not aspirated. All the voiced stops lack the breathy release that may be present in their voiceless cognates. Although the release of the /b/ is not aspirated, it can vary in the degree of force of the plosion. The /b/ can be strongly exploded, weakly exploded, or not exploded (imploded). In addition, the /b/ can be partially devoiced; the vocal fold vibration is decreased before the sound is ended.

/b/ is strongly exploded if the /b/ initiates a stressed syllable. Pronounce the following examples out loud:

buy	abide
bait	abate
bound	abound
bode	abode
bar	debar

/b/ is weakly exploded if the /b/ initiates an unstressed syllable. Pronounce these examples:

besides
rabid
rabbit
rubber
before

/b/ is usually unexploded when final in a word or phrase. Check these examples out loud:

He's a slob.
Don't grab.
That's the rub!
Don't touch that knob.
Get that cab!

There is usually no explosion of the /b/ if the next sound is a consonant. These words will illustrate the principle. Try them out loud:

Ga*b*e *t*alked.
Nothing will kill cra*b*grass.
She ro*b*s every customer.
Is the ca*b* *f*ull?

Before voiceless consonants and at the end of phrases, /b/ is usually partially devoiced. Pronounce these words and phrases out loud; check to see if the /b/ is fully voiced throughout:

lobster
mobster
Cub Scout
cab full
hubcap
Knob Hill

Specific Warnings

Sometimes the letters *p* and *b* appear in the spelling of words, but they are not to be pronounced; *p* and *b* can be silent letters.

1. If *p* precedes *n* at the beginning of a word, the *p* is silent.

   pneumatic, pneumatology, pneumonia

2. If *p* precedes *t* at the beginning of a word, the *p* is silent.

   ptomaine, Ptolemy, ptyalin

3. If *p* precedes *b* in the middle of a word, the *p* may be silent. (But note that in *upbraid,* the *p* is *not* silent.)

   cupboard, clapboard

4. If *b* follows *m* at the end of a word, the *b* is silent.

> aplomb, comb, climb, dumb, limb, lamb, plumb, thumb, tomb

5. If a suffix is added to a word ending in *mb*, the *b* is silent. (But note that in *limber*, the *b* is not silent because it was not made out of *limb* + a suffix.)

> climbing, combing, dumber, plumber

Common Deviations or Problems in the Articulation of /p/ and /b/

We now turn our attention to faulty production of the bilabial stop sounds. There are six dangers, or common problems, associated with these two phonemes. As we look at each of these deviations, check to see if you have that problem with these sounds.

1. *Incomplete closure.* Incomplete closure of the articulators on stop sounds results in sloppy, indistinct speech. If your lips are too stiff or too lazy to close completely for the /p/ and /b/, the sounds will not be clear and crisp. Have you ever heard a careless speaker pronounce the word *obvious* without quite closing the two lips firmly and completely to form the /b/? The temptation to slacken the articulation on /p/ and /b/ is especially great if they are followed by other consonants. Check to be sure that your stop is complete and the lips are *firmly* pressed together for /p/ and /b/ in these examples:

> flapjacks
> capful
> subvert
> caps
> cabs
> abduction
> subsidize
> substitute
> substantial
> hopefully
> optimum
> It's what's u*p f*ront that counts.
> The clu*b f*aces bankruptcy.
> The solution is o*bv*ious.
> We want to*p v*alue.

2. *Omission.* Some speakers do not stop at articulating /p/ and /b/ slackly; they omit the sounds altogether. Some speakers omit these sounds when they occur at the ends of words—especially if the /p/ or /b/ is preceded by another consonant. Check your pronunciation of these words to be sure the final sounds are not dropped:

wasp
clasp
bulb
yelp
pulp

Remember that the /p/ and /b/ do not always explode, but the air stream must be stopped by the two lips or the sound has not been articulated. Many people seemed to be tempted to omit these sounds after an /m/; the /b/ especially suffers omission after /m/. Check your pronunciation of these words to see if you face that problem:

ample	amble
rumple	rumble
simple	symbol
limper	limber
simper	ember
pamper	member
scamper	membership
hamper	remember
amplitude	number
contemptible	slumber
	cucumber
	September
	emblem
	combination

The /p/ and /b/ are in danger of being omitted if the preceding syllable contains a /p/ or /b/. Check your pronunciation of these words:

capable
capably
probably
unflappable
unstoppable
grabbable
preposition
proposition

3. *Overaspiration.* The amount of air released on the /p/ varies, and the amount of force with which /b/ is released also varies. This variation depends on the position of the sound in the syllable and on the sound that precedes or follows. But you should be careful not to *over-explode* /p/ and /b/.

4. *Substitution of a bilabial fricative.* Some languages have a phoneme that is a fricative sound formed by the two lips. The two lips are

puckered, but never completely, firmly pressed together, and the sound produced is not a stop plosive, but a voiced friction noise. If you first learned a language with such a phoneme, it is possible you are using that sound to substitute for the English /b/. Be especially careful of using this substitution in the middle of words or phrases. Check your pronunciation of the following words and phrases to be sure that you firmly press your two lips together and release the /b/ in a little plosion:

hobby	habit
hubby	table
flabby	babbling
rubber	bubble
cabbage	webbing
rubbish	rumble

5. *Substitution of labiodental stops.* If /p/ and /b/ occur before /f/ or /v/, there is a temptation to make the /p/ or /b/ in the same place as the following sound. That would mean that, instead of being articulated by the two lips, the /p/ or /b/ would be articulated by the upper teeth and the lower lip (as the /f/ and /v/ are). Some modification of the /p/ and /b/ will be made in preparation for the next sound, but the articulation should still be made by the two lips and should clearly be a stop sound. Check your pronunciation of these examples:

[pf]	[pv]
cup*f*ul	to*p v*alue
cap*f*ul	si*p v*enom
stopga*p f*eatures	dee*p v*ault
Ho*p f*orward.	gul*p v*isibly
Sto*p f*irst.	The sloo*p v*eered.
He has a ro*p*e *f*etish.	It's a chea*p v*acation.
It's too much to ho*p*e *f*or.	Hel*p v*erify the results.
The pu*p f*ainted.	Sto*p v*ulgar displays.

[bf]	[bv]
ob*f*uscate	ob*v*ious
ob*f*uscation	ob*v*erse
we*b*-*f*ooted	ob*v*iate
tu*b*ful	su*b*vert
Pro*b*e *f*or clues.	su*b*version
The bi*b f*ell off.	Ro*b* Vince.
Bo*b f*easts; Bar*b f*asts.	Bo*b v*olunteers.
Get to the ca*b f*irst.	What a dra*b v*oice!
The ro*b*e *f*its poorly.	The tri*b*e *v*anished.

6. *Unvoicing of /b/.* Before voiceless sounds and as the final sound in a phrase, /b/ may be slightly *de*voiced. That is, vocal vibration may

decrease before the sound is finished. But the /b/ should not be completely *unvoiced*. The word *tribe*, for example, should certainly not sound like *tripe*, and *Abe* should not be turned into *ape*. Check your pronunciation of these pairs of words. Be certain that the final /b/ sound is a voiced sound.

[p]	[b]
cap	cab
mop	mob
gap	gab
gape	Gabe
trip	Trib (short for *Tribune*)
weep	Weeb (an uncommon name)

Materials for Practicing /p/ and /b/

peat	beat	happy	abbey	sop	sob
pin	bin	rupee	Ruby	cup	cub
pay	bay	dappled	dabbled	rope	robe
peg	beg	appeal	Abeel	rip	rib
pad	bad	crumple	crumble	gap	gab
pole	bowl	ample	amble	cop	cob
poor	boor	Harpur	harbor	crap	crab
pump	bump	staple	stable	lope	lobe

1. Never buy a pig in a poke.
2. He played basketball for a private school.
3. I got into trouble by leaping and ripping the tapestry.
4. Mr. Blake was probably disturbed by that shibboleth.
5. Perry has been stationed at an army post near Budapest, Alabama.
6. Except for a couple of brilliant cab drivers, no one has ever robbed me.
7. The symbolism in the play is far from simple.
8. No one is ever absolutely beyond help.
9. Our president was quite unhappy over the bad publicity we received.
10. Don't punctuate your sentences with great bursts of air on the plosive sounds.
11. Everybody believes in "Power to the People." Everybody disagrees on what powers to which people!
12. A government's power lies in its ability to decide which people will pay and which people will collect.
13. It was obvious to everybody present that the baby was absolutely unbearable.
14. Stopgap measures may bring temporary respite, but remember that long-term planning is best.

15. It probably sounds subversive, but I hate to subsidize an incompetent membership.
16. Stop fooling around. Quit grumbling, and prepare better exercises than this rubbish!
17. Bob voted in the last election, but his habit of picking losers is unbroken.
18. You can probably bribe Vince, but don't stoop to blackmail.

/t/ and /d/

Production of the Stops /t/ and /d/

If you raise the velum to prevent the air from escaping through the nose, block the air stream at the front by pressing the tip of the tongue against the gum ridge, and then release the air by quickly dropping the tongue tip, you will produce a lingua-alveolar (tongue-gum ridge) stop. There are two lingua-alveolar stops in American English. One is voiceless (produced without vocal fold vibration); it is represented in both IPA and the dictionaries by /t/. The other lingua-alveolar stop is voiced (produced with vibration of the vocal folds); it is represented in both IPA and the dictionaries by /d/. In making these sounds you must be careful to narrow the tongue to a point, to press the tongue tip firmly against the upper gum ridge, and to make the release a quick one.

Allophones of the Stops /t/ and /d/

There are five allophones (variations) of the /t/ phoneme. Three of these allophones differ in the amount of breath released when the sound is produced. They parallel the three allophones of /p/ in this regard (see p. 55). Each of these allophones can be represented in IPA. The strongly aspirated allophone is [tʰ]; the weakly aspirated allophone is [tᶜ]; and the unaspirated allophone is [t⁼].

/t/ is strongly aspirated if the /t/ initiates a stressed syllable. Note that there is a strong puff of breath released when you produce the /t/ in these words:

two	into
tire	retire
take	partake
tend	contend
tone	intone

/t/ is weakly aspirated after /s/ in the same syllable. Note the difference in aspiration when /s/ precedes the /t/:

tile	style
tanned	stand
take	steak

tore	store
tuck	stuck
toll	stole

The /t/ is also weakly aspirated if the /t/ initiates an unstressed syallable. Note that there is a puff of breath when you release the /t/ in the following words, but there is not as great a puff of air as when initiating stressed syllables. Try these words out loud:

tomato	(Compare the stressed syllable: toe.)
today	(Compare the stressed syllable: two.)
after	(Compare the stressed syllable: turn.)
taboo	(Compare the stressed syllable: tab.)

/t/ is usually unaspirated when final in a phrase. Say these words and phrases as you usually do and you will probably discover that there is no puff of air on the release of the /t/:

rat	It's a hit!
wrote	I'm still in debt.
caught	They're on the mat.
put	Is it straight?
got	What a fight!

Also, there is usually no aspiration of /t/ if the next sound is a consonant. But the /t/ must stop, even if it doesn't explode. Pronounce these words and phrases, for example:

utmost
atmosphere
gut reaction
boat show
cat burglar
hit play

We have said that /t/ is a voiceless stop, but there is an allophone of /t/ that does have some voicing. It is not voiced sufficiently to be a /d/, which is a totally voiced stop, but some voicing is clearly present on this allophone of /t/. This allophone occurs only between vowels, which are themselves voiced sounds. It is doubtless the influence of the surrounding sounds that gives the semivoiced characteristic to this allophone. Between vowels, initiating an unstressed syllable, the /t/ is likely to be the voiced allophone. The IPA symbol for this sound is [t̬]; the little *v* under the /t/ indicates the presence of voicing. Check your pronunciation of the following words and phrases. You will probably discover that the allophone of /t/ you are using is the voiced /t/—and, although it isn't a /d/, it does bear a resemblance to a /d/.

city	one a*t* a time
pre*tt*y	Le*t* it go.
bu*tt*er	when i*t* is ready
ba*tt*er	I heard tha*t* a plan was devised.
ma*tt*er	He hi*t* a home run.

Now pronounce these pairs of words to see the difference between the voiced /t/ and a /d/ in the same context:

plotting	plodding
matter	madder
mutter	mudder
betting	bedding
otter	odder

We have said that the /t/ is a lingua-alveolar stop. It is made by placing the tongue tip on the gum ridge. That is true, except that there is one allophone of the /t/ made in another place. If the /t/ comes before one of the two "th" sounds in English, then the /t/ is made with the tongue under the upper teeth in preparation for the sound to follow. Check your production of the /t/ when you say the following examples. If necessary, look in a mirror to see where the tongue goes when making the /t/ sound.

Pu*t* the ball down.
She's a*t* the park.
Tha*t* thought had occurred to me.
Se*t* the table.
No*t* this time!
You're no*t* thinking!

There are five allophones of the /d/ phoneme. The /d/ is a voiced stop, so it is not aspirated. The /d/ can, however, vary in the degree of force of the plosive release. The /d/ can be strongly exploded, weakly exploded, or not exploded (imploded). In addition, the /d/ can be partially devoiced, and there is an allophone of the /d/ made with the tongue on the upper teeth.

/d/ is strongly exploded if the /d/ initiates a stressed syllable. Pronounce the following examples out loud:

door	adore
dent	indent
day	today
deck	bedeck
due	subdue

/d/ is weakly exploded if the /d/ initiates an unstressed syllable. Pronounce these examples:

delay   (Compare with the stressed syllable: D.)
candid   (Compare with the stressed syllable: did.)
madam   (Compare with the stressed syllable: dam.)
Sunday   (Compare with the stressed syllable: day.)
haddock   (Compare with the stressed syllable: dock.)

/d/ is usually unexploded when final in a word or phrase. Do you explode the /d/ at the end of these phrases?

> She can't stand the sight of blood.
> I'll lie in the shade.
> I'm addicted to rich food.
> You've got it made.
> I'd rather be popular than good.

There is usually no explosion of the /d/ if the next sound is a consonant. Try these examples out loud:

> Good food; good show; good day. Goodbye.
> I want a grand piano.
> I would love to know.
> Advertising is a good business.

/d/ is usually partially devoiced before voiceless consonants and at the ends of phrases. Pronounce these examples. Check to see if the /d/ is fully voiced throughout:

> headstone
> codfish
> madcap
> cold feet
> bold fool
> That's good.

The /d/ phoneme (like its cognate /t/) changes the place of its articulation before the two "th" sounds. This allophone of /d/ is made with the tongue at the back of, or under, the upper teeth. Check your own production of the /d/ when you say the following examples out loud:

> width
> breadth (Be sure to get the /d/ in; the word is not breath.)
> She had the nerve to tell!
> We led the parade.
> You would think so.

Specific Warnings

1. Sometimes the letters *t* and *d* appear in the spelling of words, but they are not to be pronounced.

2. In some words ending in the spelling *tle,* the *t* is silent. Here are some examples:

> bristle, thistle, whistle, epistle, wrestle, castle, hustle

3. In some word ending in the spelling *ten,* the *t* is silent. Note these examples:

> often, soften, hasten, chasten, listen, glisten, fasten, moisten

4. In some other words also, the *t* is a silent letter:

> Chris*t*mas, ches*t*nut, mor*t*gage

5. In a few words, *d* is a silent letter:

> We*d*nesday, han*d*kerchief, han*d*some

6. The spelling *-ed* represents three different pronunciations indicating the past tense. When the past-tense morpheme is added to a word ending in a voiceless sound, *-ed* represents a /t/; *-ed* represents a /d/ when the past-tense morpheme is added to a word ending in a voiced sound; but the *-ed* represents the syllable [ɪd] when the past tense morpheme is added to a word ending in /t/ or /d/. Say these words aloud to check out this principle: *roped, robbed, rated.* Again, try this list to hear each of the three: *laughed, loved, parted.*

Common Deviations or Problems in the Articulation of /t/ and /d/

Let us look now at the common problems or faults associated with the production of the lingua-alveolar stop sounds. There are seven dangers related to these two phonemes we want to warn you about. As we discuss each of these deviations, check to see if you have that problem with these sounds.

1. *Incomplete closure.* The alveolar sounds occur very often in English speech, and so any slackness in their articulation is quite noticeable. Lazy articulation of the alveolar sounds will interfere with your ability to be understood. The /t/ and /d/ are *stop* sounds; the air stream must be stopped completely. If you articulate the stops correctly, for an instant no air at all is coming out; it is *stop*ped. To stop the outgoing breath stream completely, you must get good, firm contact of the articulators. For /t/ and /d/, you must press the tongue tip firmly against the gum ridge. If you do not get that firm contact, these sounds will not be clear and crisp, and your speech will have a lazy, careless, slovenly character. Check to be sure that the air is completely stopped and the tongue tip is firmly pressed against the upper gum ridge for /t/ and /d/ in these examples:

> metal   medal
> betting   bedding
> center   sender

plant	planned
I hit it.	I hid it.
a coat	a code
That looks . . .	mad looks
kits	kids
He let her go.	He led her away.
I'm not bitter.	I'm not a bidder.

2. *Dentalization.* The customary place to articulate the /t/ and /d/ sounds in American English is the gum ridge. If you put your tongue on the teeth instead (or just at the point where the teeth and gum meet), you have dentalized these alveolar sounds. We told you earlier that both /t/ and /d/ have an allophone made on the teeth (when the sound occurs before one of the two "th" sounds), but dentalization of /t/ and /d/ at any other time distorts the sounds. This change in tongue placement gives a fricative quality to a sound that is supposed to be a stop. The /t/ that results sounds a bit like /ts/, and the dentalized /d/ sounds something like /dz/. Check to be sure that your tongue tip goes to the gum ridge—about a quarter of an inch behind the teeth—when you make the /t/ and /d/ sounds. Pluck that point on the gum ridge with your tongue tip (and be sure the tongue is pointed to a tip, not flattened into a blade). The /t/ and /d/ should be quick, firm clicks—not prolonged, breathy explosions. Try these words out loud to check for dentalization:

toll	dole
tense	dense
team	deem
tuck	duck
tout	doubt
tab	dab

3. *Omission.* Because /t/ and /d/ are used so often in our words, the tendency to leave out these sounds is a serious problem. One very common fault is to leave these sounds off at the ends of words—especially if the /t/ or /d/ is preceded by another consonant. Check your pronunciation of these words and phrases to be sure that the final /t/ and /d/ are not dropped:

last	laughed	lapped	lacked	lashed	latched
cost	coughed	copped	cocked	quashed	scotched
gold	gunned	gummed	ganged	garaged	gorged
band	bland	blamed	banged	massaged	botched

The /t/ and /d/ are in danger of being omitted in the middle of words, especially after other consonants. Check your pronunciation of these words to see if you face that problem:

center	molting	master
venting	halter	Easter
hunter	helter	Buster
renting	altar man	
Can't he?	filter	
cinder	molding	Mazda
vending	hauled her	eased her
under	held her	buzzed her
rending	alderman	
candy	filled her	

The omission of /t/ and /d/ when they occur between two other consonants (the three consonants together are called a consonant cluster) is very common, but it is a mark of lazy articulation. We will deal with consonant clusters at length later in the book. But now you should check to see if you omit the /t/ and /d/ between two other consonants in the following words:

lofts	costs	concepts	corrects
crafts	casts	corrupts	conducts
lifts	lists	accepts	respects
softly	costly	abruptly	exactly
swiftly	ghostly	ineptly	correctly
hands	handle	wilds	wildly
spends	spindle	colds	coldly

4. *Nonstandard assimilations.* Assimilations are changes in sounds caused by neighboring sounds. (See pp. 256–262 for a fuller explanation.) Many assimilations occur in the Standard Dialect. Some assimilations, however, are still nonstandard. If you change a /t/ or /d/ into the following sound, you are substituting the next sound for the /t/ or /d/; essentially, you anticipate the next consonant, omit the /t/ or /d/, and double the next consonant. Here are some examples. Remember, we are telling you what to avoid, not what to imitate! Rather than write these errors in phonetic (IPA) symbols for you, we will spell them out in regular spelling and then translate them.

thap present	that present
hop potato	hot potato
lipe blue	light blue
streak car	street car
ik could	it could
if feels	it feels
coug go	could go
hab been	had been
Rev Foxx	Redd Foxx

Did you try these errors out loud to see what we mean? Remember, when stops are doubled, there is only one closure—which is held a little longer than usual and then released. Also, remember that these assimilations are nonstandard.

5. *Addition of* /t/. Some people add a /t/ to the ends of words where it does not belong. This problem is not very common, but it does still occur. Instead of saying *once*, they say *oncet;* instead of saying *twice*, they say *twicet*.

6. *Substitution of a glottal stop for* /t/ *or* /d/. The glottis is the space between the vocal folds. Some languages have a phoneme that is a stop made by the vocal folds. If you close the vocal folds, build up the air pressure, and then release the air in an explosion at the vocal folds, you have produced a glottal stop. We do not have such a phoneme in English, but the sound is sometimes heard as a nonstandard substitute for /t/ and /d/. The glottal stop is most often substituted for the /t/ or /d/ before /l/ or /n/ when the /l/ or /n/ is syllabic (that means the /l/ or /n/ provides the carrying power for a final syllable without a vowel being present in that syllable). The glottal stop sometimes appears as a substitute for these two stops before other consonants as well. Check your pronunciation of these examples for the glottal stop substitution:

mental	written	Let me go.
metal	rotten	What way?
fundamental	kitten	Not much.
beetle	bitten	It was just one.
battle	batten	It used to be true.
bottle	button	It was never verified.
settle	mutton	That may be so.
subtle	mittens	What lazy kids!
kettle	cotton	
little	mountain	
hospital	fountain	
piddle	shouldn't	
paddle	couldn't	
pedal	wouldn't	
poodle	didn't	
middle	hadn't	
meddle		
saddle		
straddle		
riddle		
ladle		
yodel		
fiddle faddle		

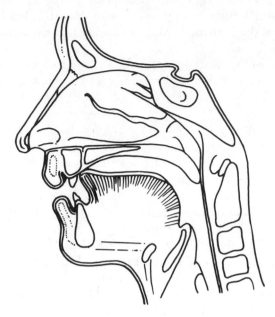

FIGURE 2–2. *Diagram of the mouth showing contact point for /t/, /d/, /l/, and /n/. The /n/, however, is produced with a relaxed and lowered soft palate.*

When /tl/, /tn/, /dl/, or /dn/ form a final syllable without a vowel, the tongue goes up to the gum ridge for the stop and stays there for the /l/ or /n/. The tongue must stay in firm contact with the gum ridge. The plosion then occurs with the tongue tip still in firm contact with the gum ridge: over the side of the tongue for /l/ and up through the nose for /n/. Say the preceding words and phrases again out loud. Be certain that you hold your tongue tip firmly against the gum ridge continuously on these combinations. The tongue does not drop down (thus releasing a plosion and forming a vowel) between the /t/ or /d/ and the /l/ or /n/.

7. *Unvoicing of /d/.* Like the other voiced stops, /d/ may be slightly devoiced before voiceless sounds and as the final sound in a phrase, but even in final position it should not be totally *un*voiced. You should not make the kind of mistake made by one of our students who read aloud to her class about a horse who was to be *shot* when the author had written about a horse who was to be *shod*.

Materials for Practicing /t/ and /d/

dear	tear	shudder	shutter	aid	ate
den	ten	medal	metal	bud	but
dapper	tapper	plodding	plotting	bad	bat

dot	tot	ladder	latter	heard	hurt
doubt	tout	bidder	bitter	node	note
daunt	taunt	ruder	rooter	Swede	sweet
dub	tub	herding	hurting	loud	lout
dame	tame	contended	contented	tied	tight

1. The Transit Authority pressed him into an untenable position.
2. One should do his best, even in an unimportant speech.
3. The priest recommended an hour of meditation every day.
4. Are hereditary factors or environmental factors more important in developing personality?
5. According to the teacher, improvement will depend on interest, effort, and practice.
6. There is no substitute for drill to develop precise articulation.
7. I took the achievement test, but I didn't do well on it.
8. "Liberty, equality, and fraternity" was a revolutionary motto.
9. The speaker developed a devastating analysis of the current trend.
10. What lawyer today would talk about "the quality of mercy"?
11. Should prostitution be legalized in the United States? I don't think so.
12. The plaintiff demanded restitution, but he didn't get it.
13. The rules on substitutions are not consistent.
14. I would have entered the contest, but I didn't know about it.
15. It isn't that I don't understand her; I just can't stand her!
16. I plan to do my term paper during Easter vacation.
17. What kind of neurotic would own ten poodles?
18. I've told her twenty times and she still can't remember it.
19. She dropped him like a hot potato!
20. The audience laughed as the alderman accepted the degree.
21. I wonder why politicians are not trusted and don't get respect.
22. All Fred's friends laughed when he got slapped.
23. He's not totally against progress; he's just opposed to change.
24. I didn't expect to be rejected, and I'm pretending it didn't happen.
25. Don't you think this edition could be greatly improved?

These sounds, /n/, /l/, /d/ and /t/, are all made on the gum ridge. If you have a problem with dentalizing them, be careful to place the tongue tip in the proper place as you read the words across the line. The tongue tip should go to the same spot to make all four initial sounds.

nigh	lie	die	tie
know	low	dough	toe
nip	lip	dip	tip
nor	lore	door	tore
napper	lapper	dapper	tapper
not	lot	dot	tot

nil	Lil	dill	till
nick	lick	Dick	tick
knee	lee	D	tee
near	leer	dear	tear
numb	Lum	dumb	Tum
gnu	lieu	do	too
nab	lab	dab	tab
Nome	loam	dome	tome
noon	loon	dune	tune
ne'er	lair	dare	tare

1. Touch the tip of the tongue to the alveolar ridge.
2. Do not explode it; tap it.
3. The tendency to dentalize the /t/ and /d/ is not too unusual in New York City.
4. Do not let the tongue tip slide forward.
5. We do not want a nuclear explosion. Cut down on the fallout.
6. Do not touch the teeth on the /t/ sound.
7. It will be necessary to practice until proper placement feels natural.
8. One must undo an old habit and replace it with a new one.
9. Let nothing deter you.
10. Do not limit your practice to laboratory sessions.
11. No one else will be able to establish new speech patterns for you.
12. Whenever you talk, try to do your best.
13. Listen carefully and critically to your own speech.
14. Learn to control the release of the air efficiently.
15. Make clear articulation a habit.
16. Spend some time each day practicing your speech.
17. Twenty sessions of five minutes each is doubtless better than one session of a hundred minutes.
18. Try to train your ears as well as your tongue.
19. Do you feel it when your tongue goes too far forward on these sounds?
20. If you are frantic doing these exercises repeatedly, devise your own.

Between vowels, /t/ often becomes somewhat voiced and therefore, sounds a little like a /d/. Many careful speakers want to make a very clear distinction between /t/ and /d/ between vowels, and for them we pass along a trick given us by the late Dr. Claude Wise. The voiceless sound /t/ can have aspiration in contrast with the voiced /d/. Therefore, to insure making the distinction, you can add a tiny puff of breath after the medial /t/ and before the next vowel. That is, put a tiny /h/ between the /t/ and the following vowel. For *bitter,* think *bit her;* for *better,* think *bet her;* for *butter,* think *but her.* Of course, the /h/ should be tiny—that is, shorter than a regular /h/. Try these pairs to get the distinct /t/:

bit her	bitter
bet her	better
but her	butter
sit he	city
wit he	witty
pit he	pity
mat her	matter
pat her	patter
fat her	fatter
bet he	Betty
let he	Letty
fret hing	fretting
bet hing	betting
get hing	getting
it his easy	It is easy.
not has easy	not as easy
what ha day	What a day!

Work for Clear, Firm Stops

1. I shudder every time I think about it.
2. We prefer shutters at the windows.

3. We are plodding along, but progress should be faster.
4. Malcontents were plotting against the authorities.

5. That old house needs a protective coating of paint.
6. Coding messages is an interesting, but difficult, task.

7. I hate to be patted on the head.
8. You ought to be put in a padded cell.

9. Puritans were particular about what puddings they would eat.
10. I'm putting this episode into your permanent record.

11. The student pleaded with the instructor to change the grade.
12. Pleated trousers are a relatively recent innovation.

13. Adam had marital problems too.
14. We live in the shadow of the atom bomb.

15. It really wasn't nearly as bad as I expected it to be.
16. She broke the baseball bat over his head.

17. It was an effort, but we weighed her.
18. Waiter, will you bring me the check?

19. Today one should bet on a mudder.
20. That is no reason for him to mutter constantly.

21. I plan to audit the course.
22. Ought it to take much time?

23. I don't think I can mend it.
24. I told him I meant it.

25. The artist bowed in response to the tumultuous ovation.
26. It will be his last bout in the Garden.

27. My reach wouldn't exceed my grasp, if I had a ladder to stand on.
28. Do you know Mormons by the name of Latter Day Saints?

29. Why are they herding so many students into one class?
30. Sadists enjoy hurting others.

31. The painting was sold to the highest bidder.
32. Are you bitter because you lost?

33. What's the matter?
34. I'm madder than a wet hen!

35. Are Columbia men ruder than most college students?
36. Their rooters displayed neither sportsmanship nor courtesy.

/k/ and /g/

Production of the Stops /k/ and /g/

If you raise the velum to prevent the air from escaping through the nose, block the air stream by pressing the back of the tongue against the soft palate, and then release the compressed air quickly by dropping the tongue from the soft palate, you will produce a lingua-velar (tongue and soft palate) stop. There are two lingua-velar stops in English: one that is voiceless, represented in IPA and in the dictionaries by /k/, and one that is voiced, represented in IPA and in the dictionaries by /g/.

Allophones of the Stops /k/ and /g/

There are three allophones of the /k/ phoneme. These allophones, like those of the other voiceless stops, vary in the amount of breath released (the degree of aspiration) when the sound is produced. Each of these allophones can be represented in IPA. The strongly aspirated allophone is [kʰ]; the weakly aspirated allophone is [kᶜ]; and the unaspirated allophone is [k⁼].

/k/ is strongly aspirated if the /k/ initiates a stressed syllable. There is a strong puff of breath released on the /t/ in these words, for example:

kin	akin
cur	occur
cute	acute
cause	because

/k/ is weakly aspirated after /s/ in the same syllable. Note the difference in aspiration when /s/ precedes the /k/:

Chi	sky
key	ski
kin	skin
care	scare
Kate	scate

The /k/ is also weakly aspirated if it initiates an unstressed syllable. Note that there is a puff of breath when you release the /k/ in the following words, but there is not as great a puff of air as when /k/ initiates stressed syllables.

confused	(Compare the stressed syllable: Kahn.)
packing	(Compare the stressed syllable: King.)
commit	(Compare the stressed syllable: come.)

/k/ is usually unaspirated when final in a phrase. Say these words and phrases as you ordinarily do, and you will probably discover that there is no puff of air on the release of the /k/:

take	Buy me a pack.
peak	Just one more piece of cake.
oak	I'm already broke.

Also, there is usually no aspiration of /k/ if the next sound is a consonant. Pronounce these examples:

actor	Take more than one.
lackluster	Dick took his share.
bookmark	Back to nature!
back seat	Look for the silver lining.

There are four allophones of the /g/ phoneme. Like the other voiced stops, /g/ is not aspirated, but it does vary in the degree of force on its release. The /g/ can be strongly exploded, weakly exploded, or not exploded. In addition, the /g/ can be partially devoiced.

/g/ is strongly exploded if the /g/ initiates a stressed syllable. Pronounce the following examples out loud:

go	ago
get	forget
gassed	aghast
glow	aglow
grand	aggrandizement

/g/ is weakly exploded if the /g/ initiates an unstressed syllable. Pronounce these examples out loud:

biggest	(Compare the stressed syllable: guest.)
haggle	(Compare the stressed syllable: gull.)
beggar	(Compare the stressed syllable: girl.)

/g/ is usually unexploded when final in a phrase. Check this principle out as you read these sentences out loud:

> Give me a hug.
> Don't damage the flag.
> We've been hit by a plague.
> Everyone was agog.
> Forgive me if I brag.

There is usually no explosion of the /g/ sound if the next sound is a consonant. Read these examples out loud:

> Your dog bit me.
> She dug me. What did she dig you?
> It's the big league from now on.
> We lost the big one.

/g/ is usually partially devoiced before voiceless consonants and at the ends of phrases. Read these sentences out loud: Is each /g/ fully voiced throughout?

> It was a big harvest.
> One *egg* sunnyside up.
> The *gag* fell flat.
> *Eggnog* should not affect you like that.
> Humility is still in vogue.

Specific Warnings

The spellings *kn* and *gn* at the beginnings of words in English represent the /n/ sound. The *k* letter and the *g* letter are silent. Note these examples, and pronounce them out loud:

knack	gnarl
knave	gnash
knead	gnat
knee	gnaw
kneel	gnome
knell	Gnostic
knife	gnu
knit	
knob	
knock	
knoll	
knot	
know	
knuckle	

There is no /k/ or /g/ phoneme at the beginning of any of those words.

The letter g before m or n at the end of a word is silent. Pronounce these words out loud, remembering that the /g/ phoneme does not occur at the end of these words:

diaphragm	sign	reign	impugn	ensign
paradigm	align	arraign		
phlegm	assign	deign		
	benign	feign		
	consign	campaign		
	design	champagne		
	malign			
	resign			

In the preceding words, the g remains a silent letter when some suffixes are added to the words, and it is pronounced when other suffixes are added. In general there is no /g/ if the suffixes -ing, -ment, or -er are added; in general there is a /g/ if the suffixes -al, -ance, -ant, -atic, -ation, -ia, -ify, or -ity are added. Check these examples by pronouncing them out loud:

WITHOUT /g/	WITH /g/
alignment	signal
assigning	malignance
signer	malignant
consignment	phlegmatic
resigning	resignation
designer	insignia
arraignment	signify
feigning	malignity
campaigner	

Common Deviations of the Stops /k/ and /g/

There are four common deviations associated with the phonemes /k/ and /g/. As we discuss each of these problems, check to be sure you do not have that problem with these sounds.

1. *Incomplete closure.* As in the case of the other stops, it is necessary to block the air stream completely on /k/ and /g/. Careless speakers pronounce such words as *acceptable, accede,* and *succulent* without making a complete stop on the /k/. The back of the tongue is not pressed firmly enough against the soft palate to completely stop the outgoing air. You have probably also heard people who do not fully close the /g/ in such words as *ignition, cognition,* and *recognize.* For these sounds to be stops, the air stream must be completely stopped. Check to be certain

you are making clear, complete stops for the /k/ and /g/ sounds in these words and phrases:

uncle	bungle
bicker	bigger
Buckley	ugly
bucking	bugging
vicar	vigor
fictitious	ignore
activate	aggravate
archangel	argyle
actually	agonize
accept	segment
accident	agreement
accupuncture	agriculture
a lack	a lag
evoke	a vogue
opaque	a plague

2. *Omission.* There seems to be a great temptation to leave out /k/ and /g/ sounds altogether, especially at the ends of words and in certain other contexts. We will give you some words where there is a danger of omitting these stops. Do not yield to the temptation. Check your pronunciation of these words and phrases out loud:

FINAL /k/	FINAL /g/
back	bag
Huck	hug
Rick	rig
plaque	plague

/ks/	/gz/
leaks	leagues
racks	rags
bricks	brigs
accede	exact
access	exalt
accent	exert
accelerate	exist
accident	exotic
succeed	exult
success	big zoo
succinct	zigzag zone
except	big zero
excel	flag zealot

/kt/	/gd/
decked	begged
joked	jogged
whacked	wagged
lacked	lagged
chucked	chugged
tact	tagged
plucked	plugged
locked	logged

/sk/	/sks/	/skt/
ask	asks	asked
mask	masks	masked
bask	basks	basked
cask	casks	casked
disc	discs	disked
risk	risks	risked

Here are some words where the /k/ and /g/ come before a variety of consonants and consonant groups. All contain a temptation to omit the /k/ or /g/:

/k/	/g/
arctic	signify
tactic	significance
explain	extinguish
explicit	recognition
extent	recognize
extensive	ignite
express	ignition
extinct	ignoble
explore	big boy
exploit	peg bent
explosion	Hug Mary.
export	Tag Prince.
extort	stag party
expulsion	pig pen
extra	
disc brakes	
blackboard	
rag doll	
bleak picture	

3. *Overaspiration.* The amount of air released on the /k/ varies, and the amount of force with which /g/ is released also varies. We explained

these variations when discussing the allophones of these stops. But we must add a word of warning here: Be careful not to overexplode /k/ and /g/.

4. *Unvoicing of* /g/. Like the other voiced stops, /g/ is slightly *de*voiced before voiceless sounds and as the final sound in a phrase. But the /g/ should not be completely *un*voiced. Even when the last word in a phrase or sentence, *lug* should not sound like *luck* and *stag* should not sound like *stack*.

Materials for Practicing /k/ *and* /g/

Kaye	gay	meeker	meager	lock	log
coast	ghost	racket	ragged	back	bag
cause	gauze	anchor	anger	Rick	rig
crime	grime	lacquered	laggard	muck	mug
crape	grape	Becker	begger	Beck	beg
crypt	gripped	ankle	angle	leak	league
clue	glue	backing	bagging	hawk	hog
class	glass	pokey	pogy	hack	hag
clean	glean	bucking	bugging	luck	lug

1. The Clarks have a cottage and garden in the country.
2. A government employee, he still kept his membership in the key club.
3. The crowd found the combat gripping, but the combatants themselves were cool and calculating.
4. Every society has its own golden calf. Is ours success?
5. He is not an ignorant man, but he did not recognize the governor.
6. In such a struggle, there is rarely a victor; one must be rugged and clever merely to survive.
7. Above being a common crook, a smuggler is a racketeer and a rogue.
8. To prevent students from haggling over exam grades, some professors keep all questions exceptionally vague.
9. Actually, I cannot accede to your request because I would be an accessory to your crime.
10. The thieves took out my car's ignition and broke the lock on the trunk.
11. I couldn't detect his agony—except for his groans.
12. The house was *almost* perfect: the back porch sagged and the roof leaked.
13. I begged him for an extension, but he got angry and walked away.
14. Actually, I'm very unlucky; some time ago, all my luggage was taken from my locker.
15. I'm going to buy a ticket to a rugged, picturesque place.

16. I can't accept charity, but I would be glad to get a job.
17. His first act as governor was to go out and wave a flag.
18. If gas gets any more expensive, I'll have to get a horse and buggy.
19. The dog growled, and my guest knocked over the bookcase.
20. The college orchestra and chorus give a concert version of "The Music Man" in August.
21. I liked the work at first, but my interest lagged and I offered my resignation.
22. I gather that doctors and chiropractors don't always agree.
23. A big group of people was saved by his quick reaction to the explosion.
24. Rock could be the classical music of the future—I guess.
25. I think you are exaggerating the significance of Rock.

FRICATIVES

If you bring two articulators together (not enough to completely close off the outgoing air stream) and squeeze the breath between the two articulators, you will produce a frictionlike noise. These frictionlike noises or sounds are called fricatives. There are ten fricative consonants in American English. They are the first sound in the words: *wheel* (if you pronounce the first sound *hw* as we do), *feel, veal, thin, then, Sue, zoo, she,* and *he;* the tenth sound never occurs in English words as the first sound in a word, so we must give you a key word with the sound in the middle: the /ʒ/ (zh) in *azure.*

As we analyze the fricative sounds, we will look at two individual sounds and at four pairs of cognates.

/ʍ/ (hw)

Production of the /ʍ/ (hw)

Several movements are involved in the production of this fricative sound. You must raise the velum to prevent air from escaping through the nose, pucker the lips as if you were going to make the /u/ vowel (the first sound in the word *ooze*), let the tip of the tongue rest behind the lower front teeth, and raise the back of the tongue toward the velum. Together with these simultaneous movements, you emit the air in a friction-type noise without the vocal folds vibrating. The sound produced is a voiceless bilabial fricative; the IPA symbol for this sound is /ʍ/, and the dictionary symbol is hw. Some phoneticians consider this sound the voiceless cognate of the /w/. It sounds like an *hw* combination, except that it has no voicing. Like the /w/, the /ʍ/ always occurs at the beginning of syllables—never at the end. This voiceless bilabial fricative is the first sound in most words beginning with the spelling *wh*—as pronounced by many, if not most, speakers of Standard American English. You may notice that we have hedged that sentence with several qualifiers; we will explain those evasions immediately.

Allophones of the /ʍ/ (hw)

We said that many, if not most, speakers of Standard American English use this sound to distinguish such words as *wheel* and *we'll*, *where* and *wear*, and *whether* and *weather*. The use of /ʍ/ seems to be declining, both in the United States and Great Britain. In parts of the eastern United States, especially in New York City and other urban areas, the /ʍ/ sound is rarely used and /w/ is regularly used in its place on *wh* words. These writers (one a Southerner and the other a Midwesterner) both live in New York City, but they continue to include the /ʍ/ in their idiolects. We prefer not to use the /w/ on these *wh* words, simply because doing so results in so many homophones (words that sound alike but differ in spelling and meaning). Check your own pronunciation of the following pairs of words. Do you use /ʍ/ (hw) to begin the first word of each pair, or do you begin both words in each pair with /w/? In either case, the use of /w/ for all these words is so widespread among speakers of the Status Dialect that its use certainly cannot be labeled nonstandard. Still, out of curiosity, check to see whether you use the /ʍ/ (hw) or not.

whee	we
what	watt
whine	wine
where	wear
whale	wail
why	Y
whet	wet
wheel	weal
which	witch
whey	way
white	wight
whit	wit
whirred	word
whirled	world
whir	were
while	wile
whether	weather
Whig	wig
whisk	Wisk
whacks	wax
whys	wise
why'd	wide

Specific Warnings

In some words beginning with the spelling *wh,* the initial sound is not /ʍ/ (h̯w) or /w/. Instead, in these words, the initial sound is /h/. The words *who, whose, whom, whole, whore,* and *whoop*—and the words formed from them—all begin with the /h/ sound.

Common Deviations or Problems in the Articulation of /ʍ/ (h̯w)

There are two dangers associated with this phoneme: slack articulation at the lips and substitution of /v/ for /ʍ/.

1. *Inadequate lip tension and movement.* You must round the lips to make the /ʍ/ sound. Earlier, we said to pucker the lips. If you do not tense the lips enough, the articulation will be slack and inexact. To be sure you get sufficient tension and rounding of the lips, look in the mirror as you say the words *ooze, you,* and *whim.* The lips should be puckered (or pursed) for the beginning of all three words. The lips should be as tightly rounded for /ʍ/ (or /w/) as for the vowel in *ooze* and *you.* Checking for adequate lip rounding in the mirror, pronounce these words out loud:

> whip
> whim
> whelp
> whimper
> whimsy
> whisper
> wheat
> whiff
> whistle
> whisky
> whiz

2. *Substitution of /v/ for /ʍ/* (h̯w). Some speakers who learned English as a second language (and some speakers whose speech patterns were influenced by those who learned English as a second language) substitute /v/ for the /ʍ/ (and for /w/). The /ʍ/ fricative is made by forcing air between the two lips, which have been tensed into a pucker; the /v/ is made by squeezing air between the upper teeth and the lower lip. Checking in a mirror as you pronounce these words, be sure that the initial sound in the first word of each pair is articulated by the two lips; the initial sound in the second word of each pair should be articulated by the upper teeth and lower lip.

> while   vile
> whine   vine
> why   vie

wheel	veal
whale	vale
whet	vet
whim	vim

Materials for Practicing /ʍ/ (hw)

1. She didn't tell me the whys and wherefores.
2. I don't know whether to change the whole wheel or just the tire.
3. Why did the bridesmaids wear white dresses?
4. Meanwhile, the dervish kept whirling and the witch kept mixing potions.
5. Why in the world did she whack him with a broom?
6. The dog's whines were drowned out by the whir of the engine.
7. I couldn't decide which place to go—to Gimbel's white sale or to Macy's "Whale of a Sale."
8. Pleasure-wacky people today would start their Declaration, "Whee, the people . . . ."
9. Whisper to me whatever you want to say.
10. Do you prefer white bread or whole wheat?
11. I know what I'll do, but who knows where or when?
12. The more whisky she drank, the more whimsical she became.
13. It's wicked to whet my appetite when I'm trying to diet.
14. Why did they want you to shave off your whiskers?
15. I know what to buy, but I don't have the wherewithal!

/h/

Production of the /h/

If you bring the vocal bands together enough to cause friction, but not vibration, and huff the air through while keeping the velum raised to prevent the air from escaping through the nose, you will produce the glottal fricative. The glottis is the space between the vocal folds; hence, the name. This sound occurs in English only at the beginning of a syllable, and the lips and tongue are in the position of the vowel that follows while the /h/ is produced. Pronounce the words *he, had,* and *who* and you will see that the lips and tongue are already in position for the following vowel when the /h/ is uttered. We represent this sound in both by IPA and the dictionaries by the symbol /h/.

Allophones of the /h/

There are two allophones of the /h/ phoneme. The voiceless allophone, or variation, is the more common of the two. When /h/ occurs between vowels in the middle of a word, the /h/ is sometimes voiced. The /h/ absorbs voicing from the surrounding vowels. Compare your own pronunciation of the words *half* and *behalf*. The first began with a voiceless, aspirate (breathy) /h/; the second probably had a voiced (and much less breathy) /h/ in the middle. The IPA symbol for the voiced allophone is [ɦ]. Pronounce the following pairs of words and phrases out loud. The words in the left-hand column will begin with a voiceless /h/; those in the right-hand column will probably contain the [ɦ] allophone.

half	behalf
hold	behold
head	behead
hind	behind
harsh	Be harsh.
head	ahead
hit	a hit
habit	rehabilitation
hooves	behooves
how	anyhow

Specific Warnings

Not every word that is spelled with the letter *h* contains the /h/ phoneme. Some words preserve the silent *h* of their French origin. Pronounce these words out loud, remembering that the *h* letter is silent:

heir	heirloom
hour	hourly
honor	honorable
honest	honesty

There are some words spelled with the letter *h* that some speakers of the Standard Dialect pronounce with /h/, whereas other speakers of the Standard Dialect do not. Either pronunciation, therefore, is "standard." Do you pronounce an /h/ at the beginning of these words?

herb   homage   humble

When the unstressed form of a form word (see pp. 263–266 for a discussion of form words) beginning with /h/ occurs in the middle or at the end of a phrase, the /h/ is often omitted. This omission, especially in conversational speech, should not be considered nonstandard. Read the following phrases out loud—as you would say them in conversation. Each time, check to hear if you pronounce the /h/ or not:

I told him.
How could he do it?
I found her weakness.
That's his job.
Where have they gone?
It has not been finished.

We had gone by then.
We forgave her.

The /h/ phoneme never occurs at the end of a syllable. The *h* letter at the end of a written word or syllable is silent. Pronounce these examples out loud:

Ah!
Allah
blah
Torah
Sikh
hutzpah
matzoh
pariah
hurrah
huzzah
Hanukkah
hallelujah

Common Deviations of the /h/

There are two common problems associated with the /h/ sound: (1) omission and (2) overaspiration.

1. *Omission.* In some areas of the United States (especially in metropolitan New York) the /h/ is omitted by most speakers in such words as hue and human. Even cultivated speakers make homophones (words that sound alike) of *hue* and *you* and of *human* and *Youman.* In most of the United States, however, the omission of the /h/ in such words is considered nonstandard and should be avoided.

In the middle of words, the spelling *h* is silent if it initiates an unstressed syllable, but it is sometimes pronounced /h/ if it initiates a stressed syllable. The *h* in *prohibit,* for example, is pronounced because it initiates the stressed syllable of the word; the *h* in *prohibition,* however, is not pronounced because it initiates an unstressed syllable. To add to the confusion, the *h* in *exhibit, exhaust, exhaustion, exhilarant, exhilarate,* and *exhort* is silent.

Be especially careful not to omit the /h/ in the middle of words, and be wary of an /h/ after consonants in the middle of words. Try the following examples aloud:

exhale	inhuman	withheld	dishearten
exhalant	unholy	bathhouse	disharmony
exhaling	unhurried	withhold	mishap

2. *Overaspiration.* If too much air is pushed through on the /h/ sound, your speech will sound breathy. Move off the /h/ quickly and on to the next vowel. Do not huff and puff too forcefully on the /h/ phoneme.

Materials for Practicing the /h/

hear	ear
heal	eel
heat	eat
hate	ate
he	E
hail	ale
how	Ow!
had	add
hand	and
high	I
head	Ed
Harry	airy
Hugh	you
held	Eld
who	Oo!
hit	it
hid	id
hide	I'd
Hoyle	oil
hasp	asp
has	as
he's	ease
his	is
hers	errs
hug	Ugh!
hickey	ickey
heavens	Evans
hold	old
honed	owned
haste	aced
heist	iced
hell	el
him	M
hacked	act
hanker	anchor
who's	ooze
Huss	us
hot	Ott
handsome	and some
haughty	Ought he?

1. The halfback was late getting back to the huddle.
2. Henry thinks humility is his greatest virtue.
3. How many wives did Henry the Eighth behead?
4. Behold I show you a great mystery: how he passed the exam.
5. She's inhuman; she wants to get ahead.
6. Who will speak in behalf of the honor system?
7. My huge debts keep me humble.
8. Such habitual behavior must be inherited.
9. Those who used to agree with us are heretics; those who have never agreed with us are heathen!
10. Hugh has no sense of humor.
11. If it is humanly possible, she'll humiliate her husband.
12. What adhesive holds them together?
13. Hospital rates are higher than those of the Waldorf-Astoria Hotel.
14. I've heard there's a Huguenot church in Greenwich Village.
15. Anyhow, it is an unhealthy relationship.
16. Why withhold your support? He's going to win anyhow.
17. The house is totally unheated.
18. Whoever gets behind Hubert will be hurt.
19. It ill behooves any of us to be hasty to criticize another human being.
20. One who gives with an unhappy heart is no humanitarian.

/f/ and /v/

Production of the Fricatives /f/ and /v/

If you raise the velum so no air can escape through the nose, bring the edges of the upper teeth and the lower lip together, and force the air out between the upper teeth and lower lip, you will produce a labiodental (lip and teeth) fricative. There are two labiodental fricatives in English: one that is voiceless and one that is voiced. The voiceless cognate is represented in IPA and in the dictionaries by /f/; the voiced cognate is represented in IPA and in the dictionaries by /v/.

Allophones of /f/ and /v/

There is only one form of the /f/ and only two allophones (variations) of the /v/.

In all positions in our words (at the beginning, in the middle, at the end), the /f/ sound is produced in the same way: the upper teeth and lower lip are brought together, and the air is forcibly squeezed out between them.

The /v/ is articulated in the same way as the /f/, except that the vocal folds are vibrating. When initiating syllables, when between vowels, and when at the end of a syllable before another voiced consonant, /v/ is fully voiced. Check your pronunciation of these words to be sure the /v/ is fully voiced:

very	Avery	saved
vermin	savor	naval
vengeance	leaving	evil

Before voiceless consonants and at the ends of phrases, /v/ is partially devoiced. (The IPA symbol for devoicing is a little circle under the letter.) Check to hear if the /v/ is partially devoiced in the following examples:

five tons
five pounds
Give testimony.
Believe somebody.
He has no leave time left.
Relieve Kitty.
I can't carve turkey.
They gave cheerfully.

Specific Warnings

Just a reminder: the little, common word *of* is spelled with an *f*, but it is pronounced with a /v/.

Common Deviations or Problems in the Articulation of /f/ and /v/

There are five common problems associated with these two fricative sounds: (1) slack articulation, (2) omission, (3) unvoicing /v/, (4) the substitution of /w/ for /v/, and (5) the substitution of /b/ for /v/.

1. *Slack articulation.* To produce these two sounds, you must bring the upper teeth and the lower lip together. They must touch. If you only raise the lower lip a little, you will produce a bilabial fricative rather than a labiodental fricative; that is a different kind of sound altogether. If your lips are too lazy to move, you will have to work to get them used to articulating. Slack articulation of the /f/ and /v/ creates the impression of careless, slovenly speech. Checking to be certain the upper teeth and lower lip *touch*, pronounce these words out loud:

feel	leaf	vague	gave
fine	knife	vast	starve
fall	off	veer	Reeve
fool	aloof	vile	alive

2. *Omission.* Many speakers are tempted to omit /f/ and /v/—particularly before other consonants. Of the two sounds, /v/ is more often

omitted because the voiced cognate is always the less forceful one to begin with. It is also true that many speakers who omit these sounds are not aware at all of doing so. Check carefully, while pronouncing these examples, to be sure that the /f/ and /v/ are not omitted.

lifetime	slaveship
off-white	evening
afternoon	love story
laugh meter	leave time
graph paper	prove troublesome
It's half time.	Give me some.
Cough syrup, please.	Love me or leave me.
It's a rough time.	I have to go.
There's enough work.	I've delivered it.
What a golf course!	I've canceled them all.

3. *Unvoicing of* /v/. Like other voiced consonants, /v/ may be slightly devoiced before voiceless sounds and as the final sound in a phrase. But the /v/ should not be completely *unvoiced*. *Save* should not become *safe,* for example, and *have* should not become *half.* Check to be sure that, as you pronounce these words out loud, the final /v/ is clearly a voiced sound:

safe	save
strife	strive
proof	prove
life	live (adj.)
leaf	leave
serf	serve
belief	believe
waif	wave
grief	grieve
Duff	dove
shelf	shelve
plaintiff	plaintive
half	have

4. *Substitution of* /w/ *for* /v/. Some speakers who learned English as a second language substitute /w/ for /v/. The /w/ is articulated by puckering the two lips, but the /v/ is articulated by bringing the upper teeth and lower lip together. Check to see if you make a distinction between these sets of words:

wail	vale
wane	vain
won't	vaunt
wary	vary

wend	vend
went	vent
west	vest
wet	vet
wicker	vicar
wide	vied
wile	vile
wine	vine
wince	Vince
wiper	viper
Weiss	vice
worse	verse
woo	voodoo

5. *Substitution of* /b/ *for* /v/. Some speakers who learned English as a second language (especially those who first spoke Latin-American Spanish) substitute /b/ for /v/ in English. This confusion is understandable, because of the phonemic system of their first language. Check to be sure you articulate the first sound in the words starting with /v/ with the upper teeth and lower lip touching. Use a mirror to check your articulation of the /v/.

bale	vale
bane	vain
ban	van
bend	vend
Bender	vendor
berry	very
beer	veer
banish	vanish
bet	vet
bile	vile
boat	vote
bow	vow
buy	vie
bicker	vicar
boo, booh	voodoo
imbue	in view
Eban	even
a boat	a vote
Cabot	Cavett
Hubbard	hovered
Abie	A-V
Graber	graver

saber	savor
labor	laver
Bieber	beaver
gibbon	given
a Boyd	avoid
ribbon	riven
a bale	avail
abide	divide
about	devout

Materials for Practicing /f/ and /v/
INITIAL /f/ AND /v/
CONTRAST

feel	veal
fine	vine
fairy	very
first	versed
few	view
face	vase
fast	vast
fear	vear
file	vile
faught	Vought
focal	vocal
fire us	virus
fender	vendor
fault	vault
fie	vie

MEDIAL /f/ AND /v/
CONTRAST

infest	invest
defied	divide
refile	revile
a fur	aver
proof it	prove it
infighting	inviting
surface	service
rifle	rival
surfer	server
define	divine
safer	savor
leafing	leaving
refuse (v.)	reviews

FINAL /f/ AND /v/
CONTRAST

leaf	leave
safe	save
waif	wave
belief	believe
serf	serve
life	live (adj.)
strife	strive
proof	prove
grief	grieve
fife	five
shelf	shelve
half	have
relief	relieve
a buff	above
reef	Reeve

1. I may be very foolish, but I do not fear the future.
2. My friends think I'm naive—just because I believe everything I hear.
3. My staff couldn't get enough information to develop a brief.
4. Frieda tore her velvet dress on the shelves.
5. My wife has a vast store of information on trivia.
6. Victor may be a fool, but he would never deceive anybody.
7. Have you read *Leaves of Grass?*
8. Why was Valerie so furious? She hadn't gotten a whiff of the scandal!
9. Because of the layoffs, they've taken to drink.
10. I've told everything I know, and that should be enough.
11. Wouldn't it be fine if every revolver in America would vanish over-night?
12. They called me subversive because of my friends.
13. I'd love to be invisible for just a few hours.
14. Don't laugh. She fell because the pavement is so uneven.
15. They've started to investigate his involvement in the fraud.
16. I've heard the D.A. vowed to produce proof.
17. I've bet five dollars on the fifth race. Now they've revised the odds.
18. I'm not really very brave—just foolhardy.
19. It's obvious to everybody who knows him he's in difficulty.
20. Evidently, the service has gone from bad to worse.
21. *Twelfth Night* is one of my favorite plays.
22. I will not move; I am not the driver.

23. Save your money. The raffle is fixed.
24. It was hanging above the door for more than five days.
25. He could have proved himself a live wire.
26. Mardi Gras is one last carefree fling before pleasures are shelved.
27. A fifth of a cupful is quite enough.
28. I've left the cover of the manuscript at home.
29. Mother always laughs while Father carves the fowl.
30. She forgot and sang the same verse twice.
31. Leaving nothing to the imagination, the devil made the offer quite obvious.
32. It is very foolish to strive against overpowering odds.
33. Would you be very comfortable at a rendezvous with a rival?
34. Somewhat given to violence, that fraternity is called the home of the brave.

Here are some sentences that contrast /v/ and /b/:

1. I'd rather move in a covered wagon than in a moving van. Bandits!
2. Eventually, everybody will be required to vote.
3. Above all, be virtuous—whatever that means.
4. The bureaucrats on the Zoning Commission took a dim view of his log cabin.
5. Don't get involved with little vices; think big.
6. I get bored very easily when I watch TV.
7. Bertha's always vulgar—even in private.
8. I told Victor to work on verbal skills.
9. Every time Barbara said, "It's all over," it revived our romance.
10. Bob is a very devout Seven-Day Hedonist.
11. Be very careful about what you vow you'll never do.
12. Bill has twelve more days of classes at Brooklyn College.
13. Have you been in service? No, but I've been in the Boy Scouts.
14. The firemen believe the blaze started in the oven.
15. I've done my best on every sentence. I've practiced; I've listened; I've thought. I may face reverses, but it's getting better!

Here are a few sentences that contrast /v/ and /w/:

1. I'm willing to wait; I just hope it's not in vain.
2. I won't ever get involved again!
3. I was shoveling snow when I began to quiver all over.
4. Who would have thought David would grieve so over a dog?
5. I've never felt worse; it was stupid behavior.
6. I want them to prove it to me.
7. The duty of a vassal is to work; the job of a serf is to serve.
8. Hoping to make his own wine, Dad has bought some grape vines.

9. The second verse was even worse than the first.
10. Unable to woo and win her, he tried voodoo.

Production of the Fricatives /θ/ (th) and /ð/ (th)

If you raise the velum so no air can escape through the nose, bring the upper teeth and the blade of your tongue together, and let the air ooze out between the upper teeth edges and the tongue, you will produce a linguadental (tongue and teeth) fricative. The tongue may be placed either against the inside surfaces of the upper front teeth or beneath the edges of the upper front teeth. There are two linguadental fricatives in English: one is voiceless, represented in IPA by /θ/ and in the dictionaries by th; and one is voiced, represented in IPA by /ð/ and in the dictionaries by *th*.

Allophones of /θ/ (th) and /ð/ (th)

There are no standard allophones (variations) of these two phonemes. Be sure your tongue is at the bottom of the upper teeth and the air comes oozing out rather than in a plosive burst.

Specific Warnings

Both linguadental fricatives in English are represented in regular spelling by the digraph (letter combination) *th*. You cannot tell from the spelling whether the word contains the voiceless or the voiced cognate. Sometimes *th* does not represent either sound. Note the words *courthouse, outhouse,* and *Thomas*.

Common Deviations in the Articulation of /θ/ (th) and /ð/ (th)

There are five common problems, or dangers, associated with these sounds: (1) omission, (2) unvoicing of /ð/, (3) raising the sounds, (4) substitution of /f/ and /v/, and (5) substitution of /s/ and /z/.

1. *Omission.* Some speakers omit these sounds at the ends of words. Check your pronunciation of the following phrases to be sure the final /θ/ (th) and /ð/ (th) are not omitted:

both of them	tithe our income
birth of the Blues	bathe a child
south of Boston	teethe all year
path of least resistance	clothe a family
wrath of God	wreathe a door

The /θ/ (th) and /ð/ (th) are in danger of being omitted if the next sound is a consonant. Checking for omission of /θ/ (th) and /ð/ (th), pronounce these examples out loud:

birthday	breathe freely
bathroom	bathe daily
pathway	clothe children
cloth coat	soothe Tom
mouth to mouth	tithe faithfully
oath taken	lathe machine
with Tom	writhe frantically
My tooth hurts.	seethe constantly
north wind	Don't mouth your words.
South side	Wreathe your face in a smile.

The greatest temptation to omit /θ/ (th) and /ð/ (th) is when they appear in consonant combinations. Speakers who are careless (lip and tongue lazy) tend to avoid the extra trouble of putting these sounds in when they occur in difficult combinations. And there is no question that it does take extra care and effort to get the sounds in. When one syllable ends with a consonant and the next syllable starts with a consonant, the consonants are said to be abutting. We have already noted that you may be tempted to omit /θ/ and /ð/ when either is the first of two abutting consonants (when either ends one syllable and another consonant starts the next syllable). The reverse is even truer: when either /θ/ or /ð/ begins a syllable after another syllable ending in a consonant or consonants, there is great danger of omission. Read aloud the following phrases, and be careful not to omit the abutting /θ/ (th) or /ð/ (th).

Just think.	What's that?
fix things	Why ask that question?
complex theology	It's the truth.
fast thinking	miss the point
six thrills	Pick the winner.
past thirty	muff the answer
rough thrust	I can't stand this!

The greatest temptation to omit /θ/ and /ð/ comes in consonant clusters —that is, in groups of consonants that lack vowels between them. Pronounce the following groups of words aloud, and check to be sure you do not omit the /θ/ (th) or /ð/ (th):

/θs/ (ths)	/ðz/ (thz)	[ðd] (thd)
breaths	breathes	breathed
bath's	bathes	bathed
deaths	writhes	writhed
Booth's	soothes	soothed
earth's	seethes	seethed
myths	mouths (verb)	mouthed
youth's	truths	clothed

/θm/(thm)   /ðm/(thm)
anthem   rhythm

/sθ/(sth)

aesthetic
anesthesia
anesthetic
anesthetist
anesthesiologist

/fθ/(fth)	/fθs/(fths)	/pθ/(pth)	/pθs/(pths)
fifth	fifths	depth	depths

/dθ/(dth)	/dθs/(dths)	/lθ/(lth)	/lθs/(lths)
width	widths	wealth	wealth's
breadth	breadths	health	health's
hundredth	hundredths	stealth	stealth's

/nθ/(nth)	/nθs/(nths)	/ksθ/(ksth)	/ksθs/(ksths)
seventh	sevenths	sixth	sixths
ninth	ninths		
tenth	tenths	/ŋ(k)θ/(ngkth)	/ŋ(k)θs/(ngkths)
eleventh	elevenths	length	lengths
month	months	strength	strengths

2. *Unvoicing.* Although the /ð/ (th) will be slightly devoiced before voiceless sounds and when it is the last sound in a phrase, it should never be completely unvoiced. *Soothe* should never be turned into *sooth,* for example, and *teethe* should never become *teeth.* Try these phrases out loud and check for unvoicing of the /ð/ (th):

I can hardly breathe.
I wish he'd bathe.
Watch that wrestler writhe!
Larry is using the lathe.

3. *Raising.*[2] Raising the tongue behind the teeth on the production of the two "th" sounds produces a distortion. To the untrained ear, the resulting /θ/ (th) sounds like a /t/, and the resulting /ð/ (th) sounds like a /d/. Actually, the people who raise the tongue on these sounds do not articulate a real American English /t/ or /d/, but the distortion is great enough to sound that way. Remember that /t/ and /d/ are articulated by the tongue tip on the gum ridge. The tongue is not raised that

---

[2] The phonetic symbol for raising is ⊥; it is placed to the right and a little above the symbol for the sound—that is, [θ⊥] and [ð⊥].

high on these distortions; it is raised up behind the teeth, but it never gets as high as the gum ridge. Still, when raised that high, the sounds do sound more plosive than fricative. And those who raise the tongue up on the inner surfaces of the teeth on the /θ/ and /ð/ are thought to say *"dis, dat, dese, and dose";* "Come wit me," "I'll go witcha," and "nuttin' doin'." If the tongue is not placed at the bottom of the upper teeth, the sounds will be distorted. The tongue does not have to be under the teeth to produce these sounds, but the blade of the tongue must be at the bottom of the teeth. If you have difficulty with this distortion, we suggest you use a mirror and make sure that the tongue is under the upper teeth. Check your production of /θ/ (th) and /ð/ (*th*) on the following list of examples:

thigh	thy
thin	then
ether	either
mouth (n.)	mouth (v.)
teeth	teethe
cloth	clothe

He's at the school.
Hit the road.
I read the book.
I made that mistake.
I'll take this one.
Who'll go with you?
You can't soothe my feelings.
Now it will be smooth sailing.
It's no bother; I'll get another one.
Birth and death are mysteries.
I think those are the right ones.

4. *Substitution of* /f/ *for* /θ/ (th) *and* /v/ *for* /ð/ (*th*). In some nonstandard (although thoroughly self-consistent) dialects of American English, speakers substitute /f/ for /θ/ and /v/ for /ð/—especially in the middle and at the ends of words. Check your own pronunciation of these words and phrases to see if you make this substitution. If necessary, watch in a mirror as you say the words.

death	other
birthday	another
with ease	whether to go
with me	smoother worker
pathway	I'd rather not.
North Pole	It's no bother.
both of us	Either I do or I don't.

5. *Substitution of /s/ for /θ/* (th) *and /z/ for /ð/* (th). Some speakers who learned English as a second language substitute /s/ for /θ/ and /z/ for /ð/. Their first language, doubtless, did not have the /θ/ and /ð/ phonemes (many languages do not), and they have substituted a sound they were used to for the unfamiliar new phonemes of English. Remember that /θ/ (th) and /ð/ (*th*) are made with the tongue at the bottom of the upper teeth and, although they are friction noises, they are not hissing noises like /s/ and /z/. Read aloud the following words to see if you make this substitution:

sinking	thinking	Z	thee
seems	themes	Zen	then
saw	thaw	Zayre	there
sought	thought	Xanadu	than I do
sick	thick	(Auld Lang) Syne	thine

Thank you; my hopes sank.
I think I'll take it, or I'll sink trying.
A good girl is a myth—not a miss.
The end ran a straight path and caught the pass.

I resemble them a little.
The breeze is so strong I can hardly breathe.
Every minute she writhes, her temperature rises.
The cop seized her; she just seethed.

Materials for Practicing /θ/ (th) *and* /ð/ (*th*)

INITIAL /θ/ (th)   thank, thatch, thaw, theater, theft, theism, theist, theme, thence, theocracy, theology, theory, therapy, thermal, thesis, thespian, thick, thicket, thief, thigh, thimble, thin, thing, think, third, thirty, thirsty, thistle, thong, thorn, thorough, thrash, thread, threat, three, threshold, thrift, thrill, thrive, throat, throb, throne, throng, throttle, through, thrust, thug, thumb, thump, thunder, thwart

MEDIAL /θ/ (th)   Athens, atheist, aesthetic, author, breathy, catholic, earthy, ether, either, Elizabethan, frothy, Gothic, Martha, method, mythical, nothing, pathetic, pathology

FINAL /θ/ (th)   breath, booth, birth, broth, bath, death, both, earth, tooth, forth, myth, moth, mouth, south, north, cloth, truth, health, month, ninth, width, length, wealth, worth

INITIAL /ð/ (*th*)   than, that, thee, the, then, there, thereafter, thereby, therefore, therein, these, they, their, them, this, thine, those, thou, though, thy, thus

MEDIAL /ð/ (*th*)　　either, mother, father, bother, farther, other, breathing, feather, rather, gather, soothing, smoother, smother, leather, heathen, further, bathing, southern, northern

FINAL /ð/ (*th*)　　bathe, clothe, breathe, lathe, soothe, mouth (v.), teethe, writhe, smooth

1. They are planning to go home for Thanksgiving.
2. Was that the brand that you ordered?
3. The Crofts are going to the theater tonight.
4. I want to thank you for suggesting a title for my theme.
5. I don't think it fair that the instructor allowed them three extra days on the assignment.
6. We know nothing about the authorship of the material in our files.
7. I'm leaving for Athens in the morning.
8. There's a wealth of information on both topics.
9. Three fifths of the students who responded to the survey admitted that they had cheated.
10. "Is this the face that launched a thousand ships?"
11. Even if it doesn't ruin them, it will cause them a lot of trouble.
12. I live on the South Side, but I'm going to move on Thursday.
13. I'd rather associate with someone who bathes regularly.
14. We got eight thousand answers to the ad, and only five thousand of them were threatening.
15. The Egyptian dancer writhed for an hour but stayed fully clothed.
16. Although we sat there through the whole lecture, none of us accepted his theories.
17. Soothing irate professors is a hard thing to do.
18. One sometimes finds that he must further his career by telling a few half-truths.
19. There are many paths to success—all of them crooked.
20. Both of them in the experiment went to great lengths to continue to breathe.
21. Thomas offered thousands of suggestions—all of them worthless.
22. I'm not an atheist, but I don't believe in the infallibility of authors.
23. It's pathetic that there are so few enthroned monarchs left.
24. Although she's a pathological liar, she has a method to it.
25. My mother and father had a smooth marriage for more than thirty years.

/t/ AND /θ/ (th) CONTRAST		
taught	thought
tin	thin
tinker	thinker

torn	thorn
tick	thick
ting	thing
tie	thigh
true	threw
trust	thrust
trill	thrill
team	theme
bat	bath
hat	hath
rat	wrath
wrought	Roth
pit	pith
wit	with
pat	path
boat	both
boot	booth
suit	sooth
dirt	dearth
toot	tooth
root	Ruth
fort	forth
brought	broth
bet	Beth
set	Seth
Myrt	myrth

Here are some sentences that contrast /t/ and /θ/:

1. I'd like to tinker with Rodin's "The Thinker."
2. Every paragraph in his theme teems with smut.
3. She was enchanted with his charm and wit.
4. I forgot to thank you for the tank top.
5. Struggling through the blackberry thicket, I lost my ticket home.
6. The roof was quite thin and made entirely of tin.
7. Don't be a big eater just before taking ether.
8. I thought I had taught you better than that!
9. It took both of them to open the throttle on their boat.
10. With unmitigated gall, she dismissed my story as mythical.

/d/ AND /ð/ (*th*)	dare	there
CONTRAST	doze	those
	Ds	these
	day	they

die	thy
dine	thine
den	then
Dan	than
dough	though
dismiss	this miss
discharge	this charge
disappointment	this appointment
disappearance	this appearance
disagreement	this agreement
disapproval	this approval
discuss	this cuss

Here are some sentences that contrast /d/ and /ð/ (*th*):

1. He wasn't there. How dare he?
2. He laid a new piece of metal on the lathe.
3. I fed her a line about liking feathers.
4. The new breed of young people are "yearning to breathe free."
5. The room is not in disarray; this array of artifacts is valuable.
6. One day soon they will understand.
7. These students will not accept Ds and Fs.
8. Not 'till then did I go into the den.
9. The minister said my prosperity is tied to the tithe.
10. Having never seen another cow, I couldn't find her udder.

/f/ AND /θ/ (th)	fin	thin
CONTRAST	fink	think
	first	thirst
	fie	thigh
	Fred	thread
	fret	threat
	free	three
	fro	throw
	frill	thrill
	deaf	death
	reef	wreath
	roof	Ruth
	oaf	oath
	half	hath
	stiff	Stith
	laugh	lath
	miff	myth
	trough	troth

Here are some sentences that contrast /f/ and /θ/ (th):

1. To the day of his death, he was deaf as a post.
2. The captain threw a wreath on the reef as we hit it.
3. Ruth sunbathes in the nude on the roof every day.
4. When praying, the minister still says "hath" about half the time.
5. Mrs. Stith has a stiff upper lip and a sharp tongue.
6. I won't take an oath unless that other oaf does too.
7. Why did you laugh when the carpenter broke the lath?
8. Nothing but strife ever comes out of the mouth of that babe.
9. I live north of Philadelphia.
10. Fly around the earth? Not on your life!
11. Both of them brought us a loaf of bread.
12. I found the leaf underneath our table.
13. It isn't perfect, so it's not worth it.
14. It looked better when she took that ugly cloth off of it.
15. That goofy guy stayed at the kissing booth all day.

/s/ and /z/

Production of the Fricatives /s/ and /z/

If you raise the velum so no air comes out through the nose, line up your front upper and lower teeth, lightly touch the tongue tip against the lower or near the upper gum ridge, and shoot the air stream out of the grooved tongue over the tongue tip and between the front teeth, you will produce a lingua-alveolar fricative. We know that is a long sentence, because the number of necessary movements makes a long list; perhaps you had better read it again—a couple of times.

There are two lingua-alveolar (tongue and gum ridge) fricatives in English. One is voiceless and is represented in both IPA and the dictionaries by /s/. The other is voiced and is represented in both IPA and the dictionaries by /z/.

If you read that first sentence carefully, you noticed that the tongue tip can go to one of two places to make these sounds. Most people articulate these sounds with the tongue tip under the alveolar ridge (and, therefore, somewhat in back of the upper front teeth). But the sounds can be made satisfactorily with the tongue tip on the lower gum ridge (just in back of the lower front teeth). When the /s/ is blended with other sounds that are made on the alveolar ridge (the upper gum ridge), the /s/ is made in the upper position—by all speakers.

Allophones of /s/ and /z/

There are no variations of /s/. There are only two variations of /z/. The /z/, as we have said, is a voiced consonant. It is often fully voiced.

But it also has an allophone, like the other voiced consonants, that is partially devoiced. Before voiceless consonants and as the last sound in a phrase, the /z/ is partially devoiced.

Specific Warnings

When we discussed the problems associated with spelling in English, we looked at each sound of the language and the various ways of spelling each sound. (See p. 38.) There are six different ways to spell /s/ and six to spell /z/. Spelling is certainly not a guide to knowing which of these sounds to use and when to use them.

There is an interesting contrast in a group of words based on these two contrasting sounds. The words are in pairs, and the two words in each pair differ in whether they end in /s/ or /z/. (Remember, we are talking about sounds now—not about spelling. The words in the pair may be spelled exactly alike!) This sound difference is important, because it marks the difference in the function of the two words in the pair. The word ending in /s/ is a noun (or occasionally an adjective), and the word ending in /z/ is a verb. Pronounce these pairs of words out loud. In the column on the left are the nouns (*close* is the only adjective) ending in /s/; in the column on the right are the verbs ending in /z/. (In the last pair, the distinction is maintained consistently only in the southern part of the United States. If you pronounce both words of the last pair with /s/, don't worry. That pronunciation is standard; the difference is regional.) Now try these pairs of words aloud:

advice	advise
device	devise
use	use
abuse	abuse
misuse	misuse
diffuse	diffuse
excuse	excuse
refuse[3]	refuse
close	close
house	house
blouse	blouse
grease	grease

Common Deviations of Problems in the Articulation of /s/ and /z/

The sounds /s/ and /z/ are high-frequency noises (the whole family of hissing sounds is called the sibilants) and are not too pleasant at best.

---

[3] Some nouns and adjectives are distinguished from verbs by a shift of stress on the two syllables. (See p. 310.) The noun *refuse* differs from the verb *refuse* both in final sound and stress.

Distortions of these sounds, known as lisps, are common and quite notice-able. The /s/ should be short and sharp (but not whistled), and the /z/ should be voiced and correctly articulated.

Although there are a number of other distortions of these sounds, there are seven deviations that are most common: (1) the lingual protrusion lisp, (2) the dental lisp, (3) the lateral emission lisp, (4) the whistling (or high-frequency) lisp, (5) the overaspirated /s/, (6) lack of adequate aspiration and friction, and (7) unvoicing of the /z/.

1. *Lingual protrusion lisp.* The name of this distortion tells you exactly what it is. The tongue is thrust out between the teeth so that these sibilants resemble the /θ/ (th) and /ð/ (*th*) sounds. This problem is the one commonly thought of as "the lisp." If you have a lingual protru-sion lisp, you will have to work to replace your present habit with conventional placement of the tongue. *Sing* should not sound like *thing.* These pairs of words are in clear contrast to each other:

/s/ AND /θ/ (th)		
CONTRAST	sing	thing
	sin	thin
	sink	think
	sank	thank
	sick	thick
	sought	thought
	sacker	Thacker
	suds	thuds
	saw	thaw
	sunder	thunder
	some	thumb

/z/ AND /ð/ (*th*)		
CONTRAST	Z	thee
	Zen	then
	Syne (Auld Lang)	thine

2. *Dental lisp.* The dental lisp results from incorrect placement of the tongue tip on the teeth. If you have discovered that you tend to dentalize the alveolar consonants /t/, /d/, /l/, and /n/, check to see if you also dentalize the /s/ and /z/. If you do place the tongue on the teeth when making these sounds, the /s/ and /z/ will be distorted.

3. *Lateral emission lisp.* The lateral emission lisp is that sound devia-tion in which the air stream comes over the sides of the tongue rather than through the center over the tongue tip. (You football players—and fans—know what lateral means. The pass goes to the side, rather than forward. The lateral emission lisp is a problem like that. The air comes out of the sides of the mouth, rather than out the front of the mouth.) This problem can be the result of pointing the tongue (tip or blade) up toward the alveolar ridge and failing to tense the sides of the tongue

against the sides of the hard palate or against the inner surfaces of the side teeth. The air, therefore, escapes over the sides of the tongue, similar to the production of a correct /l/ sound. To correct this distortion, (1) tense the tongue as you place it in either position to make the /s/ or /z/ (remember we said that you can produce these sounds in two places); (2) line up the front upper and lower teeth to help you in focusing the breath over the top of the tongue tip and out through the center of the mouth; and (3) seal off the air on each side with the sides of the tongue.

4. *Whistling (or high-frequency) lisp.* As we noted earlier, the sibilants are high-frequency sounds, but the /s/ and /z/ should not "whistle." Usually this deviation results from too much tension of the tongue; it may be that as you attempt to position the tongue correctly, you make it too tense. Just relaxing the tongue slightly may correct the whistling noise.

If you make the sounds on the upper ridge, it may be that you are pulling the tongue too far back in the mouth; if so, pull the tongue up a little closer to the teeth (but not on them) to correct this distortion. If you make the sound on the bottom ridge, your tongue tip may be too high—that is, too near the lower teeth; if so, lower the tongue slightly to correct the distortion.

5. *The overaspirated /s/.* The overaspirated /s/ results from pushing too much air through on the sound and from prolonging the sound, if you sssssssssssee what we mean. Of course /z/ should be given its proper duration in the final position in a word, but /s/ is never a long sound. Move on to the sound that follows. In a phrase such as "The grass is green," for example, you should practice *the-gra-siz-green,* getting off the /s/ quickly and getting on to the next sound.

6. *Lack of adequate aspiration and friction.* Although some speakers push too much air through on these sounds—especially the /s/ and, thus, produce overaspirated sounds, other speakers fail to emit enough air on the sounds. The sounds then not only lack friction, they are almost inaudible. If this is your problem, work for adequate tension of the tongue and adequate air pressure.

7. *Unvoicing of the /z/.* Although the /z/ will be slightly devoiced before voiceless sounds and as the last sound in a phrase, it should not be completely unvoiced. Even at the end of a sentence, *his* should not sound like *hiss, fleas* like *fleece, pays* like *pace,* or *cards* like *carts.* Pronounce the following examples out loud to check for unvoicing of the final /z/:

I broke two ribs.   (not *rips!*)
My attention lags.   (not *lacks!*)
There are two beds.   (not *bets!*)

Cheating never pays.	(not pace!)
They're my wards.	(not warts!)
We may lose.	(not loose!)
My cat purrs.	(not purse!)
Pass the peas.	(not peace!)

Materials for Practicing /s/ and /z/

INITIAL /s/ AND /z/	sag	zag
	Sue	zoo
	sown	zone
	see	Z
	sip	zip
	sap	zap
	sink	zinc
	said	Zed
	seal	zeal
	scion	Zion
	sane	zany
	sell it	zealot

MEDIAL /s/ AND /z/	looser	loser
	racing	razing
	busing	buzzing
	lacy	lazy
	prices	prizes
	rice's	rises
	hearses	hers is
	eyes her	icer

FINAL /s/ AND /z/	cease	seize
	curse	curs
	price	prize
	false	falls
	once	ones
	lice	lies
	moose	moos
	mace	maze
	ice	eyes
	loose	lose
	hearse	hers
	lace	lays
	race	raise
	place	plays
	waltz	walls
	rice	rise

INITIAL, MEDIAL, AND FINAL /s/	sap	passer	pass
	same	Macy's	mace
	sum	mussing	muss
	sail	assail	lace
	set	Tesser	Tess
	sign	nicer	nice
	sake	casing	case
	sought	tossing	toss
	seep	piecing	piece
	sell	lesson	less
	sub	busing	bus
	sob	bossing	boss
	sigh	icing	ice
	suck	cussing	cuss

MEDIAL AND FINAL /z/	buzz	buzzing
	muse	music
	daze	daisy
	ease	easy
	raze	razing
	rise	rising
	boose	boosing
	freeze	freezer
	wise	wiser
	cruise	cruiser

Remembering to articulate the alveolar sounds with a firm tongue tip on the gum ridge and to give the /s/ no more duration than you give to /t/ and /d/, try the following sequences:

dick	tick	stick
dare	tare	stare
dough	toe	stow
dock	tock	stock
deem	team	steam
dill	till	still
Dan	tan	Stan
die	tie	sty
doubt	tout	stout
dub	tub	stub
dint	tint	stint
damper	tamper	stamper
Dall	tall	stall
dale	tale	stale
dead	Ted	stead

deal	teal	steal
dear	tear	steer
durn	turn	stern

We want to shoot a thin stream of air over the center line of the tongue tip on the /s/. Because the tongue tip is sharply pointed for the /t/, which is made on the alveolar ridge, and because the /s/ shoots the air out over the tip just under the alveolar ridge, we can work for a tight, forward-focused, brief /s/ in these pairs of words:

stead	said
steed	seed
steal	seal
stale	sale
store	sore
stand	sand
steak	sake
steam	seem
stage	sage
stag	sag
still	sill
stick	sick
stoop	soup
stuck	suck
stir	sir
stone	sown
stalk	Salk

The /s/ occurs at the beginning of words blended with several other consonants. Here are some words, contrasting initial solo /s/ with initial /s/ blends. If you have difficulty with a lateral lisp, do not practice the /sl/ blend words until you have received instructions and assistance from your instructor.

/sn/ AND /s/ CONTRAST	snap	sap
	snake	sake
	sneak	seek
	snail	sail
	snag	sag
	snip	sip
	snob	sob
	snooze	Sue's
	snort	sort
	snoop	soup
	snow	sew
	sneeze	seize

/sk/ AND /s/ CONTRAST	scale	sale
	scold	sold
	scanned	sand
	skip	sip
	scad	sad
	sceptic	septic
	scheme	seem
	scoop	soup
	scope	soap
	score	sore

/sp/, /s/, AND /sw/ CONTRAST	speed	seed	Swede
	spell	sell	swell
	spun	sun	swung (!)
	spin	sin	swim (!)
	spank	sank	swank
	spur	sir	swerve (!)
	spay	say	sway
	spine	sign	swine

/sl/ AND /s/ CONTRAST	slat	sat
	slash	sash
	slam	Sam
	slater	satyr
	slave	save
	sled	said
	sleep	seep
	slick	sick
	slew	sue
	sleigh	say
	slide	side
	sling	sing
	slub	sub
	slur	sir
	sly	sigh

Now try these sequences. Work to get a good /s/ and not a /ʃ/ (sh).

rate	trait	straight
rap	trap	strap
ray	tray	stray
rip	trip	strip
rain	train	strain
rue	true	strew
ride	tried	stride

ripe	tripe	stripe
raid	trade	strayed
ruck	truck	struck

If you have a problem with lateral emission of the air, try these sequences (reading across, of course.) Refer back to p. 106 for a review of suggestions to correct this problem.

team	steam	seem
Ted	stead	said
take	steak	sake
tear (n.)	steer	seer
to	stew	sue
tanned	stand	sand
tick	stick	sick
tow	stow	sew
tougher	stuffer	suffer
tie	sty	sigh
tag	stag	sag
teed	steed	seed
tat	stat	sat
tore	store	sore
top	stop	sop
tone	stone	sown
tock	stock	sock
tinker	stinker	sinker
Tet	stet	set
tuck	stuck	suck
tack	stack	sack

Here are some sentences for /s/ and /z/ practice. Don't try tongue twisters. These sentences contain /s/ and /z/, but they are not "loaded." They are the kinds of sentences you might say in everyday conversation.

1. Stop, look, and listen!
2. It's all the same to me, of course.
3. But it isn't the same thing.
4. I've already said I was sorry.
5. We've chosen our silver pattern.
6. Spring is his favorite season.
7. I'm concerned about whether it is constitutional.
8. Many of us have strong feelings about civil liberties.
9. Ozzie is afraid of snakes.
10. Nobody seemed to understand the lecture, but everybody took copious notes.
11. I lost my gloves, but Eddie gave me his.

12. Who says that crime never pays?
13. Spring is sprung; the grass is rizz.
    I wonder how far Vassar is.—*Burma Shave*.
14. Star light, star bright;
    First star I've seen tonight.
15. He can certainly perform mysterious tricks with those cards.
16. The audience liked the last scene best of all.
17. It takes me all week to read the Sunday *New York Times*.
18. The assignment was to read all of *Tom Jones*.
19. He's a master of the art of telling little harmless lies.
20. If he's working on a Ph.D., he's dying by degrees.
21. She's having a hard time raising money for her fees this semester.
22. Are you absolutely sure Susan works for the CIA?
23. Please select your purchase. The store is closing.
24. I'm not fooled by her saccharine sweetness or her pseudosaintliness.
25. I cease to be amazed at superstition in the twentieth century!

/ʃ/ (sh) and /ʒ/ (zh)

Production of the /ʃ/ (sh) and /ʒ/ (zh)

If you raise the velum so no air can escape up through the nose, round the lips slightly, line up the front upper and lower teeth, place the front of the tongue blade either near the back of the alveolar ridge or behind the lower gum ridge, press the sides of the tongue against the sides of the hard palate or against the inner surfaces of the side teeth, and shoot the air stream out of the grooved tongue over the center of the front of the tongue blade and between the teeth, you will produce a lingua-post-alveolar fricative. Because that sentence is a paragraph long, and because each of those movements is important to the production of these two sounds, you should read that sentence again—a few times.

There are two lingua-postalveolar fricatives in English. One is voiceless; it is the consonant in the middle of assure. It is represented in IPA by /ʃ/ and in the dictionaries by sh. The other lingua-postalveolar fricative is voiced; it is the consonant in the middle of azure. It is represented in IPA by /ʒ/ and in the dictionaries by zh.

You will notice several differences between the production of these two sounds and of /s/ and /z/. These sounds are also hissing noises and are in the sibilant family of sounds, but they do differ from /s/ and /z/. First, the lips are usually spread for /s/ and /z/; they are slightly rounded (pursed) for /ʃ/ (sh) and /ʒ/ (zh). Second, the air stream is shot out over the tongue tip on /s/ and /z/ but comes over the front of the tongue on /ʃ/ (sh) and /ʒ/ (zh). Also, the groove of the tongue is wider on /ʃ/ (sh) and /ʒ/ (zh) than on /s/ and /z/, and the entire tongue is pulled farther back on /ʃ/ (sh) and /ʒ/ (zh).

Allophones of /ʃ/ (sh̪) and /ʒ/ (zh̪)

There are no allophones of /ʃ/ (sh). There are only two allophones (variations) of /ʒ/ (zh̪). Like other voiced consonants, the /ʒ/ (zh̪) is usually fully voiced. However, also like other voiced consonants, it has an allophone that is partially devoiced. Before voiceless consonants and as the last sound in a phrase, the /ʒ/ (zh̪) is partially devoiced.

Specific Warnings

The /ʃ/ (sh̪) phoneme can occur at the beginning, in the middle, and at the ends of English words. The /ʒ/ (zh̪) phoneme generally occurs only in the middle and at the end of English words. On a few words we have borrowed from French we have kept the French pronunciation and thus start the word with /ʒ/ (zh̪). Note these borrowed words with /ʒ/ (zh̪) preserved at the beginning:

> jabot
> genre
> gendarme

French names that begin with this sound are also pronounced with /ʒ/ (zh̪). Note these examples:

> Gide
> Genet
> Giraud
> Jacques
> Jeanne d'Arc

Common Deviations

There are three common distortions of the /ʃ/ (sh̪) and /ʒ/ (zh̪) sounds: (1) dentalization, (2) lateral emission of the air, and (3) unvoicing of the /ʒ/ (zh̪).

1. *Dentalization.* If you dentalize the /s/ and /z/ sounds, it is likely you will also make the /ʃ/ (sh̪) and /ʒ/ (zh̪) with the tongue touching the front teeth. Placing the front of the tongue on the teeth will distort these sounds. Correct tongue placement (with the front of the tongue back of the gum ridge—whichever one you use, upper or lower) is essential to production of conventional sounding /ʃ/ (sh̪) and /ʒ/ (zh̪). Pronounce the following words and check to be sure the tongue is not *on* the teeth, not touching the teeth at all:

shield	leisure
share	Zsa Zsa (Gabor, of course)
shrink	genre

2. *Lateral emission.* The sounds /ʃ/ (sh̪) and /ʒ/ (zh̪) are sibilants; they are in the hissing family. Any distortion of a sibilant, as we said

earlier, is a lisp. And if you have a particular kind of lisp on /s/ and /z/, you may (probably will) also have that problem with /ʃ/ (s̪h) and /ʒ/ (z̪h). The most common is the lateral lisp—where the air comes out over the sides of the tongue rather than over the center. As in the case of the /s/ and /z/, the air should come over the center of the tongue on /ʃ/ (s̪h) and /ʒ/ (z̪h). Check your pronounciation of these phrases to see if the air is coming out of the sides of the mouth:

He dashed out.	I am under no barrage!
My diction is good.	The job has no prestige.
What's Tom's mission?	I found a treasure.
Her reputation is tarnished.	I'm going to Asia.

3. *Unvoicing of the* /ʒ/ (z̪h). The /ʒ/ (z̪h) will be slightly devoiced when it comes before voiceless sounds or is the last sound in a phrase. But it should not be totally unvoiced. If you tend to unvoice voiced consonants, you should check to be certain that you do not unvoice /ʒ/ (z̪h). *Vision* should not rhyme with *fission,* and *mirage* should not rhyme with *Dear Osh.*

Materials for Practicing /ʃ/ (s̪h) *and* /ʒ/ (z̪h)

INITIAL, MEDIAL, AND FINAL /ʃ/ (s̪h)			
	sheen	luscious	flesh
	shack	ashamed	blush
	sharp	machine	wash
	shirk	conscience	finish
	shadow	caution	wish
	shallow	anxious	blemish
	shout	issue	brandish
	shrimp	ocean	lush
	shut	mission	gnash
	sure	passion	harsh
	sugar	patient	gauche

MEDIAL AND FINAL /ʃ/ (z̪h)		
	azure	menage
	confusion	camouflage
	casual	entourage
	vision	mirage
	occasion	corsage
	pleasure	prestige
	usual	garage

INITIAL /ʃ/ (s̪h) AND /s/ CONTRAST		
	shag	sag
	shake	sake
	Shall he?	Sally
	sham	Sam
	shame	same

shank	sank
she	see
sheet	seat
sheer	sear
sheep	seep
shelf	self
shift	sift
shimmer	simmer
shin	sin
shine	sign
shingle	single
ship	sip
shock	sock
shod	sod
shoe	sue
shoot	suit
shop	sop
short	sort
shot	sot
show	sew
shower	sour
shuck	suck
shun	sun
shuttle	subtle
shy	sigh

FINAL /ʃ/ (sh) AND /s/ CONTRAST	rush	Russ
	gush	Gus
	leash	lease
	push	puss
	Cornish	cornice
	ash	ass
	brash	brass
	clash	class
	gash	gas
	lash	lass
	mash	mass

FINAL /ʒ/ (zh) AND /z/ CONTRAST	rouge	ruse
	beige	bays
	liege	Lees

1. She never seems to agree with my decisions.
2. Various pressure groups determined the outcome of the election.
3. I'm going to the garage to have the car washed.

4. Will you show us where the treasure is hidden?
5. Harsh punishments are usually reserved for felons.
6. Occasionally he comes with his entire entourage.
7. At the last session of the English Parliament, there was great confusion in the Commons.
8. The corsage complemented the gown, which was beige.
9. Such intrusions are usually rather embarrassing.
10. We offered to furnish the professor with a new set of illustrations.
11. The doctor cautioned me to use sugar substitutes.
12. We should be free from unreasonable search and seizure.
13. The dinner was delicious, as usual.
14. I assure you that I will not shirk my duties because failure would damage my prestige.
15. Without twinge of conscience, they shrieked with pleasure.
16. It's shameful for candidates to evade the issues facing this nation.
17. She blushes but feels no shame.
18. How do you measure depth of devotion?
19. I'm sure I don't have the cash to buy you a Persian rug.
20. After she claimed to have had a vision, the neighbors made her garage a shrine.
21. I wish I had more leisure time.
22. I'm anxious to know the neighbors' reaction to the new massage parlor.
23. Charlotte says her new washing machine makes washing a pleasure.
24. The anesthesia left the patient in fair condition.
25. The gendarmes were not very helpful when I had my collision in Paris.
26. Ske kept her composure and showed no emotion when I told her about my fetish.
27. We have been barraged with books of that genre.
28. The shaky regime could not stand derision.
29. I was astonished at her profession.
30. Occasionally we need to go in a fresh direction.

AFFRICATES

An *affricate* is, phonetically, a combination of two consonants—a stop and a fricative—but it is, phonemically, a single sound. In other words, an affricate functions in the language as a single unit, and speakers of English do not recognize an affricate as two separate sounds. Separate and distinct phonemes function individually; they cannot be divided into smaller sound units. Even though affricates require us to make two kinds of movements to produce them, they cannot be divided; they are indivisible. They function as a single unit.

The word *hit* is made up of three phonemes: the initial fricative consonant /h/, the vowel (represented in IPA by /ɪ/ and in the dictionaries by ĭ), and the final stop consonant /t/. We can add another sound /s/ to the word to make it *hits*. Now the syllable ends with a stop and a fricative. But this stop and fricative are separate units; we can take them apart and leave one off. They are, therefore, a combination of two consonants, but not an affricate. They are still two phonemes—not one. But look at the word *hitch*. This word also has three phonemes. The first two are the same ones we had in the word *hit*, but the third one is a different phoneme. The last sound in the word *hitch* is an affricate represented in IPA by /tʃ/ and in the dictionaries by ç̧h. You cannot divide that last sound in the same way you could divide /t/ and /s/; it is one sound indivisible!

Look at another example. The word *head* also has three sounds in it: the initial consonant /h/, the vowel (which we represent in IPA by /ɛ/ and in the dictionaries by ĕ), and the final stop /d/. Again you can add another sound to make the word plural: /z/. The word is now spelled *heads*, and the syllable ends with a stop (/d/) and a fricative (/z/). But, clearly, the /d/ and /z/ are separate phonemes and can be divided. Compare the word *heads* with its four phonemes with the word *hedge*, which has three phonemes. *Hedge* has the same first two sounds as the word *head*, but the last sound is a voiced affricate represented in IPA by /dʒ/ and in the dictionaries by j. It is one sound and cannot be pulled apart into other phonemes.

In summary, then, consonant combinations that combine a stop and a fricative, such as /ts/ and /dz/, are not affricates because each individual sound retains its own identity. Affricates, on the other hand, are articulated as half stop–half fricative, but are perceived as single sounds (phonemes). There are two affricates in English. One is voiceless and is the first and last sound in the word *church*. The other is voiced and is the first and last sound in the word *judge*.

/tʃ/ (ç̧h) and /dʒ/ (j)

Production of /tʃ/ (ç̧h) and /dʒ/ (j)

If you raise the velum to prevent air from escaping through the nose, stop the outgoing air stream by firmly touching the tip of the tongue to the alveolar ridge and the blade of the tongue to the area just back of the ridge, bring the sides of the tongue into contact with the sides of the palate or the inner surfaces of the back teeth (to prevent the air from escaping over the sides of the tongue), and then drop the tongue tip quickly—shooting the air out the center over the grooved blade of the tongue—you will produce an affricate. As we said, there are two affricates in English: one voiceless, which we represent in IPA by /tʃ/ and in the dictionaries by c̮h; and one voiced, which we represent in IPA by /dʒ/ and in the dictionaries by j.

Perhaps it would have been easier to tell you to produce the voiceless affricate by putting your tongue in the position to form a /t/, making a good firm stop, and releasing the air quickly in a /ʃ/ (s̮h). Does it work? Actually, that is what we told you before—in slightly more detail. It might also have been easier to follow if we had told you to make the voiced affricate by putting your tongue in the position to form a /d/, making a good firm voiced stop, and then releasing the air in a /ʒ/ (z̮h).

Allophones of /tʃ/ (c̮h) and /dʒ/ (j)

There are no variations of the /tʃ/ (c̮h). And there are only two varieties of the /dʒ/ (j): the regular, voiced sound and a partially devoiced allophone that occurs before voiceless consonants and at the ends of phrases.

Specific Warnings

Beware of English spelling! There are five different ways to spell /tʃ/ (c̮h) and six ways to spell /dʒ/ (j). In addition, the letters *ch* do not always represent /tʃ/ (c̮h). Look at the words *yacht, archangel,* and *Chanukkah.* (See p. 38.)

Common Deviations of the /tʃ/ (c̮h) and /dʒ/ (j)

There are four common distortions associated with the affricate sounds: (1) incomplete closure, (2) dentalization, (3) lateral emission of the air, and (4) unvoicing of the /d/.

1. *Incomplete closure.* Affricates are single sounds, but they start as stops and end as fricatives. The first danger you should be warned against, then, is not making a complete stop to begin the affricate sound. Failure to block the air stream completely on the affricates, as on the six stop consonants, is a mark of careless speech. The name *Fitchen* should not sound like *fission,* and *ledger* should not be pronounced as a variation of *leisure.* In the following pairs of words, the first begins in a fricative /ʃ/ (s̮h) and the second begins with an affricate /tʃ/ (c̮h). Be sure that you begin the affricate sound with a complete stop.

share	chair
Shane	chain
sheer	cheer
sheep	cheap
ship	chip
shin	chin
shied	chide

shop	chop
shows	chose
shoes	choose
shuck	chuck

In the following pairs of words, the first ends in the fricative /ʃ/ (sh), and the second ends in the affricate /tʃ/ (ch). Make the distinction by being certain that the affricate begins with a complete stop of the air stream.

marsh	march
wash	watch
bash	batch
cash	catch
hash	hatch
leash	leech
wish	witch
mush	much
crush	crutch
hush	hutch

We cannot offer you pairs of words to contrast the fricative /ʒ/ (zh) and the affricate /dʒ/ (j). Still, you should pronounce the following words out loud to be certain you make a complete closure at the beginning of the /dʒ/ (j) affricate. The words in the left-hand column begin with /dʒ/ (j); the words in the right-hand column end in /dʒ/ (j).

jab	gage
genius	pledge
Jim	huge
job	strange
junk	grudge
jail	lunge

2. *Dentalization.* The affricates should begin with the tongue tip firmly on the gum ridge. If you have found that you have a tendency to dentalize the /t/ and /d/, check to see if you also dentalize the /tʃ/ (ch) and /dʒ/ (j). It is likely that you do. If so, you will have to work to pull the tongue tip back to the alveolar ridge where it belongs for these sounds in American English. Use the preceding /tʃ/ (ch) and /dʒ/ (j) words to check for dentalization.

3. *Lateral emission.* The affricates belong to the family of high-frequency hissing noises called sibilants. If you have a problem of emitting the air over the sides of the tongue on the other four sibilants—

/s/, /z/, /ʃ/ (s̲h̲), and /ʒ/ (z̲h̲), it is likely that you also have a problem with lateral emission of the air on the two affricate sounds. Here are a few examples. Check the affricates as you pronounce them to see if the air is coming out of the sides of the mouth on these sounds.

> to China
> Tough, chump.
> No chance!
> Don't chance it.
> Did he jump?
> to join us
> dumb jury
> no joke
> Judge not, Judge Knott.
> in just a minute
> Keep in touch.
> I'm in dutch!

If you have a problem with lateral emission, see p. 106 for suggestions.

4. *Unvoicing of* /dʒ/ (j). Like other voiced sounds, /dʒ/ (j) will be slightly devoiced before voiceless sounds and when final in a phrase, but it should not be completely unvoiced. *Ridge* should not become *rich, besiege* should not become *beseech,* and *edging* should not become *etching.* Read aloud some of the contrasting words in the practice materials that follow to check on unvoicing.

Materials for Practicing /tʃ/ (c̲h̲) and /dʒ/ (j)

INITIAL /tʃ/ (c̲h̲) AND /dʒ/ (j) CONTRAST		
	cheap	jeep
	chip	gyp
	chunk	junk
	char	jar
	choke	joke
	cheer	jeer
	chinks	jinx
	chain	Jane
	choice	Joyce
	chive	jive
	chump	jump
	chest	jest
	choose	Jews
	chill	Jill
	chock	jock
	chutes	Jutes
	chin	gin
	chug	jug

MEDIAL /tʃ/ (c͜h) AND /dʒ/ (j) CONTRAST		
	etching	edging
	lunches	lunges
	riches	ridges
	batches	badges
	searching	surging
	breeches	bridges
	lecher	ledger
	beseeches	besieges

FINAL /tʃ/ (c͜h) AND /dʒ/ (j) CONTRAST		
	march	Marge
	match	Madge
	etch	edge
	rich	ridge
	lunch	lunge
	search	surge
	batch	badge
	leech	liege
	cinch	singe
	perch	purge
	wretch	Reg(inald)
. . . him pinch		impinge

Here are some sentences for practicing /tʃ/ (c͜h) and /dʒ/ (j):

1. It's a question seldom asked, even in speech classes.
2. A change in address must be reported at once.
3. He left the judge, determined to seek his revenge.
4. He got it off his chest by confessing to the student board.
5. The politicians were accused of gerrymandering.
6. The performer is quite agile. No one else has such grace.
7. He has a vivid imagination; he should be watched.
8. Two cars in every garage is no longer a joke.
9. He sends Madge casual messages. Would you deliver them?
10. I hate pigeons. You're not well adjusted.
11. I'll meet you at the general's house.
12. "Righteous indignation" may be a cloak for malicious vengeance.
13. He was ordered to squelch the rumors about the stranger.
14. He placed just above the median. The coach is pleased.
15. Who's catching a cold? The doctor urged us to get flu injections.
16. The cheering section was slow to catch on. They jumped to conclusions.
17. Nature speaks to all men; the Church speaks to a few.
18. Discourtesy was a major factor in his failure.
19. The mob surged into the street. Urchins followed them.
20. He ripped his breeches in the second match.

21. The soldier has asked for a hardship discharge.
22. Omitting lunch saves time for study. Cheating is inexcusable.
23. Each jar of peanut butter was judged individually.
24. Who could have chosen a better arrangement?
25. Each citizen has a responsibility to the general welfare.

NASALS

There are three nasal consonants in English. All the other phonemes of the language are made with the velum raised, so that the air cannot escape up through the nose. On these three sounds, however, the velum is lowered. The outgoing air, therefore, is emitted through and resonated in the nose.

All three of the nasals are articulated by blocking the air stream at some point in the mouth. They differ in the amount of oral (mouth) resonance they have because all three use all of the nose for resonance. Each of the nasal consonants (unlike French, there are no nasal vowels in English) is articulated at the place of articulation of one of the pairs of stops. The bilabial /m/ is articulated by the two lips, as are /p/ and /b/; the lingua-alveolar /n/ is articulated with the tip of the tongue on the gum ridge, as are /t/ and /d/; and the lingua-velar /ŋ/ (dictionaries use n͡g to represent this sound) is articulated with the back of the tongue against the soft palate, as are /k/ and /g/.

The nasal sounds have great resonance, when articulated properly. For this reason, they have great carrying power (sonority). Indeed, they have so much carrying power that some final syllables have no vowel at all, and the final nasal sound carries the syllable (provides the sonority for the syllable). When this occurs, the nasal sound is called *syllabic m, syllabic n,* or *syllabic ng.* The nasals are humming sounds, and they should be given ample nasal resonance. Lightly touch your thumb and first finger to each side of your nose while you make each of the three nasal sounds. You should be able to feel good reverberation on these sounds.

/m/

Production of the /m/

By closing the two lips, as you would to make /p/ and /b/, you make /m/, a *voiced bilabial nasal.* But, instead of stopping the air completely as you do to form /p/ and /b/, you lower the velum so the air can pass out through the nasal passages. The vocal folds vibrate, and the vibrated air is resonated in the whole mouth and the nose. You should get good resonance on this humming sound.

Allophones of the /m/

There is only one standard allophone of the /m/ phoneme. After a voiceless consonant in the same syllable, the /m/ is partially devoiced. The phonetic symbol for this allophone is [m̥]—the little circle representing devoicing. To check on this allophone for yourself, pronounce the following pairs of words. You will discover that when the /m/ follows the voiceless /s/, the /m/ is [m̥].

mart	smart
mash	smash
mall	small
mile	smile
mother	smother
myth	Smith

Some speakers occasionally articulate the /m/ with the upper teeth and lower lip, if the sound occurs before /f/ or /v/; however, this variation (represented in IPA by [ɱ]) is usually considered a distortion of the /m/.

Specific Warning

There are six ways to spell /m/ in English.

Common Deviations or Problems in the Articulation of /m/

There are six common problems associated with the production of the /m/ phoneme: (1) denasality, (2) inadequate duration, (3) severe nasality on neighboring vowels, (4) substitution of a nasalized vowel for /m/, (5) substitution of /n/ for /m/, and (6) substitution of [ɱ] before abutting /f/ and /v/.

1. *Denasality.* If you do not get enough nasal resonance on the nasal sounds, you have the problem of *denasality.* We have only three nasal sounds in English, and they should be well hummed up through the nose. Denasality (the lack of adequate nasal resonance) is a cold-in-the-head quality. It may result from colds, adenoids, or some other obstruction of the nasal resonator—or from faulty speech habits. The nasals are long, resonant, humming, continuant (sounds that, unlike stops, can be sustained—held onto) consonants. Full nasal resonance is necessary for brilliant tone and good projection. If you have a problem with denasality, you should consult a physician and a speech therapist. On your own, you can work to give adequate duration (nasals are two-beat sounds) and full resonance in the nose on the /m/. If possible, tape record your pronunciation of the following words. When you play the tape back, listen to be sure the /m/ sounds do not sound something like /p/ or /b/.

my	(not *pie* or *buy*)
mare	(not *pear* or *bear*)
more	(not *pore* or *bore*)
may	(not *pay* or *bay*)
me	(not *P.* or *be*)
mill	(not *pill* or *Bill*)
aim	(not *ape* or *Abe*)
come	(not *cup* or *cub*)
game	(not *gape* or *Gabe*)
cam	(not *cap* or *cab*)
bomb	(not *bop* or *Bob*)
psalm	(not *sop* or *sob*)
trim	(not *trip* or *Trib*)
gam	(not *gap* or *gab*)
some	(not *sup* or *sub*)
flam	(not *flap* or *flab*)
lamb	(not *lap* or *lab*)
rum	(not *Rupp* or *rub*)

2. *Inadequate duration.* The problem of inadequate duration is related somewhat to denasality. Certainly inadequate resonance will result from inadequate duration, but they are not the same thing. This problem is simply the result of not maintaining the sound long enough. The sound may be articulated properly, but it is cut off—that is, cut short. The /m/ is cheated. Read the preceding list again, this time checking to be sure that your final /m/ (especially) is a two-beat sound. You should hold onto the /m/ for two counts. For example, in pronouncing the word *time,* pat your foot as you say the word. The *tie* part of the syllable should get the first beat (or pat) and the /m/ should get the second beat (or pat). If the syllable is not getting that second beat for the /m/, you are giving it inadequate time (duration). Work for good humming and adequate duration on the /m/.

3. *Severe nasality on neighboring vowels.* The velum (soft palate) is lowered only on the production of the three nasal sounds in English. For all the other sounds (including the vowels), the velum is raised to close off the nasal passages. Obviously we do not talk a word at a time or a single sound at a time. Our speech flow is connected in phrases. The movements to make sounds, therefore, are not separate sets of movements, but a continuous set of overlapping movements. While we are making one sound, we are getting ready for the next sound; and we are still finishing the last sound as we produce the present one. Many different movements occur at the same time, and the movements for the sounds overlap.

It is not only normal, but inevitable, that there will be a little nasal resonance on vowel sounds that come before or after nasal consonants. If you say the word *him,* for example, you will begin to drop the velum (getting ready for the nasal consonant /m/) while you are still uttering the vowel (represented in IPA by /i/ and in dictionaries by ĭ). On the other hand, if you say the word *me,* you will not be able to get the velum completely raised and the nasal passages completely closed off before you start to utter the vowel (represented in IPA by /i/ and in dictionaries by ē.

Now, having said all that, and having conceded that some nasalization of vowels next to nasal consonants is inevitable, we must tell you that *excessive* nasalization of those vowels is a distortion and a problem. How much is excessive? It's a logical question. If most or all of a vowel before or after a nasal consonant is uttered with the velum lowered so that the air stream escapes in part through the nose, the sound becomes quite unpleasant. In short, get as little nasal resonance on the vowels before and after nasal consonants as you possibly can. If most or all of a vowel has nasal resonance (is nasalized), it has excessive nasalization. Vowels, in English, are oral rather than nasal sounds.

Some vowels seem to offer more temptation toward nasalization than others. These are the vowels and diphthongs (diphthongs are vowel combinations that sound like one sound) that present the most tempting opportunities for excessive nasalization:

Key Word	IPA Symbol	Dictionary Symbol
bet	/ɛ/	ĕ
bat	/æ/	ă
bait	/eɪ/	ā
bite	/aɪ/	ī
bout	/aʊ/	ou

Pronounce these pairs of words out loud. Compare the way you say the *vowel* in the two words of each pair. There should not be a great difference. Make the vowels as much alike as you can.

hem	head
ham	had
aim	aid
I'm	I'd
Baum	bowed

You must train yourself to direct the air consciously through the mouth or through the nose. The word *how,* for example, because it has no nasal sounds in it, should have no nasal resonance, and no air should come through the nose while it is being pronounced. You could hold your nose, then, and the pronunciation of the word *how* would not be affected. As a further check, pronounce the word *how* out loud with no nasal resonance. If you are not sure, hold your nose while you say the word, and then say the word without holding your nose. There should be absolutely no difference in the way the word sounds. (If you feel air trying to come through the nose while you say the word *how*, you have a real nasality problem!) Now you have pronounced the word *how* aloud with no nasal emission of air at all; next, pronounce the sounds /nd/ aloud with full nasal resonance on the /n/. Finally, try the word *hound* all together— with as little nasality on the /ɑu/ (ou) diphthong as you can achieve. Work to make the diphthong in *hound* as much like it was in *how* as you can. AND work to get as much good nasal resonance on the /n/ in *hound* as you can muster. The secret of solving this problem of excessive nasality on neighboring vowels is this: Work for good resonance in the nasal cavity on the nasal sounds—/m/, /n/, and /ŋ/ (n͡g), and work for as little nasality on the vowels and diphthongs as possible.

4. *Substitution of a nasalized vowel for oral vowel* + /m/. When a vowel or diphthong is followed by a nasal consonant, some speakers drop the nasal consonant altogether and simply nasalize the vowel or diphthong. This substitution of one nasalized vowel or diphthong for both an oral sound plus a nasal consonant is a mark of very careless speech in our language. Nasalized vowels are characteristic of French and Portuguese, but they should be avoided in English. Check your own pronunciation of each of the following words or phrases to be certain that you get good nasal consonants, but no nasalized vowels, in each:

> humble
> somewhere
> emphatic
> teamwork
> hemp
> New Hampshire
> same time
> triumph
> home free
> impossible
> I can't climb.
> I'm clumsy.
> a bomb threat
> Calm down.

5. *Substitution of* /n/ *for* /m/. Assimilation is the adapting of sounds to be more like their neighboring sounds, and there are many standard assimilations in English. To change /m/ to /n/ in order to make it easier to say before another sound is not standard, however. There are several

contexts that offer the greatest temptation to make this substitution. You may be tempted to substitute /n/ for /m/ before abutting alveolar consonants. (Abutting consonants are those that come right after another consonant but are in a separate syllable.) The sounds /t/, /d/, /l/, and /n/ are made on the gum ridge, and careless speakers are likely to turn /m/ to /n/ (which is on the gum ridge, remember) before these sounds. Pronounce the following material out loud. Check to be certain you make a real /m/ and not an /n/. The lips must close completely and you must hum up through the nose to make the /m/ sound.

/m/ BEFORE ABUTTING /t/	sometime
	dumb test
	came today
	calm teacher
	a timetable
	my hometown
	a claim ticket
	You seem tired.
	I hear him talking.
	I'm turning it in.
/m/ BEFORE ABUTTING /d/	the same day
	some dogs
	the dumb dog
	room decor
	Sam didn't.
	The flame died.
	Does it seem tasteless?
	I'm dead tired.
/m/ BEFORE ABUTTING /l/	slim lead
	extreme lack
	some lady
	a grim lesson
	so prim looking
	a dream location
	the same logic
	You seem lifeless.
	I'm leaving.
	See if fame lingers.
/m/ BEFORE ABUTTING /n/	some nights
	grim necessity
	a sham nevertheless
	hymn number three
	cream nougats

to seem natural
a tame neighborhood
a glum negotiator
I'm not going.
I'm never wrong.

You may be tempted to substitute /n/ for /m/ before several other abutting consonants. Check your pronunciation of these words and phrases to
be sure the /m/ is a real /m/.

/m/ BEFORE ABUTTING /θ/ (th)	something
	the same thought
	Some think so.
	the same thrill
	a dumb theory
	a crime thriller
	The groom threatened.
	calm through it all
/m/ BEFORE ABUTTING (s)	theme song
	themselves
	to blame somebody
	another bomb scare
	a prime suspect
	I'm single.
	Not another drum solo!
	The alarm sounded.
/m/ BEFORE ABUTTING /z/	Who's clumsy?
	You seem zealous.
	another time zone
	It was all sham zest.
/m/ BEFORE ABUTTING /ʃ/ (sh)	Yes, I'm sure.
	Give me some sugar.
	Slam shut the door.
	The lamb shivers.
	some shallow thinking
	You don't seem shocked.
/m/ BEFORE ABUTTING /j/ (y)	I'm your assistant.
	a dream yacht
	Don't slam your door.
	I'm used to that.
	That's some youngster!

/m/ Before Abutting /w/	teamwork
	some weariness
	the same waterproof watch
	the dumbwaiter
	The climb wore me out.
	The chasm widened.

/m/ Before Abutting /ʍ/ (hw)	somewhere
	same whitewash
	some wherewithal
	I'm whipped.

/m/ in Final /md/ Combination	I screamed.
	It's doomed.
	She was framed.
	We roomed at the dorm.
	She claimed the reward.
	They chimed in.
	It wasn't aimed at you.
	She damned everyone.

6. *Substitution of* [ɱ] *for* /m/ *before abutting* /f/ *and* /v/. We have mentioned this nonstandard substitution before. If you make the /m/ by bringing the upper teeth and lower lip together, you will form this distortion of /m/. You may be tempted to use this sound before syllables beginning with /f/ or /v/. Check your pronunciation of the following words and phrases.

comfort
comfortable
a team vehicle
the same voting district
farm for sale
climb fifty steps
room vacancy
some variety of joke
Come fast!
You come first.
I'll name Virgil chairman.
I'll get home very fast.

Materials for Practicing the /m/

mill	limber	limb
mock	calmer	calm
muss	summer	some

mate	tamer	tame
muck	coming	come
main	naming	name
milk	climate	climb
might	timely	time
mead	deeming	deem
mud	dumber	dumb
moot	tomblike	tomb
mat	tamborine	tam
make	Cambridge	came
mass	Sammy	Sam
mad	damnable	dam

1. My Mary's asleep by the murmuring stream.
2. My name is Ozymandias, king of kings.
3. Can common people appreciate good music?
4. He didn't mean to alarm you.
5. They're doomed. They put a bomb in the Capitol dome.
6. Even though he is handsome, they should not have chosen that madman to lead them.
7. Many observers are unimpressed by that kind of maneuvering.
8. There is only temporary comfort in self-deception.
9. There must always be time to dream.
10. Some of the students are visions, but many others are sights.
11. The big game is the main event of the autumn season.
12. I'm grumbling because I left another umbrella at the terminal.
13. I manage to survive from term to term.
14. Why bemoan your fate or blame others for it?
15. The mechanic moaned. The motor was simply covered with grime.
16. She went at him with a broom when he stumbled home.
17. She removed the ham from the oven, but would not let me touch it.
18. I'm very sure he's the informer.
19. Sometimes, complex things seem simple and simple things seem complex.
20. From womb to tomb, man dreams of the impossible.

/n/

Production of the /n/

The sound /n/ is a *voiced lingua-alveolar nasal.* It is made by pressing the tongue tip against the gum ridge—the same articulation you would use to make /t/ and /d/. But, instead of stopping the air completely as you would to form /t/ and /d/, you lower the velum so the air can pass out through the nasal passages. The vocal folds vibrate, and the vibrated air is resonated in the area of the mouth behind the upraised tongue and the nose. You should get good resonance on this humming sound.

Because of the differences in their places of articulation, the /m/ and /n/ sound different; they have different amounts of oral resonance. The /m/ uses the whole mouth for resonance, but the /n/ uses only part of the mouth for resonance. Both, of course, use the nose for amplifying the sound.

Allophones of the /n/

There are two allophones of the /n/ phoneme. All three nasal consonants in English are voiced sounds, but /n/, like /m/, is partially devoiced if it follows a voiceless consonant in the same syllable. The symbol in IPA for this allophone is [n̥]. To identify this allophone for yourself, pronounce the following pairs of words out loud. You will discover that, after the voiceless /s/, /n/ is slightly devoiced.

no	snow
knees	sneeze
knicker	snicker
knack	snack
need	Sneed
nail	snail
nap	snap

The other allophone of the /n/ phoneme occurs when /n/ is followed immediately by one of the two "th" sounds in English. Before both /θ/ (th) and /ð/ (th), the /n/ is made with the tongue on the teeth. Before any other sounds, an /n/ made in this way would be a distortion (dentalization). But, anticipating the linguadental articulation for the "th" to follow, the /n/ becomes a linguadental sound too. The symbol for this allophone is [n̪]—the little tooth under the symbol indicating dentalization. Check your own pronunciation of these words and phrases, and see if you do not use the dental allophone of /n/ before /θ/ (th) and /ð/ (th).

ninth
tenth
eleventh
month
in the class
on the desk
in this house
when that occurred
down the drain

Specific Warning

There are five different ways to spell /n/ in English.

Comon Deviations or Problems in the Articulation of /n/

There are eight common problems associated with the production of the /n/ phoneme: (1) denasality, (2) inadequate duration, (3) severe nasality on neighboring vowels, (4) substitution of a nasalized vowel for an oral vowel + /n/, (5) dentalization, (6) substitution of /m/ for /n/ before abutting /p/ or /b/, (7) substitution of [ɱ] for /n/ before abutting /f/ or /v/, and (8) substitution of /ŋ/ (ng) before other abutting consonants.

1. *Denasality*. Denasality is the lack of adequate nasal resonance on the nasal sounds. If you tended to denasalize the /m/ (see p. 123–124), it is likely you will also denasalize the /n/. Check your pronunciation of the following list of words; if possible, tape record them. When you play them back, listen to be sure that the /n/ sounds do not sound something like /t/ or /d/.

know	(not *toe* or *dough*)
knee	(not *tea* or *D*)
name	(not *tame* or *dame*)
nick	(not *tick* or *dick*)
nigh	(not *tie* or *die*)
ten	(not *Tet* or *Ted*)
men	(not *met* or *med*)
moon	(not *moot* or *mood*)
June	(not *jute* or *Jude*)
can	(not *cat* or *cad*)
ban	(not *bat* or *bad*)
con	(not *cot* or *cod*)
refrain	(not *re-freight* or *refrayed*)
pain	(not *pate* or *paid*)
brine	(not *bright* or *bride*)
bone	(not *boat* or *bowed*)
bun	(not *but* or *bud*)
Ann	(not *at* or *add*)
Ben	(not *bet* or *bed*)
crown	(not *kraut* or *crowd*)
down	(not *doubt* or *Dowd*)
fan	(not *fat* or *fad*)

Did you sound as if you had a cold in the head when reading those words with /n/? If so, you have a problem of denasality. Refer to p. 124 for ways to deal with this problem.

2. *Inadequate duration.* The nasal sounds are long sounds. They give good resonance to the voice—brilliant tone and carrying power. Take advantage of them. Don't cheat them! Reread aloud the preceding list of words, and check to be sure you give a two-beat duration to the /n/ sounds. If, when you pronounce it, the word *ten* does not have two foot-tapping beats, then you are cutting it too short. Work for adequate duration of the /n/.

3. *Severe nasality on neighboring vowels.* We discussed this problem in some detail when dealing with distortions of the /m/. (See pp. 124–126.) We would remind you here that some nasalization of vowels before and after nasal consonants is inevitable, but we would also remind you that excessive nasalization of these vowels is a distortion—and it is an unpleasant distortion to have to listen to. Such nasalization gives a harsh quality to the sound, and completely untrained ears can hear it. If most or all of a vowel before or after /n/ is nasalized, the nasalization is excessive.

Pronounce these pairs of words out loud. Compare the way you say the *vowel* in the two words of each pair. There should be little difference between them. Make the vowels as much alike as possible.

hen	head
hand	had
gain	gait/gate
fine	fight
town	tout
bin	bid
Ben	bed
ban	bad
crane	crate
sign	sighed/side
gown	gout
pin	pit
pen	pet
pan	pad
brain	braid
line	lied
down	doubt

If you discover that you nasalize the vowels next to /n/ excessively, review the suggestions we gave for this problem on pp. 124–126.

4. *Substitution of a nasalized vowel for an oral vowel + /n/.* Some speakers do not stop at just nasalizing the vowel before the /n/; they proceed to drop the /n/ consonant altogether and let the nasalized vowel stand in for the original oral vowel and the nasal consonant /n/. The poor distorted vowel has to do double duty! In French and in some other lan-

guages, nasal vowels are part of the phonemic structure. In English they are not. This substitution of a nasalized vowel for both an oral vowel (or diphthong) and a nasal consonant is a mark of careless speech in English. The /n/ must be articulated. The tongue tip must touch the gum ridge, and the voiced consonant must be resonated in the nose. Check your pronunciation of all the following material to be sure you are getting in a good nasal consonant for /n/ and that you are not using a nasalized vowel substitute.

> unreal
> unbelievable
> insane
> onion
> canyon
> unconcerned
> no conscience
> It's all gone.
> It's done.
> I can't go.
> I won't do it.
> Iona College. I own a college?
> It's no fun anymore.
> He's incompetent.

5. *Dentalization.* Speakers who tend to dentalize /t/, /d/, and /l/ in all positions often dentalize the /n/ as well. Like /t/, /d/, and /l/, the /n/ will be made with the tongue on the teeth when it occurs before one of the two *th* sounds. In all other positions, however, the /n/ should be made on the gum ridge. Check to see if you put your tongue on your teeth to make the /n/ sound in the following words and phrases:

> not
> neat
> nod
> Nate
> knoll
> loan
> been
> den
> stun
> green
> disdain

6. *Substitution of /m/ for /n/ before abutting /p/ or /b/.* If one syllable ends with an /n/ and the next syllable begins with either /p/ or /b/, some speakers change the /n/ to /m/. This assimilation is understandable

(/m/ is articulated with the two lips as /p/ and /b/ are), but it is non-standard. Check to see if you face this temptation in the following material:

> unpolished
> unprovoked
> unbending
> unbecoming
> It can be said.
> It can prove useful.
> He's unpopular.
> He's unbelievable.
> When buying groceries . . . .
> When people meet . . . .

The /n/ before /p/ and /b/ should be articulated with the tongue tip pressed against the gum ridge. No substitutes, please.

7. *Substitution of* [ŋ] *for /n/ before abutting /f/ or /v/.* This variation of /m/ (made by the upper teeth and lower lip) is not generally considered a standard allophone of /m/. It certainly is not accepted as an allophone of /n/. This assimilation, of course, can easily be explained: the /f/ and /v/ are made by bringing the the upper teeth and lower lip together. But, however easy it is to explain, [m] for /n/ is nonstandard. Check to see if you make this substitution with this material:

> unfair
> inviolate
> confide
> convince
> confess
> convey
> unfriendly
> involved
> inflate
> invent
> confused
> unverified
> He can fix anything.
> She can visit the children.
> In fact, she stays over when visiting.

8. *Substitution of /ŋ/ (ñg) for /n/.* Before certain other consonants, you may be tempted to replace /n/ with /ŋ/—the third nasal consonant (represented in the dictionaries by ñg). Of course, this substitution is more likely before /k/ and /g/, which are articulated at the same place as the /ŋ/ (ñg), but it may occur before other consonants as well. Check

your pronunciation of this material to determine whether you make this substitution.

/n/ BEFORE ABUTTING /k/	incomplete
	concave
	unkind
	unconscious
	You can keep it.
/n/ BEFORE ABUTTING /g/	engrave
	ungrateful
	ingrained
	I can get it.
/n/ BEFORE ABUTTING /s/	concerned
	construction
	insipid
	in spite of it
/n/ BEFORE ABUTTING /ʃ/ (ṣh)	conscious
	insure
	influential
	Let the sunshine in.
/n/ BEFORE ABUTTING /r/	unreliable
	unruly
	unreported
	Fire when ready.
/n/ BEFORE ABUTTING /j/ (y)	union
	onion
	in your car
	Can you wait?

Materials for Practicing the /n/

Ned	tenet	den
need	deny	dean
no	owner	own
nut	tunnel	ton
gnat	tanner	tan
knack	canning	can
knock	Conner	con
nog	goner	gone
note	toner	tone
nick	kinfolk	kin
nap	panning	pan
nips	spinning	spin

net	tennis	ten
nice	signer	sign
night	timely	time
gnaw	awning	on
name	mainly	main
nose	zoning	zone
numb	money	Munn
node	donor	Doane
knit	tenacious	tin
nude	do not	dune

1. I need some human contact.
2. In any case, we must uphold the constitution.
3. Frankly, I found all the nonsense infuriating.
4. Ann works downtown for a venerable institution.
5. I can go if I want to.
6. Mr. Brown has found out that his invitation was counterfeit.
7. The candidates, Tweedledum and Tweedledee, have begun to re-sort to name calling.
8. Who could be lonely with wind and rain for companions?
9. Nancy's defense lawyer urged her to confess.
10. I can cook two dishes—in case I have to.
11. In fact, the union representative mentioned a new plan.
12. Nobody is consistently mean.
13. Athletes are not all brawn and no brain.
14. My brother went to the barn dance.
15. Mr. Jones telephoned to inquire about you.
16. I wouldn't call him henpecked; he wants Helen to decide every-thing.
17. I never see a morning—to say nothing of the dawn!
18. In case he was involved, I gave them all unconditional pardons.
19. I am not conscious of a need for life insurance.
20. I don't spurn any reasonable offer—no matter how strange.
21. Nudity may be natural, but it's generally frowned upon.
22. I can see you are beginning all over again.
23. The cunning gunner quickly left the scene.
24. No, he's not unbalanced, but he's not unprejudiced either.
25. The nasal consonants should be given full nasal resonance on their emission.

/ŋ/ (n͡g)

Production of the /ŋ/ (n͡g)

The sound /ŋ/ (n͡g) is a *voiced linguavelar nasal*. It is made by lower-ing the velum so air can pass out through the nose, arching the back of

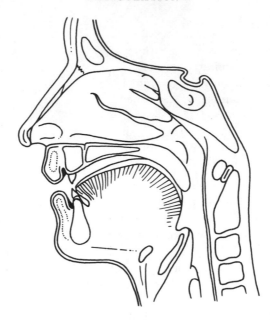

FIGURE 2–3. *Articulatory adjustments for* [ŋ]. *Note relaxed (lowered) soft palate.*

the tongue against the soft palate (the articulation you would use to make a /k/ or /g/), vibrating the vocal folds, and resonating the vibrated air in the nasopharynx and nose. You articulate this nasal sound with the tongue in the position for /k/ and /g/, but you do not stop the air completely (as you do on /k/ and /g/); you use the raised tongue to redirect the air up and out through the nose. This sound has less oral resonance than the other two nasal sounds in English. Where /m/ used all the mouth as a resonator and /n/ used about two thirds of the mouth as resonator, this nasal sound has only a little oral resonance. because of the place where the tongue is raised. You should, however, get good nasal resonance on this sound.

Allophones of the /ŋ/ (n͡g)

There is only one standard allophone of the /ŋ/ (n͡g) phoneme. And remember, this is *one* sound—even though we use two letters most of the time to represent the sound. Like other voiced consonants, the /ŋ/ (n͡g) will be slightly devoiced before voiceless consonants. If you pronounce the word *sing* and give full voicing to the "ng" sound at the end of the word and then pronounce aloud the phrase *sing her song again,* you will notice that the /ŋ/ (n͡g) before /h/ is partially devoiced—getting ready for the coming voiceless /h/. Also, like other voiced consonants, the /ŋ/ (n͡g) is partially devoiced at the ends of phrases.

Specific Warnings

There are three spellings for the /ŋ/ (n͡g) sound. In the word *lank,* the /ŋ/ is spelled *n;* in the word *tongue,* the /ŋ/ is spelled *ngue;* the most common spelling is the one found in the word *thing: ng.*

The spelling *ng* does not always represent the /ŋ/ phoneme, however. Here are four lists of words—all spelled with *ng* and none pronounced with /ŋ/:

ingest	engage	congratulate	range
ingenious	engross	incongruous	grange
ingenue	engender	conglomeration	strange
inglorious	engine	congestive	lunge
ingot	engineer	congenital	plunge
ingraft	engraft	congenial	hinge
ingrain	engrain	congeal	singe
ingress	engorge		impinge
ingulf	engulf		longevity
ingrate	engrave		
ingratitude			
ingratiate			

Sometimes the spelling *ng* represents only the sound /ŋ/—a single nasal sound. And sometimes it represents that nasal sound + /g/. Compare the words *singer* and *finger.* The *ng* in the first word stands for /ŋ/ alone; the *ng* in the second word stands for /ŋg/. On pp. 143–145, we will explain this contrast. One other observation is that the /ŋ/ (ng) phoneme occurs, in English, only in the middle and at the ends of words—never at the beginning.

Common Deviations or Problems in the Articulation of /ŋ/ (n͡g)

There are six common problems associated with this sound: (1) denasality, (2) inadequate duration, (3) severe nasality on neighboring vowels, (4) substitution of a nasalized vowel for an oral vowel + /ŋ/, (5) substitution of /n/ for final /ŋ/, and (6) /ŋ/ click (or /ŋ/ confusion).

1. *Denasality.* We defined denasality as the lack of adequate nasal resonance on the nasal sounds. If you discovered that you tended to denasalize the /m/ and /n/ (see pp. 123–124 and p. 132), it is likely that you will also denasalize the /ŋ/ (n͡g). Check your pronunciation of the following words and phrases to see if you denasalize the /ŋ/ (n͡g). The /ŋ/ (n͡g) should not sound like /k/ or /g/.

wrong
young
bang

king
stronger
hunger
strangle
mingle
elongate
bungalow
angular
singular
longing to go
completely hung up
"The Star-Spangled Banner"
flinging out a challenge

If you sound like you have a "cold in the head" on these phrases, you probably have a problem of denasality. Refer to our suggestions for coping with this problem on p. 124.

2. *Inadequate duration.* Like the /m/ and /n/, the /ŋ/ (n͡g) needs proper nasal resonance. These sounds give good carrying power to the voice and provide a musical element to the sound of your speech. Don't cheat the /ŋ/ (n͡g) sound. It is a long sound; give it its full amount of time.

3. *Severe nasality on neighboring vowels.* We discussed this problem in some detail in the section on distortions of /m/. (See pp. 124–126.) Before and after /ŋ/ (n͡g), some nasalization of the vowel is inevitable. But you should be careful to keep this amount of nasalization to a minimum. You want to work for good nasal resonance on the nasal consonants and good *oral* resonance on the vowels.

Pronounce these pairs of words out loud. Compare the way you say the *vowel* in the two words of each pair. There should be little difference in the vowel sound of the two words. Work to make them as much alike as possible.

swing	swig
rang	rag
tongs	togs
brink	brick
blank	black
dunk	duck
long	log
tongue	tug
sang	sag
wing	wig
hung	hug
bang	bag

ring	rig
rung	rug
slang	slag
slung	slug
gang	gag
lung	lug
among	a mug

Did you find that you have a problem with nasalizing the vowel in these words? If so, refer to our suggestions on pp. 124–126.

4. *Substitution of a nasalized vowel for an oral vowel* + /ŋ/. This problem was also a danger associated with the other two nasal consonants. It involves leaving out the nasal consonant completely and simply nasalizing the preceding vowel to make up the difference. It is not an acceptable substitute in English. The /ŋ/ (n͡g) must be articulated; the movements involved in making the "ng" sound must be made. That means all the movements—not just dropping the velum down! Check your pronunciation of the following sentences to see if you use a nasalized vowel in place of an oral vowel and the /ŋ/ (n͡g).

> We need strong leaders.
> It's the wrong thing to do.
> The pianist was banging away.
> I need a drink.
> We have an elected king.
> She flung the ring at him.
> Hang it all.
> The gang hid the loot.
> The throng ganged up on him.
> She's not too young.

5. *Substitution of* /n/ *for final* /ŋ/ (n͡g). In informal speech situations, especially in southern areas of the United States, many educated, cultivated speakers use *in* in place of *ing* in such words as *coming* and *going*. The use of *in* is widespread, but generally, educated speakers are expected to use *ing*—especially in more formal situations. We would encourage you not to be hasty in judging speakers who do use *in* for *ing*, but we would also encourage you to use *ing* yourself.

Check your pronunciation of these *ing* words:

> seeing
> giving
> getting
> taking
> wrapping

hopping
hanging
joking
talking
losing
earning
reading
going
doing
being
dying
bowing

6. /ŋ/ (n͡g) *click or* /ŋ/ (n͡g) *confusion.* Sometimes, in English, the /ŋ/ (n͡g) phoneme is followed by a /k/ or /g/ sound. Sometimes it is not followed by either of these sounds. Some people who have learned English as a second language and many speakers in the metropolitan New York area demonstrate confusion about when a /k/ or /g/ should follow /ŋ/ (n͡g) and when it should not.

There seem to be two sources of confusion with regard to this sound. One is the influence of a language that does not include the pronunciation of both /ŋ/ and /ŋg/. The other is spelling, which contributes to the confusion because, although /ŋ/ is a single sound, it is usually represented in our spelling by the two letters *n* and *g*. It is also sometimes spelled *ngue* (in words such as *meringue* and *tongue*) and in other words is represented by the single letter *n* (as in words such as *blink* and *bank*). Do you know whether you have this problem? Are you sure you know when to include /k/ or /g/ and when not to? You can check yourself right now. Pronounce the following material out loud. Listen each time to see if a /k/ or /g/ was pronounced in the word or phrase.

Hang it up.
Bring it here.
Sing a new one.
on Long Island
boring
hanging
strongly
a real swinger
Swinging is for apes.
I hung around for a while.
"Hanger" and "hangar" sound alike.

Did you pronounce a /k/ or /g/ in any of the examples? If you did, you have added the sound where it does not belong. And you have, therefore, an "NG Click." But let us doublecheck the results. Read the following list of words and phrases. Check again to see if any example contains a /k/ or /g/ sound as you pronounce it.

the fickle finger of fate
Look Back in Anger
What a language!
I've bungled it.
I tried every angle.
every single time
the youngest member
stronger

What did you discover this time? Did all the examples have a /g/ after the /ŋ/ (n͡g) sound? They did? No, that is not an "NG Click." The words contain both an /ŋ/ (n͡g) and /g/. If you did not include any /g/ sounds in these words, then you are confused about when to include /g/ and when not to. Let us try one more experiment. Pronounce the following list of words and phrases out loud. Again, listen to be sure whether you include a /k/ or /g/ after the /ŋ/ (n͡g) sound.

bank
banker
drunk
drunkard
wrinkle
tanks
think
Lincoln
anchor
a trim ankle
cranky

Did you hear something different this time? We hope so. This time every word or phrase contained a /k/ after the /ŋ/ (n͡g).

Can you see any pattern here at all? There is one. Maybe the following four generalizations will make the pattern clear to you.

1. When a word ends in the spelling *ng* or *ngue*, the word ends in the single nasal consonant /ŋ/. No /g/ or /k/ is ever sounded in these words, even if the next word begins with a vowel. The addition of the extra sound is considered substandard. Check your own pronunciation of *sing it*, *hang on*, and *calling all cars* to be certain that you do not add /k/ or /g/ after the nasal sound.

2. When you add a word-forming suffix to a word that ends in *ng* or *ngue*, there is usually no /g/. When the *ng* spelling is in the middle of a word and you can divide the word into a root word ending in n͡g and a

suffix, the *ng* represents the one sound /ŋ/ (n͡g). *Singer*, for example, can be divided into the root *sing* and its suffix *er*. There is, therefore, no /g/. In the word *finger*, on the other hand, there is a /g/ after the medial /ŋ/ (n͡g) because the word cannot be divided into root and suffix. Compare the word *singer* and *single*. The first, as we have noted, has no /g/, but the second is pronounced with /ŋg/ (n͡g + g) because it is not based on the root *sing*. Check your own pronunciation of the words *kingly, longing, hanger, swinger, strongly, haranguing,* and *slangy* to be certain that you do not insert a /g/ or /k/ after the nasal sound.

There are two groups of exceptions to the principle we have just explained. The comparative and superlative forms of the adjectives *long, strong,* and *young* are all pronounced with /ŋg/. *Longer, stronger, younger, longest, strongest,* and *youngest* contain /g/ after the /ŋ/ (n͡g). The second set of exceptions to this principle involves those words formed by adding *ate, ation,* or *al.* Such words as *elongate, prolongation,* and *diphthongal* are pronounced with /ŋg/.

3. When *ng* occurs in the middle of a word and is followed by sounds that do not constitute a word-forming suffix, the word will be pronounced with /ŋg/ (n͡g + g). *Linger, finger, anger, language, English, singular, single, distinguish,* and *angular* are all examples of this generalization.

You should be aware of two exceptions to this third /ŋ/ (n͡g) principle. The word *gingham*, although it cannot be divided into root and suffix, does not contain a /g/. You should also note that the words *length, strength, lengthen,* and *strengthen* are pronounced either with /ŋ/ (n͡g) or /ŋk/ (n͡g + k). Whether you pronounce these words with a /k/ or not, be careful not to substitute /n/ for /ŋ/ (n͡g). This nonstandard pronunciation *strenth* for *strength,* is more common in the South than elsewhere, but it is heard in other parts of the country as well. You should avoid it.

4. When the spelling *nc, nk,* or *nx* ends a syllable, the syllable contains /ŋk/ (n͡g + k). Pronounce these examples out loud:

nc	nk	nx
anchor	bank	lynx
Lincoln	link	minx
zinc	bunk	Manx
uncle	shrink	sphinx
distinct	cranky	larynx
succinct	ankle	pharynx
instinct	twinkle	Bronx
tincture	thinker	anxious

Just for review purposes, here are the generalizations in summary:

1. Word ending in *ng* or *ngue:*   /ŋ/ (n͡g) only; no /k/ or /g/
2. Root ending in *ng* + suffix: /ŋ/ (n͡g) only; two exceptions

3. Root (indivisible) word with   /ŋg/ (ng + k); two exceptions
   ng in middle:

4. Syllable ending in *nc, nk,* or *nx:*   /ŋk/ (ng + k)

Apply these principles in the exercises that follow.

Materials for Practicing the /ŋ/ (n͡g)

sing	singer
sing	single
swing	swinging
sung	bungle
sang	wrangler
hearing	hearings
Kong	Congo
singing	swimmingly
hung	hungry
hang	hangar
rating	tingle
dung	dungarees
ring	ringer
strong	strongly
laughing	finger
linking	linger
bang	banged
prolong	elongation
sting	distinguish
slang	languish
king	kingly
long	longer
young	youngest

1. Sing a song of six pence.
2. His youngest brother is studying to be a con man.
3. Staying in training seems to be difficult.
4. Do you go swimming often?
5. Seeing Ann isn't so easy since she moved to Long Island.
6. After finding out the questions, I still gave the wrong answers.
7. I'm remaining in town for the holidays.
8. As long as you are coming anyway, bring it with you.
9. I haven't the strength to swim the length of the pool.
10. There was a long line of men standing at the gate.
11. She can never seem to hang up the phone.
12. Is there a single standard for judging all entrants?
13. "Younger Than Springtime" is a beautiful song.
14. He's been working on all the angles.

15. Mr. Cunningham has been laughing all through the performance.
16. Running away is no answer to one's problems.
17. Practicing every day is necessary for improving your language habits.
18. Did you know that some people elongate diphthongs into triphthongal glides?
19. There's not a single gangster among us.
20. Nothing is as important to him as being on time.
21. The teacher wrongly accused the youngster of being involved.
22. The evening wasn't as boring as I thought it would be.
23. It may be the wrong thing to do, but I'm hanging in there!
24. Amazing as they may be, I wouldn't call his drawings art!
25. His daring act left the audience gasping and begging for more.
26. As long as I live, I will never forget her nasal twang.
27. Teaching is an art, and learning, an adventure.
28. I don't think you are handling it correctly.
29. Telling all he knows? That won't take him long!
30. We have prolonged these exercises long enough; now we're leaving it up to you.

THE LATERAL

A lateral sound is one on which the air is emitted over the sides of the tongue and comes out the sides of the mouth. There is only one lateral sound in English, which we represent in IPA and the dictionaries by /l/.

/l/

Production of the /l/

To form the /l/ continuant consonant, you close off the nasal passages by raising the velum, touch the tip of the tongue to the gum ridge, and allow the air to pass over the sides of the tongue out of the mouth. The /l/ is a voiced sound (produced with vocal fold vibration). The /l/ is a *voiced lingua-alveolar lateral*. The point of articulation for the /l/ is the same as for /t/ and /d/—tongue tip to gum ridge. However, on /t/ and /d/, the tongue is held against the insides of the back teeth to prevent the air from coming out over the sides of the tongue. The sides of the tongue are dropped down on /l/ to let the air come out over the sides. The tongue tip is held on the gum ridge to divide the air stream in two.

Allophones of the /l/

There are four allophones of the /l/ phoneme: (1) light /l/, (2) dark /l/, (3) devoiced /l/, and (4) dental /l/.

The "light /l/" occurs at the beginning of a syllable (either alone or after another consonant in a blend) before vowels formed by the tongue in the front of the mouth. The light /l/ is articulated as we indicated earlier, but with this addition: the back of the tongue is low in the mouth. Pronounce these words containing light /l/ before front vowels and diphthongs:

leap
lip
late
let
lack
blight
loud
lot

The phonetic symbol for light /l/ is [l̩].

The "dark /l/" occurs at the beginning of a syllable (either alone or after another consonant in a blend) before vowels formed in the back of the mouth. Unlike the light /l/, the dark /l/ is produced with the back of the tongue raised toward the soft palate—about as high in back as for the vowels in the words *took* and *stood* (represented in IPA by /ʊ/ and in the dictionaries by ŏŏ. Pronounce these words containing dark /l/ before back vowels and diphthongs:

Luke
look
glow
law
loin

The dark /l/ occurs at the ends of all words in all dialects of American English. Pronounce these words containing dark /l/ at the ends of words (either as the final consonant or before the final consonant):

full
feel
hell
help
yelled

Generally, Americans use the dark /l/ allophone in the middle of words, although many Southerners use the light /l/ in the middle of a word if it comes before a front vowel, as in such words as *Lily, yelling*, and *truly*. Which allophone do you use in those words? The dark /l/ is represented in IPA by [ɫ].

In summary, then, on the first two allophones of /l/: There is a difference in sound (a difference in acoustic quality) caused by a difference in the position of the back of the tongue. The back of the tongue is low on light /l/ and is raised toward the soft palate on dark /l/. The position of the tip of the tongue is the same for both allophones. The sounds that follow the /l/ and their position in the word determine which of the two allophones Americans will use.

Another allophone of /l/ is partially devoiced. After the voiceless sounds /p/, /k/, /f/, and /s/ (in an initial consonant blend), the /l/ is slightly devoiced. The IPA symbol for devoicing is a little circle underneath the phonemic symbol, so devoiced /l/ is represented [l̥]. Pronounce the following sequences and check for the devoicing of the /l/:

play	clay	flay	slay
plop	clop	flop	slop
plane	claim	flame	slain
plaque	claque	flack	slack
platter	clatter	flatter	Slatter
plink	clink	Flink	slink

Dental /l/ (represented in IPA by [l̪]) is the fourth allophone of the /l/ phoneme. It occurs before either of the two *th* sounds. Anticipating the dental articulation of the coming sound—(either /θ/ (th) or /ð/ (*th*)), we make the /l/ with the tongue on the teeth as well. Read the following examples aloud. You should find that you use the dental allophone of /l/ before the two "th" sounds.

> wealth
> health
> stealth
> Tell the truth.
> Will they come?
> Sell that one.
> Now he'll think twice.

Specific Warnings

Some words spelled with *l* do not contain the /l/ phoneme. Some speakers, with the best intentions, are misled by the spelling and put in an /l/. Such mispronunciations are called "spelling pronunciations." We do want you to be precise in your articulation, but pronouncing silent letters is not "being precise." Pronounce the following lists of words out loud. You should discover, as you pronounce them, that the spelled *l* is silent.

balk	alms	solder	calf	halve	could
calk	calm	salmon	half	salve	would
chalk	balm		behalf		should
Falk	embalm				
stalk	palm				
talk	qualms				
walk	psalm				
	almond				

Common Deviations or Problems in the Articulation of /l/

There are six common problems associated with the articulation of /l/: (1) slack articulation, (2) omission, (3) confusion of light and dark /l/, (4) dentalization, (5) labialization, and (6) confusion of /l/ and /r/.

1. *Slack articulation.* You have probably heard a speaker whose /l/ sound, especially in the middle of words, was not distinct. It is quite likely that the speaker was simply not touching the gum ridge with the tongue tip to form the sound. Aiming the tongue in the right direction is not enough. The tongue must touch the gum ridge. No matter where the /l/ is in the word (beginning, middle, or end) and no matter what sound comes before or after the /l/, the tip of the tongue must firmly press against the gum ridge to articulate the /l/. Try the following words out loud, and check to be sure that your tongue tip presses against the alveolar ridge on the /l/ sounds.

relevant
challenge
tranquillity
quality
analysis
William
silence
inland
truly
million
violent
violate
silly
delicate
swelling
boiler

In addition to the /l/ in the middle of words, there is another place where the /l/ is in danger of being articulated slackly, or half-heartedly. This distortion is especially common in the South. In words where the /l/ comes before the final consonant, some speakers fail to touch the gum ridge with their tongue tips on the /l/. Because the /l/ will be a dark /l/, the back of the tongue will be raised up toward the soft palate. Without firm tongue-tip articulation and with the tongue humped up in the back of the mouth, this distorted /l/ may sound more like the vowel in the word *took* (/ʊ/ in IPA and o͝o in the dictionaries) or like the first sound in the word *above* (/ə/ in both IPA and the dictionaries) than like an /l/. Distorted in this slovenly way, the word *help* would become *hĕ o͝op* (/hɛʊp/ in IPA) or *hĕəp* ([hɛəp] in IPA). In both cases, the /l/ is distorted and the pronunciation is nonstandard.

2. *Omission.* Some speakers do not stop at loosely articulating the /l/ and thus distorting it. They omit it altogether. Yield not to the temptation of omission! The temptation is greatest when the /l/ (it will be a dark /l/) comes before another consonant. Practice the following words and phrases out loud, and check to be sure you include the /l/. Articulate it by touching the tip of your tongue to the alveolar ridge.

all right
already
all-round
all gone
almost
all-knowing
all hail
all week
all kinds
all fours
all hands on deck
all clear
tall man
soldier
shoulder
million
railroad

As a further check, pronounce these pairs of words out loud. Make the distinction clear by articulating a good tongue-tip-to-gum-ridge /l/.

odor	older
code	cold
goad	gold
Mick	milk
boat	bolt
wed	weld
jade	jailed
defied	defiled
aw, man	all man
sewed my shirt	sold my shirt

3. *Confusion of light and dark /l/.* Confusion with regard to the *light and dark* /l/ is another problem sometimes associated with this sound. Some speakers for whom English is a second language always use the *light* /l/ no matter where the sound occurs. They could correct this element of a foreign accent by becoming aware that there are two forms of the sound, that they are made with the back of the tongue in a slightly

different position, and that the two allophones have different acoustic qualities. Some native speakers of American English also confuse the two forms by using the *dark* [ɫ] in all positions.

4. *Dentalization.* When an /l/ sound comes before either the voiced /ð/ (*th*) or voiceless /θ/ (*th*) sounds, the /l/ will be made with the tongue on the teeth. We noted this standard allophone of the /l/ earlier. But dentalization of the /l/, except before these sounds, is a distortion. If you discovered that you tend to dentalize /t/ and /d/, you may also dentalize the /l/. Check your pronunciation of the following examples to be certain you do not put your tongue on the upper teeth or between the teeth when you make the /l/.

> hill and dale
> Ted tells everything.
> All I want to know is. . . .
> Let me do it.
> "Hello Dolly"
> Gold is useless.
> The Big Apple

5. *Labialization.* This word simply refers to a kind of misarticulation on which articulation is made by the lips (*labia*) rather than the customary articulators. If lip movement is substituted for tongue movement in the formation of the /l/—that is, if you do not lift your tongue tip to the gum ridge but instead raise the back of the tongue and pucker your lips as if for /u/ (the vowel in *boot*) or /w/—then you are said to have labialized the sound. This distortion is associated in many people's minds with "baby talk" and you should practice to get your tongue moving to the customary spot to make the sound if you have this problem.

This distortion is represented in phonetics as [lʷ]. Although the labialized distortion can occur on /l/ in any context, the greatest danger, of course, is in an initial consonant blend after /p/ or /b/—both bilabial sounds. Remember, the /l/ is made with tongue movement, not lip movement. *Lead* should not sound like *weed; laid* should not resemble *wade; plead* and *bleed* should not become *pwead* and *bweed;* and *played* and *blame* should not become *pwayed* and *bwame.*

6. *Confusion of /l/ and /r/.* Speakers of English who learned English after speaking an Oriental language may have some difficulty hearing and making the difference between /l/ and /r/. Although these two sounds are quite separate phonemes in the English language, they are not separate phonemes in Oriental languages. Those whose first language is Japanese, Chinese, or Korean are likely to think of /l/ and /r/ as allophones of the same phoneme—rather than as separate, different sounds.

There is a difference in the articulation of the /l/ and /r/ phonemes in American English. The /l/ is made with the tip of the tongue *touching* the *gum ridge*. It touches firmly. As long as the /l/ is being sounded, the tongue is held against the ridge. Then, the tongue pushes off to go into position for the following sound. The /r/, on the other hand, is made with the tongue tensed up in the middle of the mouth and the tip pointing up to the area just *behind* the alveolar ridge—but not touching it. From this position, the tongue slides to the position for the vowel that follows the /r/. The /l/ tongue tip touches the gum ridge; the /r/ tongue tip points up to the area back of the gum ridge. If you have this problem, you will have to work to feel where the tongue goes to make these sounds, to feel the difference in tension between the two sounds, and to see the difference both in lip and tongue position between the two sounds. (The difference in tension will affect the jaw and lips.)

The following pairs of examples provide a contrast for the /l/ and /r/ sounds. Try them out loud:

leap	reap
limb	rim
late	rate
led	red
land	Rand
light	right
lout	rout
lewd	rude
look	Rook
load	rode
law	raw
lot	rot
lug	rug
alone	a roan
alive	arrive
sully	surrey
jelly	Jerry
belong	be wrong
flee	free
fly	fry
play	pray
plowed	proud
bleed	breed
blessed	breast
cloud	crowd
clipped	crypt

Materials for Practicing the /l/

led	teller	dell
lip	pillow	pill
leave	velar	veal
Luke	cooling	cool
late	tailor	tail
loaf	Foley	foal
log	galling	gall
lug	gullet	gull
lame	melee	mail
limb	miller	mill
light	tiling	tile
lap	pallid	pal
lobe	bowling	bowl
leap	peeling	peel
lick	killer	kill
law	already	all
live (adj.)	alive	vile
loot	toolbox	tool
lease	ceiling	seal
lace	sailor	sale
Lee	reeling	eel
lack	calendar	Cal
lid	dilly	dill

INITIAL /w/ AND /l/ CONTRAST	we	Lee
	wick	lick
	wait	late
	wet	let
	wag	lag
	Watt	lot
	womb	loom
	woe	low
	Wong	long
	one	lung
	wowed	loud
	wine	line
	work	lurk
	awake	a lake
	a way	allay
	be wise	belies
/l/ AND /bl/ CONTRAST	lead	bleed
	link	blink

	lame	blame
	lend	blend
	land	bland
	lack	black
	lot	blot
	Lou	blue
	low	blow
	light	blight
	luster	bluster
	lank	blank
	lake	Blake
	lose	blues
	lined	blind
	lair	Blair
	lone	blown
	lock	block
	leak	bleak
/l/ AND /pl/ CONTRAST	luck	pluck
	lace	place
	land	planned
	lane	plane/plain
	loom	plume
	lad	plaid
	lump	plump
	ledge	pledge
	lead	plead
	lug	plug
	lot	plot
	light	plight
	Loy	ploy
	loud	plowed
	lack	plaque
	lied	plied
	Lee's	please
	late	plate
	lop	plop
	lacquered	placard
	latitude	platitude
	laud	applaud
/bl/ AND /pl/ CONTRAST	bleed	plead
	bleat	pleat
	blink	plink
	blaze	plays

black	plaque
blank	planned
blot	plot
bloom	plume
blouse (v.)	plows
blush	plush
blunder	plunder
blight	plight

1. Let me call you sweetheart. You call everyone darling.
2. I'll sell it to you for a dollar.
3. Don't be silly. Of course, I'm willing.
4. Most lovers think jealousy should be a felony.
5. She knelt at the altar rail.
6. As the ball sailed between the goal posts, the team set a field goal record.
7. The Long Island Railroad is asking for help from the federal government.
8. Leonard has failed the oral examination again.
9. We'll sail for Europe on the first of April.
10. It is a delicate matter to expose a friend's fallacy.
11. Are all the lectures in this college dull?
12. No one told me there were so many scholarships available.
13. Sally belongs to a mutual admiration society.
14. You can't pull the wool over my eyes.
15. Why do you like to study the fraternity files?
16. I'll tell you no lies, but I'm likely to tell little fibs.
17. I'll be glad to call you in the morning.
18. His refusal to take the pledge should have been a clue.
19. Don't let them bluff you. Claim you're a civilian!
20. I know a million ways to make a million—all of them illegal.
21. The Oval Office should be made of glass.
22. Would you believe the place has a fifty-foot pool?
23. Everything was all right—'till I got the bill.
24. I told her in the hallway.
25. I've already violated my sacred pledge.
26. The railroads should be given all kinds of help.
27. We climbed to the top of the hill and played there.
28. Where there's a will, there's a relative.
29. I'd like to allay your fears, but it would be all lies.
30. Will you be able to think up more examples?

GLIDES

When we defined vowels and consonants at the beginning of this chapter, we said that these two kinds of sounds differ in the way they are produced and in the way they are used. In general, of course, this is true: there are differences between vowels and consonants in terms of production and function. Now, however, we have to qualify those statements a little bit.

We have a group of sounds that clearly function in the language as consonants. They act like consonants. They do the things consonants do: they begin and end syllables rather than serve as the peak of sonority (carrying power) of the syllables. *However,* in terms of their production, they are not formed the same way as the other consonants.

Consonants in this group are not nearly so obstructed as the rest of the consonants. (Remember, we said vowels are relatively open sounds, and consonants are either partially or completely obstructed.) In terms of the way these sounds are made, these consonants don't quite match the definition we gave you.

The glides differ from the other consonants in two major regards: (1) the articulators move from one position to another in the formation of these sounds, and (2) there is less obstruction of the air stream on glide sounds than on most of the other consonants. In connection with the first difference, you should remember that glides always glide into a vowel. They never appear in final position in a syllable or before a consonant. Because of the second difference, glides are sometimes called semivowels. In fact, each of the glides moves from the position of one of the vowels and is, therefore, no more obstructed than its related vowel.

/w/

Production of the /w/ *Glide*

If you put your lips and tongue in position for the vowel in the word *boo,* let the vocal folds vibrate, and glide from this position into the next vowel, you will produce the *voiced bilabial* (two-lip) *glide.* In both IPA and the dictionaries, this sound is represented by /w/. Let us be a little more specific about how the sound is formed. Pucker the lips and, letting the tongue tip rest behind the lower front teeth, raise the back of the tongue toward the soft palate. Close the velum so no air will escape up through the nose, and let the vocal folds vibrate.

This sound is the voiced partner (cognate) of the /ʍ/ (hw) sound, but it lacks the fricative nature of its voiceless cognate.

Allophones of the /w/

There are only two allophones (variations) of this phoneme. We told you this is a voiced sound, and a well-voiced allophone is usually heard. However, a partially devoiced allophone occurs in initial consonant blends after the voiceless consonants /s/, /k/, and /t/. The symbol for this devoiced allophone in IPA is [w̥]. Compare the following pairs of words. You should be able to detect the devoicing of the /w/ after the voiceless consonants.

wire	choir	wipe	swipe	wine	twine
ween	queen	wear	swear	we'd	tweed
wick	quick	well	swell	win	twin

Specific Warnings

Words beginning with the spelling *wr* are pronounced with /r/ only; the letter *w* is silent. If you pronounce the following examples, you should discover that none of the words contains a /w/:

wrack	wretched
wrangle	wriggle
wrap	Wright
wrath	wring
wreak	wrinkle
wreath	wrist
wreathe	writ
wreck	write
wren	writhe
wrench	written
wrest	wrong
wrestle	wrought
wretch	wry

The letter *w* is silent in the middle of the words *answer, toward, sword,* and *two. Answer* is pronuonced /ænsɚ/ (*ăn-sər*). *Toward* is a one-syllable word pronounced [touɚd] (*tōrd*) or [tɔɚd] (*tôrd*). *Sword* rhymes with *toward,* and *two* sounds like *to* and *too.*

Like the other two glides, /w/ occurs only at the beginning of syllables —never at the end of a syllable. The *w* spelling, however, can occur at the end of syllables. When it does, the *w,* of course, is silent. Here are four lists of words spelled with silent *w.* The words are listed according to the vowel (or diphthong) in the syllable with the silent *w.*

/o/ (o)	/aʊ/ (ou)	/u/ ($\overline{oo}$) OR /ju/ ($\overline{yoo}$)	/ɔ/ (ȏ)
row (a line)	row (a fight)	dew	saw
low	cow	few	draw
blow	how	flew	flaw
grow	now	brew	claw
flow	plow	crew	craw
bow (a knot)	bow (v.)	pew	jaw
sow (v.)	sow (n.)	mew	gnaw

tow	Dow	grew	law
sew	pow!	Jew	paw
strew	vow	new	maw
shew	wow	threw	raw
window	fowl	lewd	straw
yellow	jowl	stew	yawl
below	owl		awl
pillow			shawl
minnow			awful
tallow			lawman
			awkward

Comon Deviations or Problems in the Articulation of /w/

There are four common problems associated with the /w/ phoneme: (1) slack articulation, (2) omission, (3) substitution of /v/ for /w/, and (4) addition.

1. *Slack articulation.* If you do not round your lips enough and have enough tension of the lips when you produce this sound, the articulation will be careless and the sound will be weakened almost beyond recognition. We hope you do not have lazy lips. (Did you find that you had slack or lazy articulation on /p/, /b/, and /m/—three other sounds formed by the two lips? Have you worked sufficiently on lip movement to produce a firm, clear /p/, /b/, and /m/?) Unless you get sufficient lip movement and lip tension (the lips must be puckered to make this sound), you will not produce a clear /w/.

Pronounce the following sequences out loud. We are working for labial movement. To produce the /p/, /b/, and /m/, of course, the lips have to close completely. The lips do not close completely on /w/, but they must close down to a tight, round circle. Try these sequences out loud:

peak	beak	meek	weak
pie	buy	my	Y
pay	bay	may	weigh
peal	Beale	meal	weal
pate	bait	mate	wait
pail	bail	mail	wail
pet	bet	met	wet
P	be	me	we
pit	bit	mit	wit
pear	bare	mare	wear
Poe	bow	mow	woe
pill	bill	mill	will
penned	bend	mend	wend
purr	burr	myrrh	were

pest	best	messed	west
pile	bile	mile	wile
packs	backs	Max	wax
pain	bane	mane	wane
pelt	belt	melt	welt
pall	ball	mall	wall

Try to develop the sensitivity to feel the proper lip tension for the /w/ sound. If necessary, get a mirror and look to see where the lips are for the vowel in *ooze,* and (if that is pursed enough) get the same lip position for the beginning of /w/. The greatest temptation to slack articulation of the /w/ occurs in initial consonant blends—when /w/ follows /k/, /s/, /t/, or /d/. Check your pronunciation of these pairs of words. Be careful to get good lip rounding for the initial /w/, and then listen, look, and feel to check to see if you get equally good articulation of the second word (where the /w/ follows another consonant).

/w/ AND /kw/ CONTRAST	wad	quad
	wit	quit
	wake	quake
	wail	quail
	waver	quaver
	wilt	quilt
	work	quirk
	wire	choir
	ween	queen
	wick	quick
	west	quest
	Wyatt	quiet
	will	quill
	well	quell
	wench	quench
	wash	quash
	wary	quarry

/w/ AND /sw/ CONTRAST	wash	swag
	wane	swain
	wallow	swallow
	wan	swan
	warm	swarm
	wag	swart
	wart	swash
	watt	swat
	way	sway
	wear	swear

wet	sweat
wetter	sweater
we'd	Swede
weep	sweep
well	swell
welling	swelling
welter	swelter
wig	swig
will	swill
wine	swine
wing	swing
wipe	swipe
wish	swish
witch	switch

/w/ AND /tw/ CONTRAST

waddle	twaddle
wane	twain
weak	tweak
weed	tweed
wig	twig
will	twill
wine	twine
win	twin
Winkle	twinkle
wit	twit
witch	twitch

/w/ AND /dw/ CONTRAST

well	dwell
welling	dwelling
wharf (?)	dwarf

2. *Omission.* Some speakers go beyond loosely articulating the /w/ and omit it from some words completely. The /w/ most in danger of omission is the one after an abutting consonant. Pronounce these words, and listen to be sure the /w/ is not left out.

awkward
teamwork
homework
unworthy
stalwart
onward

The /w/ in the middle of a word is in some danger—even if it is preceded by a vowel or diphthong. Pronounce these words out loud, and check for the omission of /w/:

way*w*ard
sea*w*orthy
lee*w*ard
for*w*ard

3. *Substitution of /v/ for /w/*. Some speakers who have learned English as a second language (and others who learned English from someone for whom English was a second language) confuse /v/ and /w/, often substituting the /v/ for the /w/. The two phonemes are separate and distinct in English; they are not variations of each other. They are formed in very different ways. The /v/ is articulated by the upper teeth and the lower lip; the /w/ is formed by tensely rounding the two lips and suddenly opening them as you utter the next vowel.

Here are some pairs of words that contrast the /w/ and /v/. Check to see if you are tempted to make the words with /w/ in the same way you make the words with /v/.

wail	vale
wane	vain
wan	von
wary	vary
Walt	vault
want	vaunt
wend	vend
went	vent
west	vest
wet	vet
wicker	vicar
Weiss	vice
Y	vie
wile	vile
Willa	villa
wine	vine
wiper	viper
wiser	vizor
wow!	vow
we	V
worse	verse
we're	veer

If you have difficulty making this distinction, work on articulation of the /w/ by being sure your tongue and lips are in the position for the vowel in the word *do*. Look in the mirror to see the position of the lips as you utter that word *do*. The lips should be slightly protruded and tensed into a little circle. That is exactly the position from which the /w/

starts. Therefore, we will try a word beginning with /w/ right after that vowel in *do* (the vowel is represented by o͞o in the dictionaries and by /u/ in IPA). Be sure to hold your lips in the position of the last sound in the word *do* as you begin the /w/ of the next word. (The /w/, being a glide, does not keep the lips in that position but slides into the next vowel position.) Now, remembering these instructions, try saying "Do well" out loud. Could you feel that the /w/ started out right where the /u/ (o͞o) was? If so, then try these other phrases—all of which have an /u/ (o͞o) followed immediately by a /w/. The /u/ (o͞o) should give you the proper jumping off place for the /w/.

> you want
> who would
> too wise
> two wives　　(a tough one!)
> to wed
> Sue will
> new one
> do one
> too wet
> to win

4. *Addition.* Some speakers insert a /w/ sound if a syllable ends with /o/ (the vowel at the beginning of the word *own*) or /u/ (the vowel at the beginning of the word *ooze*) and the next syllable begins with a vowel. Because the lips are rounded for the vowels /o/ and /u/, it is easy to voice the glide /w/ as the lips and tongue move to the position for the next vowel. Understandable though the insertion may be, it is nonstandard and should be avoided. Check your own pronunciation of these words and phrases. If you insert a /w/, the words in the left-hand column will sound like the ones in the right-hand column:

you are	you war
you ate	you wait
doing	do wing
knew it	new wit
sewing	so wing
know it	no wit
no air	no wear
go in	go win

Materials for Practicing the /w/

1. Watch out! It's getting worse.
2. What does the weather vane on the church steeple symbolize?
3. Many humanitarians have been men of vast wealth.

4. Victory is its own reward.
5. It comes in various widths and a wide variety of lengths.
6. A wise voter will check on a candidate's views.
7. I look forward to working with you.
8. I told her to beware of her wayward son.
9. I want to believe mankind is going onward and upward forever.
10. It was an awkward moment when the queen's face began twitching.
11. The choir sang well enough to suit me; I didn't awaken.
12. I think it unwise to swagger so much.
13. You're not unwelcome or unwanted, but you are one hour early.
14. Teamwork was the secret of their winning ways.
15. You warned me, but it was worse than I expected.
16. Winston doesn't do his homework very often.
17. The witch had a twinkle in her eye as she swore I'd become rich.
18. I'm told Wilma just won't eat quail.
19. Dr. Vest went to Greece without hotel reservations.
20. A swarm of policemen quelled the riot; several of the rioting dwarfs were hurt.
21. Their mother swears she can't tell the twins apart.
22. I want to spend a quiet evening with the family.
23. Thanks to the well-informed voters, the reformers made a clean sweep.
24. Water is the only thing that can quench my thirst.
25. Vera's always very willing; I just wish she were more able.

/j/ (y)

Production of the /j/ (y)

If you put your tongue in the position for the vowel in the word *beet,* let your vocal folds vibrate, and glide from this position into the next vowel, you will produce the *voiced linguapalatal glide.* This sound is represented in IPA by /j/ and in the dictionaries by y. The sound is made by letting the tongue tip rest behind the lower front teeth, raising the front of the tongue nearly to the hard palate, raising the velum, and vibrating the vocal folds. The lips will be in the position for whatever vowel follows. This sound, like the other glides, always precedes a vowel and never is at the end of a syllable.

Allophones of /j/ (y)

There are only two allophones (variations) of the /j/ (y) phoneme. It is a voiced sound and the fully voiced allophone is the most common. It does have a partially devoiced allophone, however, which occurs in initial consonant blends after the voiceless consonants /t/, /k/, /p/, /f/, and /h/. The symbol for this devoiced allophone in IPA is [j̥]. Compare the following pairs of words. You should be able to detect the devoicing of the /j/ (y) after the voiceless consonants.

Yuma	tumor
you	cue
you	pew
you'd	feud
you	Hugh

Common Deviations or Problems in the Articulation of the /j/ (y)

There are four common problems associated with this sound: (1) omission, (2) confusion of /u/ and /ju/ ($\overline{oo}$ and y$\overline{oo}$), (3) substitution of /dʒ/ (j) and (4) addition.

1. *Omission.* There is a temptation to omit the /j/ (y) in the middle of words after /l/ and /n/. Indeed when /l/ or /n/ abuts /j/ (y), careless speakers tend to omit the second of the two abutting consonants. Check your own pronunciation of the following words and phrases to be sure you do not omit the /j/ (y) phoneme after the /l/ or /n/.

/j/ (y) AFTER ABUTTING /l/		
	million	hellion
	billion	rebellion
	trillion	Collier
	pavilion	stallion
	civilian	battalion
	billiards	halyard
	William	galleon
	Hilliard	
	Will you try?	
	I'll tell you.	
	Did it fill you up?	
	sell your car	
	a swell year	

/j/ (y) AFTER ABUTTING /n/		
	onion	union
	Bunyan	communion
	grunion	canyon
	minion	companion
	pinion	lanyard
	opinion	banyon
	dominion	*Agnus Dei*
	filet mignon	lorgnette
	Can you go?	
	in your car	
	a fine year	

As we explained earlier, /j/ (y) slides from the position where the vowel in *eat* is made. That is, the tongue is in the position used for the vowel in *eat* (represented in IPA by /i/ and in the dictionaries by ē) as the /j/ (y) glide begins. Ordinarily, the tongue then slides into the position for the vowel that follows the /j/ (y). But what happens if the vowel after the /j/ (y) is an /i/ (ē) vowel? And what happens if the sound just before the /j/ (y) is the /i/ (ē) vowel? Well, of course, some people take the easy way out and omit the gliding consonant /j/ (y)! Granted, it does take extra effort to get the /j/ (y) in. Check your own pronunciation of the following words and phrases to be sure you do not omit the /j/ (y).

> ye
> year
> yeast
> yield

Now compare these pairs of examples. Do you include the /j/ (y) in the second phrase of each pair, or do you omit it?

he earns	he yearns
the ear	the year
the el	the yell
the awning	the yawning
Say "S."	Say yes.

2. *Confusion of* /u/ (o͞o) *and* /ju/ (yo͞o). Many people are confused about when to use the vowel /u/ (the opening sound in the word *ooze*) and when to precede that vowel with the glide /j/ (y). Here are some general principles to guide you:

1. In initial position in the word, the spellings *u, eu,* and *ew* are pronounced /ju/ (yo͞o).
2. Generally, after /p/, /b/, /k/, /m/, /f/, /v/, and /h/, the spellings *u, eu, ew, iew,* and *ue* are pronounced /ju/ (yo͞o).
3. After /t/, /d/, and /n/, the spellings *u, eu, ue,* and *ew* are pronounced either /u/ (o͞o), /ju/ (yo͞o), or /ɪu/. (See p. 186 for a discussion of the vowel /ɪ/.) Although the use of /u/ (o͞o) predominates nationally, the most careful speakers use either /ju/ (yo͞o) or /ɪu/. We would encourage you not to use the /u/ (o͞o), because it results in a number of unnecessary homonyms.

The following words contain /u/ (o͞o):

> to, too, two, do, noose

The following words contain /ju/ (yo͞o):

> uniform, unity, unify, union, eulogy, usury, uranium, usage

Words in the left-hand column are pronounced with /u/ ($\overline{oo}$); those in the right-hand column are pronounced with /ju/ (y$\overline{oo}$).

coo	cue
poor	pure
do	dew
booty	beauty
who	hue
moo	mew
food	feud
voodoo	view do

Check your pronunciation in the following sentences of the sound you use after /t/, /d/, and /n/:

1. Tuesday there will be a meeting of the Tuna Packers Association.
2. Do you read the *Daily News?*
3. How many students were involved in the incident?
4. He wrote the words to the song, but he used an old tune.
5. The note will come due next week.
6. The police are on duty twenty-four hours a day.
7. It is impolite to call me stupid.
8. All of the duly elected officers have been impeached.
9. Mr. Newley has written a new play.
10. What can I possibly do with a bushel of tulip bulbs?
11. I'm so poor I can't afford to be pure.
12. I said "phooey" and a few other choice words.
13. Do you get up early enough to see dew on the grass?
14. I was in no mood to be patient when the cat mewed all night.
15. Who painted the room this horrible hue of green?
16. He pooh-poohed religion, but he was in the family pew every week.
17. The poor director could not get the bird to coo on cue.
18. The pirate prized her beauty above all the booty he had found.
19. Do you know when the note is due?
20. In just two days it will be Tuesday!

3. *Substitution of* /dʒ/ (j) *for* /j/ (y). Some speakers, including many who learned English as a second language, substitute the /dʒ/ (j) sound —the first sound in the word *jet*—for the voiced linguapalatal glide /j/ (y). The two sounds are articulated in very different ways. The /j/ (y) is made with the tongue tip behind the lower front teeth and the front of the tongue lifted up tensely almost to the hard palate (although it does not touch the palate). The /dʒ/ (j) is made with the tongue tip and blade firmly pressed against the gum ridge and the back of the gum ridge—from which point it pushes away, dropping down. Check your own pronunciation of the following pairs of words. The first word in each pair begins with /j/ (y) and the second word begins with /dʒ/ (j):

yak	Jack
yard	jarred
yaw	jaw
yea	Jay
year	jeer
a yearning	adjourning
yell	jell
yellow	Jello
yerk	jerk
yes	Jess
yet	jet
you	Jew
yoke	joke
yowl	jowl
Yules	Jules
yacht	jot
Yale	jail
yam	jam
you know	Juno

4. *Addition.* Some speakers add the /j/ (y) sound if a syllable ends in the vowel /i/ (ē) (the first sound in the word *eat*) or in the three diphthongs ending in the vowel /ɪ/ (ĭ) (/ɪ/ is the first sound in the word *it*). These three diphthongs are the last sounds in the words *buy, boy,* and *bay.* Because the tongue is already in the position for the /i/ (ē) or /ɪ/ (ĭ) vowel, it is easy to glide with voicing to the position of the next vowel; in that way, /j/ has been articulated. If the next syllable is a stressed syllable, it is especially easy to fall into this problem. However easy it may be, it is not considered standard. In the old Popeye cartoons, you remember, Popeye often said, "I yam!" But Popeye was noted for his brawn—not his brains or his speech patterns. In the left-hand column, there are a few phrases that contain the temptation to add a /j/ (y). If you add the /j/ (y), the phrase will sound like the phrase in the right-hand column.

see it	see yit
be over	be yover
I am	I yam
my arm	my yarm
joy in	joy yin
toy is	toy yiz
may eat	may yeat
Say "S."	Say yes.

Materials for Practicing /j/ (y)

INITIAL /j/ (y)   unite
                     union
                     yards
                     yon
                     use
                     yonder
                     yell
                     you
                     eulogy

MEDIAL /j/ (y)   disunite
                     communion
                     billiards
                     galleon
                     misuse
                     beyond
                     Daniel
                     review

INITIAL AND MEDIAL /pj/ (py)   pure   impute
                                 pew   impugn
                                 pupil   compute

INITIAL AND MEDIAL /bj/ (by)   butane   imbue
                                 beauty   abuse
                                 beautiful   abusive

INITIAL AND MEDIAL /tj/ (ty)   tune   platitude
                                 tuba   constitute
                                 tutor   gratuity

INITIAL AND MEDIAL /dj/ (dy)   dew   induce
                                 duty   endure
                                 duly   unduly

INITIAL AND MEDIAL /kj/ (ky)   cue   accuse
                                 cute   accute
                                 cure   incurable

INITIAL AND MEDIAL /fj/ (fy)   few   confuse
                                 fuse   infuse
                                 future   refute

INITIAL AND MEDIAL /mj/ (my)   muse   amused
                                 mute   immutable
                                 music   immune

INITIAL AND MEDIAL /nj/ (ny) new   anew
                               nuisance   renew
                               nuance   annuity

1. Are you familiar with the *Saturday Review?*
2. Youth today are not confused, but they're confusing.
3. Yesterday he yawned in my class again!
4. The yield of yellow corn has doubled in the last year.
5. William has been told a million times to keep his opinions to himself.
6. In all humility, I think this volume will endure.
7. His battalion was ordered to put down the rebellion.
8. The leaders of my union would have led Daniel *into* the lions' den.
9. The eulogy was delivered by a young priest from the Humane Society.
10. I'm told the yearly take on illegal gambling is over nine billion dollars.
11. Beauty is in the eye of the beholder, and Cupid produces myopia.
12. Have you any use for a deserted canyon?
13. She yelled her abuse until it was almost humorous.
14. It is your duty to go on this futile mission.
15. How can you refuse to recognize his genius?
16. We use millions of them every year.
17. Seniors at the institute gave a huge donation.
18. It takes a sense of humor to play the tuba.
19. I think your uncle has visited every vineyard in Europe.
20. In my opinion, it's the best in years.

/r/

Production of the /r/ *glide*

Because the /r/ sound is made by different people in different ways and in different regions in different ways, it is difficult to describe this consonant with exactness. In addition, because the /r/ is a glide, which implies continuous movement of the tongue from the sound that precedes it to the sound that follows it, the surrounding sounds cause variation in the production of /r/.

If you put your tongue in the position for the vowel in the word *burr* (see pp. 231–237 for a discussion of the vowels /ɝ/ and /ɚ/), let the vocal folds vibrate, and glide immediately into the vowel that follows, you will produce a *lingua-postalveolar glide*, which we represent by /r/. More specifically, the sound is formed by pointing the tensed tip of the tongue upward to a position just in back of the alveolar ridge or by slightly curling the raised tongue tip back toward the palate, closing the velum, and vibrating the vocal folds. From this position the tongue slides

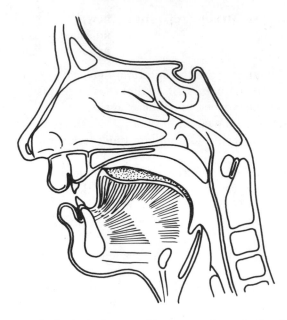

FIGURE 2–4. *Articulatory adjustments for retreflex* [r].

toward the position of the vowel that follows. If the following vowel is made in the back of the mouth, more than likely the tongue tip will be slightly retroflexed on the /r/. If the vowel following is made in the front of the mouth, more than likely the tongue tip will be slightly turned toward the alveolar ridge. You should remember in forming this sound that there should be a minimum of lip movement. The sound is articulated chiefly by the movement of the tongue.

Allophones of the /r/

There are three allophones of the /r/ glide in American English. The /r/ consonant, you remember, like the other two glides, occurs only before vowels and never occurs at the end of a syllable. (Its related vowels —and there are two of them—*do* occur at the ends of syllables.) When gliding into most vowels, the /r/ has almost no friction. This frictionless allophone is the most common form of the /r/ heard in the United States. Its IPA symbol is simply [r].

After /t/ and /d/ in initial consonant blends, the /r/ has a fricative quality. Because there is a narrower opening between the tongue and the back of the gum ridge than on other /r/s, this allophone pushes the air through the opening more forcefully; the result is a more fricative type of sound. The opening is narrower because it has just been closed off by the articulation of the preceding /t/ or /d/ and the tongue does not drop down as much as on other allophones of /r/. The symbol in IPA for the fricative allophone is [ɹ]. If you compare your pronunciation of the words *rip, trip,* and *drip,* you will notice that the /r/ in *rip* is far smoother and the /r/ in trip and drip far rougher (or more fricative). Can you hear the difference?

There is one other allophone of the /r/ in American English. The /r/, like the two other glides, is a voiced sound, but it is partially devoiced in initial consonant blends after voiceless consonants (/p/, /t/, /k/, /θ/, /f/, and /ʃ/). If /s/ is added before the /p/, /t/, or /k/, however, the /r/ is not devoiced. You can check out this allophone for yourself. Read aloud the following sequences. In the first word of the sequence, the /r/ should be frictionless and voiced. In the next three words, the /r/ should be slightly devoiced because of the voiceless preceding sound. (After the /t/, the /r/ will be both devoiced and fricative.) Listen for yourself.

rye	pry	try	cry
raise	praise	trays	craze

Now compare these pairs of words. In each pair, the first word will contain the voiced allophone and the second will contain the slightly devoiced allophone (represented in IPA by [r̥]).

red	thread
Red	Fred
rug	shrug
row	throw
rill	frill
rink	shrink

We have one more set of sequences for you to check aloud. In this set, each sequence has /r/ in initial position in a word, then /r/ after a voiceless stop (where the /r/ will be devoiced), and then an initial consonant cluster where /s/ has been added before the voiceless stop and the /r/. In this last word, the devoicing is not present; the /s/ siphoned off the extra air. Test these words—out loud— for yourself:

rat	Pratt	Spratt
rap	trap	strap
ream	cream	scream
ray	pray	spray
rain	train	strain
rue	crew	screw

Common Deviations or Problems in the Articulation of /r/

There are six common problems associated with the /r/ phoneme: (1) trilled or flapped /r/, (2) excessive friction, (3) excessive retraction, (4) labialization, (5) addition, (6) confusion of /r/ and /l/.

1. *Trilled or flapped* /r/. In certain other English-speaking countries, the /r/ is either trilled or flapped against the ridge or palate. In the United States, however, trilling or flapping the /r/ is uncommon and is considered an affectation. We advise against it.

2. *Excessive friction.* If you push the air stream with considerable force through the opening between the tongue tip and the palate when making the /r/, the sound will possess a fricative quality. In the speech of most Americans, fricative /r/ is unsual except in the consonant combinations /tr/ and /dr/. Even in those combinations you should be careful not to attack the /r/ sound with too much force. The slight devoicing of the /r/ that occurs after the voiceless sounds in the combinations /pr/, /tr/, /kr/, /fr/, /θr/, and /ʃr/ seems to increase the danger of excessive friction. If you have discovered that you tend to overaspirate some consonants, check to be certain that you do not push too much air through on the /r/, especially in these combinations.

3. *Excessive retraction.* In many parts of the United States, especially in the Midwest, the /r/ is often produced with the tongue tip turned backward toward the palate. If this retroflexion is excessive, the vowels that surround the /r/ will be distorted. You may have read a story in which an author spelled *very* as "vurry" and *American* as "Amurrucan" to represent this kind of pronunciation. If you produce the /r/ with the tongue tip curled back toward the palate, check to be certain that you do not pull the tongue back so far that the vowels are noticeably distorted. Some speakers use another form of retracted /r/ that sounds a great deal like the retroflex we have just discussed. In this variation the tongue tip remains low in the front of the mouth and the back of the tongue is raised toward the soft palate. This retraction of the tongue, like excessive retroflexion, markedly changes the quality of the adjacent vowels and should be avoided.

4. *Labialization.* The labialized /r/ results from excessive lip movement in forming the sound and produces a distorted consonant that sounds something like /w/. If you discovered that you tended to labialize the /l/, you may also discover that you substitute lip movement for tongue movement on the /r/. Pronounce the word *red* and listen to determine if it sounds like *wed*. Next, check with a mirror to see if you are moving your lips as you pronounce the /r/. When /r/ is the initial sound in a word, the lips will be in the position for the sound that follows while the /r/ is being uttered. In the word *reed*, then, the lips should be spread for the vowel in the word and should not move while the /r/ is being emitted. Most people who have difficulty with the labialized deviation of /r/ do not lift the tongue tip up to the alveolar ridge or the palate but instead let the tongue tip lie low in the front of the mouth and raise the back of the tongue up toward the soft palate (in the position of /u/ and /w/). To correct this distortion, you must raise your tensed tongue tip toward

the proper spot and prevent the lips from moving. (Tongue tension is essential!)

5. *Addition.* This problem is also called "intrusive *r*" because the *r* intrudes where it does not belong. The space between two successive vowels that occur in separate syllables (that is, one syllable ends in a vowel, and the next syllable begins in a vowel) is called hiatus. A *hiatus* is a little pause or break to separate the two vowels and indicate they are in different syllables. Granted, it is easier to separate syllables by having them start with consonants! But it is possible to have syllables *end* with a vowel or diphthong rather than with a consonant, and it is also possible to have a syllable *start* with a vowel or diphthong rather than with a consonant. It is when you have both such syllables together that some people run into trouble. They want to add an /r/ to help them keep the syllables separated. This is the added, or intrusive, /r/. Let us look at an example to help make this problem clearer. The word *going* has two syllables. The first ends with the /o/ phoneme (actually, here it will be the diphthongal allophone, but it doesn't matter), and the second syllable starts with the /ɪ/ (ĭ) vowel—the vowel in the word *it*. Between these two syllables, some people are tempted to insert an /r/— transforming the word into *goring*. The two syllables that present the problem do not have to be in the same word. The words *idea of it* are transformed into *idear of it* with the addition of the intrusive *r*.

Pronounce the examples that follow. Check to hear if you add an /r/ at the hiatus.

> the *idea* of it
> a *law* office
> I *saw* it.
> He ate a *raw* egg.
> It will *thaw* out.
> Can you *draw* a face?
> *Cuba* is a neighbor.
> *Atlanta* is lovely.
> the *cawing* of the crows
> *Drawing* is not difficult.
> a *flaw* in the plan
> the *Shah* of Persia
> *Utah* is unique.
> *Emma* and Mary
> *law* of the land
> The *comma* is out of place.
> *Medea* is a witch.

We recognize that there are educated, cultivated speakers who add the /r/ to words and syllables. President Kennedy talked to the nation about "Cuber." But the pronunciation was a source of amusement to many and an annoyance to some; the vast majority of Americans certainly noticed it and found it strange. We think it best to become aware of this habit if you have it and to omit the added /r/.

6. *Confusion of /r/ and /l/.* We have already discussed this problem in relation to the /l/ phoneme. See pp. 151–152 for an explanation of and suggestions for this problem.

Materials for Practicing the /r/

INITIAL AND MEDIAL /r/		
	round	around
	rate	berate
	root	uproot
	wrecked	direct
	robe	disrobe
	ride	deride
	Rome	aroma
	rise	arise
	rage	enrage
	rye	awry
	rive	arrive
	ravel	unravel
	ranged	deranged
	real	unreal
	rode	erode
	rest	arrest
	rear	career

INITIAL /r/ AND /tr/		
	rain	train
	rim	trim
	rip	trip
	raid	trade
	rue	true
	rash	trash
	Rio	trio
	right	trite

INITIAL /r/ AND /dr/		
	rill	drill
	raw	draw
	ream	dream
	rug	drug
	rive	drive
	rain	drain
	rear	drear
	round	drowned

INITIAL /r/ AND /kr/	reek	creek
	ram	cram
	rum	crumb
	ruse	cruise
	rave	crave
	ripped	crypt
	ride	cried
	rest	crest

INITIAL /r/ AND /gr/	raze	graze
	rid	grid
	reeve	grieve
	ripe	gripe
	rope	grope
	round	ground
	rub	grub
	Rand	grand

INITIAL /r/ AND /fr/	round	frowned
	rock	frock
	rend	friend
	ride	fried
	runt	front
	wrench	French
	rank	frank
	rail	frail

INITIAL /r/ AND /θr/ (thr)	rift	thrift
	rob	throb
	rush	thrush
	roan	throne
	rash	thrash
	wrong	throng
	rue	through
	rive	thrive

If you have a tendency to labialize the /r/, the following words will be especially difficult for you to pronounce. The /p/ and /b/, of course, are bilabial sounds (articulated by the two lips). The articulation of the /r/ (made by tongue movement) takes place at the same time the lips are producing the /p/ or /b/; the /p/ or /b/ and the /r/ are *not* produced as successive sounds (the /r/ *after* the /p/ or /b/). You need your lips to make the /p/ or /b/, and if you are used to using the lips to also produce the /r/, you are in trouble. You couldn't produce both at the same time with the lips. So you need to get your tongue into the act. Remember, the tongue starts from the position of the vowel in *her* and slides from there into position for the next vowel. Try this sequence to help get the feeling; be sure to hold your tongue in the position of the last sound in the word *her* as you begin the /r/ of the next word. Then we can try to put a /p/ or /b/ in front of the whole thing. Try to say *her reach*. Did you feel that the /r/ started off (in the word *reach*) right where the vowel at the end of the word *her* was? If so, try these sequences to help us get ready for the /br/ and /pr/ combinations.

her room	room	broom
her reach	reach	breach
her right	right	bright
her rig	rig	brig
her ring	ring	bring
her reading	reading	breeding
her ride	ride	bride
her races	races	braces
her racket	racket	bracket
her rake	rake	break
her raid	raid	braid
her rain	rain	brain
her reef	reef	brief
her risk	risk	brisk
her roach	roach	broach
her root	root	brute

her raise	raise	praise
her ram	ram	pram
her ray	ray	pray
her rank	rank	prank
her reach	reach	preach
her recision	recision	precision
her reference	reference	preference
her repair	repair	prepare
her reparations	reparations	preparations
her rest	rest	pressed

INITIAL /r/ AND /br/

rig	brig
reefer	briefer
rite	bright
red	bread
wrought	brought
rave	brave
rue	brew
rim	brim

INITIAL /r/ AND /pr/

ride	pride
roof	proof
rinse	prince
rune	prune
raid	prayed
rye	pry
reach	preach
rest	pressed

INITIAL /r/ AND /ʃr/ (shr)

rude	shrewd
rink	shrink
rill	shrill
rub	shrub

INITIAL /r/ AND /spr/

ray	spray
rout	sprout
ring	spring
rightly	sprightly

Be careful not only to get a good /r/ in these words, but a good /s/ as well. Don't turn /s/ into /ʃ/ (sh).

INITIAL /r/ AND /str/

raid	strayed
wrangle	strangle
Ruggles	struggles
rip	strip
rate	straight
rain	strain
wrong	strong
rest	stressed
raw	straw
range	strange
ride	stride
rap	strap
ring	string
reek	streak
ray	stray
ripe	stripe
roll	stroll
rut	strut
rive	strive
rider	strider
rife	strife
ream	stream
wrapping	strapping
rand	strand

INITIAL /r/ AND /skr/   reach   screech

                                 rub   scrub

                                 ream   scream

                                 rue   screw

Here are some sentences with /r/ in various positions and combinations.

1. He would rather be Right than President.
2. I have been reading *Pride and Prejudice*.
3. If I broke it, I'm very sorry.
4. The customer is always right.
5. The new director will present his first play on Friday.
6. He eats french fries three times a day.
7. She's absolutely treacherous. Beware of her.
8. They sent me a crate of Florida oranges.
9. We'll cross that bridge when we come to it.
10. The train leaves at three o'clock and will arrive around five.
11. Pronounce the words carefully, but not pedantically.
12. The store is demanding proof of payment.
13. The company will try to make other arrangements for the irate passenger.
14. His demands were pretty unrealistic.
15. We had a grand time on our trick-or-treat expedition.
16. Straight-laced and prudish, she brands everything obscene.
17. It was a horrible day for the Macy's parade.
18. He may be crass and greedy and treacherous, but he's my friend.
19. Those small-fry operators want to destroy everything we have constructed here.
20. He thinks he's patriotic because he carries a flag around and cries when he hears the "Star-Spangled Banner."
21. Not very happy? I'm miserable!
22. The wrestler groaned a lot to prove the match was real.
23. I'm afraid she's just stringing him along.
24. She trapped him into the marriage by threatening suicide.
25. His approach is ridiculous: he'll take anything for a trade-in.
26. I hear it all right, but I don't grasp your meaning.
27. So my precious baby is still crawling at fourteen. What does that prove?
28. Bring your rich uncle. I want to drive his Rolls-Royce.
29. I'm sorry I don't have a very good reason for it.
30. Don't be afraid. He'll approve anything.
31. You're probably ready to create your own sentences.

3
The Sounds of American English: Vowels

W E HAVE already defined vowels as speech sounds that are emitted with relatively little obstruction of the air stream. Vowels, then, are not articulated in the same way as consonants. They are distinguished one from another by slight changes in resonance in the oral cavity (mouth). By shifting the tongue around in the mouth, by changing the shape of the opening formed by the lips, and by varying the amount of muscular tension and the time we hold onto the sounds, we produce the different vowels of American English.

We cannot be nearly so exact in describing the formation of vowels as we were for consonants, because we cannot be precise in describing the height to which the tongue is raised on any given sound, in pinpointing the exact area of the mouth to which the tongue is pulled forward or back, or in depicting the exact degree to which the lips are rounded. Vowels are influenced by the consonants that precede and follow them, and different people produce the same vowels differently. We will have to discuss the production of each vowel in rather general terms, and you will have to train your ears to recognize the slight differences that will distinguish one vowel from another.

Distinctive Features: Classification of Vowels

Every sound in the language can be identified (set off from all other sounds in the language) on the basis of a group of distinctive characteristics. These distinctive features, or components, are the means of classifying and describing sounds. Consonants, you remember, are distinguished from each other on the basis of three classes of features. Two of those classes are irrelevant in distinguishing vowels. All vowels are voiced; they are made out of tones produced by the vocal folds. Too, all vowels are emitted through a rather open passage out of the mouth. Unlike consonants, vowels cannot be classified by whether or not they have voicing (they all do) or how they are emitted (they are all emitted in relatively the same way). On all the vowels, the velum is raised to prevent air from

179

escaping through the nose; we have no nasal vowels in English. (In languages such as French and Portuguese, whether vowels are emitted orally or nasally is a distinguishing feature.)

Each vowel in American English can be described (or classified) in terms of five classes of basic characteristics: (1) lip position, (2) tongue elevation, (3) tongue position, (4) duration, and (5) tension. Although it may not take all five characteristics to distinguish a given vowel from all the other vowels of the language, it does take all five characteristics to describe the vowel fully.

For example, to identify or classify the vowel at the end of the word *boo*, you would note its characteristics: /u/ (o͞o) is a tense, long, tightly lip-rounded, high (the back of the tongue raised high—nearly to the soft palate), back (the tongue raised in the back of the mouth) vowel. These five descriptive features pinpoint, or classify, this vowel.

Let us look at each of these classes of characteristics separately.

LIP POSITION

If you look in a mirror at the position of your lips as you pronounce the vowels in the words *moo, me,* and *ma,* you will notice that the lips are tightly rounded for the first, unrounded and spread for the second, and unrounded and quite open for the third. Vowels may be classified as to whether or not they are uttered with the lips rounded. In general, the lips are more or less spread for the vowels formed by raising the tongue in the front of the mouth, and they are more or less rounded for the vowels formed by raising the tongue in the back of the mouth. Furthermore, there is a parallel between the amount of lip rounding and the degree to which the tongue is raised in the back of the mouth: the higher the tongue to form the vowel, the more tightly the lips are rounded.

The way you shape the opening of the mouth with your lips affects the resonance of the vowels. It is theoretically possible to produce recognizable back vowels without the usual lip rounding, but the resonance of the vowels is clearly affected. The sound is different and distorted, if recognizable, and we certainly do not advise it.

TONGUE POSITION

When you form all the vowels, your tongue tip remains behind your lower front teeth. It is the rest of the tongue that moves around in the mouth to produce the different vowels. If you raise the front of the tongue high in the mouth up near the hard palate and, while the vocal folds are vibrating, slowly lower the front of the tongue until the tongue lies flat in the mouth, you will produce a number of vowel sounds that are called *front vowels.* Similarly, if you round the lips tightly and raise the back of the tongue high up in the back of the mouth near the soft palate and, while the vocal folds are vibrating, slowly lower the tongue and gradually relax the rounding of the lips, you will produce a number of vowel sounds that are called *back vowels.* In addition to the front and back vowels, there is a group of vowels made with the center of the tongue raised up in the center of the mouth; these vowels are called, logically enough, *central vowels. Front, back,* and *central vowels,* then, refer to the area of the oral cavity (mouth) in which the tongue is raised to produce the vowel.

TONGUE ELEVATION

Each vowel in each of the three groups of vowels (back, front, and central) can be further described in terms of the relative height to

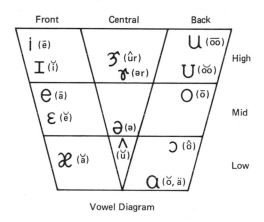

Vowel Diagram

which the highest part of the tongue is raised to make the sound. For example, the vowel in the word *be* is made with the front of the tongue raised very high in the mouth. The vowel /i/ (ē) is therefore called a *high* front vowel. The vowel at the beginning of the word *ooze,* on the other hand, is made with the back of the tongue raised very high in the mouth. The vowel /u/ (o͞o) is a *high* back vowel. Another example is the vowel at the beginning of the word *up,* which is made with the center of the tongue raised up to the middle of the mouth; this vowel /ʌ/ (ŭ) is a *mid* central vowel. For a clearer understanding of the relative positions and heights of the vowels, see the vowel diagram.

DURATION

The duration of a vowel, of course, is how long you hold it. A vowel is a sound that can be sustained or prolonged. How long you prolong a vowel depends on three factors: (1) the nature of the vowel itself (some vowels are inherently longer—in English, at least—than other vowels); (2) whether the vowel occurs in a stressed syllable (and, if so, the degree of stress); and (3) the vowel's position in a syllable and its neighboring sounds.

We said that some vowels are naturally longer (in English) than other vowels. Some might dispute that statement, because theoretically you could hold on to any vowel for a long time. But, in connected speech, some vowels are given longer duration than others. True, there are other factors involved here, but /u/ (o͞o) is ordinarily held longer than /ʊ/ (o͝o). Poets know the value of using long and short vowels (we are not talking about diacritics in the dictionaries, but about the length of time a vowel lasts!) to suit their purposes in poems. Edgar Allen Poe wrote an essay about the use of sounds and the choice of sounds to create certain moods. You must give vowels their proper length to catch the music and rhythm built into our speech patterns.

Another factor determining the length of time a vowel gets is syllabic stress. We make some syllables stand out by giving them more stress (prominence) than other syllables. We accomplish this stressing of the syllable by increasing loudness, raising pitch, *and* increasing the duration of the vowel. We stretch out syllables we want to stand out. Stressed syllables are longer, because the vowels are held longer. You can check this out for yourself. Say the words *no* and *piano* out loud. Is the *o* in each of equal length? No, because in the first word the syllable is stressed and in the second it is unstressed.

Finally, how long a vowel will be sustained depends also on what position it has in a syllable and in a word and on what sound follows. Try the words *row* and *romance* out loud. The /o/ phoneme of the first word is longer than the /o/ of the second word. This is partly so because the first is in a stressed syllable and the second in an unstressed syllable. However, another explanation is that the /o/ is final in the first word and it is not final in the second. Maybe we should have had you use the word *robot* as the second (contrast) word. There the difference is not in stress, but in position, and still *row* contains a longer vowel. To check on the effect of the sound that follows, pronounce the words *rope* and *robe* aloud. Which one has the longer /o/? You are right. The /o/ in *robe* is the longer one. If a voiced consonant comes after the vowel at the end of the syllable, the vowel will be longer than when the vowel is followed by a voiceless sound. Compare *right* and *ride, lace* and *lays,* and *have* and *half.* In each case, the syllable terminated by a voiced consonant contains a longer vowel.

TENSION

Vowels differ in the amount of tension there is in the oral cavity when they are formed. The tongue, of course, has muscles, and these muscles— like others—can be tensed or relaxed. To form some vowels, you tense the side-to-side muscles of the tongue, but to form other vowels you do not tense them. Say the words *eat* and *it* aloud. Can you feel the tongue tension on the vowel in the first word? Can you feel the tongue relax to make the vowel in the second word? Try the two words out loud again, but this time as you say them, put your thumb and forefinger on your neck under your jawbone. Hold them there lightly as you pronounce the two words. Now can you feel the tension on the first word? Do you feel the tightening for /i/ (ē) and the relaxing for /ɪ/ (ĭ)? If you are producing these vowels properly, you will be able to detect the marked difference in tension.

The Fourteen Vowel Phonemes

We will now look at fourteen vowel phonemes in some detail. For each sound, we will explain the correct (customary) production of the sound, discuss any allophones the sound may have, describe the common deviations or problems associated with the sound, and provide exercises for use in improving your own production of the sound.

FRONT VOWELS

/i/ (ē)

Production of the /i/ (ē)

If you lift the front of the tongue nearly to the hard palate while the tip of the tongue rests behind the lower front teeth, tense the tongue, spread the slightly tensed lips into a smile, and emit the air stream through the mouth with the vocal folds vibrating, you will produce the highest front vowel, the vowel sound in the word *beat*, which is represented in IPA by /i/ and in the dictionaries by ē. The sound /i/ is classified as a *tense high front vowel*.

Allophones

In unstressed syllables, /i/ (ē) may become either /ɪ/ (ĭ) (the shorter, more relaxed, and lower front vowel of the word *it*) or /ə/ (the neutral first vowel in the word *above*). Compare your pronunciation of the words *even* (where the first vowel is the stressed syllable) and *event* (where the first vowel is the unstressed syllable). In the word *event*, did the initial /i/ (ē) remain /i/ (ē), or did it change to /ɪ/ (ĭ)?

In final position in a word in an unstressed syllable, the /i/ (ē) may remain /i/ (ē) or it may be pronounced /ɪ/ (ĭ). The vast majority of Americans pronounce the final, unstressed /i/ (ē) an /i/ (ė̄); many Southerners use the allophone /ɪ/ (ĭ). Pronounce the following words.

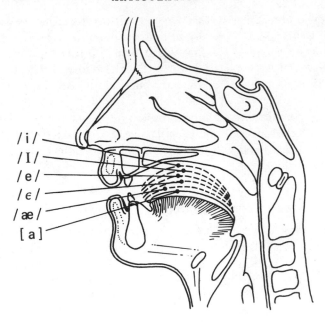

/i/
/I/
/e/
/ɛ/
/æ/
[a]

FIGURE 3–1. *Representative tongue positions for front vowels.*

Each has the phoneme /i/ (ē) in an unstressed final syllable. Do you use /i/ (ē) or /ɪ/ (ĭ) in the final syllable?

> worry, hurry, happy, money, honey, funny,
> coffee, marry, silly, Billy, really

In the middle of such words as *beautiful, pitiful, easily, medicine,* and *citizen,* speakers of the Standard (or Status) Dialect do not use /i/ (ē). They use either /ɪ/ (ĭ) or /ə/. For *beauty,* they will use /i/ (ē) in the final syllable probably, but when the *ful* suffix is added and the /i/ (ē) becomes the middle of the word, they no longer use /i/ (ē).

Deviations or Problems in the Production of /i/ (ē)

There are two common problems or distortions associated with this sound: (1) diphthongation or triphthongation, and (2) inadequate tension:

1. *Diphthongation or triphthongation.* In the South and Southwest of the United States, there is a tendency on the part of some speakers to "drawl," which means that they elongate their vowels into diphthongs and triphthongs. Diphthongs are blends of two vowels and triphthongs are blends of three vowels. The greatest temptation to add an extra sound (or two) after the /i/ (ē) occurs when the consonant /l/ follows in the same syllable. Then, /i/ (ē) may turn into /iə/ (remember /ə/

is the little vowel at the beginning of the word *above*) or even /ijə/. (ē should not become ēə or ēyə.) Check your pronunciation of the following words. Do you detect an extra sound (or two) after the /i/ (ē) and before the /l/?

feel, kneel, wheel, meal, keel, deal

Let's check again. You probably will not elongate the vowel before a /t/ sound. Let's compare a few pairs of words to see if the /i/ (ē) is the same in both words. Pronounce the pairs, and check to hear if the vowels are alike and the /i/ (ē) is pure:

feet	feel
wheat	wheel
meet	meal
neat	kneel
seat	seal
peat	peel
beat	Beale
heat	heal

2. *Lack of adequate tension.* Unless the /i/ (ē) sound has adequate tension, it will lack its distinctive character and sound like the more relaxed vowel /ɪ/ (i). Many speakers who learned English as a second language have difficulty getting enough tension in the production of this vowel. The tongue must be very tense and the front of the tongue must be raised very high in the front of the mouth. You should be able to feel the tension in the muscles. (See pp. 182–183.)

Materials for Practicing /i/ (ē)

INITIAL /i/ (ē)

eager
eagle
ear
Easter
easy
ego
eke
equal
ether
Eve
even

MEDIAL AND FINAL /i/ (ē)

beach	be
feed	fee
agreed	agree
he'd	he

keen	key
lied (a song)	Lee
meat	me
neat	knee
peer	pea
scene	see
wield	we

1. It is not easy to describe a beautiful woman.
2. For the life of me, I don't understand that scene.
3. For the meal we are about to receive, increase our appreciation.
4. He's a big wheel in the city machine.
5. Honey, please don't consider me in your plans.
6. Every charity in the country sends me an appeal.
7. I still can't believe Harvey Lee's a thief!
8. Not really easy—just eager to please.
9. Even in his sleep, he's dreaming up illegal schemes.
10. We received a meager sum of money.
11. She's not conceited—just pleased with herself.
12. The teacher gave decent lectures this week.
13. How did Eve feel—after leaving Eden?
14. Our team has never been defeated.
15. We must not yield to that beastly intrigue!

/ɪ/ (ĭ)

Production of the /ɪ/ (ĭ)

If you allow the front of the tongue to relax into a position slightly lower and farther back than the height it assumed for /i/ (ē), relax the lips slightly but continue to leave them spread, and emit the air stream through the mouth with the vocal folds vibrating, you will produce the vowel in the word *bit*, which we represent by /ɪ/ in IPA and by ĭ in the dictionaries. The /ɪ/ (ĭ) is classified as a *lax high front vowel*. It is usually shorter in duration than /i/ (ē).

Allophones of the /ɪ/

In addition to the most common variation of the /ɪ/ (ĭ) described here, there is one other allophone of this phoneme. It occurs in some unstressed syllables and sometimes even in stressed syllables before the dark /l/. This unstressed form of /ɪ/ (ĭ) differs from the usual allophone of /ɪ/ (ĭ) in that it is made with the lips in neutral position rather than spread—as for /ɪ/ (ĭ) generally; *and* it is made with the tongue pulled back to the center of the mouth—toward the position for /ə/, the first vowel in *above*. Indeed, it sounds like a hybrid sound—half /ɪ/ (ĭ) and half /ə/! The IPA symbol for this allophone of /ɪ/ is [ɨ].

Many Americans use this variation in both syllables of the word *children*. Some use it in words like *milk* and *built*. It is common in connected speech in phrases such as *I can go* and *I will go*. The vowel in *can* can be weakened to [ɪ], as can the vowel in *will*. This sound is very common in the past-tense ending (spelled *-ed*) after /t/ and /d/ and in the plural and possessive endings added after any of the six sibilants sounds. How do you say the words *rated* and *roses*, for example? Do you use this allophone of /ɪ/ in the second syllable?

Common Deviations or Problems in the Production of /ɪ/ (ĭ)

There are three common problems or distortions associated with this phoneme: (1) diphthongation or triphthongation, (2) substitution of /i/ (ē) for /ɪ/ (ĭ), and (3) substitution of /ɛ/ (ĕ) for /ɪ/ (ĭ).

1. *Diphthongation or triphthongation.* We have already discussed this problem in relation to the /i/ (ē). It is probably even more of a temptation on the /ɪ/ sound. Speakers who tend to elongate their vowels and turn one sound into two or three can have a field day with the /ɪ/ (ĭ). *Hit*, which has three sounds—the middle of which is a vowel /ɪ/ (ĭ)— can be turned into [hɪət] (hĭət) or even [hɪjət] (hĭyet). This last version has a good /j/ (y) sound in the middle of it. Our advice, if you have this problem, is: get off the sound quickly; don't hold on to the sound long enough to let it turn into two or three sounds. Move on, and tack on the consonant.

2. *Substitution of /i/ (ē) for /ɪ/ (ĭ).* You have probably heard a student from another country say *eat* for *it*, *seat* for *sit*, and *team* for *Tim*. One lovely lady came to us for assistance on this problem recently because she had provoked gales of laughter in a New York department store when she tried to buy a sheet for her bed.

The /ɪ/ (ĭ) sound is very difficult for many who learned English as a second language. Many languages do not contain this phoneme, and speakers of those languages are not accustomed to hearing or making this sound. The Romance languages have only one phoneme where English has two—/i/ (ē) and /ɪ/ (ĭ), and that sound is about halfway between our /i/ (ē) and /ɪ/ (ĭ). If they use the sound from their language in English, native speakers will recognize the sound as "different" and probably identify it as the other one of the two—whichever it is. So the sound these speakers use will sound reversed to native speakers all the time!

The difference between /i/ (ē) and /ɪ/ (ĭ) is not only height of the tongue (the /i/ is higher, you remember), but also tension and duration. You must relax the tongue muscles to produce a good /ɪ/ (ĭ), and you must shorten the sound /ɪ/ (ĭ) and lengthen the /i/ (ē).

Here are some words to check for the contrast between these two high front vowels. Listen, feel, and see the difference between the two vowels:

INITIAL /i/ (ē) **AND** /ɪ/ (ĭ) **CONTRAST**	each	itch
	eat	it
	e'en	in
	eel	ill
	ease	is
MEDIAL /i/ (ē) **AND** /ɪ/ (ĭ) **CONTRAST**	leave	live
	leak	lick
	meal	mill
	peal	pill
	seems	Simms
	seal	sill
	feel	fill
	meat	mit
	leafed	lift
	heat	hit
	seep	sip
	leap	lip
	reach	rich
	cheat	chit
	peach	pitch
	deep	dip
	seen	sin
	green	grin
	bean	been
	heat	hit
	greet	grit
	feet	fit
	bead	bid
	peak	pick
	steal	still
	team	Tim
	easy	Izzy
	tease	'tis
	sheen	shin
	cheap	chip
	jeep	gyp
	Jean	gin
	neat	knit
	heed	hid
	reek	Rick

3. *Substitution of* /ɛ/ (ĕ) *for* /ɪ/ (ĭ). In the substitution already discussed, a higher, more tense vowel was substituted for the /ɪ/ (ĭ) vowel. In this substitution, on the other hand, a lower vowel is being used. The

tongue is lowered from the position for /ɪ/ and relaxed down to (or almost to) the position for /ɛ/—the vowel in the word *Ed,* which is represented in dictionaries by ĕ. Have you heard someone say "Set down" for "Sit down"? Or perhaps "It's on the sell" for "It's on the sill"? This substitution, although not very common, does occur. Check your pronunciation of the following pairs of words to be sure you do not make this substitution.

/ɪ/ (ĭ) AND /ɛ/ (ĕ) CONTRAST		
	ill	el
	will	well
	hill	hell
	sill	sell
	bill	bell
	dilly	deli
	fill	fell
	nil	knell
	quill	quell
	till	tell
	sit	set
	bid	bed
	bit	bet
	hid	head
	mitt	met
	lid	led
	wit	wet
	slid	sled

Materials for Practicing /ɪ/ (ĭ)

ill	still	silly
ink	blink	stinky
inn	sin	any
is	whiz	Izzy
it	split	gritty

1. "How are you called?" is an idiom in Spanish.
2. I did not mean to imply that you were ignorant—just stupid.
3. There are clear indications that it will end in disaster.
4. I agreed with the teacher's interpretation, and still he flunked me.
5. I'll speak to him this evening.
6. Penniless and weary, he ended up on skid row.
7. I believe that he is the most creative person I know.
8. I resent a person with a holier-than-thou attitude.
9. We react emotionally rather than logically.
10. She is completely out of touch with reality.
11. He complained that the meat was full of gristle.

12. Eager to please, the minister rewrote the sermon.
13. Is he coming in his new automobile? No, he's still driving the old one.
14. Dick is the leader in the class that meets on Wednesday evening.
15. Some of our citizens are easily influenced by demagogues.
16. I did indeed think it was a ticklish situation!
17. Many voters want a simple answer to every difficult question.
18. I think I've got this problem licked.
19. Am I to infer that you disagree with me?
20. He admits that women are his weakness; I think he's addicted.

/e/ (ā)

Production of the /e/ (ā)

If you open the lips a bit more and spread them a bit less than for producing the /ɪ/ (ĭ), lift the front of the tongue to a position slightly below the height it assumed to produce /ɪ/ (ĭ), and emit the air stream through the mouth with the vocal folds vibrating, you will produce the first vowel in the words *chaotic* and *detente*. We represent this sound by the IPA symbol /e/ and by the dictionary symbol ā. The tongue is tense, and this phoneme is of very long duration in stressed syllables. Indeed, it is so long (as we will see in a moment) that it is actually a diphthong in stressed syllables—rather than a pure vowel. Because the sound /e/ (ā) is made with the tensed front of the tongue raised midway up in the front of the mouth, it is classified as a *tense mid front vowel*.

Allophones of the /e/ (ā)

There are two allophones of this phoneme in American English. The pure vowel [e] occurs only in unstressed syllables and is, therefore, the less common allophone. It is heard in the word *peyote* as the vowel in the first syllable. Contrast that vowel with the /e/ (ā) phoneme that occurs in the word *pay*, where the diphthongal allophone occurs. Another contrast would be between the pure vowel allophone used in the words *birthday* and *holiday* with the diphthongal allophone used in the word *day* alone. The names of the days of the week that include the unstressed syllable *day* in their names are pronounced with the pure vowel, as opposed to the diphthong form of the phoneme. (They can also be pronounced with /di/ (dē) or /dɪ/ (dĭ). *Monday* is not Mon-day, however, with the second syllable containing the stressed diphthongal allophone.

The more common allophone of the /e/ (ā) phoneme is the diphthong represented in IPA by [eɪ]. In this variation of the phoneme, the sound is a vowel blend made of two vowels (even though they are perceived by native listeners as one sound). The first of the two vowels is the longer and stronger one, but the second is clearly heard. We start with the

/e/ (ā) vowel, but raise the tongue in a continuous movement toward the high front vowel /i/ (ē). We do not get the tongue as high as /i/ (ē), nor do we hold the second vowel of the diphthong as long as /i/ (ē) is usually held. For that reason, the diphthong is represented with [ɪ] as the second vowel. If you have difficulty hearing or producing this diphthong, it might be wise to think of the second element in the diphthong as an /i/ (ē).

Pronounce the word *aim* in slow motion to check on what your tongue does as it makes the word. The word has two phonemes in it: /e/ and /m/. The first phoneme, however, is not a pure vowel sound in American English; phonetically, it is a diphthong. You should be able to tell that the front of your tongue moves on the "*a* sound" upward toward the position of /i/ (ē). This tongue movement while the /e/ (ā) is being made produces the diphthongal allophone of the sound. Remember that this is the variation of the phoneme that will occur most often in American English, because native speakers use this diphthongal allophone for the "long *a*" in any stressed syllable.

Common Deviations or Problems in the Production of /e/ (ā)

There are four problems commonly associated with this sound: (1) diphthongation and triphthongation, (2) lowering, (3) substitution of /æ/ (ă) for /e/ (ā), and (4) substitution of the pure vowel allophone for the [eɪ] allophone.

1. *Diphthongation and triphthongation.* Turning single sounds into two or even three sounds is clearly a distortion. And this vowel suffers from drawlers as much as any. The temptation is greatest before the /l/ in the same syllable. Get off the /e/ (ā) before you turn it into [eə] (āə) or [ejə] (āyə)! Here are some sequences. Use them to check for the problem and also for practice. Try to keep the /e/ (ā) phoneme (it will be the standard diphthongal allophone in each word) consistent across the sequence. Listen, especially, for a difference in the /e/ (ā) before /l/ in the last word of each sequence.

Kaye	Kate	kale
pay	pate	pale
hay	hate	hale
Faye	fate	fail
way	wait	wail
tray	trait	trail
bay	bait	bail
stay	state	stale
day	date	dale
gray	great	grail
fray	freight	frail

may	mate	male
gay	gate	gale
ray	rate	rail
nay	Nate	nail

2. *Lowering.* If you lower the tongue slightly from the position required for /e/ (ā), relax the tongue muscles, and shorten the sound somewhat, you will produce a sound very close to the vowel in *egg* rather than the vowel in *age*. Indeed, you may be actually substituting the /ɛ/ (ĕ) vowel for the /e/ (ā). The sound /e/ (ā) is a tense sound, and relaxing the tongue will distort it, changing it into (or almost into) /ɛ/ (ĕ). Read the following pairs of words aloud, and check to be sure you clearly differentiate /e/ (ā) from the more lax and slightly lower vowel /ɛ/ (ĕ).

yell	Yale
bell	bale
sell	sale
well	wail
tell	tale
Vel	vale
dell	dale
fell	fail
hell	hail
jell	jail
Nell	nail
pell-mell	pale male

For some unknown reason (or maybe for a reason known only to Freud), some speakers substitute the /ɛ/ (ĕ) for /e/ (ā) in the word *naked*. Maybe *nekkid* sounds worse to them. It certainly does to us; it is non-standard.

3. *Substitution of* /æ/ (ă) *for* /e/ (ā). Some speakers, particularly in the East, substitute /æ/ (ă) for /e/ (ā). Again, the place of greatest temptation seems to be before /l/ in the same syllable. Check your own pronunciation of *pail* and *pal*. Is there a clear distinction between them? Here are a few words for you to check this contrast. Read them aloud and be sure the /e/ (ā) is [eɪ].

Al	ale
pal	pail
gal	gale
Cal	kale
Hal	hail
mal-	male
Sal	sail
Val	vale

4. *Substitution of a pure vowel for* [eɪ]. Most native speakers of English do not confuse the two allophones of /e/ (ā). For people who have learned English as a second language, however, there may be some difficulty with the diphthongal allophone. Many other languages do not have this sound; many other languages have pure vowels for phonemes. And speakers of those languages might easily transfer into English the phoneme from their first language that was closest to our "long *a.*" Speakers who learned English as a second language may also make the /e/ (ā) with a bit more tension of the tongue than those who learned English as a first language here in the United States.

If you have this problem, you should work first on ear training, so you can perceive the difference between the two allophones of the phoneme, and then work to elongate the sound for the diphthongal allophone. When working to elongate the diphthong variation, remember that the tongue moves from the position of the first vowel to the second in one continuous movement.

Materials for Practicing /e/ (ā)

1. Hail, fellow, well met.
2. Bill Bailey, won't you please come home?
3. We were sailing along on Moonlight Bay.
4. Is life a tale told by an idiot?
5. The motion failed for lack of a second.
6. Sally knows the jailer very well.
7. The mailman was late this morning.
8. Tony Zale was a famous pugilist.
9. I'm afraid she's naked as a jaybird.
10. He wasn't a failure, though he wasted his talents.
11. I may be sent to a new station.
12. My neighbors portrayed me as a callous ape.
13. That display of malice takes the cake!
14. You made a mistake. He's been in jail—not in Yale.
15. Macy's is having a "Whale of a Sale."
16. I wouldn't say she is ancient—just on the edge of old age.
17. Ray wept as the bell tolled its baleful news.
18. Frankly, I wouldn't take Jane's tale at face value.
19. Is his confidence faith, foolishness, or naiveté?
20. James explained the plan in great detail.

/ɛ/ (ĕ)

Production of the /ɛ/ (ĕ)

If you open the lips just a bit more than you did for forming the /e/ (ā), allow the front of the tongue to relax into a position slightly lower and farther back than the height it assumed for the /e/, and emit the air stream through the mouth with the vocal folds vibrating, you will produce the vowel in the word *bet*—which is represented in IPA by /ɛ/ and in the dictionaries by ĕ.

Both /e/ (ā) and /ɛ/ (ĕ) are mid front vowels, but /ɛ/ (ĕ) is more lax in its tongue tension than /e/ (ā), lower in tongue position than /e/ (ā), and usually shorter in duration than /e/ (ā).

/ɛ/ (ĕ) is classified as a *lax mid front vowel*.

Allophones of the /ɛ/ (ĕ)

Before the consonant /r/ and the vowel /ɚ/ (see pp. 235–237), the /ɛ/ (ĕ) shows an interesting variety. The sound varies by dialect and idiolect. There is no consistency in the production of this sound—either in any specific region of the country or even in the speech patterns of a single person.

Before /r/ and /ɚ/, /ɛ/ may become /æ/ (ă)—the vowel sound in the words *add* and *cat*—in words like *care, Mary, carry, marry, vary, various, variable, harry, harried, carrot, stare, stairs,* and *fair*. You are more likely to hear this pronunciation in the South than in the rest of the country.

Before /r/ and /ɚ/ (an unstressed *r*-vowel that can occur alone in unstressed syllables or—as in some of these cases—after another vowel), In words like *dairy, Mary, vary,* and *area,* /ɛ/ (ĕ) may become /e/ (ā). Again, you are more likely to hear this variation in the South than in the rest of the United States.

In some words, you will notice, the /ɛ/ (ĕ) can turn into either /æ/ (ă) or /e/ (ā). Words such as *Carey, Mary, vary* (and the words derived from *vary*), and *again* (where the vowel is not followed by /r/) fall into this group.

Out of curiosity (and to prove our point about the lack of consistency in the use of these variations), pronounce the following words aloud.

ARR	AR	ER	ERR	EAR	AIR	ERE
marry	Mary area		merry	air		
Harry, harry	declare				hairy Claire	
carry, carrot	Carey, care vary, various	very				
parry	parent			pear		

arry	bare	bear			
	fare		fair, fairy		
	wary, beware	wear		where	
	stare		stairs		
				there	their
	dare, daring		dairy		
arrow	spare, sparing				
	Gary, garish				
arry	glare, flare		lair, flair, Blair		

Listen carefully for changes in the vowels. Which vowel—/ɛ/ (ĕ), /æ/ (ă), or /e/ (ā)—do you use in each word? If necessary (or if possible), tape record the words and play them back to hear the differences (if any).

Common Deviations or Problems in the Production of /ɛ/ (ĕ)

There are four common problems or distortions associated with this phoneme: (1) diphthongizing and triphthongizing, (2) substitution of /e/ (ā) for /ɛ/ (ĕ), (3) substitution of /ɪ/ (ĭ) for /ɛ/ (ĕ), and (4) substitution of /æ/ (ă) for /ɛ/ (ĕ).

1. *Diphthongizing and triphthongizing.* If you have a tendency to "drawl" your vowels and diphthongs out—elongating them into two or three extra sounds, you may have this problem with the /ɛ/ (ĕ) vowel. Pronounce the word *yes* out loud. Do you hold onto the vowel and get a little *uh* sound (/ə/) before the /s/? Try the word *well*. Is there a little *uh* (/ə/) or even a little *yuh* (/jə/ or yə) after the /ɛ/ (ĕ) and before the /l/? The first is a diphthong and the second is a triphthong. And /ɛ/ (ĕ) is a single vowel! Make it short, and move on to the following consonant quickly.

2. *Substitution of /e/ (ā) for /ɛ/ (ĕ).* In a few words, as we noted before, /e/ (ā) is an acceptable variant of /ɛ/ (ĕ). If this substitution is made on other words, however, it is a distortion and is nonstandard. This distortion is more common in the South than in the rest of the country. Speakers who make this substitution use the higher, more tense mid front vowel for the lower, more lax one. Perhaps you have heard someone say *haid* for *head* or *laig* for *leg*; they were making this distortion of the /ɛ/ (ĕ) sound. Be sure to use the /ɛ/ (ĕ) in such words as *leg, keg, egg, bed, measure,* and *pleasure*.

3. *Substitution of /ɪ/ (ĭ) for /ɛ/ (ĕ).* This distortion, although common in the South, Midwest, and Southwest is nonstandard. If you substitute the high front lax vowel for the mid front lax vowel, you get this distortion. Ordinarily, this substitution of /ɪ/ (ĭ) for /ɛ/ (ĕ) occurs before consonants made on the upper gum ridge. Anticipating the coming

consonant, the speakers lift the tongue to the higher /ɪ/ (ĭ) position and thus replace the lower /ɛ/ (ĕ) vowel with the higher vowel sound. This distortion is most likely to occur before nasal sounds, however. *Ten soldiers* are not *tin* soldiers, and a *hem* is not a *him*.

Pronounce the following contrasts aloud to hear whether you make a distinction between /ɪ/ (ĭ) and /ɛ/ (ĕ)— or if you are tempted to substitute /ɪ/ (ĭ) for /ɛ/ (ĕ) in some (or all) of the words.

/ɪ/ (ĭ) AND /ɛ/ (ĕ) CONTRAST		
	Min	men
	Minnie	many
	been	Ben
	tin	ten
	pin	pen
	din	den
	him	hem
	lint	lent
	mint	meant
	rinse	rents
	since	cents
	tint	tent
	whim	when (!)
	bit	bet
	hid	head
	git	get
	forgit	forget
	lit	let
	lid	led
	rid	red
	lift	left
	kit	kettle
	pinned	penned
	wind	wend
	timber	member

4. *Substitution of* /æ/ (ă) *for* /ɛ/ (ĕ). Another distortion you may sometimes hear is the substitution of the vowel in *add* and *had* (/æ/ in IPA and ă in the dictionaries) for the /ɛ/ (ĕ). In this case, the speaker is dropping the tongue down and back from the usual position for /ɛ/ (ĕ). The result is that *yes* may sound something like *yass* and *guess* something like *gas*. Try these contrasts out loud:

/æ/ (ă) AND /ɛ/ (ĕ) CONTRAST		
	mat	met
	Yassir	yes sir
	gas	guess
	blast	blessed

bass (fish)	Bess
last	lest
bat	bet
cattle	kettle
massed	messed
past	pest
lag	leg
mag	Meg
bad	bed
bag	beg
Cagney	keg
knack	neck
pack	peck
rack	wreck
racked	wrecked

Materials for Practicing the /ɛ/ (ĕ)

INITIAL AND MEDIAL /ɛ/ (ĕ)	edge	ledge
	ebb	deb
	end	lend
	egg	leg
	ember	member
	ere	there
	etch	wretch
	Ed	bed

If you tend to substitute /e/ (ā) for /ɛ/ (ĕ), try these sequences. Try to match the vowel from the first word when you pronounce the second (temptation) word:

Ed	egg
bet	beg
pet	Peg
met	Meg
let	leg
kettle	keg
Ed	edge
led	ledge
pled	pledge
red	regular
pled	pleasure
med	measure
tread	treasure

Here are some words that contrast /ɛ/ (ĕ) and /e/ (ā).

/ɛ/ (ĕ) AND /e/ (ā)
CONTRAST

let	late
get	gate
led	laid
bread	braid
fleck	flake
wet	wait
bet	bait
tread	trade
met	mate
fed	fade
pled	played
Rhett	rate
dead	Dade
mess	mace
less	lace
rest	raced
behest	be hasty
held	hailed
meld	mailed
felled	failed
heaven	haven
men	main
den	Dane
tent	taint
rend	rained
edge	age
ebb	Abe
el	ale
Ed	aid
etch	H
edged	aged
Eck	ache
S	ace
M	aim
Epps	apes

If you tend to substitute /ɪ/ (ĭ) for /ɛ/ (ĕ), especially before /n/ and /m/, try these sequences. You will probably get a good /ɛ/ (ĕ) before the stop sounds. Therefore, pronounce the first word, with the /ɛ/ (ĕ) before a stop, and then try to make the vowel the same as you pronounce the second word, with the /ɛ/ (ĕ) before a nasal.

bed	Ben
dead	den
fed	fen

head	hen
Ked	Ken
med	men
Ted	ten
Tet	tenth
whet	when
jet	gem
head	hem
let	Lem
fed	fem
stead	stem
ebb	ember
ebb race	embrace
met Bert	member
educate	emulate
Edna	Emma

Here are some sentences for practicing /ɛ/ (ĕ):

1. You can sing "Git Along, Little Doggies," but you should say "Get Along!"
2. Women outnumber men in the United States.
3. Ed has moved into a penthouse. The rent is exorbitant.
4. Ten and ten and two are twenty-two.
5. Yes, there is an echo in the auditorium.
6. I meant every word I said.
7. Please make an extra effort to be ready on time.
8. I guess I will lend him a few dollars from my paycheck.
9. He told me he was the sinner on the football team: I think he meant that he was the center.
10. The speaker used no gestures until the end of his speech.
11. Emma broke both legs in the accident.
12. I always meant to become a member, but I honestly haven't been well.
13. Unless he is excellent at pretending, his head is really empty.
14. She said, "It was a business doing pleasure with you."
15. The rest of the debt must be paid by the tenth of the month.
16. According to the ledger, we had misplaced ten dollars and ten cents.
17. We left the wrecked car on the edge of the cliff.
18. How do you measure intensity of feeling?
19. When did you get back from the demonstration?
20. The boss blessed me as I tendered my resignation.
21. She says eating eggs will raise my cholesterol level.

22. I will treasure this pen and pencil for the rest of my days.
23. I begged and pled for an end to the contest.
24. Mary has had various suitors, but none suited her and she never married.
25. I don't care what the rest of the world thinks; I pledge you my friendship.

/æ/ (ă)

Production of the /æ/ (ă)

If you raise the front of the tongue to a position slightly below and behind the height it assumed for producing the /ɛ/ (ĕ), open the lips without much tension, and emit the air stream through the mouth with the vocal folds vibrating, you will produce the *low front vowel* that occurs in the words *add* and *mad*. We represent this phoneme by /æ/ in IPA and by ă in the dictionaries.

When you make this sound, the tongue is raised low in the front of the mouth (although the tongue tip is behind the lower front teeth, you remember, on all the vowels). That is why the vowel is classified as a *low front vowel*. The lips are neither spread nor rounded, but the jaw is dropped and relaxed and the lips are quite open.

Allophones of the /æ/ (ă)

The phoneme /æ/ (ă) has a variant form, or allophone, that is heard mostly in New England. This second vowel, which can be used interchangeably with the [æ] (ă), is a lower front vowel than the [æ] (ă). It is about halfway between the vowel sound in *at* ([æ] in IPA) and the vowel sound in *alms* (/ɑ/ in IPA and ä in the dictionaries). This allophone is represented in IPA by the symbol [a].

Some people use the [æ] allophone in some words and the [a] allophone in others. You might check your own idiolect. Do you use the same form of this phoneme in the words *at* and *ask?* Or *cad* and *Cathy?*

This lower (in tongue elevation) vowel [a] is used by some speakers of American English as the first sound in the phonemic diphthongs heard in the words *buy* and *bough*, *I* and *ouch*, *eyes* and *out*. (See pp. 239–240 and pp. 245–246.)

Common Deviations or Problems in the Production of /æ/ (ă)

There are four common distortions or problems associated with the /æ/ (ă): (1) raising, (2) nasalizing, (3) diphthongizing, and (4) substitution of /ɑ/ (ä) for /æ/ (ă).

1. *Raising*. Not long ago one of our students told us that nothing was inevitable but death and Texas. The pronunciation of *Texas* for *taxes* is

an extreme example of raising the vowel, because the speaker actually substituted /ɛ/ (ĕ) for the /æ/ (ă). Most speakers who distort the vowel by tensing and raising the tongue do not go that far. You can check in the mirror to see if you raise the tongue on this sound. Watch to see where the tongue is when you pronounce the /ɛ/ (ĕ); then watch to see if it drops considerably to from the /æ/ (ă). It should drop so that the tongue is *almost* flat in the mouth on the low front vowel.

As you pronounce the following pairs of words and phrases, check to be sure you get a good distinction between /ɛ/ (ĕ) and /æ/ (ă). Listen and look for any raising of the /æ/ (ă) vowel toward the position of /ɛ/ (ĕ).

/ɛ/ (ĕ) AND /æ/ (ă) CONTRAST		
	Ed	add
	led	lad
	left	laughed
	mess	mass
	deft	daft
	pest	past
	bet	bat
	Beth	bath
	less	lass
	hell	Hal
	men	man
	neck	knack
	heck	hack
	fleck	flack
	leg	lag
	bed	bad
	said	sad
	peck	pack
	wreck	rack
	beggar	bagger
	Becker	backer
	wreck it	racket

A word that gives some Southern speakers trouble is *can't*. If these speakers tend to use a raised form of /æ/ (ă) anyway, the /æ/ (ă) before /n/ *really* gets lifted up. The common word *can't* gets the most extreme treatment of all; it becomes *cain't* [kemt]. Perhaps the extra lifting and tension of the tongue give it extra emphasis. In any case, it is considered nonstandard. Some pairs of words follow in which the sounds /æ/ (ă) and /e/ (ā) are contrasted. Be sure that the /æ/ (ă) is relaxed and low: the tongue is *almost* flat in the mouth—lifted *very* slightly in the front.

/æ/ (ă) AND /e/ (ā) CONTRAST

can	cane
ran	rain
man	main
fan	feign
van	vain
ban	bane
plan	plain
Dan	Dane
Jan	Jane
Chan	chain
pan	pain
bran	brain
Strand	strained
panned	pained
planned	planed
Rand	rained
in grand	ingrained
fanned	feigned
plant	plaint
ant	ain't
pant	paint
fantasy	faint
canned	caned

2. *Nasalizing.* Many speakers who raise and front the /æ/ (ă) also nasalize the vowel, producing a particularly unpleasant sound. Be especially careful when the vowel precedes a nasal consonant. Listen to your own pronunciation of such words as *can, Sam,* and *bang* to see if you detect excessive nasalization of the vowel. Next, pronounce the word *cad,* being certain not to raise and nazalize the vowel, and then pronounce the word *can,* trying to get the same open, oral vowel you produced in *cad.* Try the same procedure with *sad* and *Sam* and with *bad* and *bang.*

Reread the material on nasalization on pp. 124–126 and on pp. 133–134. Then try these sequences. If you get a good, relatively low, relaxed vowel in the first word, try to match that vowel (without adding nasality) in the second word.

cad	can
add	Ann
had	hand
mad	man
fat	fan
rat	ran
dad	Dan

begat	began
plaid	plan
lad	land
sad	sand
cab	cam
dab	dam
jab	jam
lab	lamb
pap	Pam
sad	Sam
dab	damp
stab	stamp
wrap	ramp
bad	bang
fat	fang
Gad	gang
hat	hang
jackal	jangle
Mackel	mangle
pad	pang
rack	rang
sag	sang
Tad	Tang

3. *Diphthongizing*. If you tend to drawl, you probably elongate the vowel /æ/ (ă). Some speakers stretch the simple vowel not just into a diphthong but into a triphthong. Have you ever heard someone say /mæjən/ (măyən) for *man?* Probably the substitution of the diphthong /æə/ (ăə) for the pure vowel is more common, but it is no more acceptable. Remember to move on to the next consonant; do not try to hang on to the vowel.

4. *Substitution of* /ɑ/ (ä) *for* /æ/ (ă). If you learned English as a second language, you may have difficulty with this phoneme of the English language. Your first language may not have had this phoneme in its sound system, and you may therefore substitute a vowel from that language for the unfamiliar sound. The /ɑ/ sound (represented in the dictionaries by ä) is a vowel sound made with the tongue lying relatively flat (unraised) in the mouth. It is a separate phoneme in English from the /æ/ (ă) sound, because the two cannot often be substituted for each other without changing the meaning. That is why it is important for you to be able to distinguish between the two sounds, to make them both, and to use them at the right times.

Remember that the tongue is in a different position on the two sounds. The tongue tip will be behind the lower front teeth on both sounds, but the front of the tongue will be raised slightly in the front of the mouth to produce the /æ/ (ă). The tongue will *not* be raised noticeably to produce the /ɑ/ (ä). If you are in doubt about what you are doing with your tongue on these sounds, check by using a mirror.

The following pairs of words contain a contrast between these two vowels. The first word of each pair will have an /ɑ/ (ä), and the second word will have an /æ/ (ă).

bond	band
clock	claque
cot	cat
con	can
Dodd	Dad
Don	Dan
dolly	dally
fond	fanned
hot	hat
job	jab
cop	cap
lots	lats
mop	map
mock	Mack
knob	nab
pond	panned
pot	pat
Ron	ran
sock	sack
sop	sap
psalm	Sam
togs	tags
top	tap
von	van

/ɑ/ (ä) AND /æ/ (ă)
CONTRAST

Materials for Practicing the /æ/ (ă)

1. They passed the bandstand late in the afternoon.
2. Sam had a very bad time at the party.
3. His problem is that he cannot analyze facts.
4. I am not particularly happy with either candidate.
5. His car was badly damaged in the accident.
6. I will catch the last bus back home.
7. A few inaccurate answers kept me from passing the course.
8. After the excursion there was sand on the blanket.
9. There will be a mass meeting of the faculty this afternoon.
10. There are several aspects of the case I do not understand.

11. Dad thinks my present income is adequate.
12. Mr. Thatcher became rather angry with me.
13. His hostile attitude and nefarious activities were only two factors which led to his dismissal.
14. We have had a very happy time in Paris.
15. Francis is handsome, but he is not practical.
16. I think Ann is in the laboratory.
17. Allen has a habit of playing pranks on people.
18. He is too passive to be a good actor.
19. Ask me no questions and I'll not have to lie.
20. They mocked and laughed because I couldn't get the hang of it.
21. The students demanded one last chance.
22. I absolutely can't stand that pack of crackers!
23. Tad was the champion but refused the plaque.
24. His constant use of slang added to his handicaps.
25. I would rather enter a wrestling match with a bear than take that class.

Here are some sentences containing both /æ/ (ă) and /ɑ/ (ä):
 1. Mr. Dodd's a happy man. Today he's a Dad!
 2. It seems odd to add an extra lock, but I can't afford to lack one.
 3. Shall I stand when the band plays Mrs. Bond's song?
 4. The boss prodded him about his padded expense account.
 5. A real tragedy: he mistook an adder for an otter.
 6. My body is badly out of shape, but I plan to drop some flab soon.
 7. A foul: the quarterback was socked after he was sacked.
 8. Is it a fact that all blondes like bland food?
 9. The cop put on his cap before going back out.
10. My captain is as brilliant as the Wizard of Oz was.
11. What was in the bag Mr. Bassey threw into the bog?
12. A terrible crash! A cadillac rammed a Honda.
13. Some top executives tapped the company funds.
14. I am tired of giving alms to wealthy charities.
15. Rats are always attracted to a rotten mess.

BACK VOWELS

/ɑ/ (ä)

Production of the /ɑ/ (ä)

If you let the tongue lie low in the mouth, open the unrounded lips rather wide, and emit the air stream through the mouth with the vocal folds vibrating, you will produce the low back vowel in the words *arm* and *alms*. We represent this sound in IPA by /ɑ/ and in the dictionaries by ä.

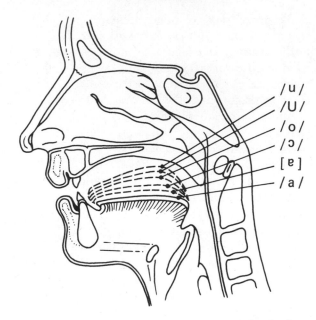

F IGURE 3–2. *Representative tongue positions for back vowels.*

It is no accident that the physician asks you to say *ah* when he wants to look down your throat. When you produce the /ɑ/ (ä), you open the mouth wider and drop your tongue lower than when making any other vowel in English.

Allophones of the /ɑ/ (ä)

The vowel /ɑ/ (ä) has a variant form that is used by some speakers in place of the /ɑ/ (ä) in "short *o*" words such as *odd, hot, pot,* and *stop.* This second vowel is a higher back vowel than the first. It is formed with the tongue slightly raised in back from the position of /ɑ/ (ä) and with the lips slightly less open and more rounded than in the production of /ɑ/ (ä). This variant is ordinarily short and lax.

This sound is represented in IPA by [ɒ]. As we will see later, this sound is an allophone of another vowel, in addition to the /ɑ/ (ä).

Pronounce some of the "short *o*" words aloud. Do you pronounce *hot, lot, got, stop, rot,* and *odd* with the "wide open" [ɑ] (ä) or with the slightly raised and rounded [ɒ] (ŏ)? The use of this allophone is not considered nonstandard, but the vast majority of Americans use [ɑ] (ä) on these words.

A third variation, or allophone, of /ɑ/ (ä) occurs after /w/ (the sound and not just the spelling) and before /r/ or /ɚ/ (ər)—the unstressed *er* vowel heard in the second syllable of *other.* Sometimes, before

/r/ (depending on the dialect and the idiolect) and always before /ɚ/ (ər), if there is a /w/ before the /ɑ/ (ä), the sound changes to [ɔ] (ô) —the vowel in the word *raw*. The little /ɚ/ is represented by the letter *r* when it follows a vowel or diphthong in the same syllable. The word *car*, for example, has three sounds: /k/, /ɑ/, and /ɚ/. Because that /ɑ/ (ä) is not preceded by /w/, the /ɑ/ (ä) remains [ɑ] (ä). But compare your pronunciation of the word *car* with that of the word *war*. Listen to the vowel in each word. Is the vowel exactly the same in the two words? No. After /w/ and before /ɚ/, the ɑ shifts to [ɔ] (ô)— the vowel at the beginning of the word *ought*. When /ɑ/ (ä) occurs before the consonant /r/, which means that /ɑ/ (ä) will end one syllable and /r/ will begin the next syllable, you may use either the usual form of /ɑ/ (ä) or that allophone made with the tongue raised in back and the lips somewhat tensed and rounded—[ɔ] (ô). Check your own pronunciation of the word *Warren*. Which of the allophones of /ɑ/ do you use—[ɑ] (ä) or [ɔ] (ô)?

Pronounce the following words to listen for this [ɔ] (ô) allophone of /ɑ/ (ä):

/wɑ/ BEFORE /ɚ/	war	
	warm	(See p. 292 for more examples.)
	wart	
	ward	
	quart	
	quarter	
	warn	
	swarm	
	swarth	
	warship	
	warmth	
	warmblooded	
	warmhearted	(Note the two allophones, one in each syllable!)

/wɑ/ BEFORE /r/	Warren
	warrant
	warrantee
	warranty
	Warrick
	warrior

Common Deviations or Problems in the Production of /ɑ/ (ä)

There are two common problems associated with the production of this sound: (1) raising and fronting, and (2) the substitution of /ɔ/ for /ɑ/.

1. *Raising and fronting.* The most common distortion of the /ɑ/ (ä) is that of raising and fronting the vowel by pulling the tongue up and forward toward the position used in forming the vowel /æ/ (ă) and its allophone [a]. If the sound is made with undue tension, with the lips slightly spread, and with the tongue slightly lifted toward the front of the mouth, the sound will be distorted. The /ɑ/ (ä) should be open, free, and relaxed. Drop the tongue and open the mouth to form it. *Stop* should not sound like *stap* nor *are* like [æɚ] (ăər).

2. *Substitution of* [ɔ] (ô) *for* /ɑ/ (ä). We have noted that in one context, /ɑ/ (ä) does become [ɔ] (ô): after /w/, before /ɚ/ (ər), and sometimes before /r/. In other contexts, however, substituting the /ɔ/ (ô) phoneme (the vowel in the word *awe*) for the /ɑ/ (ä) is non-standard. *Lard* should not become *lord; ardor* should not become *order; stark* should not be turned into *stork; are* should not become *or;* and *far* should not become *for.* Check your own pronunciation of these words, and listen for this substitution. For more examples of /ɑ/ (ä) before /ɚ/, see pp. 293–294.

Materials for Practicing the /ɑ/ (ä)

odd	ah	hah
ox	alms	palms
occupy	art	dart
otter	ark	park
obvious	arch	march
oblong	arm	harm
opposite	arbor	harbor

1. He was not qualified for a career in the army.
2. My partner will buy up the option.
3. Popeye and Olive were always in trouble.
4. No, my father was not a locksmith.
5. The guard was unable to prevent the robbery.
6. The golfer responded with an oath.
7. Obligations should be met without argument.
8. I don't object to giving alms, but I wouldn't give him a farthing!
9. The sergeant parked his car and ordered the private to guard it.
10. Fort Knox would be a golden opportunity.
11. Don't you think it odd that he wants to be shot off in a rocket?
12. Robert's not calm; he's preoccupied.
13. It's obvious our congressman has stock in an oil company.
14. Dogmatic? He's an ardent agnostic.
15. Exhausted, Robert was temporarily out of ardor.
16. Your charm won't work, but there's no harm in trying.
17. I've been warned that I can't expect a pardon.

18. Bart has had to station guards at the country club. That's par for the course.
19. Why should he be alarmed that his partner is coming?
20. Charlie's smart remarks marred the reunion.
21. It's not that Carl is tardy; he just operates in a different time zone.
22. What this farm needs is a pretty red barn.
23. The prices at the supermarket jarred me into cost consciousness.
24. She didn't have the heart to tell me we were parting forever.
25. Either you are or you are not.
26. He said the used car had belonged to a warmhearted schoolmarm. I found it hard to believe.
27. My reputation was tarnished by a few heartless remarks.
28. The bouncer took his arm and barred him from the club.
29. Sometimes a little ardor is in order.
30. After ten children, Mrs. Stark has some doubts about the stork.
31. It's much too far away for a quick trip to the garden.
32. The lord of this house prefers lard to Crisco.
33. They are neither gnarled nor straight.
34. Mort's new store is called the M-Mart.
35. The alarmed harpist said the pains were short but sharp.

/ɔ/ (ô)

Production of the /ɔ/ (ô)

If you raise the back of the tongue up slightly toward the soft palate, round the lips a bit more than you did in forming [ɒ], and emit the air stream through the mouth with the vocal folds vibrating, you will produce the low back vowel in the words *all* and *ought*. This vowel is classified as a *tense low back vowel*. The "short o" allophone of /ɑ/ (ä), which we discussed earlier, is a *lax* low back vowel. We will see a little later that this lax vowel is also an allophone of the tense low back vowel /ɔ/ (ô). This tense low back vowel phoneme is represented in IPA by /ɔ/ (not quite an *o*, you see) and in the dictionaries by ô.

To form this vowel correctly, you must achieve slight tension of the tongue and lips, rounding the lips into a vertical ellipse.

Allophones of the /ɔ/ (ô)

As we noted earlier, the [ɒ] is used as an allophone, or variant form, of this vowel in some regions. An author trying to represent these dialectal differences with regular spelling might spell the word *forest* as *fawrest* or *fahrest* to indicate the difference in pronunciation. Check your own pronunciation of such words as *forest, dog, hog, log, Laura, Pauline,* and *called* to see which of the vowels you use in these words. Either is acceptable, but most speakers of American English use the

/ɔ/ (ô), and in many parts of the country the [ɒ] would be thought an affectation.

Common Deviations of Problems in the Production of /ɔ/ (ô)

There are three common distortions of the vowel /ɔ/ (ô): (1) substitution of /o/ for /ɔ/ ô; (2) retraction; and (3) diphthongizing. The last two distortions often occur together.

1. *Substitution of /o/ for /ɔ/ (ô)*. Many languages do not include this phoneme. If you first learned a language that does not contain this sound in its phonemic system and then learned English, the vowel /ɔ/ (ô) may give you some difficulty. You may substitute the vowel /o/ in its place. Although in some dialects of American English there are words that can be pronounced with either of these vowels, they are separate phonemes in the language, and there are many words that depend on these vowels to distinguish between them. If you say the word *bought* in a sentence such as "I bought it," do you say *bought* like *boat?* If so, you may use the pure vowel /o/ rather than the more common allophone of /o/—the diphthongal allophone. But neither allophone of /o/ should be substituted for /ɔ/ (ô).

Check your pronunciation of these pairs of words. They are distinguished from each other by the use of either /ɔ/ (ô) or /o/. The words containing /ɔ/ (ô) are in the left-hand column.

/ɔ/ (ô) AND /o/ (ō)

CONTRAST	
bought	boat
caught	coat
wrought	wrote
naught	note
Saul	soul
awed	owed
saw	so, sew
flawed	flowed
vault	volt
fawn	phone
lawn	loan
fall	foal
called	cold
gnaw	know, no
off	oaf
laud	load
law	low
claws	clothes
raw	row
hall	whole, hole

walk	woke
Falk	folk
or*	oar*
horse*	hoarse*

2. *Retraction.* The distortion that we label retraction of the /ɔ/ (ô) is produced by doing two things: first, by puckering the lips excessively so that they are noticeably protruded, and second, by pulling the tongue back in the mouth. You may have heard someone imitating the stereotyped impression of "New Yorkese" by asking for *cawfee* and for a *chawklet mawlted* or complaining that something was *awwful*. The retracted /ɔ/ (ô) is a tense, grating sound and should be avoided. If you tend to retract the vowel, you should relax the lips slightly and open the mouth a bit wider, being certain that the lips are not protruded and do not move and you should lift the back of the tongue to a position about halfway between /ɑ/ (ä) and /o/.

3. *Diphthongizing.* Another deviation results from replacing the pure vowel /ɔ/ (ô) with a diphthong. If you add the /ə/, the first vowel in the word *above*, to the /ɔ/ (ô), you have the diphthong [ɔə] (ôə). This elongation, common in the greater New York area, might be called a "Northern drawl"! Combined with retraction of the /ɔ/ (ô), it is a particularly unpleasant distortion to most American ears. In such words as *ought, taught, call, tall, talk, dog, coffee, awful, chocolate,* and *malted,* do not hold on to the /ɔ/ (ô); move on to the next consonant.

Materials for Practicing the /ɔ/ (ô)

all	tall	taw
oft	soft	saw
Ong	wrong	raw
awes	claws	claw
ought	naught	gnaw
off	cough	caw
orgy	Georgie	jaw
awed	laud	law

1. It was an ordeal, but I taught the class.
2. The wrestler lost points for stalling.
3. All of the pledges suffered horribly.
4. The author was quite proud of his lyrics for the song.
5. Most coffins cost a fortune!
6. Paul is going to Europe in August.
7. Please call a taxi for me about eight in the morning.
8. I'm sorry that we ar losing our foreign trade.

* This distinction is not maintained in all dialects of American English. A Southern speaker is more likely to preserve the difference in these words.

9. We're learning to talk in flawless English.
10. I drank orange juice, coffee, and a chocolate malted for breakfast.
11. Because of recent reforms, it is easier to adopt an orphan.
12. I ought to buy that dog from my lawyer.
13. I thought everybody in the dorm had heard of Pauline.
14. Caught in the act, he was mortified.
15. She ordered me to tell her all the morbid details.
16. He lost his train of thought after that long pause.
17. Chalk up another win for California.
18. I fought because those were my orders.
19. What's the cost of an eight-by-ten glossy photo?
20. We lost all our home games—and the coach also.

/o/ (ō)

Production of /o/ (ō)

If you raise the back of the tongue up about midway in the back of the mouth toward the soft palate, round the lips more than you did to form /ɔ/ (ô), and emit the air stream through the mouth with the vocal folds vibrating, you will produce the tense mid back vowel we represent by /o/ in IPA and by ō in the dictionaries.

This vowel phoneme is the first sound in the word *obey* and the last sound in the word *tomato*. It is the second of the two phonemes in the word *no*. The vowel /o/ (ō) is classified as a *tense mid back vowel*.

Allophones of /o/ (ō)

There are three variations of this phoneme. If you read aloud the key words we just gave you, you probably discovered that the /o/ (ō) in *obey* and *tomato* is somewhat different from the /o/ (ō) in *no*. There is a difference in length and purity. The /o/ (ō) in *no* lasts much longer than the /o/ (ō) in *obey*, because *no* is a stressed syllable and the /o/ (ō) in *obey* is an unstressed syllable. When the "long o" is held as long as we Americans stretch it in stressed syllables, it ceases to be a pure vowel sound; it is a diphthong—a blend of two vowels. The difference is not phonemic (it does not change the meaning); the pure vowel and the diphthong are allophones (variations) of the same phoneme. However, if you substitute one allophone for the other, native speakers will notice the difference.

In American English, the /o/ (ō) is heard as a pure vowel in unstressed syllables. The symbol for this allophone in IPA is [o]; dictionaries have represented the allophone as ô. This allophone would be heard in the following words, for example:

> obey, omit, omission, opine, Odessa, obese, hallow, hollow, follow, piano, yellow, window, hotel, fellow

In American English, the /o/ (ō) is heard as a diphthong in stressed syllables. The symbol for this allophone in IPA is [ou]; the dictionary symbol is ō. As you can guess from the IPA symbols, the diphthongal allophone of /o/ is two vowels blended together—the pure vowel /o/ and a second weaker, shorter vowel that is almost the oo in *ooze*. To represent the second vowel, we use the phonetic symbol for the vowel in the word *foot*, because the second vowel of the diphthong is not as long or quite as tense as the vowel in *ooze*. Still, if you have difficulty with this sound, it might be wise for you to think of the second vowel as an /u/ (oo)—the vowel in *ooze*. This [ou] (ō) allophone is heard in all stressed syllables in American English, so it is used far more often than the pure vowel allophone. Here are only a few·words in which the diphthongal allophone is heard:

> know, grow, blow, show, boat, soul, beau, load, own, bone, both, broke, host

Before the vowel /ɚ/ (ər) (see pp. 292–293.), an interesting dialectal variation occurs. In New York City and other portions of the Northeast, /o/ (ō) becomes /ɔ/ (ô) before the r-vowel. In other portions of the country, the use of /ɔ/ (ô) instead of /o/ (ō) before /ɚ/ (ər) seems to be increasing. We certainly cannot label this substitution nonstandard, although we confess it still sounds strange to our ears. Do you make a contrast in the following words and phrases, or do you use the /ɔ/ (ô) vowel in both words of each pair?

/ɔɚ/ (ôər) AND /oɚ/ (ōər) CONTRAST

or	oar
for	four/fore
horse	hoarse
border	boarder
morn	mourn
morning	mourning
Tor	tore
rawer	roar
lord	lowered
nor	know 'er

Common Deviations and Problems in the Production of /o/ (ō)

There are five common problems associated with this phoneme: (1) substitution of /ə/ for /o) (ō), (2) substitution of /ɚ/ for /o/ (ō), (3) substitution of [o] (ô) for [ou] (ō), (4) centering, and (5) triphthongizing.

1. *Substitution of /ə/ for /o/ (ō)*. In most unstressed syllables, the vowel will be reduced to /ə/. (See pp. 263–266.) The syllables containing the pure vowel allophone of /o/ (ō), therefore, differ from most of the unstressed syllables of American English. Some speakers tend to substi-

tute the more common vowel for unstressed syllables—the /ə/—for the unstressed form of /o/ (ō). This substitution is nonstandard. Pronounce the following words. Do you use the [o] (ȯ) or the /ə/ (the first sound in the word *above*) in the last syllable of these words?

> yellow, fellow, mellow, window, follow, hollow, hallow, pillow, shadow, bellow, piano, cello

There are at least two words with the unstressed /o/ occurring in *both* the first and last syllables. Do you substitute the /ə/ for the [o] (ȯ) in either or both of the syllables of these words?

> potato, tomato

2. *Substitution of /ɚ/ (ər) for /o/ (ō)*. Some speakers substitute the unstressed -*er* sound heard in the word *mother* for the [o] in unstressed syllables. Check the two lists we gave you in the first problem associated with this sound. You may find you are tempted to make this substitution. It is considered nonstandard.

3. *Substitution of* [o] (ȯ) *for* [ou] (ō). Many languages use the pure vowel [o] consistently and never use the diphthong heard in English. If you learned English as a second language, you may substitute the pure vowel allophone for the diphthongal variation of /o/ (ō) in stressed syllables. If you fail to add the second vowel, the off-glide, you will not give the phoneme its customary duration (length)—which will affect the rhythm of your words and sentences. Pronounce the word *no*. Now pronounce the word in very slow motion as you watch your lips in a mirror. (You probably cannot see the tongue movement.) You should see the lip opening close down considerably during the production of this sound, and you should be able to feel the tongue pull up in back as it moves from the [o] position to the [u] position. During the diphthong, the lips and tongue *move* from one position to another in a continuous movement, as the two different vowels are blended together.

4. *Centering*. Some speakers pull the entire diphthong [ou] forward in the mouth by lifting the tongue in the center of the mouth rather than in the back of the mouth. This centering of the vowel (in its diphthongal form) results in a distortion that causes *home* to sound something like *hum, most* like *must*, and *soak* like *suck*. We consider this substitution nonstandard and suggest you avoid it. Here are a few more pairs of words that contrast the /o/ (ō) with the /ʌ/ (ŭ)—the vowel in the word *up*:

/o/ (ō) AND /ʌ/ (ŭ) CONTRAST	mode	mud
	goat	gut
	comb	come
	roam	rum
	tomes	Tums

Gomer	gummer
choke	chuck
rowed	Rudd
goal	gull
roan	run
phone	fun
sown	sun
bone	bun
Nome	numb
dome	dumb
known	none

5. *Triphthongizing.* In its most usual form, the /o/ (ō) is a diphthong, as we have observed. Adding another sound to this diphthong would turn it into a triphthong (three vowels combined into one sound). Especially before /n/ and /1/, some speakers are tempted to add the little vowel /ə/ on to the /o/ (ō). (And, if you have a tendency to drag the vowel out in this way, be careful you do not have a /w/ between the /o/ (ō) and the added /ə/. That adds insult to injury—or, more accurately, compounds the distortion.) Check your own pronunciation of these words:

/o/ (ō) BEFORE /n/   bone
cone
Doan/Done
phone
hone
Joan
moan
known
pone
roan
sown
shown
tone
stone
won't

/o/ (ō) BEFORE /1/   bowl
coal
dole
foal
goal
hole
cajole

mole
knoll
pole
rolled
soul
shoal
toll
stole
volt

Because you are most likely to add the /ə/ (or the /wə/) before a consonant in the same syllable—especially the /n/ or /l/—you can check the vowel /o/ (ō) you use when no consonant follows and then try to match that vowel in words where /n/ or /l/ follows the /o/ (ō). Try these pairs of words with that in mind. Remember to try to match the vowel in the first word when pronouncing the second word:

/o/ (ō) AND /on/ (ōn) CONTRAST		
	bow	bone
	blow	blown
	Coe	cone
	dough	Doan/Done
	foe	phone
	grow	grown
	ho	hone
	Joe	Joan
	low	loan
	Moe	moan
	know	known
	Poe	pone
	roe/row	roan
	sew/so	sown
	show	shown
	toe	tone
	stow	stone
	woe	won't

/o/ (ō) AND /ol/ (ōl) CONTRAST		
	bow	bowl
	Coe	coal
	dough	dole
	foe	foal
	go	goal
	ho	hole
	Joe	cajole
	Moe	mole
	know	knoll

Poe	poll/pole
roe/row	roll/role
sew/so	soul
show	shoal
toe	toll
stow	stole

Materials for Practicing /o/ (ō)

oh	float	flow
owed	rowed	roe
oaf	loaf	low
oak	soak	sew
own	blown	blow
oar	door	dough
oat	tote	toe

1. Of all the folks I have known, he was the most cooperative.
2. I do not believe he will grow any more.
3. The owner could not agree that the cloth should be torn.
4. The speaker did not know how bored the audience really was.
5. Open the door slowly.
6. The crowd roared the chants they had learned by rote.
7. Fort Knox is where the gold is stored.
8. Is it only the cheerleaders who are hoarse all the time?
9. She insisted that I row toward the shore.
10. I'm told you're an expert on Indian folklore.
11. The old grad did not omit a single detail from the story.
12. Both of them always cry on my shoulder.
13. Jo-Ann implored and swore, but the hotel clerk could not find our reservations.
14. Stephen was not the only martyr who's been stoned.
15. Obeying the chairman's orders, we gave him a standing ovation.
16. Joe is exploring possibilities in Ohio.
17. The whole team poured onto the floor when the goal was disallowed.
18. I'm told the new location will be on the West Coast.
19. I took an oath never to eat another potato.
20. How long have you known this fellow?
21. I've grown more and more weary of this thorough analysis.
22. Some movers! A window was broken and the piano smashed.
23. He spoke of order, but I couldn't follow him.
24. I've known him for more than ten years.
25. The friendship was restored—when we chose to forget the whole thing.

/ʊ/ (ŏŏ)

Production of /ʊ/ (ŏŏ)

If you lift the back of the tongue up in back toward the soft palate farther than you did in forming the /o/ (ō), round the lips even more than you did on the /o/ (ō), and emit the air stream through the mouth with the vocal folds vibrating, you will produce the lax high back vowel heard in the word *look* that we represent in IPA by /ʊ/ and in the dictionaries by ŏŏ.

This vowel has much the same relation to the vowel sound in the word *Luke* (represented in IPA by /u/ and in the dictionaries by ōō) as the /ɪ/ (ĭ) vowel has to /i/ (ē). (See pp. 183–187.) Just as /ɪ/ (ĭ) is formed with the tongue slightly lower and more lax than when forming /i/ (ē), so /ʊ/ (ŏŏ) is made with the tongue slightly lower and more lax (less tense) than when forming /u/ (ōō). Another parallel is that /ʊ/ (ŏŏ) and /ɪ/ (ĭ) are usually short sounds, whereas /u/ (ōō) and /i/ (ē) are usually long sounds.

This vowel is classified as a *rounded lax high back vowel.*

Deviations and Common Problems in the Production of the /ʊ/ (ŏŏ)

There are four common problems associated with this sound: (1) centering, (2) diphthongizing, (3) substitution of /u/ (ōō), and (4) substitution of /o/ (ō).

1. *Centering.* Some speakers make this vowel with the tongue too low and too far forward. Usually, speakers who center the /ʊ/ (ŏŏ) not only raise the tongue in the center of the mouth, rather than in the back, but also relax the lips somewhat. Carried to an extreme, centering may result in the actual substitution of the central vowel /ʌ/ (ŭ)—heard in the words *mud* and *hut*—for the /ʊ/ (ŏŏ). *Look* should not sound like *luck, took* like *tuck,* or *shook* like *shuck.*

Try these pairs of words and phrases out loud. Does the first word tend to sound like the second word? There should be a clear contrast. The first word contains /ʊ/ (ŏŏ) and the second word contains /ʌ/ (ŭ).

/ʊ/ (ŏŏ) AND /ʌ/ (ŭ) CONTRAST	
book	buck
hook	Huck
hood	Hud
look	luck
puss	pus
put	putt
shook	shuck
stood	stud
took	tuck
Buddhism	Bud isn't

2. *Diphthongizing.* Like other vowels, /ʊ/ (ŏŏ) can be stretched into a diphthong by adding /ə/. Be careful not to drawl this vowel. It is a relatively short sound. Move on to the next consonant, and keep the vowel pure.

3. *Substitution of* /u/ (ōō) *for* /ʊ/ (ŏŏ). Many languages do not have this vowel as a separate phoneme of the language. If you learned English as a second language, you may not be used to hearing the distinction between the vowels in the word *foot* (/ʊ/ or ŏŏ) and the word *food* (/u/ or ōō). And you may substitute the /u/ (ōō) for the /ʊ/ (ŏŏ)—using the one sound for both sounds. Many English words depend on these two vowels for the contrast in meaning. (Although it *is* true that a few words can be pronounced with either sound.)

Pronounce these words and phrases. Be sure that there is a clear contrast between the vowel in the first word and the vowel in the second word. Remember that the words in the left-hand column contain /ʊ/ (ŏŏ)—on which the tongue is lower and more relaxed and the lips slightly less tightly rounded than for /u/ (ōō), the vowel in the right-hand column.

/ʊ/ (ŏŏ) AND /u/ (ōō) CONTRAST		
	could	cooed
	cookie	kooky
	full	fool
	good	gooed
	hood	who'd
	look	Luke
	putsch	pooch
	pull	pool
	soot	suit
	should	shooed/shoed
	wood	wooed

4. *Substitution of* /o/ (ō) *for* /ʊ/ (ŏŏ). When the r-vowel /ɚ/ (See pp. 235–237.) follows, some speakers substitute /o/ (ō) for /ʊ/ (ŏŏ). This substitution, of course, is nonstandard. The /o/ (ō) is made with the tongue raised lower in the back of the mouth than for /ʊ/ (ŏŏ), and the lips are not as rounded (as tightly puckered) on /o/ (ō) as on /ʊ/ (ŏŏ). Remember, /ʊ/ (ŏŏ) is almost /u/ (ōō)—the vowel in *ooze*. If in doubt, just remember the /ʊ/ (ŏŏ) before /ɚ/ will sound much more like /u/ (ōō) than like /o/ (ō).

Pronounce these pairs of words and phrases. Check to be sure that the first word or phrase does not turn into the second one.

/ʊɚ/ (ŏŏər) AND /oɚ/ (ōər) CONTRAST		
	poor	pour/pore
	boor	bore/boar
	tour	tore

dour	door
Cours	cores
gourmet	Gore may
lure	lore
moor	more
sure	shore
your	yore
adjure	a jore(?)

Materials for Practicing /ʊ/ (ŏo)

1. I understood every word of the bulletin.
2. He may be foolish, but he is not crooked.
3. Few tourists ever get to Brooklyn.
4. The poor rookie had trouble enduring the hazing.
5. I would appreciate it if you would return my book.
6. She shook her head as the butcher quoted the price.
7. Mr. Cooke takes a little coffee in his sugar.
8. She made them put back every book they took.
9. We put the Girl Scout cookies in a bushel basket.
10. I had understood this was a good neighborhood!
11. It looks like I'll enjoy what you've got cooking.
12. I'm not exactly a gourmet cook.
13. I endured the rural life as long as I could.
14. Cardinal Cooke's sermon was full of the papal bull.
15. For goodness sake, put an end to this!

/u/ (o̅o)

Production of /u/ (o̅o)

If you raise the back of the tongue nearly to the soft palate, round the lips tightly, and emit the air stream through the mouth with the vocal folds vibrating, you will produce the highest back vowel, heard in the words *ooze* and *Sue*. We represent this sound in IPA by /u/ and in the dictionaries by o̅o. Produced with the lips and the back of the tongue tense, /u/ (o̅o) is usually a long vowel in its duration. The vowel /u/ (o̅o) is classified as a *rounded tense high back vowel*.

Allophones of the /u/ (o̅o)

Although /u/ (o̅o) and /ʊ/ (ŏo) are separate phonemes, there are a few words in which [ʊ] (ŏo) is a standard variation of /u/ (o̅o). Whether these words are pronounced with /u/ (o̅o) or /ʊ/ (ŏo) depends on a person's dialect or idiolect. These words are all spelled with *oo*. Note, for example, how you pronounce the words *coop, hoof, whoop,*

hoop, roof, and *room.* Which vowel did you use? Were you consistent on the entire group of words?

Common Deviations or Problems in the Production of /u/ (o͞o)

There are four common distortions associated with this sound: (1) substitution of /ʊ/ (o͝o) for /u/ (o͞o), (2) substitution of /ju/ (yo͞o) for /u/ (o͞o), (3) centralizing, and (4) diphthongizing.

1. *Substitution of /ʊ/ (o͝o) for /u/ (o͞o).* If you fail to purse (pucker) the lips tightly enough and to get enough tension of the tongue, you may lower the vowel /u/ (o͞o) to the position and relaxation of the lax high back vowel /ʊ/ (o͝o). Although there are a few words on which /ʊ/ (o͝o) seems to function as a standard allophone of /u/ (o͞o), as we mentioned earlier, this substitution generally is nonstandard. *She wooed* should not sound like *She would,* and *a new suit* should not sound like *a new soot.*

2. *Substitution of /ju/ (yo͞o) for /u/ (o͞o).* When we discussed the /j/ (y) phoneme, we mentioned that some speakers are confused about when to use /u/ (o͞o) and when to use /ju/ (yo͞o). At that time, we gave you some principles to guide you in deciding which times to use which sounds. (See pp. 165–166). Some speakers, intending to be precise—or perhaps elegant—use /ju/ (yo͞o) in place of /u/ (o͞o)—at the wrong times! We noted the sounds that often are followed by /ju/ (yo͞o): /t/, /d/, and /n/. We also noted the sounds that *are* followed by /ju/ (yo͞o) if the word is spelled with *u, eu, ew, iew,* or *eu:* /p), /b/, /k/, /m/, /f/, /v/, and /h/. If a speaker uses /ju/ (yo͞o) after /s/, /z/, /l/, or /θ/ (th), however, it is considered an affectation—and nonstandard. Are you tempted to use the /ju/ (yo͞o) instead of /u/ (o͞o) in these words:

suit, resume, absolution, enthusiastic?

3. *Centralizing.* Some speakers distort the /u/ (o͞o) by attempting to make it with the tongue too far forward in the mouth and the lips too relaxed. In this case, they raise the tongue in the center of the mouth rather than at the back. The effect is to distort and "flatten" the sound. Work for adequate lip rounding and correct tongue placement.

4. *Diphthongizing.* As we said earlier, /u/ (o͞o) is a long sound. Unless you are careful, it can easily be turned into a noticeable diphthong. If you start with the tongue in a position too low and too relaxed to produce a good /u/ (o͞o) and slide slowly up to the customary spot, you will, of course, produce a diphthong. Substitution of a diphthong may also result from starting in the customary tense high position and relaxing the tongue into a lower spot. Another diphthongal distortion results from adding the little neutral vowel /ə/ (the first sound in the word *above*) to the vowel /u/ (o͞o). This last substitution—/uə/ (o͞oə)

for /u/ ($\overline{oo}$)—is most likely to occur before /l/ and /n/ in the same syllable.

Check your own pronunciation of the following words. Are you tempted to turn the /u/ ($\overline{oo}$) vowel into a diphthong?

cool	boon
drool	buffoon
fool	croon
ghoul	dune
Jules	June
pool	lampoon
spool	moon
tool	soon
stool	spoon

To avoid drawling, move definitely (not slowly and deliberately) to the right place to form the sound, and hold the tongue in that place until you move on to the next sound.

Because you are less likely to make the vowel into a diphthong when it occurs alone at the end of a word, try the following pairs of words aloud. Try to match the vowel from the first word in the second word when the /u/ ($\overline{oo}$) is followed by /l/ or /n/:

/u/ ($\overline{oo}$) AND /ul/ ($\overline{oo}$l) CONTRAST

coo	cool
Drew	drool
foo	fool
goo	ghoul
who	who'll
poo	pool
too	tool

/u/ ($\overline{oo}$) AND /un/ ($\overline{oo}$n) CONTRAST

boo	boon
coo	coon
do	dune
goo	goon
Jew	June
Lou	loon
Sue	soon

Materials for Practicing /u/ ($\overline{oo}$)

ooze	choose	chew
oolong	too long	too
umiak	loom	lieu
oomph	zoom	zoo

1. Louise, a pessimist, spreads doom and gloom.
2. The charges were based purely on rumor, but she was accused.

3. Who would have believed so few would show up for duty?
4. Truth should not be the exception—but the rule.
5. His shrewish wife is on another crusade.
6. His case will be reviewed in June.
7. Junior may be ignorant, but he's no fool.
8. Having to do that paper was cruel and unusual punishment.
9. I wouldn't mind doing it, if I had the right tools.
10. The tune he requested was "Blue Moon."
11. You can't be neutral; you must choose sides.
12. He ordered the troops into another useless battle.
13. Everyone knew the effort was futile.
14. A few truthful rumors can ruin a good neighborhood.
15. Who's going to help you review for the exam?

Here are some sentences containing both /u/ (o͞o) and /ʊ/ (o͝o):

1. I was a fool to foot the bill.
2. Should I buy a new pair of shoes?
3. Look for St. Luke's Hospital.
4. Who expected the hood to fly off?
5. I hate to pull trash out of the pool.
6. It was foolish, but I stood on the stool. I should have known better.
7. The baby "gooed" as the Mother said, "Good baby."
8. The troupe sold cookies to raise money.
9. No more food! I'm full!
10. I'm not too lazy; I just need a push.
11. How *could* you chew those beetle nuts?
12. Brooklyn is not too far away.
13. The crowd booed as the referee put the player out of the game.
14. Sue took my books back to the library.
15. I assure you: sugar should not be so refined.
16. I shook in my boots.
17. The soot of New York does not suit me very well.
18. Should she have shooed the flies toward the food?
19. That foolish book is full of errors.
20. If I had known she was interested, of course I would have wooed her.

CENTRAL VOWELS

/ʌ/ (ŭ)

Production of the /ʌ/ (ŭ)

If you lift the center of the tongue slightly toward the palate, keep the lips unrounded, and emit the air stream through the mouth with the vocal folds vibrating, you will produce the stressed low central vowel heard in the words *up* and *come*. We represent this sound by /ʌ/ in IPA

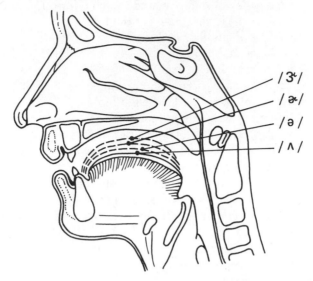

/ 3˞ /

/ ɚ /

/ ə /

/ ʌ /

FIGURE 3–3. *Representative tongue positions for central vowels.*

and by ŭ in the dictionaries. It is ordinarily a short sound. This vowel is classified as the *stressed low central vowel.*

Common Deviations or Problems in the Production of /ʌ/ (ŭ)

There are four common problems associated with /ʌ/ (ŭ): (1) fronting and raising ,(2) raising, (3) retracting and raising, and (4) substitution of /ɑ/ (ä) for /ʌ/ (ŭ).

1. *Fronting and raising.* The most common distortion of the /ʌ/ (ŭ) is fronting and raising the sound before consonants made in the front of the mouth. Pulling the tongue up and forward in the mouth on the formation of this vowel results in its sounding like /ɪ/ (ĭ) or /ɛ/ (ĕ). The word *just,* then, would sound a great deal like *gist* or *jest.* Perhaps you have heard someone say, "Gist a minute," or "Jest a minute." Pronounce the following list of words. Check your own pronunciation to be sure you do not distort the vowel in this way.

such
cover
judge
hush
mush
shut
brush
lush
hut

hutch
budge
fudge
clutch
judge
smudge
rush
much

2. *Raising.* Some speakers distort the /ʌ/ (ŭ) vowel by raising the tongue further up in the center of the mouth than is customary to form the sound. They do not turn this central vowel into a front vowel (as in the first distortion discussed); it is still a central vowel, but it is not the *same* central vowel. There is a sound that is an uncommon allophone of the stressed *er* vowel (the vowel in the words *stir* and *her*, represented in IPA by /ɝ/ and in the dictionaries by ûr); that allophone is a tense, high central vowel, but it has no *r*-coloring. (See p. 231.) When the tongue is raised up relatively high in the center of the mouth and tensed a bit, this allophone of /ɝ/ (ûr) is produced. When this sound is substituted for /ʌ/ (ŭ), the /ʌ/ (ŭ), of course, is distorted.

3. *Retracting and raising.* Some speakers pull the tongue up and back in the mouth on the formation of this vowel. If you raise the tongue up rather high in back, leaving the tongue somewhat lax, you will produce some variation of the /ʊ/ (o͝o) vowel. Indeed, this distortion sounds like a substitution of /ʊ/ (o͝o) for /ʌ/ (ŭ). To check your pronunciation for this distortion, and to be sure you make a good contrast between /ʌ/ (ŭ) and /ʊ/ (o͝o), read the contrasts on p. 218.

4. *Substitution of* /ɑ/ (ä) *for* /ʌ/ (ŭ). There are many languages that do not contain the /ʌ/ (ŭ) sound at all. If you learned English as a second language, it is possible—even likely—that the language you learned first does not include this sound in its phonemic structure. If so, you may have difficulty distinguishing this sound from others made near to the position for the /ʌ/ (ŭ) vowel. The most common problem of this sort is the substitution of /ɑ/ (ä) for /ʌ/ (ŭ). To contrast the two vowels, you will have to train your ear and your tongue. Remember, the /ɑ/ (ä) is made with the tongue almost flat in the mouth. There is a slight raising of the tongue in the center of the mouth to form the /ʌ/ (ŭ). That little bit of raising of the tongue in the center of the mouth makes the difference. But the difference, small as it is, is important in English. These are two separate phonemes; they cannot be substituted for each other without changing the meaning of the word.

Pronounce these pairs of words. They show the contrast between the two vowels /ɑ/ (ä) and /ʌ/ (ŭ). Listen and feel the difference. If you have this problem, you will have to work to make the correct difference.

/ɑ/ (ä) AND /ʌ/ (ŭ) Contrast

bomb	bum
Bock	buck
Bonn	bun
bobble	bubble
cot	cut
clock	cluck
dock	duck
Don	done
fond	fund
got	gut
hot	hut
jog	jug
lock	luck
mock	muck
mod	mud
knob	nub
not	nut
pot	putt
rob	rub
rot	rut
rod	Rudd
sock	suck
psalm	sum/some
Tom	Tum

Materials for Practicing /ʌ/ (ŭ)

1. God must have loved poor people. He (or She) made so many of us.
2. "Hello Dolly" had a long run on Broadway.
3. The curtains shut out the light; the vandals shot out the light.
4. Why do modern men envy mud huts?
5. If you model after me, you'll just muddle through.
6. "Judge not, so you will not be judged."
7. Fudge, with or without nuts, is my undoing.
8. My son has not done his homework.
9. It's lots of fun if it's done right.
10. John Donne was not a Hungarian poet.
11. Justice is not only blind; it is deaf and dumb as well.
12. "Love thy brother" does not endorse incest.
13. It's odd he didn't come on up.
14. It must be causing the hum, but it won't harm the stereo.
15. The love of money is not the root of *all* evil; the lack of money is one of the roots too.
16. I wonder what bums put that bomb in the bank.

17. With a lot of luck, I may not need a lock on the door.
18. The mugger shot past me without shutting the door or looking back once.
19. Her blunder was believing the blonder you are the more fun you have.
20. My dumb broker gave me poor instructions; now I'm stuck with worthless stock.
21. The posher the theater the more unctious the usher.
22. Mrs. Hopper lives on the Upper West Side.
23. Don has done nothing to deserve this punishment.
24. It was utter nonsense for Judd to adopt an otter.
25. The umpire had a wan look when the other side won the game.
26. His collar was the color of a chunk of coal.
27. My body-building buddy is not a mumbling, stumbling idiot.
28. I'd love to know what the robber wanted with our rubber duck.
29. You can come—on the assumption you're going to calm down.
30. Yes, I begrudge the ten dollars, since I've never seen a duller show.
31. Just a minute. I think Bud got the gist of it.
32. Don't cause trouble. It was just a little joke—a tiny jest.
33. There was such a commotion when the judge jumped over the hedge.
34. Shut the door to the shed, and cover the window. I'm shivering.
35. His little brush with the law didn't mesh with the rest of his undertakings.

/ə/

Production of /ə/

The unstressed equivalent of /ʌ/ (ŭ) is the short neutral central vowel heard in the first syllable of the word *above* and in the second syllable of the word *sofa*. In both IPA and the dictionaries, this sound is represented by /ə/. This vowel is a lax vowel—formed with the lips and tongue relaxed, the lips unrounded, and the tongue raised slightly up toward the middle in the center of the mouth. We classify this vowel as a *lax mid central vowel*.

Allophones of /ə/

The /ə/ is the most frequently used vowel in our language. The vowel has a name: *schwa*, because we cannot pronounce the sound itself by itself. The sound is so short in duration it cannot be uttered alone; it is an unstressed vowel and exists only in unstressed syllables. There must be another syllable pronounced in addition to the syllable in which /ə/ occurs or it is not /ə/. To identify the phonetic symbol and the sound, phoneticians gave the sound a name by which they could identify it. The word *schwa* (according to Claude Wise, the late great Louisiana

State University phonetician) is a German modification of the Hebrew word *sheva,* meaning "little" or "weak." The Hebrew language also includes this vowel in its phonemic system; the vowel pointing (representation in Hebrew) is : .

The schwa is the vowel in most unstressed syllables in American English. No matter what the vowel in a syllable or word in its stressed form, the vowel usually is reduced to this neutral little central vowel when the syllable is not stressed. Compare the word *land* with the second syllable of the word *England.* Is the vowel the same when you pronounce the words aloud? No. The vowel in the word *land* is /æ/ (ă); the vowel in the second syllable of *England*—if the second syllable has a vowel at all—is /ə/. The difference, of course, is that *land,* a one-syllable word, is stressed; in the word *England,* the stress is on the first syllable, and the second is unstressed.

There are four variations of the unstressed vowel in English: /ɪ/ (ĭ), /ɨ/, /ʊ/ (o͝o), and [o] (ŏ)—in addition to the /ə/.

The tense high front vowel /i/ (ē) is often weakened to /ɪ/ (ĭ) or /ɪ/ in unstressed syllables. The vowel /ɛ/ (ĕ) also may be weakened to either of these two sounds rather than to /ə/. Check for yourself. Pronounce the word *plenty.* The second syllable probably ends with a short /i/ (ē). Now pronounce the word *plentiful.* Is the vowel in the middle syllable /ə/, /ɪ/ (ĭ), or /ɨ/? It could be any of three variations of the unstressed vowel; all are standard. Now try the word *roses* out loud— as you ordinarily say it. Repeat the word, listening closely. What is the vowel in the second syllable? Hopefully, it is not the stressed vowel /ɛ/ (ĕ) but one of the three variations of the unstressed vowel: /ə/, /ɪ/ (ĭ), or /ɨ/. (See p. 186 for a discussion of /ɨ/.) You probably could not care less, but Eleanor DiMichael uses /ɨ/ as the second syllable of the word *roses,* and Robert King uses /ɪ/.

The tense high back vowel /u/ (o͞o) is often weakened to /ʊ/ (o͝o) in unstressed syllables. Pronounce the word *to.* The vowel, of course, is the tense high back vowel /u/ (o͞o). Now try the famous line "To be or not to be" aloud as you would say it in regular conversation. What vowel did you now use in the word *to?* Now it is in an unstressed syllable —or should be—and the vowel will no longer be the stressed vowel /u/ (o͞o). Did you use /ʊ/ (o͝o) or /ə/? Either is standard. Only in such unstressed syllables does the /ʊ/ (o͝o) vowel occur at the end of a syllable—or, for that matter, at the beginning of a syllable—in English.

We noted earlier in this book, when discussing the /o/ (ō) phoneme, that the pure vowel allophone of the /o/ (ō) phoneme could occur in unstressed syllables. And we gave a number of examples of words containing this sound: *tomato, piano, yellow,* and others. Indeed, the unstressed vowel /ə/ is nonstandard in these words. But there are many words in the Standard Dialect of American English in which the /o/ (ō) *is* weakened to /ə/. Pronounce the following words, and check on the beginning vowel in each word. In these words, the weakened vowel is /ə/:

    o'clock
    official
    officiate
    offensive
    oppose
    opponent
    occasion
    occur
    opinion

Common Deviations and Problems in the Production of /ə/

There are three major problems associated with the /ə/: (1) substitution of a strong (or stressed) vowel for /ə/, (2) omission, and (3) addition.

1. *Substitution of a strong (or stressed) vowel for /ə/.* It is nonstandard to substitute /i/ (ē) for /ə/, /ɪ/, or /ɨ/ in such words as *beautiful, plentiful,* and *bountiful.* It is nonstandard to substitute /ʌ/ (ŭ) for /ə/ in either the stressed or unstressed forms of such words as *of, was,* and *from.* It is nonstandard to substitute /u/ (o͞o) for /ə/ or /ʊ/ (o͝o) in such words as *regular* and *regulate.* And please note that there is neither an /u/ (o͞o) nor an /ʊ/ (o͝o) in the middle of the words *simile* and *similar.* It is nonstandard to substitiute the [o] (ȯ) for /ə/ in such words as *opinion, official, violent,* and *violate.* Our last example of nonstandard substitutions of strong, stressed vowels for the unstressed vowels is the substitution of /e/ (ā) for /ə/ in such words as *around, about, arise,* and *account.*

2. *Omission.* Some careless speakers omit /ə/—especially when it occurs between consonants in the middle of a word or when beginning a syllable after a syllable ending with a vowel or diphthong. Pronounce these words, which offer a temptation to omit the schwa between consonants:

    bakery
    cabinet
    corridor
    delicate
    family
    federal
    mercury
    parade
    police

similar
suppose
support
traveler
unity
veteran

The following words also offer a temptation to omit the unstressed vowel. This time the vowel in danger occurs after a syllable ending in a vowel or diphthong. Do not yield to the temptation. At least, check to see if you are tempted and usually do omit the vowel.

poem	pious
poetry	diet
lion	quiet
scion	period
Zion	area
liable	sodium
riot	simian
Ryan	criteria
jewel	media
cruel	medium
society	delirious
variety	stowaway

3. *Addition.* Just as some speakers are tempted to leave out the /ə/, so others are tempted to put in an extra /ə/ occasionally. Have you ever heard anyone turn the two-syllable word *athlete* into a three syllable word by adding a schwa between the /θ/ (th) and the /l/? Or have you heard someone add an /ə/ after the /θ/ (th) in *athletics?* These additions are, of course, nonstandard.

Materials for Practicing /ə/

assault	sociable	sofa
agree	permanent	boa
affair	specify	soda
oppose	prominent	coma
offend	delegate	cola

1. The police said the crime occurred in the area of the stadium.
2. The editor has said all along it is dangerous to express an opinion.
3. The stowaway was questioned for a long period of time.
4. Canada and America have a lot in common.
5. Of course there are some honorable politicians and public officials.
6. I think I support every charity around.

7. How he got elected again is a mystery to me.
8. Some of my students have been in a coma the whole term.
9. Yes, I'm consistent. I'm violently opposed to violence and completely intolerant of intolerance.
10. I suppose we should use the same criteria to judge all of them.
11. She's not manic-depressive. She's occasionally happy, but generally depressed.
12. He's been awfully quiet about that famous diet lately.
13. I'm always a little suspicious of one who announces his piety.
14. It would take a miracle for the president to present an interesting speech.
15. Is disobedience to law ever justified in this society?

/ɝ/ (ûr)

Production of /ɝ/ (ûr)

If you lift your tongue tip upward to a position just in back of the alveolar ridge, curl the raised tongue tip back slightly toward the hard palate, lift the middle of the tongue up near the hard palate, leave the lips unrounded, and emit the air stream through the mouth with the vocal folds vibrating, you will produce the stressed tense high central vowel heard in the words *sir* and *her*. In IPA, this sound is represented by /ɝ/; in the dictionaries, it is represented by ûr. This stressed vowel is tense and long. The amount of retroflexion (curling back) of the tongue (which gives the sound its "*r*-coloring") varies greatly from person to person and region to region. We classify this sound as a *tense high central vowel*.

Allophones of /ɝ/ (ûr)

There is a variant form, or allophone, of this vowel heard mostly in New England and New York City, which we represent in IPA by [ɜ]. If you arch the center of your tongue in the center of your mouth, as you would on /ɝ/, but let your tongue tip lie low in the front of your mouth rather than curl it back behind the upper gum ridge, you will produce this allophone. Many Southerners as well as Easterners use this variation in place of /ɝ/. Probably because of the influence of radio and television, however, the use of this allophone (an *r*-less variation) seems to be decreasing even in New York City.

Common Deviations or Problems in the Production of /ɝ/ (ûr)

There are four problems associated with the production of this vowel: (1) excessive retraction, (2) substitution of [ɜɪ], (3) substitution of /ɔɪ/, and (4) omission of "*r*-coloring" before a vowel.

1. *Excessive retraction.* If you pull the tongue tip too far back toward

the palate or the center of the tongue too far back in the mouth, you will distort the vowel. This distortion is more common in the Midwest and Southwest than in the rest of the United States. Some authors, to indicate this vowel distortion, have noted that people said *vurrry, purrrty,* or *Amurrrica.*

2. *Substitution of* [ɜɪ]. Some speakers who use the r-less variation of the vowel turn the vowel into a diphthong before consonants. They add the front vowel /ɪ/ (ĭ) as an off-glide after the vowel before the consonant. The word *heard,* then, becomes [hɜɪd].

3. *Substitution of* /ɔɪ/ (oi). This distortion is not heard as frequently as the preceding distortion, but it is still heard occasionally. This distortion also is used by speakers who ordinarily use the r-less variation of the vowel ([ɜ]). Substituting this diphthong for the vowel when it occurs before a consonant creates a number of homophones (sound alike words). It is nonstandard. Check the following pairs of words to be sure you make a clear distinction between them. The word in the left-hand column will contain /ɝ/ (ûr); the word in the right-hand column will contain /ɔɪ/ (oi).

/ɝ/ (ûr) AND /ɔɪ/ (oi) CONTRAST		
	learn	loin
	hurt	Hoyt
	bird	Boyd
	purrs	poise
	verse	voice
	Kern	coin
	Earl	oil
	Berle	boil
	curl	coil
	furled	foiled
	early	oily
	adjourning	adjoining
	Herman	Hoyman

4. *Omission of r-coloring before a vowel.* Even in dialects and idiolects that omit the r-coloring when it is final in a word or syllable before a consonant, the r-coloring is restored when the sound is followed by a vowel. In the sentence "She has a fur coat," the allophone [ɜ] might logically appear in the word *fur.* A consonant follows the /ɝ/ vowel, and the r-coloring may disappear. In the sentence "She left the fur on the seat," the r-less allophone should not appear. The r-coloring is restored for linking with the following vowel. This reappearing r-coloring, by the way, is called "linking R." To omit it before a vowel is nonstandard. Read each of these sentences aloud. There is a "linking R" possibility in each of them. Listen for it. Do you include or omit the r-coloring?

I told her about it.
Wearing fur is immoral.
That "curr" is my best friend!
They were even at the turn.
I prefer a new one.
Will it occur again?
It did not deter anyone.
What can I confer on you?
I will defer any more examples.

Materials for Practicing /ɝ/ (ûr)

err	dirty	myrrh
ermine	purple	burr
early	burly	cur
earn	servant	her
erstwhile	nervous	fur
Erwin	mercy	sir

If you tend to labialize the /r/ phoneme (see pp. 172–173), you may also use the lips to make the related vowel /ɝ/ (ûr). The /ɔɪ/ (oi) substitution results from using the lips instead of forming the vowel with the correct tongue placement. The /ɝ/ (ûr) vowel is made with the tongue lifted higher in the center of the mouth than it is on the central vowel (/ʌ/ (ŭ). If you substitute /ɔɪ/ (oi), you will lift the back of the tongue up in back as you purse the lips. Both of these movements (tongue and lips) distort the /ɝ/ (ûr) sound. To get the "feel" of the central position, first say a word containing the /ʌ/ (ŭ); then check to see where the tongue and lips are to form that sound. Then, by lifting the tongue up in the *center* toward the palate from the place where you made /ʌ/ (ŭ), and by keeping the lips from rounding and tensing, you can make a good /ɝ/ (ûr) in the same context. Then move on to /ɝ/ (ûr) alone. We are using alveolar sounds before these vowels, because they get your tongue moving in the right neighborhood. Try these sequences, remembering our instructions:

/ʌ/ (ŭ) AND /ɝ/ (ûr) CONTRAST

ton	turn	earn
done	durn	earn
Lund	learned	earned
dud	dirge	urge
luck	lurk	irk
a Tully	attorney	Ernie
doth	dearth	earth
tuck	Turk	irk

Tum	term	Irma
stub	disturb	herb
duck	Dirk	irk
Tully	Turley	early
tub	turban	urban
tux	Turks	irks
enough	a nerve	Irv
tummy	determine	ermine
this tub	disturb	herb
stun	stern	earn
Lux	lurks	irks

1. The early bird can have the worm.
2. The quarterback turned before hurling the spheroid across the field.
3. For the third time, I refer you to your textbook.
4. I urge you to come to the rehearsal this evening.
5. They were deterred by their fear of violence.
6. She not only spurned his advances; she gave him a sermon.
7. The meeting adjourned without determining what to do next.
8. The driver averted a tragedy by swerving sharply to the right.
9. We are certain that you are informed and concerned about public affairs.
10. He never shirks a burden, and he serves without pay.
11. She may be earnest, but she erred.
12. Urchins followed us everywhere in the urban areas.
13. You don't deserve a third chance.
14. He curves the grades, but is it worth learning nothing?
15. My grades this term are worse than the term before.
16. Perversely religious, he would neither confirm nor deny that the earth is flat.
17. So-called "dirty words" do not disturb me.
18. I admit I squirmed a little when the nurse gave me the injection.
19. Our reserve quarterback suffered a few reverses.
20. It's male politicians who skirt the issue and throw the dirt.
21. I'm stunned the teacher is so stern.
22. Did Professor Gulley really go to the girly show?
23. She forgot and burned the buns.
24. A pert little girl, she putts well.
25. She's so curt; her remarks are always cutting.
26. My cat Anathema has such poise; she purrs all the time.
27. I'm not averse to music, but a voice she does not have.
28. I've learned to like roast pork loin.
29. Earl consumes gallons of olive oil.
30. Of course he's surly; his reputation is soiled.

/ɚ/ (ər)

Production of /ɚ/ (ər)

The unstressed equivalent of the stressed vowel /ɜ/ (ûr) is the short neutral vowel with an r-coloring heard in unstressed syllables. It is heard, for example, in the first syllable of the word *perhaps* and the second syllable of the word *other*. The dictionary symbol is ər, and the IPA symbol for the sound is /ɚ/. You will note that the IPA symbol is a schwa with a little *r* hook on it. Like the schwa, this vowel is used in unstressed syllables, and like the /ɜ/ (ûr), it is r-colored. It is more lax and shorter than the /ɜ/ (ûr), made with the lips unrounded and the center of the tongue raised up toward the center of the mouth and the tip of the tongue curled back toward the palate behind the upper gum ridge. The air is emitted through the mouth with the vocal folds vibrating. As in the case of the stressed vowel /ɜ/ (ûr), the amount of retroflexion (curling back) of the tip of the tongue varies greatly.

Allophones of /ɚ/ (ər)

The unstressed /ɚ/ (ər) vowel occurs in three contexts in American English: (1) alone as the vowel of an unstressed syllable, (2) before final consonants in a syllable, and (3) in final position after vowels and diphthongs.

In the words *perhaps* and *other*, the /ɚ/ (ər) occurs at the end of a syllable; it is the only vowel in the syllables in which it occurs in those two words. The /ɚ/ (ər) occupies the same position in the words *actor* and *nadir*. (Yes, even though the spelling is different, both words contain the same sound.)

Most American speakers use the /ɚ/ (ər) vowel when the letter *r* precedes a consonant. The sound would occur, then, before the final consonant in such words as *harm, heart, tired, bored,* and *word*. The word *arm* is made up of three sounds: /ɑ/ (ä), /ɚ/ (ər), and /m/. The sounds /ɑ/ (ä) and /ɚ/ (ər) form a diphthong (a two-vowel blend), but each of the vowels retains its individual identity, so this diphthong is not a phonemic diphthong (a phoneme—single sound—itself). Pronounce the following words containing /ɑ/ (ä) plus /ɚ/ (ər) before a consonant:

arm	card
harm	barred
charm	jarred
farm	marred
alarm	art
harp	heart
hard	part
lard	Bart

guard	start
garden	smart
pardon	sharp
Carl	cart
Charles	dart
Marlboro	mart
gnarled	tart
barn	darn
tarnish	varnish
schoolmarm	tardy

The unstressed vowel /ɚ/ (ər) also occurs in final position in syllables after vowels and diphthongs. Pronounce the words *ear, air, are, our,* and *ire.* The last sound in each word is the little vowel /ɚ/ (ər).

In addition to the more common vowel /ɚ/ (ər), there is a variation of this sound—an allophone—that is r-less. This little vowel without the r-coloring, of course, would be the schwa. Speakers who use the r-less /ɜ/ rather than the /ɝ/ also ordinarily use the /ə/ in place of /ɚ/. These speakers would pronounce the word *mother* as /mʌðə/ (mŭthə), but if the next word in the phrase began with a vowel, they would put the *r* back in. (The "linking-*r*" principle is applied to the stressed /ɝ/ (ûr) *and* the unstressed vowel /ɚ/ (ər).) Speakers who use /ə/ in place of /ɚ/ (ər) would also use this allophone before a final consonant in a syllable. They would therefore omit the r-coloring in such words as *card* and *harm.* They would pronounce these words simply with a lengthened /ɑ/ (ä). They would also omit the r-coloring after a vowel or diphthong, but they *would* use /ə/. *Hour,* then, would be pronounced /ɑuə/ (ouə).

Common Deviations or Problems in the Production of /ɚ/ (ər)

There are three common problems associated with this sound: (1) excessive retraction, (2) substitution of /ɔɚ/, (ôr) and (3) omission of r-coloring before a vowel.

1. *Excessive retraction.* If you pull the tongue too far back toward the back of the mouth and curl the tongue tip too far back toward the palate, you will distort the sound. This vowel is a neutral central vowel—not a back vowel.

2. *Substitution of* /ɔɚ/ (ôr). Some people who think in terms of pronouncing written letters rather than vocal sounds are led into "spelling mispronunciations." You may have heard someone say *educatawr* (/ ɛdʒukeɪtɔɚ /) for *educator* (/ ɛdʒukeɪtɚ /) or *actawr* (/ æktɔɚ /) for *actor* (/æktɚ /). This substitution results from a misunderstanding of the way language works and is pedantic, affected, and nonstandard. The /ɚ/ (ər) can be spelled many different ways: *er, or, ar, ir, ur, ure, yr,*

oar, or *re*. Note your pronunciation of the following words: *other, educator, wizard, nadir, murmur, measure, satyr, cupboard, and theatre.* You should find that the same vowel (/ɚ/) occurs in the last syllable of all the words.

3. *Omission of r-coloring before a vowel.* We have discussed the "linking *r*" before. If a speaker omits the "linking *r*" before a syllable or word beginning with a vowel, the omission is nonstandard—even in an "r-less dialect." Read these few sentences aloud. Each sentence affords you an opportunity to use the "linking *r*." Check to hear whether you omit it.

Mother is at home.
I'm suffering.
It's either a yes or a no.　　(That's *two* chances!)
Here is a picture of me.　　(Two more!)
Figure it out.

Materials for Practicing /ɚ/ (ər)

mother	humor	pleasure	scepter
father	actor	treasure	theater
bother	factor	pressure	pillar
brother	mirror	measure	tapir
murmur	murder	further	surfer
collar	comfort	dullard	labor
dollar	effort	collard	nadir
pillar	glamour	flavor	tumor
sugar	clamor	favor	similar

forbid	surmount	perform
forbade	survey (v.)	perfume
forgive	surmise	persuade
forget	survival	perhaps

1. We cannot permit you to perjure yourself.
2. You must maintain your humor to survive.
3. I would rather not search for the treasure.
4. Weather hindered the surfers from practicing yesterday.
5. We persuaded him to walk under a ladder and break the mirror.
6. The performance will be given either this week or next.
7. My brother made his sacrifice at the altar.
8. Perhaps she can't be bothered with answering the phone.
9. It is no pleasure for an actor to memorize his lines.
10. The underprivileged have difficulty in surmounting their problems.
11. I may be able to forget, but I'll never be able to forgive her.
12. You'd better believe that debtor who says, "I'll be forever indebted to you."

13. I took no pleasure in the doctor's reassurances.
14. The director tried too hard to impress the alarmed benefactor.
15. The governor may not be a perfect dullard (hardly anyone is perfect), but he's certainly no scholar either.
16. There is no need to pursue this further.
17. Better to suffer in silence than to alarm your hard-working supervisor.
18. After all, my vote may be a factor in the outcome.
19. Our distance runner is ready to run another race.
20. I'm learning to raise better ferns; it's fun.
21. I could hardly believe my ears. The senator was giving a lecture on ethics.
22. The preacher warned us to ponder our wicked ways.
23. It doesn't matter. Neither of us will bother it.
24. I'd pay top dollar for a tender and juicy steak.
25. Rockefeller and his brothers are all fairly comfortable.

The Three Phonemic Diphthongs

A *diphthong*, as we said earlier, is a blend of two vowels. Diphthongs function as vowels in the language (see pp. 47–48), but they differ from pure vowels in that the lips and tongue move during the production of the sound. This continuous movement changes the quality of the sound during its production. There are two elements in a diphthong (two simple vowels) that are melded together by continuous movement from the position of one element to the position of the other.

We have discussed two standard diphthongal allophones: [oʊ], an allophone of /o/ (ō), and [eɪ], an allophone of /e/ (ā). These diphthongs are variations of their respective phonemes, rather than separate phonemes. If you replace [o] [ȯ] with [oʊ] (ō) (or vice versa), the meaning is not affected; hence, they are merely variations of the same phoneme. The difference between [o] (ȯ) and [oʊ] (ō) or between [e] (ȧ) and [eɪ] (ā) does not distinguish one word from another. If they were separate phonemes, it would.

We have also looked at the problem of diphthongizing—turning pure vowels into diphthongs and, thus, distorting them. Even though the vowels are distorted by this elongation (and the addition of an extra vowel element), we still recognize them as the same phonemes (even if slightly out of whack).

We have three diphthongs in the language that *are* phonemic diphthongs. These do change meaning when we substitute them for other vowels, and each of them (although made up of two elements) is really a single sound—that is, a single phoneme unit in the language. These three *phonemic diphthongs* are heard in the words *bough, buy,* and *boy.*

The first is represented in IPA by /ɑʊ/ and in the dictionaries by ou; the second is represented in IPA by /ɑɪ/ and in the dictionaries by ī; and the third is represented in IPA by /ɔɪ/ and in the dictionaries by oi.

Let us look at these three sounds a little more to be clear about why they are *phonemic* diphthongs.

The vowel sound in the word *high* is represented in IPA by two symbols, because it is made up of two elements. The lips and tongue begin to make the sound at about the position for the vowel in *alms* (the tongue may be a little higher and farther front) and move toward the position for the vowel in the word *eat*. Because the tongue does not get quite as high and tense as in the production of the vowel in *eat*, phoneticians have used the symbol for the vowel in *it* to represent the second element of this diphthong. In IPA, then, the diphthong is represented as /ɑɪ/ (or ɑɪ/). We have seen each of those vowels before. /ɑ/ (ä) and /ɪ/ (ĭ) are themselves phonemes in English. Can a sound made by blending the two of them become a third phoneme—different and separate from either of them? Well, let's check. Go back to the word *high* (/hɑɪ/). Is that word the same or completely different in meaning from the word *ha* (/hɑ/)? And is the word *high* the same or completely different in meaning from the word *he* (/hi/)? (Remember, we move toward the /i/ (ē) vowel when making the /ɑɪ/ (ī) sound.) The answer is obvious. You cannot substitute /ɑɪ/ (ī) for either /ɑ/ (ä) or /i/ (ē). You cannot substitute it for /ɪ/ (ĭ) either. *Hide* and *hid* are different words in English; the change of /ɑɪ/ (ī) to /ɪ/ (ĭ) changes the meaning, so they are separate and distinct phonemes in English.

You can check on the other two phonemic diphthongs in the same way. Note that *wowed* (/ɑʊ/ or ou), *wad* (/ɑ/ or ä), *wooed* (/u/ or ōō), and *wood* (/ʊ/ or oo) are all different words in English. Hence, they each contain a distinct vowel sound (phoneme). Now look at the fact that *foil* (/ɔɪ/ or oi), *fall* (/ɔ/ or ô), *feel* (/i/ or ē), and *fill* (/ɪ/ or ĭ) are all different words in English; they, too, each contain a separate and distinct vowel phoneme.

The three phonemic diphthongs definitely function as single sounds— indivisible sounds—in the language; they are vowel phonemes too.

/ɑʊ/ (ou)

Production of the /ɑʊ/ (ou)

If you start with your lips and tongue in position for forming the /ɑ/ (ä)—the vowel in the word *alms*—and then glide from that vowel smoothly toward the position of the lips and tongue used to form /u/ (ōō)—the vowel in the word *ooze*—you will produce the phonemic diphthong heard in the words *bough* and *now*. We told you to move *toward* the position for /u/, because it is easier to explain the sound that way. The first element of the diphthong is longer than the second element. The IPA symbol for this diphthong is /ɑʊ/; it is represented in the dictionaries by ou.

You will notice that at the start of this diphthong the mouth is open wide and the lips are relaxed; the tongue is almost flat in the mouth. At the end of this diphthong, the lips are closed down into a pucker, the lips are more tense, and the back of the tongue has been raised high in the back of the mouth. The diphthong starts from approximately the position for /ɑ/ (ä) and moves almost to the postion for /u/ (o͞o).

Allophones of /ɑʊ/ (ou)

There are two allophones, or variations, of this diphthong. We have already explained one variation of the sound and have given you the phonetic symbols for this allophone: [ɑʊ]. Although we gave you this allophone first, and we have used the symbol /ɑʊ/ to represent the phoneme itself, this allophone is probably less common than the second variation of the phoneme. We chose to present the sound in this way because it is much less confusing for those of you who speak English as a second language and because it uses phonemic symbols rather than symbols of allophones.

If you have learned English as a second language, you may have some difficulty with this phoneme. You should have little trouble making a perfectly acceptable, standard variation of this phoneme if you combine the /ɑ/ (ä) and /u/ (o͞o)—sounds you probably already use in your first language.

The second variation of this phoneme is made by starting with the lips and tongue in position to form the [a] allophone of /æ/ (ă) and gliding from that position up toward the position of /u/ (o͞o). In this allophone, the sound begins with the front of the tongue raised *very* slightly; the tongue is still *almost* flat in the mouth. This variation ([aʊ]) is the more common of the two variants, but both are standard.

Common Deviations and Problems in the Production of /ɑʊ/ (ou)

There are five common problems associated with the production of this phoneme: (1) raising and fronting, (2) raising and centering, (3) nasalization, (4) substitution of /ɑ/ (ä), [a], or /æ/ (ă), and (5) substitution of /ɑə/ (äə) or [aə].

Of all the diphthongs, this one is the most frequently distorted in all sections of the United States; and of all the diphthongs, this one, when distorted, is the most unpleasant.

1. *Raising and Fronting.* If you begin the diphthong with the tongue raised too high in the front of the mouth, you will produce a flat and very unpleasant sound. If you tend to raise the /æ/ (ă) vowel, you should be especially careful in producing this diphthong. You may find that you

not only substitute [æʊ] for [aʊ] but that you substitute a diphthong initiated with a raised form of /æ/. The /aʊ/ (ou) should begin with the mouth open and the tongue relatively flat in the mouth. If you are not certain that you are producing the sound correctly, check with a mirror.

Pronounce these words, and check the placement of your tongue at the beginning of the /aʊ/ (ou) sound:

bout
out
owl
our
outline
ounce
doubt
town
proud

2. *Raising and centering.* This distortion is caused, again, by raising your tongue too high in your mouth as you begin the /aʊ/ (ou) sound. If you raise your tongue in the center of your mouth, you will produce the diphthong [ɜʊ], which (like the raised and fronted distortion) is nonstandard.

3. *Nasalization.* Many speakers who raise and front the diphthong also nasalize it. The result is that the sound is not only "flattened" but it is also "pinched" through the nose. This nasalized form is more likely to occur before the nasal consonants, but it can occur when it is neither preceded nor followed by an /m/, /n/, or /ŋ/ (n̄g). You must work to be sure that the velum fully closes off the passage to the nose, that the mouth is open, and that the air stream is emitted only through the mouth. Pronounce the word *how*. Now hold your nose and pronounce the word again. It should sound exactly the same, and you should not feel any air trying to come out of the nose while you say the word. If there is air trying to come out of the nose, then you are nasalizing the sound and you need practice to make the diphthong oral rather than nasal.

You must be especially careful about nasalizing this diphthong when it precedes a nasal consonant. There the temptation will be severe. Resist it. Work for a good *oral* diphthong and good nasal resonance on the nasal consonant that follows. Try these words aloud, and check for nasalization of the diphthong:

/aʊ/ (ou) BEFORE /n/   brown
                        down
                        found

founder
flounder
fountain
gown
ground
hound
count
lounge
mound
mount
noun
ounce
pounce
pound
round
sound
astounding
town
trounce
wound (past tense of *wind*)

4. *Substitution of* /a/ (ä), [a], *or* /æ/ (ă). This distortion is more common in the South than in the rest of the United States. It results from omission of the second element in the diphthong. If the diphthong is shortened by omitting the second vowel ([ʊ]), then /ɑʊ/ (ou) becomes simply /ɑ/ (ä) or /a/—or even /æ/ (ă) if that is the vowel they use to begin the "diphthong." Needless to say, this distortion is nonstandard. Check to hear if you tend to omit the second element in the diphthong. Say the sentence "How are you?" as you would normally say it. Listen to your pronunciation of the word *how*. Does it sound like the word *ha* or perhaps the word *half* with the /f/ left off? If so, you are not moving to the second element of the diphthong.

If you have this problem, pronounce the word *ha* followed by the word *ooze* without taking a breath or a break between them. Do it in slow motion to see and feel how the lips and tongue move from the end of *ha* to the beginning of *ooze*. Then speed up the pronunciation a little each time until the words are blended into *how's*. If you preserved the /ɑ/ (ä) from *ha* and the /u/ (o͞o) from *ooze*, you should have a complete diphthong—and not just half an /ɑʊ/ (ou).

5. *Substitution of* /ɑə/ (äə) *or* /aə/. Some speakers do not omit the second element of the diphthong entirely, but they use a substitute vowel for the second element. They replace [ʊ] with [ə]. Again, this distortion is more common in the South than in the rest of the United States, but

it does occur in other parts of the country as well. Nationally, this distortion is more likely to occur before /1/ or /ɚ/ (ər).

Try these pairs of words aloud. Do you get a complete (with [ʊ]) diphthong in the /aʊ/ (ou) words, or do they tend to sound like their partners?

/aʊ/ (ou) and /æ/ (ă) CONTRAST	owl	Al
	Cowley	Calley
	howl	Hal
	Powell	pal
	vowel	Val
	cowl	Cal

/aʊ/ (ou) and /ɑ/ (ä) CONTRAST	ours	Rs
	cower	car
	bower	bar
	power	par
	showered	shard
	tower	tar

Materials for Practicing /aʊ/ (ou)

owl	howl	how
out	rout	row
ounce	bounce	bough
hour	sour	sow

/æ/ (ă) and /aʊ/ (ou) CONTRAST	tan	town
	flat	flout
	mass	mouse
	had	how'd
	rat	rout
	scat	scout
	spat	spout
	pat	pout
	bad	bowed
	lad	loud
	cad	cowed
	lot	lout
	have	how've
	math	mouth
	catch	couch
	trance	trounce
	grand	ground
	sand	sound
	hand	hound

band	bound
Rand	round
fanned	found
brand	browned
manned	mound
panned	pound
Flanders	flounders

/ɑ/ (ä) and /ɑʊ/ (ou) CONTRAST

ha	how
ah	ow!
ma	Mao
holly	Howley
collie	Cowley
lot	lout
clot	clout
pot	pout
prod	proud
Roddy	rowdy
rot	rout
tot	tout
dot	doubt
shot	shout
Koch	couch
clod	cloud
bra	brow
Ott	out
got	gout
wand	wound (v.)
fonder	founder
are	our/hour
bond	bound
fond	found
pond	pound
Rhonda	round a . . .
Honda man	hound a man

1. He was astounded that we couldn't tell a noun from a verb.
2. The college does not allow its students to carouse during school hours.
3. How can the college increase its endowment?
4. She seemed very proud of her new gown.
5. I doubt that I'll be able to meet you at the lounge.
6. The announcer took a bow with the rest of the cast.
7. The coach frowned when the center missed the rebound.
8. The queen was crowned at the witching hour.

9. When she gets angry, she goes in the house and pouts.
10. He thinks eating flowers will increase his prowess.
11. According to the announcement, the crowd numbered over a hundred thousand.
12. The rowdy crowd in Times Square waited for the countdown.
13. I would impound every hound in New York—if I had the power.
14. Why is that clown scowling at me?
15. The secretary disavowed his earlier announcement without an ounce of remorse.
16. She paraded as a Boy Scout—until she was found out.
17. Howard's on the City Council, but he has no clout.
18. A scoundrel and a thief! He steals a towel from every hotel he enters.
19. Mr. Powell is the founder of the Anti-Maoist League.
20. He cowered in a corner as the sound of the pounding got louder.
21. She howled with glee as the rout continued.
22. How are we going to get the project off the ground?
23. The student spouted his own slogans back at the frowning teacher.
24. I'm proud to say I've lost twenty pounds.
25. Anyhow, the drought has kept me from drowning.
26. The new endowment was his crowning achievement.
27. How can I live on this allowance with my bills mounting too?
28. I have unbounding faith in the power of greed.
29. Now the county has raised the taxes on the house again.
30. I'm about to quit. At the end of an hour, I still have no outline.

/ɑɪ/ (ī)

Production of the /ɑɪ/ (ī)

If you start with your lips and tongue in position for forming the /ɑ/ (ä)—the vowel in the word *alms*—and then glide from that vowel smoothly toward the position of the lips and tongue used to form /i/ (ē)—the vowel in the word *eat*—you will produce the phonemic diphthong heard in the words *lie* and *buy*. Again, we have told you to move *toward* the lip and tongue position for /i/ (ē) rather than *to* the position for /ɪ/ (ĭ). We believe it is easier to explain the production of the sound in that way, although the phonetic representation of this diphthong is /ɑɪ/ rather than /ɑi/. The positions we give you are approximate anyway, and if you are unfamiliar with this phoneme, you will be more likely to make it correctly following these instructions.

There are two elements in this diphthong; a diphthong, you remember, is one sound made by blending two vowels together. The first element is longer and louder than the second. At the start of this diphthong, the mouth is open wide and the lips are relaxed; the tongue is almost flat in the mouth. You will move the lips and tongue in a smooth, continuous movement from this position to the final position—*during* the production of the sound. At the end of the diphthong, the lips will be slightly spread and a little tensed and the front of the tongue will be raised high in the front of the mouth. The diphthong starts from approximately the position for /ɑ/ (ä) and moves almost to the position for /i/ (ē).

This phoneme is represented in IPA by /ɑɪ/; it is represented in the dictionaries by ī.

Allophones of /ɑɪ/ (ī)

As with the phonemic diphthong /ɑʊ/ (ou), there are two allophones, or variations, of this phoneme. We have already described the first variety of the sound. The phonetic symbol for that allophone is [ɑɪ]. We have also used /ɑɪ/ to represent the phoneme itself, using the symbol for the lowest back vowel /ɑ/ (ä) to represent the first element and the symbol for the lax high front vowel /ɪ/ (ĭ) to represent the second element of the diphthong. Both of those symbols are symbols of phonemes of the language. (See pp. 205–209 and pp. 186–190.)

Of the two allophones of this sound, the [ɑɪ] is probably used less frequently than the second allophone, but both are heard throughout the United States and both are standard.

If you have learned English as a second language, you may have some difficulty with this phoneme. Your first language may not have included this sound in its phonemic structure. If you relate this sound to the two vowels of which it can be blended (/ɑ/ (ä) and /i/ (ē), you should be able to make a perfectly acceptable, standard variation of this phoneme.

The second allophone is made by starting with the lips and tongue in position to form the [a] allophone of /æ/ (see p. 200) and gliding smoothly from that position up toward the position of /i/ (ē). In this allophone, the sound begins with the front of the tongue raised *very* slightly in the front of the mouth. The tongue is still almost flat in the mouth. This variation, represented in IPA by [aɪ], is the more commonly heard of the two allophones.

Common Deviations of Problems in the Production of /ɑɪ/ (ī)

There are three common problems associated with the production of this phoneme: (1) substitution of [a], [aə], /ɑ/, *or* /ɑə/, (2) retraction, and (3) raising.

1. *Substitution of* [a], [aə], /ɑ/, *or* /ɑə/. You may have read stories in which the author spelled the word *I'm* as *Ah'm* in dialogue to represent the substitution of the vowel /ɑ/ (ä) or the combination of the vowel /ɑ/ (ä) plus the off-glide vowel /ə/ for the diphthong /ɑɪ/. This distortion is not uncommon in the South and is characteristic of the speech of the less educated, although you may hear some educated

speakers use it as well. Instead of the /ɑ/ (ä), some speakers substitute the [a] alophone of the low front vowel /æ/ (ă) or that vowel plus the off-glide /ə/. This "flattened sound" is also heard in the South, particularly in the mountain regions. We have heard huge, cheering crowds in sports arenas urging their teams to [faət, faət, faət]! Actually, you will note, these speakers are having trouble with the second vowel of the diphthong. Either they omit the second vowel altogether and leave only the first pure vowel to substitute for the diphthong, or they substitute the schwa for the second vowel /ɪ/ (ĭ). Check your own pronunciation of the personal pronoun *I* to be certain that when the tongue moves from the /a/ or /ɑ/ the front of your tongue moves up to the position of /ɪ/ (ĭ) in the front of your mouth rather than to the position of /ə/ in the center of your mouth. Use a mirror to check the tongue movement.

As you said the word *I* aloud, could you hear, see, and feel the second element of the diphthong? Is the second element (vowel) present? If, in slow motion, the word *I* does not end with a sound very much like /i/ (ē), then you are cutting off the second part of the phoneme.

If you have this problem, pronounce the word *ha* (/hɑ/) followed by the word *eat* without taking a breath or a break between them. Do it in slow motion to see and feel the lips and tongue move from the end of the word *ha* to the beginning of the word *eat*. Then speed up the pronunciation a little each time until the words are blended into the word *height*. The word *height* has three phonemes in it: /h/, /ɑɪ/ (ī), and /t/. The middle phoneme, the peak or nucleus of the syllable, is the phonemic diphthong /ɑɪ/ (ī). Without the second element of the diphthong, however, the word *height* is going to sound like *hot* or *hat*, or some variation of the two words.

2. *Retraction.* In the metropolitan New York area, many speakers pull the tongue back to the back of the mouth on the opening vowel of the diphthong. Actually, it would be more accurate to say that they raise the back of the tongue up in the back of the mouth to form the opening vowel of this diphthong. This retraction markedly distorts the vowel and therefore the phonemic diphthong. A few speakers actually substitute the /ɔ/ (ô) for the [ɑ] or [a] when they initiate the diphthong, so that the word *buy* sounds like *boy*. Most who retract the sound, however, instead substitute the sound halfway between /ɑ/ (ä) and /ɔ/ (ô)—the allophone of both represented by [ɒ] (ŏ)—for the first vowel in the diphthong. You must be certain not to round the lips on this sound. Remember that the /ɔ/ (ô) and [ɒ] (ô) are lip-rounded sounds, where as /ɑ/ (ä) and /a/ are not. And do not pull the tongue back or raise the tongue up in back as you begin this diphthong. The words *odd* (or *add*) and *I'd* should both start with the tongue and lips in about the same position. The tongue and lips should not be tensed as the /ɑɪ/ (ī) begins.

3. *Raising*. If you raise the tongue from the usual position for beginning this diphthong, you will distort the sound. The diphthong begins with the mouth open wide, the jaw relaxed and dropped, and the tongue almost flat in the bottom of the mouth. If, instead, you do not open the mouth sufficiently and raise the tongue, you may produce [æɪ] or [ɛɪ] or [ʌɪ]—depending on whether you raise the tongue in the center or the front of the mouth. The greatest temptation to distort the diphthong in this way occurs after sounds articulated with the tongue tip on the alveolar ridge or the tongue blade on or near the back of the alveolar ridge.

Pronounce these words aloud, and check to be certain that your mouth is wide open, your jaw is lowered and relaxed, and your tongue is almost flat in the bottom of your mouth as you begin the /ɑɪ/ (ī):

I'd	rye	child
tide	sigh	gyro
died	shy	night
lied	xylophone	tight
chide	try	right
strive	dry	strike
retire	rely	deny

If you tend to distort this diphthong by raising the beginning vowel, try these sequences. Try to match the vowel from the first word when you *begin* the diphthong in the other words:

odd	I'd	tide	tried	denied
Oz	eyes	lies	cries	ties
of	I've	chive	drive	strive
ah	I	shy	nigh	gyrate
are	ire	dire	lyre	desire

Materials for Practicing /ɑɪ/ (ī)

I	height	high
aisle	style	sty
Ives	dives	die
icy	spicy	spy
iris	virus	vie
eyed	dried	dry
Isis	crisis	cry
icing	slicing	sly
idling	sideling	sigh
isle	while	why
Ina	shiner	shy
I'd	fried	fry

ice	lice	lie
ides	sides	sigh
I'll	Nile	nigh
I'm	time	tie
Ike	pike	pie
ire	fire	fie
I've	rive	rye
eyes	buys	buy

In the following pairs of words, the first word of each pair contains the pure vowel /ɑ/ (ä) and the second word contains the phonemic diphthong /ɑɪ/ (ī).

/ɑ/ (ä) AND /ɑɪ/ (ī) CONTRAST

rah!	rye
bah!	buy
shah	shy
ha!	high
of	I've
odd	I'd
alm	I'm
are	ire
olive	I live
odyssey	Ida see
hot	height
Tom	time
job	jibe
rod	ride
slot	sleight
Ron	rind
tot	tight
God	guide
conned	kind
plod	plied
fond	find
plot	plight

The following pairs of words differ in that the first word of each pair contains the phonemic diphthong /ɔɪ/ (oi) and the second word of each pair contains the phonemic diphthong /ɑɪ/ (ī).

/ɔɪ/ (oi) AND /ɑɪ/ (ī) CONTRAST

oil	aisle, isle, I'll
boy	buy
coy	chi
poi	pie
coined	kind
ploy	ply

Roy	rye
toy	tie
loin	line
devoid	divide
poise	pies
voice	vice
Hoyle	heil
hoist	heist
foil	file
boil	bile
Doyle	dial
coil	Kyle
void	vied

1. I have been invited to a student riot this weekend.
2. I had no idea you would try to bribe me!
3. I plan to buy an excellent item for my collection.
4. Perhaps you can get an idea of the size of the island from this diagram.
5. Time and tide are a temptation for surfers.
6. Sy is an aspiring politician.
7. The high jumper is trying for a record height.
8. Why are you buying a hundred pounds of ice?
9. Forgive me for prying, but what are your designs?
10. We can drive it in about five hours.
11. I will not sign the contract until I've read it.
12. We defied the ban and held the biennial meeting.
13. I was reminded that I have a prior commitment.
14. The rhyme scheme defies analysis!
15. Riding up the Nile was the most exciting experience of my life.
16. This is an ideal time to remind you to acquire new habits.
17. I'm tired of bigots who "have no bias."
18. They applied calamine lotion to my poison ivy.
19. I could not quite identify the kind of smile it was.
20. I didn't mind the citation, but I was required to pay a fine.
21. My wife is quite happy—only when she is buying something.
22. I had to devise a way to find the guide.
23. Larry's nearly blind, but he would rather drive at night.
24. Why does nobody seem to admire my gigantic biceps?
25. The psychiatrist kept reminding me of my identity crisis.
26. With a little more time, I might come up with a good reply.
27. Who could deny my piety? I have no minor vices.
28. A child would not have enough guile to be President.
29. Is it a crime to strive to be happy?

30. She whined all the while. I was just beside myself!
31. Don't chime in. You might be even more unkind.
32. Next time, file a little earlier and avoid the fine.
33. It's time for you to try writing your own kind of exercises.

/ɔɪ/ (oi)

Production of the /ɔɪ/ (oi)

If you put your lips and tongue in the position for producing /ɔ/ (ô) and move smoothly into the position for producing /ɪ/ (ĭ), you will produce the phonemic diphthong heard in the words *boy* and *joy*. This sound is represented in IPA by /ɔɪ/ and in the dictionaries by oi.

The diphthong begins with the vowel [ɔ] (ô) and ends in the vowel [ɪ] (ĭ). Indeed, if you have trouble getting in the second element of the diphthong, we should tell you (as we did in discussing the phonemic diphthong /aɪ/ (ī) to move toward the /i/ (ē) vowel. That advice gives you a target to aim for and should help you get the [ɪ] (ĭ) into the diphthong.

As the diphthong begins, the lips are rounded with some tension and the back of the tongue is raised in the back of the mouth. It is important that you begin the movements required to make this sound in the customary position. Otherwise, the sound will be distorted.

Common Deviations and Problems in the Production of /ɔɪ/ (oi)

There are five common problems associated with the production of this sound: (1) substitution of /ɝ/ (ûr) for /ɔɪ/ (oi), (2) substitution of [ɜɪ] for /ɔɪ/ (oi), (3) substitution of /ɔ/ (ô) or [ɔə] (ôə) for /ɔɪ/ (oi), (4) substitution of /aɪ/ (ī) for /ɔɪ/ (oi), and (5) triphthongation.

1. *Substitution of /ɝ/ (ûr) for /ɔɪ/* (oi). Occasionally in metropolitan New York or in the South you may hear someone say *Berle* for *boil*, *Earl* for *oil*, or *furl* for *foil*. It is considered nonstandard. (See p. 232 for some other /ɝ/ (ûr) and /ɔɪ/ (oi) contrasts.

2. *Substitution of* [ɜɪ] *for /ɔɪ/* (oi). If you raise the center of the tongue high in the center of the mouth rather than the back of the tongue in the back of the mouth at the beginning of this diphthong, you will produce this distortion. (See p. 231 for a discussion of the [ɜ] allophone of /ɝ/.) Check your pronunciation of the following words to see if you make this substitution:

hoist
goiter
foil
coil
joist

moist
join
joint
point
spoil
poison

If you do distort the /ɔɪ/ (oi) in this way, you are substituting a high central vowel for a low back vowel at the beginning of the diphthong.

3. *Substitution of* /ɔ/ (ô) *or* [ɔə] (ôə) *for* /ɔɪ/ (oi). In the South, you may hear the substitution of the vowel /ɔ/ (ô) or the nonstandard diphthong [ɔə] (ôə) for /ɔɪ/ (oi). If the pure vowel is substituted, the problem is simply one of omission; the second element of the phonemic diphthong has not been included and the result is another phoneme entirely—/ɔ/ (ô). If the other version of this distortion is examined, you see that the problem still is the second element of the diphthong. This time, however, /ə/—the little neutral vowel—has replaced the second element of the diphthong [ɪ]. The /ɪ/ (ĭ) is a high front vowel—made with the front of the tongue high in the front of the mouth; the schwa is made with the center of the tongue raised in the center of the mouth. This substitution changes the sound greatly. In both versions of this distortion—either /ɔ/ (ô) or [ɔə] (ôə) substituted for /ɔɪ/ (oi)—the result is that the word *oil* will sound like a drawled version of *all*, and *boil* will resemble *ball*.

Be certain that the front of your tongue moves to the high front /ɪ/ (ĭ) position at the end of the diphthong; the tongue moves front, not center.

Read the following pairs of words aloud. The first word will be pronounced with /ɔ/ (ô), and the second word with /ɔɪ/ (oi). We have chosen words where /l/ follows the two sounds, because that context offers the greatest temptation to make this substitution.

/ɔ/ (ô) AND /ɔɪ/ (oi) CONTRAST		
	all	oil
	ball	boil
	balled	boiled
	brawled	broiled
	call	coil
	called	coiled
	fall	foil
	hall	Hoyle
	Saul	soil
	tall	toil

4. *Substitution of* /ɑɪ/ (ĭ) *for* /ɔɪ/ (oi). Another distortion of the /ɔɪ/ (oi) is heard from time to time, particularly in the South. You may

hear a few speakers still say *bile* for *boil*, *tile* for *toil*, and *pint* for *point*. This substitution, of course, is nonstandard; it replaces one phonemic diphthong with another one.

5. *Triphthongation.* When /l/ follows /ɔɪ/ (oi), some speakers turn the diphthong into a triphthong. The phoneme has two elements; these speakers stretch it into three elements. They either add a schwa off-glide at the end of the diphthong (2 + 1 = 3), or they add the schwa off-glide and change the /ɪ/ into the glide consonant /j/ (y). Thus, *oil* becomes either *oy-ul* or *oy-yul*. Maybe it would be clearer in phonetics: [ɔɪl] becomes either [ɔɪəl] or [ɔjəl]. Check your own pronunciation of these few words to see if you tend to make the diphthong into a triphthong.

oil
boil
coil
foil
Hoyle
soil
toil

Frankly, this deviation makes us recoyal (recoil)!

Materials for Practicing /ɔɪ/ (oi)

oil	boil	boy
ointment	appointment	poi
	joint	joy
	soil	soy
	coin	coy
	Reuters	Roy
	toil	toy

1. The boys were forced to eat oysters during the initiation.
2. The royal family seemed to enjoy the performance.
3. He was anointed with oil and water.
4. The most poignant moment of the play was ruined by a noise in the audience.
5. Why would anyone want to join an organization in such turmoil?
6. Joyce tried to avoid my glances.
7. Reuters and Tass were embroiled in a controversy over the story.
8. She thought the poi had poisoned her.
9. The noise seemed to be coming from an adjoining room.
10. Roy has unusual poise on the speaking platform.
11. Ointment was applied to the wounds quickly.
12. Mr. Boyd collects old coins.
13. It was too early in the season for the water to be that oily.

14. You recoiled the last time too, as I recall.
15. I will not be foiled in my attempts this fall.
16. They toiled all day trying to lay the bathroom tile.
17. Mr. Berle has a low boiling point.
18. This is not the first time you've been embroiled in a brawl.
19. Sometimes I enjoy reading the *Village Voice*.
20. No matter what your foibles, this is the kind of joint everyone enjoys.
21. I don't feel exploited, but I'm still annoyed.
22. Her eyes were moist as the royal pair passed.
23. She just pointed to the empty pint bottle in the cloister.
24. I'm rejoicing because his ploy didn't work.
25. I'm employed full-time to repair the boiler.

4
Sound Changes

IN CHAPTER 2, we talked about the forty-two individual phonemes of the language. But the truth is that, in everyday speech, we do not talk a sound at a time—first one, then the next, and so on in a one-by-one sequence. Sounds, as we have said, are made by movements, and each sound is produced by a set of movements. *But* those sets of movements overlap in connected speech. When we speak, there are simultaneous movements going on much of the time. We start the next sound before the last sound is finished, or we perform the movements for two sounds at the same time.

As you would expect, a sound uttered all by its lonesome self is one thing, but that sound uttered in combination with other sounds in connected speech will be different. That sound will have to adjust to the other sounds around it. Or, to be more exact, the movements required to make a sound will have to be modified to accommodate those movements required for the sounds that precede, follow, and overlap the sound.

"The easiest way out" is a natural tendency among human beings, and it applies to articulation of speech sounds. Speaking, like any other form of human physical activity, requires coordination. But some movements are easier to perform and easier to combine (perform simultaneously) than others. If we have a choice, we human beings will choose the easier set of movements. That is what sound change in the language is all about.

At this point, we must warn you that some changes have gained social acceptance (and thus become "Standard") and that others have not. You must learn which sound changes are socially acceptable, are in style, or are "Standard" (they are all the same) and which are not. And you will find that the difference is not in the *kind* of change (there are standard and nonstandard assimilations for example), but in the specific change itself. These differences you must simply learn on an individual change basis. (The omission of the first r when pronouncing *February* and the omission of the g when pronouncing *recognize* are both dissimilations, but the first is "standard" and the second is not.)

We will look briefly at three kinds of sound changes in our language: assimilation, dissimilation, and vowel gradation. One at a time. In succession. And not overlapping.

Assimilation

If a sound changes because of the influence of a neighboring sound, that change is labeled *assimilation*. Assimilation, of course, has to do with adjusting—with fitting in; food is assimilated into our body tissues, and newcomers are assimilated as citizens into our country. In both instances, adjustments must take place for assimilation to occur. So with sounds: Adjustments must take place if they are to fit into their environment more easily.

As we said, sounds are not produced as isolated entities in meaningful speech, and some sounds are regularly changed in certain contexts in order to make the flow of speech easier. Assimilation is not necessarily "sloppy speech"; rather, it is a regular attribute of socially acceptable speech patterns. It is true that some assimilations are considered lazy, or uneducated, or nonstandard. But assimilations do occur that are customary and acceptable. Indeed, failure to use these standard assimilations sounds affected and pedantic. (At a recent performance of the American Ballet Theatre, for example, a spokesperson for the company announced that she wanted to *ĭs-syōō* (/ɪsju/) an invitation to attend a gala. At the stilted, unassimilated pronunciation of the word *issue*, the audience smiled and giggled.)

Of course, omission of a number of sounds and assimilation of the sounds remaining is careless and nonstandard. For example, /dɪdʒʊit/ is now acceptable for "Did you eat?" but /dʒit/ (*jēt*) is what John Davenport, in his delightful *New Yorker* article (June 8, 1949), calls "Slurvian." "Slurvian" is the language of those who slur their words and treat the language with slovenly disrespect.

There are two definitions of assimilation. Assimilation is either (1) absorption and incorporation—swallowing up and including, or (2) causing to resemble—influencing to produce more alikeness. Both definitions are relevant to our discussion of sound changes, because there are two kinds of assimilation in language: (1) complete and (2) partial, or incomplete. Full, or complete, assimilation involves absorbing or incorporating a sound into an adjacent sound. Partial, or incomplete, assimilation involves a sound's becoming more like an adjacent sound. Both forms of assimilation occur in American English.

We will look at both complete and incomplete assimilation briefly.

COMPLETE ASSIMILATION

Full or complete assimilation occurs when a sound in absorbed into an adjacent sound. In full or complete assimilation, the original sound disappears; it loses its identity. It does not just change its nature, it loses its nature. It is no longer heard—in any form.

Pronounce the following material as you would in ordinary conversation:

> this shore
> less sure
> miss sugar
> horse shoe
> his shirt
> Nothing is sure.

What happened to the /s/ or /z/ at the end of each word before the word beginning with /ʃ/ (sh)? If you are not sure, try them out loud again, remembering to pronounce them as a phrase as you usually do.

Did you discover that the /s/ or /z/ disappeared? That is an example of full or complete assimilation. The /s/ or /z/ has been absorbed by its neighbor /ʃ/ (sh).

Many of our present "silent letters" are visible relics of complete assimilations that occurred long ago. We have preserved the earlier pronunciations in the spelling, long after the sound represented has disappeared into its neighboring sound by means of full or complete assimilation. Pronounce the word *cupboard,* and look at its spelling. The /p/ has been completely assimilated into the /b/; the /p/ has disappeared; the *p* letter is now silent.

Some morphemes retain the assimilated sound in the morpheme unit, and the completely assimilated sound magically reappears when a suffix is added to the root word, changing the syllable arrangement. Pronounce the following list of words, and check for the complete assimilation:

> autumn
> damn
> column
> hymn
> malign
> deign
> benign

What sound was completely absorbed into its neighbor? In the first four words, you should have discovered that the /n/ was gone; the *n* is now a silent letter in those words. And in the last three words the /g/ has disappeared; *g* is a silent letter in those words. But the /n/ and /g/ have not disappeared forever. Note this reappearance, as you pronounce these words, based on the roots you have just pronounced:

> autumnal
> damnation
> columnist

hymnal
malignant
dignity
benignancy

If you are not sure about the pronunciation of any of these words, look them up in your dictionary. What did you find as you uttered these words aloud? That's right. The /n/ and /g/ are back! So the morpheme never lost the sound; the sound remained part of the meaning unit, but it disappears (is totally, fully, and completely assimilated) in certain contexts.

INCOMPLETE ASSIMILATION

Partial, or incomplete, assimilation refers to those sound changes in which a sound is modified, or adapted, under the influence of an adjacent sound. In partial, or incomplete, assimilation, a sound changes to accommodate (or adjust itself) to a neighboring sound; the assimilated sound tries to become more like its neighbor.

Partial assimilations, which account for most of the sound changes in your speech, are classified into three types according to the direction of influence. If a sound influences the sound that follows it, the assimilation is called progressive; if a sound influences the sound that precedes it, the assimilation is said to be regressive; if two sounds influence each other to produce a third, the assimilation is reciprocal.

Progressive Assimilation

When a sound is influenced by the sound that precedes it, *progressive assimilation* has taken place. That does not sound logical until you think about it a little. The names of the kinds of assimilation are based on the *direction* of the influence. If the influence goes forward (that is, it progresses in the word), then the assimilation is said to be progressive. If the influence goes forward, then the first sound influences the second sound (the sound that comes after it). Which means, of course, that it is the second sound that does the changing. It is the second sound that *gets* influenced in the progressive assimilation.

In the word *low*, the /l/ is fully voiced; /l/ is a voiced consonant, as you know. But check your pronunciation of the word *flow* aloud. How has the /l/ changed? What accommodation did it make? Can you detect the devoicing of the /l/? It is no longer *fully* voiced. It has undergone an assimilative change. And what caused or influenced this change? The voiceless /f/ that preceded the /l/. Because the first sound (/f/) influenced the second sound (/l/), and the second sound adapted itself to be more like the preceding sound, we have an instance of progressive assimilation.

The past tense, plurals, and possessives offer the best examples of progressive assimilation in English. After the vowel was dropped from the pronunciation of most words in the past tense, the tense was indicated by the voiced /d/. The words *planned, called,* and *leered* are pronounced /pland/, /kɔld/, and /lɪɚd/. If the sound preceding the past-tense ending is voiceless, however, progressive assimilation occurs and the /d/ becomes /t/. Note that the words *passed, hoped, flunked, coughed,* and *lashed* all end in /t/.

The same kind of assimilation takes place in forming plurals and possessives. The ending /z/ is changed into /s/ after voiceless sounds. Compare the pronunciation of *cubs* and *cups, beads* and *beets, pigs* and *picks, elves* and *elf's sheathes* and *sheath's.* (The same kind of progressive assimilation also occurs in the third person singular of the present tense of the verb. Compare the pronunciation of *pegs* and *pecks, tugs* and *tucks, rides* and *writes,* and *lobs* and *lops.*)

Regressive Assimilation

When a sound is influenced by the sound that follows it, *regressive assimilation* has taken place. In this case, the influence goes backward in the word; it regresses. The second sound influences the sound before it, and it is the first sound that does the changing. It is the first sound that gets influenced and the second sound that does the influencing—in regressive assimilation.

In the word *fill,* the /l/ is fully voiced. But note what happens when you add the voiceless sound /θ/ (th). Pronounce the word *filth* and compare it with your pronunciation of the word *fill.* How has the /l/ changed? What accommodation did the /l/ in *filth* make? Well, anticipating the voiceless sound /θ/ (th) immediately following, the /l/ lost some of its voicing (its vocal vibration). The /l/ adapted itself to be more like the following sound; we have an instance of regressive assimilation.

Look at another example. Pronounce the word *sin.* Listen to the final sound in the word, and feel where the tongue goes to make the final sound (/n/). Now pronounce the word *sink.* Listen to that word as you pronounce it, and check on the sound that comes before the final /k/. Is it the same sound you had in *sin?* If not, what change has it undergone? What adaptation did it make? Try *sink* out aloud again—just to be sure. And you have found, of course, that the sound preceding /k/ in the word *sink* is not /n/ but /ŋ/ (n͡g). The /n/ has changed, influenced by the coming /k/. Because the third nasal—/ŋ/ (n͡g)—is articulated at the same spot as the /k/ and /g/, it takes less effort to form /ŋ/ (n͡g) before /k/ than to form /n/. The /n/ has undergone regressive assimilation and become /ŋ/ (n͡g). The /n/ ordinarily changes to ŋ/ (n͡g) before /k/, particularly in the same syllable. Pronounce the words *sink, sank, honk,* and *flunk;* they all contain /ŋ/ (n͡g) rather than /n/. When the letter *n* ends a syllable and the next syllable begins with /k/ or /g/, there is a good deal of variation in the use of /n/ and /ŋ/ (n͡g). Some of your friends may pronounce *banquet* /bænkwɪt/ and others /bæŋkwɪt/, just as some may say /ɪnkʌm/ and others /ɪŋkʌm/ for *income.* The only principle that can be observed here is that when the letter *n* ends a syllable before a syllable beginning with /k/ or /g/, the sound will usually be /ŋ/ if the next syllable is unstressed and final in the word, as in the words *Congress* and *ankle.*

Let us look at another example. Pronounce these pairs of words and phrases aloud:

nine	ninth
well	wealth
bread	breadth
at	at this time

What happened to the /n/, /l/, /d/, and /t/ in the second word or phrase? What change did each of these sounds undergo? How was each of them different the second time you pronounced them? The first time, hopefully, each of the sounds /n/, /l/, /d/, and /t/—was an alveolar sound—made by pressing the tongue tip to the alveolar ridge. The second time, each of the sounds was probably made in a different place; this time, the tongue was on the teeth—anticipating the position of the coming /θ/ (th). Here we have another excellent example of regressive assimilation.

In regressive assimilation, you anticipate the coming sound and get ready for it. This anticipation modifies or changes the sound being uttered.

Reciprocal Assimilation

Reciprocal is another word for mutual. If anything is mutual, of course, it is a matter of give-and-take. That is what reciprocal assimilation is all about: two sounds influence each other. The result is a third sound, different from the other two, that replaces the two original sounds. If two sounds influence each other and produce, thereby, a third sound in their place, *reciprocal assimilation* has taken palce.

If /z/ and /j/ (y) come together, they may undergo reciprocal assimilation and become /ʒ/ (zh). Check your pronunciation of the following words:

vision	leisure	division
usual	seizure	precision
usury	pleasure	derision
usurer	measure	delusion

azure	treasure	incision
casual	lesion	collision
visual	illusion	occasion
version	intrusion	explosion
	conclusion	

If the /s/ and /j/ (y) come together, they may undergo reciprocal assimilation and become /ʃ/ (sh). Check your pronunciation of the following words and note the reciprocal assimilations:

fission	profession
mission	confession
issue	conscience
passion	conscious
pension	anxious
sure	delicious
glacier	pressure
precious	ocean

If /t/ and /j/ (y) come together, they may undergo reciprocal assimilation and become /ʃ/ (sh). Pronounce the following words aloud, and note the reciprocal assimilations:

nation	mention	ration
notion	attention	patient
emotion	detention	infectious
election	caution	reflection
action	fractious	rejection
sanction	inclination	cautious

If /t/ and /j/ (y) come together, they may undergo reciprocal assimilation and become /tʃ/ (ch). Note the assimilations in the following words as you pronounce them aloud:

actual	lecture
natural	question
nature	righteous
virtue	picture
virtuous	puncture
digestion	tincture
ingestion	instinctual
congestion	manufacture

If /d/ and /j/ (y) come together, they may undergo reciprocal assimilation and become /dʒ/ (j). Pronounce the following words aloud and note the reciprocal assimilations:

gradual	adulation
graduate	module
educate	modulation
education	soldier

Because we do not speak a word at a time, but blend our words in successions of syllables called phrases or thought groups, assimilations may occur between words as well as within words. Abutting consonants can produce assimilations—interverbally as well as intraverbally! Check to see if you pronounce the following examples with assimilations at the marked spots:

> Hi*t* the line.
> a*s y*ou know
> I mis*s y*ou.
> Ea*t y*our words.
> Woul*d y*ou try?

Dissimilation

Assimilation, a sound change in which a sound becomes more like an adjacent sound, occurs more often than any other kind of phonetic change. Dissimilaton is, in a sense, the opposite of assimilation. Dissimilation is a sound change in which a sound becomes *less* like neighboring sounds; it is change to be different from the neighbor instead of conforming to the neighbor.

Dissimilation occurs when a word contains a repeated sound or at least two very similar sounds, and one of those repeated or similar sounds changes into a different sound or disappears. In assimilative changes, you remember, the two sounds were right next to each other; they were adjacent sounds, if they were involved in the assimilation. This is not so in dissimilative changes. The two sounds involved here will *not* be adjacent, but they will be in the same word.

Dissimilation is a complicated process, and usually there are other factors at work in addition to the repetition of the same or similar sounds. Let's look at two examples. If you pronounce February aloud, you will probably discover that you do not pronounce the first *r*. Instead, we say *fĕb yōō ĕ rĭ* (/ˈfɛbju ˌɛri/). Why? Well, for one thing, we have an instance of dissimilation. The two /r/s in nearby syllables give us trouble, so the first one bows out. Dissimilation, pure and simple. But not quite so pure and not nearly so simple. Another influence is that we learn the names of the months, and we recite them "January, February . . . ." What could be more natural than for *fĕb yōō* . . . to follow *jăn yōō* . . . ! Is it a case of pronunciation based on analogy (comparison)? Or is it dissimilation? Or both? Probably.

The other good example of the complexity of dissimilation is found in our pronunciation of the word *government*. Try that word out loud to check on how you pronounce it. Be sure to say it as you regularly do. What do you discover—pronouncing it as you look at the spelling of the word? That's right. The first *n* is missing. Not because you are a slovenly speaker, but because two syllables in a row ending with /n/ are difficult for anyone. And dissimilation occurs; the first *n* drops out. Dissimilation pure and simple this time? Well, not quite. Could there be another explanation for the missing /n/? Could it be an instance of *assimilation* rather than dissimilation? *Complete assimilation*, with the /n/ absorbed by the following nasal sound /m/? Or could it be called *either* complete assimilation *or* dissimilation? Again, probably.

At least we should now understand what dissimilation is. It is our effort to avoid tongue-twisters where the same sound is repeated or a similar sound occurs. Some examples of dissimilation are accepted as standard, and some are not. Both of those we just mentioned (*February* and *government*) are standard. But the pronunciation of *liberry* for *library* (a clear case of dissimilation) is nonstandard. *Supprise* for *surprise* does not raise hackles in educated, cultivated circles, but *sekketary* for *secretary* certainly will. Both, of course, are examples of dissimilation, but one is considered standard and the other is not. You will just have to use your ears and your dictionary to be able to distinguish between those dissimilations that are socially acceptable and those that are not.

Vowel Gradation

In our discussion of the individual sounds of the language, we discussed the fact that vowels have strong forms that appear in stressed syllables and that we weaken the vowels in unstressed syllables. This is a very important concept, and we must explain it in some detail here.

If you have learned English as a second language, you may have difficulty understanding why ä (/ɑ/) is not always ä (/ɑ/). In your first language, a vowel may always be the same. This is not so in English. The vowel in the word *be* will be ē (/i/), but the first vowel in the word *between* will not be that long tense high front vowel. Instead, the vowel will be shortened and weakened in that syllable (because it is unstressed) to ĭ (/ɪ/). If you do not use the weak forms of the vowels in the unstressed syllables, you will distort the sounds, mispronounce the words, and alter the natural rhythm of the phrases. You must use the lower grade (or weaker grade) of vowels in the unstressed syllables and the higher grade (or stronger grade) of vowels in the stressed syllables.

Most vowels in unstressed syllables are reduced to schwa, although /i/ (ē) may become /ɪ/ (ĭ), and /u/ (o͞o) may become /ʊ/ (o͝o). The first syllable in the word *above*, for example, is not /æ/ (ă) but /ə/; the vowel in the second syllable in the word *beautiful* may be either /ɪ/ (ĭ) or /ə/; and the vowel in the first word of the infinitive *to be* may be either /ʊ/ (o͝o) or /ə/.

Because we have so many unstressed syllables in our speech, schwa (/ə/) is the most commonly used of the vowels. Of course, not every unstressed syllable is pronounced with schwa, as we have indicated. The word *regulate,* for example, has three syllables. The stress is on the first syllable, so that vowel is the stressed vowel ĕ (/ɛ/). The yo͞o (/ju/) in the second syllable will be reduced in grade (or rank) to second-class status; it will become yo͝o (/jʊ/). It *can* be reduced further to yə (/jə/), but it cannot be reduced to schwa alone. The y (/j/) of the original yo͞o (/ju/) survives. The last syllable is an unstressed syllable, or at most it has a kind of secondary stress; in that syllable, the [e] (å) rather than the diphthongal allophone [eɪ] (ā) will be heard.

To help you understand the principle of ranking or grading vowels, let us turn our attention to an important group of words in our language: *form words.* Each form word exists as a stressed form (to emphasize the idea inherent in the word) and as an unstressed form (which simply states the idea implied in the word, without giving it special prominence). There are two forms, then, for each of these words: one stressed (using stressed vowels) and one unstressed (using the unstressed vowels: /ɪ/ (ĭ), /ɨ/, /ʊ/ (o͝o), /ɚ/ (ər), /ə/, [e] (å), and [o] (ȯ)). If necessary, refer back to the material in Chapter 3 on each of these vowels.

Form words are necessary for the form, or syntax, of our sentences but not for the central ideas. These words are articles, prepositions, conjunctions, auxiliary verbs, linking verbs, and pronouns. Because the meaning is implied in the word itself, no stress on the word is necessary—unless you intend to emphasize the implicit meaning and make it explicit. For example, the word *and* implies addition. If there is no reason to emphasize the concept of addition, you would use the weak form of the word; if, however, you wanted to underscore that idea, you would use the strong form. In the phrase *bread and butter,* you would ordinarily use the weak form [n] for *and,* but if you wanted to emphasize the fact that adding butter was unusual, you would use the strong form [ænd].

Let us look at one other example. The word *the* is a pointing word; it means *one.* Usually it is not necessary to stress the idea of oneness or uniqueness, so we usually use the weak form of this word. We say: [ðə bʊk], *the book* or [lænd əv ðə fri], *land of the free. The* in those phrases is an article, pointing to the noun—not drawing attention to itself. So we use the weak form of the word [ðə] (*thə*). (Note that in the phrase *land of the free,* there are two idea words, thought-bearing words: *land* and *free.* Those two words are made to stand out by the use of the stressed vowels in them, among other techniques. Note also that the preposition *of* is a form word and is pronounced using its weak form in this phrase, not its strong form [ɑv] (äv).) Contrast the vowel in *the* in the phrase *land of the free* and the vowel you would use in the word *the* if you read this sentence aloud: "I'm going to *the* theater tonight." This time, to emphasize the *the,* you use the strong form of the word and say [ði] (*thē*), not [ðʌ] (*thŭ*). Bob King said that with some irony more than once during his college days. The word *the* was emphasized, not to indicate that he was going to the most prestigious theater in town (a possibility when you emphasize the *one* idea), but that he was really going to *the* theater in town—the *only* one!

It is important for you to master the use of form words, because we use them so often. In the exercises, work to blend the phrases together smoothly, and use the weak form of the form words.

Materials for Practicing Unstressed Forms

ARTICLES

a	Have a ball. Run a risk. It's a game.
an	It's an old story. He's an eager applicant.
the	Here comes the bride. Where are the others? The team lost the final game. The orgy followed.

PREPOSITIONS

at	She collapsed at the dance. Meet me at nine o'clock.
for	Ask for an extra one. For goodness' sake, sing "Tea for Two."
from	It's a souvenir from Fort Knox. We work from dark to dawn.
into	The attorney is looking into the case. He will take it into court.
of	I'm not tired of school. It's the principle of the thing.
to	Are you ready to go? Give it to me.

CONJUNCTIONS

and	Life and death. A girl and a boy. Joy and pain. Forever and ever.
as	She's as pretty as a painting. It's almost as expensive!
but	But you said you would! Everyone's going, but no one's staying.
or	I want only one or two of them. You may take either or both.
than	There are more than I wanted. He said nothing other than that.

AUXILIARY VERBS

am	I am speaking at the meeting. Then I am staying home.

are	We are reading *War and Peace*. Most are reading the *Classic Comic* version.
can	He can read Sanskrit. Do you know what she can do?
could	I could have performed all night. I wish I could go.
do	How do you do? Do you want to attend?
does	Does it work? When does she perform again?
had	He claimed he had already paid. The cashier had made a mistake.
has	He has been to the farm. John has learned his lesson.
have	We have seen him often. We should have gone.
must	You must practice. Russ thought he must leave early.
shall	We shall do our part. Where shall we go?
should	What should I do now? You should write other examples.
was	It was going well. Why was he suspected?
were	We were running all the time. They were provoked.
will	Who will take my place? Anyone will be able to do it.
would	I would rather do it myself. Why would they want a new one?

Linking Verbs

am	I am tired of these materials. I suppose I am too lazy to create my own.
are	We are ready for anything. They are hostile.
was	It was a serious matter. Nick was eager to stay.
were	They were happy to escape the ordeal. All of them were pawns in the power struggle.

Pronouns

he	How could he do it? I think he erred.
her	I gave her all I had. Someone told her the supply was limited.
him	Explain it to him. Make him pay his share.
his	You shouldn't have told his wife about it. She resented his running around.
some	I need some help. Give me some money.
that	He believed that he was perfect. Everyone else thought that he should be perfected.
them	I saw them at the bar. Take them home or find them a taxi.
us	Give us your number. She tried to ignore us.
you	I'm working, you know, at the grill. Have you looked for another job?
your	I'll take your place. Always do your best.

5
Sound Combinations

THUS far in studying articulation, we have discussed individual sounds. Even when we considered sound changes, we were looking at individual sounds. But it is not just lone sounds that give us difficulty in articulation. Some combinations of sounds offer special difficulties for many speakers. And because sounds put together in groups are different from sounds uttered alone, we must look at some of the particular problems presented by difficult sound combinations.

We certainly will not give attention to all the possible sound combinations in the language in this chapter. We will concentrate on those combinations that present special stumbling blocks to many speakers of American English. Because these combinations contain problems for many speakers, you should check all of them to see if you need to work on your production of these common groups of sounds.

We will divide these problematical groups of sounds into consonant and vowel groups first. Then we will look at some groups of abutting consonants and some groups of compound consonants. The vowel combinations will be divided into nonphonemic diphthongs and nonphonemic triphthongs.

Consonant Combinations

ABUTTING CONSONANTS

Abutting consonants are two successive consonants (two consonants in a row) that belong to separate syllables. That would mean, then, that one consonant ends a syllable and the next consonant begins the following syllable. There are two instances of abutting consonants that offer particular difficulty to many speakers: consecutive stops (two different stop sounds in succession) and "doubled" stops (the same stop in abutting position—one ending and the other beginning a syllable). Let us look at each of these types of problem combinations.

Two Different Stops in Succession

You will remember that we defined stops as sounds on which the air stream was stopped completely by the articulators; sometimes the air pressure is built up at the point of blockage and then released in a little explosion. We noted that stops always stop the outgoing breath stream, but they do not always explode. When the stop sounds come together one after another, there is only one explosion, although there are two stops. You stop the first stop consonant with a good firm closure, but do not release it in a plosion. Then you stop the second stop consonant with a complete closure and release it in a plosion.

Check what you do when you say the word *act*, for example. The /k/ closes off the air stream for an instant, but you do not explode the /k/ as you would in the word *keep*. Instead, you move on to the closure for the /t/ and explode only the second plosive. The same thing occurs even if the two plosives are in different words. Note that the /t/ is stopped but not exploded and the /d/ both stopped and exploded in the words *hot dog*. Check in such words as *back door, hot drink, hop down, sad case, big caldron,* or *rib cage* to be certain that you fully obstruct the air stream for an instant on the first stop plosive and that you voice it if it should have vocal vibration.

Here are some practice materials for abutting stops. Each of the following sentences contains two different stops in succession:

1. He was in a ba*d p*osition.
2. He began to dro*p b*ehind rather quickly.
3. They mus*t b*egin at once.
4. Tom carried the pac*k d*ownstairs.
5. They said it couldn'*t b*e done.
6. The performance was qui*te g*ood.
7. Ho*p d*own from the bar, toad.
8. Be sure to pic*k g*ood examples.
9. Pupils are not allowe*d t*o do homework.
10. It's a waste*d t*wo points.
11. It was har*d t*o get him to do that.
12. I can'*t b*elieve that they have turne*d t*o alcohol!
13. They ma*de t*wo touchdowns in the las*t q*uarter of the game.
14. Don'*t b*e satisfied with slack articulation of the plosives.
15. He lived in the high ren*t d*istrict.
16. The hi*p b*one's connecte*d t*o the thigh bone.
17. Grea*t d*ay in the morning!
18. I ha*d t*rouble with the assignment.
19. That act is har*d t*o follow.
20. He sagge*d and reele*d t*oo much in the firs*t p*erformance.
21. We ha*d t*o write a term paper.
22. Everyone ha*d t*o wor*k t*o complete it.
23. I've hear*d t*errible things about that chea*p t*rinket.
24. Actually, tha*t p*roduct is qui*te g*ood.

25. With his background, he's lucky the judge didn't convict him.
26. Why did Cal decide to take part in that affair?
27. I came back to work, but I'm not going to work hard.
28. She really doesn't want David to keep believing her lies.
29. It could be called a cheap trick, but it cost Dave plenty.
30. I tried to tell him, but he just prefers his present activities.

"Doubled" Stops

If you have one syllable ending with a stop consonant, and the next syllable beginning with the same stop, you do not have two stops but one—with the difference between a single consonant and a "doubled" consonant indicated by a lengthening of the time of the closure before the release of the plosion. That means that, if you have two abutting stops (and the two are the same phoneme), you make only one stop (you block the air only once), but you block off the air stream longer than you would for the same stop sound if it were a single consonant.

In the word *bookcase*, for example, you do not stop and release the first /k/ and then stop and release the second /k/. You obstruct the air stream with the back of the tongue as you would on a single /k/, but you hold the air stream closed off for a longer time before you release it. The same principle holds true even if the two stops are in successive words. Note that *last time* is not pronounced the same as *lass time*, and *missed ten* differs from *Miss Ten*. There are two distortions associated with this principle against which you should guard. Careless speakers tend to treat doubled stops as if they were single ones, and pedantic speakers tend to stop and explode each stop in the pair.

Here are some practice materials for "doubled" stops. Each of the following sentences contains at least one example of "doubled" stops.

1. You ought to vote in this election.
2. Hit to center field.
3. I hate to attend that class.
4. The coach will pick Kim for the award.
5. We had dozens of offers of help.
6. We all hope to win the big game next week.
7. He dyed the robe brown.
8. What is a "hip person"?
9. We had to bed down in the backyard.
10. The children begged to go along, but they were turned down.
11. No one got to look at it.
12. Can't you take Kevin with you?
13. I am looking for a ride downtown.
14. No honest player would rig games for profit.
15. I forgot to pack clean shirts for the trip.

16. I pass*ed t*en cars before the crash.
17. He told me he could ty*pe p*erfectly.
18. Who would ro*b B*en of his last dollar?
19. All he had to do was qui*t t*o prove his point.
20. Ma*d d*ogs and Englishmen go out in the noonday sun.
21. Ta*ke c*are of yourself, and don't forge*t t*o write.
22. I fough*t t*o get into the show, but they insisted that I loo*k c*losely at the sign: "For Trade Only."
23. I trie*d d*riving to work, but I found taking a ca*b b*etter.
24. The Exhibition Center won'*t t*ake fa*ke c*redentials.
25. Don't dra*g g*randmother's name into tha*t t*errible argument.
26. Tha*t t*estimony is no*t t*rue.
27. I've go*t t*o get a jo*b b*efore I can pay those big gambling debts.
28. How can I rea*p p*rofits? I la*ck c*apital.
29. Wha*t t*ouching loyalty! She hi*d d*ozens of his letters.
30. Kee*p p*racticing. Gra*b b*locks of time. Wor*k c*onsistently. Ge*t t*ogether with your instructor. Rea*d d*aily and hee*d d*irections. Then you can bra*g g*reatly.

COMPOUND CONSONANTS

We defined abutting consonants as two successive consonants that belong to separate syllables; one ends the first syllable and the other begins the following syllable. *Compound consonants*, on the other hand, are consonant combinations that occur *within* one syllable, either initiating a syllable or terminating it. Although books on phonetics are not consistent in their terminology, we are going to use the term *consonant blend* to refer to a compound consonant combination of two consonants and the term *consonant cluster* to refer to a compound consonant combination of three or more consonants.

We will not give instructions and practice materials for all the possible consonant blends or consonant clusters that occur in English. We will limit our attention to those combinations that give speakers the most trouble. (We have already given you some exercises for the initial consonant blends /bl/, /pl/, /br/, and /pr/. See pp. 153–155 and pp. 175–177.) Now we turn our attention to those consonant blends and consonant clusters that, especially because of their final position, may give you the most problems.

Blends

Stop Plus Nasal

These are blends in which a nasal sound follows one of the stops. They are articulated in a special way—as a combination. When a nasal consonant follows a stop, the air stream is obstructed by the articulators for the stop in the usual way, the closure is held for a moment while the velum drops down to open the passage to the nose, and the air is then popped up through the nasal passages. Some writers call this release a nasal plosion. However, be certain you do not insert the vowel /ə/ between the stop consonant and the nasal. The nasal sound itself will "carry" the syllable; the nasal, which is providing the sonority for the syllable, is called a syllabic nasal. Also be careful not to turn /pn/ into /pm/ or /kn/ into /kŋ/ (kn͡g).

Here are some practice materials for consonant blends made of a stop plus a nasal.

/pn/

1. Open the door, please.
2. How did it happen?
3. The entire torso of the sculpture seemed misshapen to me.
4. We had a wreck on the Tappan Zee Bridge.
5. We cleaned the canvas with turpentine.
6. It seemed a curious happenstance to me.
7. Does his firm have any openings I would be interested in?
8. The little fellow couldn't wait for the watermelon to ripen.
9. What's happening?
10. The bottle was a terrible weapon.

/bn/

1. She cut the ribbon.
2. Who's Ibn Saud?
3. Abba Eban is world-famous.
4. Durban is in South Africa.
5. Mr. Rubin is a gentleman.
6. Don Fabun wrote an excellent book.
7. Why is she wearing a turban?
8. The march was led by Tobin himself.
9. Seventy per cent of Americans live in urban areas.
10. Laban is a Biblical name.

/tn/

1. They threw rotten tomatoes at the speaker.
2. She was wearing a simple cotton dress.
3. Seton Hall hasn't lost a game this season.
4. The mailman was bitten three times last week.
5. Ill-gotten gains will do you no good.
6. Why haven't you written the report?
7. He appears to be smitten by her charms.
8. Farmers fatten up the hogs before slaughtering time.

9. Have you ever eaten rattlesnake? Certainly not!
10. Batten down the hatches!
11. Put on your hat and coat.
12. Who wants to buy a Siamese kitten?
13. Button up your overcoat.
14. The Titans are at the bottom of the league.
15. He wants to straighten this mess out.
16. The president has asked us to tighten our belts.
17. The theater could use new curtains.
18. Are you certain he hasn't written in a year?
19. Mutton can taste rotten unless seasoned properly.
20. Doesn't anybody wear mittens any more? I've gotten used to them.

/dn/

1. He burst into the room suddenly.
2. This product was made in France.
3. Who let the snake into the Garden of Eden?
4. I have joined the Rod and Gun Club.
5. Auden is one of my favorite modern poets.
6. Why have you hardened your heart against me?
7. The dentist could not deaden the pain.
8. The entire university was saddened by the news.
9. It was the ship's maiden voyage.
10. Is that a symphony by Haydn?
11. It's too heavy a burden for you to bear.
12. Personally I think it's good riddance.
13. He had an answer for everything.
14. The judge refused to pardon him.
15. The suspense was maddening.
16. I saw no wooden shoes in Holland.
17. This card is laden with good wishes.
18. According to the teachers, Mr. McFadden is the principal problem.
19. The news gladdened our hearts.
20. I'm good and tired of these exercises.

/dnt/*

1. You shouldn't have done that.
2. I couldn't care less.
3. He said he wouldn't go, but he did.
4. These shoes are wooden ones. Wouldn't you like to see them?
5. Are you sure they didn't like the play?

* Yes, this is a cluster rather than a blend. But the logical time to practice on it is after mastering the *dn* blend.

6. It's true I hadn't eaten frog legs before.
7. The doctor said we shouldn't eat mutton.
8. Everyone insisted he couldn't understand the assignment.
9. The instructor didn't believe them.
10. I could tell he hadn't practiced. Couldn't you?
11. I didn't hear the phone ring.
12. The adviser insisted that pledges shouldn't be beaten.
13. The mayor didn't listen to his party's bosses.
14. Wouldn't it be better to decide for yourself?
15. Aren't you afraid of rodents?
16. I hadn't thought much about it.
17. Couldn't you make up your own examples?

/kn/

1. My faith in human beings has been shaken.
2. He lives in Beacon, New York.
3. No one has reckoned the cost of the project.
4. The phonograph is broken and should be repaired.
5. I wakened to the sound of trumpets.
6. Why did he move to Hackensack?
7. I thought the ghost was beckoning to me.
8. I think her resistance is weakening.
9. I have taken all of this I can.
10. Stephen has become a deacon now.
11. Have you eaten Canadian bacon?
12. But Seconals are dangerous, I've heard.
13. Rose got everything secondhand.
14. The thought of eating snails is sickening.
15. The day of reckoning has come.
16. The cook couldn't get the syrup to thicken.
17. I always have trouble awakening.
18. Chicken is a meal most foul.
19. They're together cheek and jowl!
20. You've been my friend through thick and thin!

/gn/

1. Could I see Mr. Riggin?
2. What agony! The toboggan crashed!
3. No, I'm not Henry Higgins.
4. We met at the Guggenheim Museum.
5. Fagin was not such a bad fellow.
6. Mr. Reagan is Right.
7. Who's left but Mrs. Dugan?

8. Is the Coogan family moving next door?
9. Have you ever been in Copenhagen?
10. You can beg and plead, but it will do you no good.

Stop Followed by the Lateral

Actually, we probably should have titled this section "stop plus lateral," because we do not produce one and then the other. When a lateral "follows" a homorganic stop (a stop made in the same place as the /l/—on the alveolar ridge), the air is released in an unusual way. The air is exploded over the sides of the tongue. (There are two stops, you will remember, that are articulated by pressing the tip of the tongue against the gum ridge: /t/ and /d/.) When /t/ and /d/ occur as a blend with /l/, they are not released (ploded) in the center, with the air popping out over the tongue tip. Instead, the air pops over the two sides of the tongue.

To make the /tl/, for example, you place the tongue tip firmly on the gum ridge, hold the tongue tip firmly against the ridge, and pop the air over the sides of the tongue. Do not let the tongue drop between the /t/ and /l/, because that will insert a vowel between the two consonants. The /tl/ and /dl/ are sound combinations—lateral plosions—and you should not conceive of them as being formed separately, but together.

There are two common distortions of these sound combinations: (1) incomplete closure, and (2) substitution of the glottal stop for the /t/ in the /tl/ combination. To produce a correct /tl/ or /dl/, the tongue tip must touch the gum ridge and press firmly against the ridge until the combination is completed. The substitution of a stop made with the vocal folds for the first portion of the /tl/ combination is rather common in the greater New York area. Check to be certain that in such words as *battle, bottle, total, futile,* and *mutilate* you make the sound with the tongue tip and not back in the throat. (See pp. 69–70.)

/tl/

1. I'm hoping to settle the case out of court.
2. I have a mutilated copy of my own.
3. We are studying the fundamentals of speech.
4. They used bottles for weapons in the street battle.
5. The subtleties of the story escaped him.
6. The children called the informer a tattletale.
7. The teacher did not think I was entitled to an A.
8. In Westerns, cattle rustlers are never gentlemen.
9. She threw a bottle of ink at me in a futile attempt to stop me.
10. They looked up the vital statistics in the atlas.
11. Do not use a glottal stop in these exercises.

12. Every time I met Tom, he was hatless.
13. Myrtle is doing volunteer work at a mental hospital.
14. He always puts a little something in the Salvation Army's kettles.
15. I wasn't startled by the influence of the Beatles.
16. It'll be a long time before I learn this.
17. Her tongue is a cutlass; she's not very subtle.
18. I prefer a metal one to plastic.
19. My wife tried to whittle down the price.
20. Enough of this prattle! It's a total waste.

/dl/

1. Handle it with care.
2. He received five gold medals in one day.
3. How can you choose between Tweedledum and Tweedledee?
4. Paddle your own canoe!
5. The warden was accused of coddling the prisoners.
6. Is yodeling good for your voice?
7. The little toddler fell constantly.
8. We ate by candlelight.
9. I read a story about a headless horseman.
10. Oddly enough, he hit the wrong pedal on the organ.
11. Stop meddling in my affairs.
12. Our senator straddles every issue. He's a Mugwump!
13. Sorry. I'm no good at riddles.
14. I'm in the middle of something important.
15. She loved her poodle a lot more than she loved me.
16. They still paddle children at that school.
17. I'm not just fiddling around or twiddling my thumbs.
18. Sandals let in the air—and the dirt.
19. Yes, the vandals have struck again.
20. A little scandal can sell a lot of newspapers.
21. I don't want to saddle you with my worries.
22. I'm entering the country fiddle contest at the fair.
23. George IV was too fat even to waddle around the palace.
24. Don't bother to ladle out any turtle soup for me!
25. I guess we'll just have to muddle through.

Stop Followed by a Fricative

When a fricative follows a stop, a firm closure is made for the stop, the air pressure is built up at the point of closure, and the air is then released through the opening of the fricative.

Check your pronunciation of the following words to be certain that you get a good firm closure on the stop and a quick accurate release on the fricative:

rips
rates
rocks
ribs
raids
rugs

You should also be certain that you get good vocal vibration on the voiced sounds /bz/ (as in *ribs*), /dz/ (as in *raids*), and /gz/ (as in *rugs*).

/ps/ AND /bz/

rips	ribs
ropes	robes
apes	Abe's
lopes	lobes
Epps	ebbs
Rupp's	rubs
sops	sobs
cops	Cobb's
mops	mobs
cups	cubs
caps	cabs
sups	subs
laps	labs
hops	Hobbs
tripe's	tribes
gaps	gabs
pups	pubs

1. How many cross-country trips have you taken?
2. We bought tubs and tubs of butter.
3. She hopes to become a star in Mr. Webb's movie.
4. It didn't take him long to learn the ropes.
5. The drapes are on fire.
6. All the tribes are constantly at war with one another.
7. Be sure to buy enough tubes of paint to finish the jobs.
8. He often rubs the lamp, but nobody appears.
9. Mr. Cobb's a friend to all the cops in the neighborhood.
10. If anyone robs him, he hopes they'll catch the thief.
11. The team can't take the subs on the out-of-town trips.
12. Now in the U.S. Navy, he hopes to get into subs.
13. After the mobs mess up the kitchen, she mops the floor.

14. There were gaps in his story, and Dean Hobbs spotted them all.
15. The more abuse he heaps upon her, the more her interest ebbs.
16. The British call bars pubs; at first, I thought they were saying "pups."
17. The Cubs are a little overactive; they broke all my cups.
18. Bill Epps has a thing for ear lobes.
19. Rupp's record is great, but he rubs me the wrong way.
20. She sobs and cries when her fibs are found out.

/ts/ AND /dz/

beets	beads
bets	beds
pats	pads
knots	nods
fates	fades
bites	bides
newts	nudes
hurts	herds
carts	cards
rots	rods
rites	rides
cats	cads
rates	raids
boats	bodes
mates	maids
bits	bids
huts	Hud's
Gert's	girds
nets	Ned's
greets	greed's
Kurt's	curds
notes	nodes
sweets	Swedes
waits	wades
totes	toads
sits	Sid's
sights	sides

1. It's not a waste of time.
2. The boats are docked in the harbor.
3. That store sells many brands of paint.
4. Birds of a feather flock together.
5. It's what's up front that counts.

6. We heard many complaints in the courtroom.
7. God's in His heaven, all's right with the world.
8. By flanking the ends, our team can run complicated pass patterns.
9. The courts' dockets are crowded.
10. I hope she accepts my invitation.
11. The administration followed a "hands-off" policy.
12. The Boy Scouts' tents are on the front lawn.
13. The tax will finance new roads.
14. There are many pads in the wrestling room.
15. One faces many hazards on a safari.
16. His doubts are well founded.
17. Her moods are constantly changing, because she broods over everything.
18. We want deeds, not words.
19. He lifts weights once a week at the gym.
20. There is more faith in honest doubt than in many creeds.
21. She bites her nails; he bides his time.
22. Hope fades. My fate's in his hands.
23. The boat's sinking. That bodes ill for all of us.
24. There are more than two sides in a controversy.
25. That's what so many fights are about.
26. She just sits there and waits while he wades in over his head.
27. It's no violation of his rights. They have the goods on him.
28. Greed's a powerful force; it greets you everywhere.
29. Hud's renting the little huts for ten dollars a night.
30. Leonard girds his courage with alcohol before all his flights.
31. That's all. The period's over.
32. She writes home often when she needs money.
33. He meets his responsibilities, but he gets no credit for it.
34. There were no grounds for a good case.
35. I must check on the rates at the hotel.
36. Her hands are trembling. She waits for an answer.
37. Pangloss proved that this is the best of all possible worlds.
38. "What's time? Leave Now for gods and apes! Man has forever."
39. "The thoughts of men are widened with the process of the suns."
40. He reads all his assignments.
41. A gentleman is one who never inflicts pain.
42. He respects the rights of other human beings and aids those in need.
43. "All have a right to an equal share in the benefits and burdens of government.
44. I thought hoods were on coats—not on the streets!
45. The cad's a devil. I hope she boots him out. But I'm not taking bets on it.

/ks/ AND /gz/

lax	lags
leaks	leagues
picks	pigs
jocks	jogs
tucks	tugs
tacks	tags
racks	rags
wicks	wigs
hawks	hogs
fox	fogs
box	bogs
hacks	hags
sacks	sags
chucks	chugs
bucks	bugs
pecks	pegs
Beck's	begs
Burke's	burg's
Lux	lugs
Volks	*Vogue's*

1. The little boy was throwing rocks at the neighbors.
2. He organized the teams into two leagues.
3. He seeks only to make his point clear.
4. Have you ever eaten fresh figs?
5. Both locks were broken.
6. Their fraternity lags behind the others in scholarship.
7. I'm told that he rigs every class election.
8. He is so nervous even the clock's ticks upset him!
9. It's a story of "rags to riches."
10. Mr. Burke's election effort bogs down every time.
11. They forgot to charge tax on the tags I bought.
12. He lacks polish, but his speech tugs at your heart.
13. Beck's Drugstore begs you to bring it back.
14. Billy's car has been in three wrecks, but it still chugs along.
15. Terry never nags at him to fix the car.

Two Fricatives

When two fricatives occur together, you must be sure to articulate both sounds and permit the air stream to come through the first closure before permitting it to come through the second. There are three dangers here: (1) omission of one of the consonants, (2) the addition of a vowel between the two consonants, and (3) unvoicing of voiced sounds.

/fs/ AND /vz/

leaf's	leaves
thief's	thieves
knife's	knives
waif's	waves
proof's	proves
half's	halves
shelf's	shelves
scarf's	scarves
strife's	strives
safe's	saves
loafs	loaves
wife's	wives
Duff's	doves

1. One's beliefs are his own business.
2. Life's a vapor that quickly vanishes.
3. The safes were supposed to be burglarproof.
4. The roof's on fire!
5. Jerry loafs around the house all day.
6. He often reads from *Leaves of Grass.*
7. A good politician, he loves a difficult campaign.
8. She lives in an adjoining county.
9. Mark believes in miracles, but he never performs any.
10. He rants and raves over insignificant irritations.
11. He thinks he deceives us, but his life's an open book.
12. His wife's motto is "Don't make waves!"
13. It's good that she saves everything; her husband just loafs all the time.
14. His story? He laughs, he loves, he leaves.
15. My lawyer says the proof's missing; that proves he's incompetent.
16. He gives a lot of his time to the club. He serves on three committees.
17. Half's not enough. I want back everything those thieves took.
18. We feast while most of the world starves. Can't the "haves" share with the "have-nots?"
19. I like your new shelves, but this shelf's warped.
20. My wife's got at least twenty scarves.
21. The more he delves into philosophy, the more he believes in nothing.
22. We've got to buy a new set of kitchen knives; this knife's not sharp enough to cut butter.
23. He thrives on controversy; strife's a medicine to him.
24. She loves everybody. That's my wife's problem too.

25. My nerves are not as good as they used to be. My staff's driving me crazy.

/θs/ (ths) AND /ðz/ (thz)

youth's	youths
breaths	breathes
wreath's	wreaths/wreathes
baths	bathes
tooth's	teethes
oath's	oaths
path's	paths
cloth's	cloths

1. Authorities were unable to reach the youth's parents.
2. For your health's sake, you should stop drinking.
3. He accepts without question many incredible myths.
4. The material comes in various widths and lengths.
5. It is 99$\frac{44}{100}$ per cent pure.
6. She bathes in goats' milk.
7. Are there any truths that are self-evident?
8. The dancer writhes six hours a night at the club.
9. Paths that are "untrod" are not paths at all.
10. Not even music soothes those savages.
11. He says his wealth's a curse, but he won't curse me with it.
12. Believing an oath's worthless, he takes oaths all the time.
13. He loathes the church, but he tithes his money anyway.
14. The path's not well marked. Those youths have stolen all the signs.
15. The earth's a tiny spaceship with problems too big for our outdated myths.
16. He mouths the right words when his wrath's not kindled.
17. I'm glad we took two wreaths with us; one wreath's ribbon was damaged.
18. Youth's worshipped in America. I wish truths were too.

Sibilant Followed by a Stop

When a stop consonant follows a sibilant at the end of a word, the sibilant is articulated in the usual way, and the stop must be fully closed. Unless a vowel immediately follows the stop in the next word, the stop will not be released with aspiration (an explosive puff of breath).

There are two common dangers, or problems, associated with this consonant combination: (1) omission of the stop consonant and (2) overaspiration of the release of the stop. Although the stop consonant does not always explode in this combination, it always *stops*. The air stream is completely obstructed for a moment. During the time that the stop is being articulated, of course, no air at all is emitted, and the time taken by the closure is necessary to indicate the presence of the stop sound. You must be sure, in these combinations, that the articulators completely block off the air for the stop sound; the stop must stop! The second danger is almost the opposite of the first. Some speakers, in an effort to be precise, overarticulate the stop sound in the combination, releasing the stop in a great puff of air. To most listeners, this sounds pedantic and affected. We do not recommend it.

/sk/

1. I only ask for what is just.
2. The risk is too great for so small a reward.
3. He said it was carved from an elephant's tusk.
4. Mr. Fiske wore his uniform to the party.
5. Everyone had his own task to perform.
6. A brisk walk is good for what ails you.
7. Nothing is more beautiful than Sounion at dusk.
8. My desk is a dreadful mess.
9. He had a flask in his pocket, but I didn't ask what was in it.
10. He must have bathed in musk oil.
11. She shouldn't have taken the mask off.
12. I want to whisk you away to some deserted island!
13. I would risk everything to bask in your smiles.
14. The farmer taught me how to husk the corn.
15. Mr. Rusk's car has disc brakes.

/sp/

1. The cookies were not crisp.
2. Have you detected a lisp in my speech?
3. No one told her that the clasp was not fastened.
4. A wasp sting can be very painful.
5. You could have heard the gasp ten miles away!
6. I told you not to grasp my hand that way!
7. Your lisp doesn't bother me.
8. There was a tiny wisp of smoke on the horizon.
9. The hasp on the trunk is broken.
10. You can grasp my meaning, if you try.

/st/

1. He lives in Westport.
2. She is the least beautiful of the sisters.
3. Roast pork is on the menu tonight.
4. The note is past due.
5. What is your worst problem in speech?
6. I want your best quality of merchandise.

7. I missed Carolyn in the crowd.
8. I haven't the least doubt we'll win.
9. The horse is now at the post position.
10. What is your next question?
11. The enemy was forced back by the advancing troops.
12. I disagreed with the last proposition.
13. I trust you will rest better tonight.
14. Voters crossed party lines to elect that candidate.
15. The famous journalist was almost blind.
16. The defendant was accused of blasphemy against God.
17. His taste buds must be dead.
18. It is a situation of the utmost gravity.
19. I attended the cast party with her.
20. They lost money on that investment.
21. You must go to the game next week.
22. They all cost more than I can afford to pay.
23. Conservatives do not trust "big government."
24. I must practice diligently and regularly.
25. You could list many more examples for practice.

/ʃt/ (sht)

1. He was lashed to the mast.
2. Mashed potatoes are somewhat fattening.
3. She secretly wished for more, but said nothing.
4. He pushed his way through the crowd.
5. Several were crushed by the stampeding mob.
6. We meshed immediately.
7. She looked crushed when I said we had rushed into it.
8. What fury was unleashed on me!
9. I looked away when the car crashed.
10. She flashed a big smile, and I hushed instantly.
11. When the stocks went up, I cashed in.
12. Eleanor laughed at the joke—but she blushed.
13. He has been punished enough.
14. She furnished the entire house in Early Tacky.
15. He brandished a knife, took what he wished, and vanished.

Clusters

Stop Between Two Continuants

When a stop consonant occurs between two continuants (consonants that, unlike stops, can be sustained), you must take care to make a firm and complete closure for the stop sound. The stop will not be released in an explosion, but will be released instead through the opening for the fricative that follows. The danger, of course, is that you will omit the stop sound altogether and combine the two continuant sounds that remain. Listen to these clusters. There should be an instant between the two continuant sounds when no air is coming out at all, because the articulators have completely stopped the air stream to form the stop sound in the middle of the cluster. *Grafts* should not sound like *graphs*. In that /fts/ cluster, the air must stop completely to represent the /t/. Otherwise, the result is not /fts/, but /fs/.

/fts/

1. Dick is studying arts and crafts at the college.
2. The posse is searching all the hay lofts in the county.
3. She lifts our spirits when she enters the room.
4. The Crofts plan to spend their honeymoon in the Virgin Islands.
5. The lawn mower left tufts of grass here and there.
6. They all ran to the left side of the ship.
7. I cross my fingers when he shifts gears.
8. He never lifts a hand to help around the house.
9. I never laughed so much in all my life.
10. She records the gifts as they come in.

/lts/

1. He tilts the machine every time he plays.
2. The coat was made from dozens of pelts.
3. The gold is stored in underground vaults.
4. Every sweet saying melts in her mouth.
5. Fearful of burglars, she always bolts the door.
6. I like the way she belts out a song.
7. He paid a fortune for those colts.
8. He wilts if she so much as looks at him.
9. Her remedy for every ailment was "a dose of salts."
10. How those clowns walk on stilts is a mystery to me.

/nts/

1. She put several new dents in the fenders today.
2. We bought six pints of sherbet for the punch.
3. One of the mints is in Denver.
4. At the party she performed unusual stunts.
5. The Senate consents more than it advises.
6. He recants every other day.
7. Larry is worse; he rants and raves every day.
8. Rents in New York City are outrageous.
9. Other than that, I have no major complaints.
10. He faints at the sight of blood; she faints at the sight of flesh.

/sts/

Distinguish between the following pairs of words by making a firm closure between the two /s/ sounds with the tongue tip on the gum ridge:

mass	masts
guess	guests
lass	lasts
Joyce	joists
Tess	tests
miss	mists
pass	past's
Bess	bests
East Side, West Side	last season, next season
first semester, last semester	most certain, least certain
best sort, worst sort	

1. I want to take the test some other day.
2. The host spoke with all the guests.
3. Last season, I played on the varsity.
4. Next summer, I'm going to Europe.
5. It was the first star for which the captain looked.
6. The car almost started.
7. She raced six times and lost them all.
8. Our senator voted against Smith's proposal.
9. Increased governmental activity has characterized this past century.
10. On the way home, she passed several tall buildings.
11. We lost several games last season. Just suppose we had won!
12. He is the worst sort of rogue. You just missed seeing him.
13. That car cost several thousand dollars.
14. We must see them tonight.
15. I cannot insist Sam take the position.
16. Of all the employees, he is least secure.
17. It was the least suitable selection.
18. She passed seven courses in basket weaving.
19. I'm told that is the best sign.
20. Mine will be the last speech of the evening.
21. There are seven tests scheduled for tomorrow.
22. Kipling wrote his *Just So Stories* for his own children.
23. He kept the rest so as to raise the price.
24. They live on East Sixth Street.
25. List some other examples.
26. I must not waste so much time.

27. I spent most of my energy on the last series.
28. Forget past setbacks. Give your best service.
29. They have wasted vast sums. The costs are unbelievable.
30. The little pests refuse to give up. How can they persist so?
31. I hope it lasts a long time.
32. He produced lists of names.
33. Our host's maid took the night off. The roast's ruined.
34. The guests hardly noticed.
35. She trusts anyone—even the worst sort of people.

/ldz/

1. That sorority holds a meeting only once a month.
2. Ruthlessly he wields his power.
3. Our contractor builds each house to the owner's specifications.
4. The child's every whim is indulged.
5. A good leader welds a group into a cohesive unit.
6. I don't understand how he holds on to his power.
7. A walk in the fields is therapy for me.
8. She shields her children from the realities of life.
9. The guild's power has been broken by the strike.
10. He fields questions like a professional politician.

/ndz/

1. He lends his name to every liberal cause that comes along.
2. The bands are massed for the big parade.
3. Wally is effective at predicting economic trends.
4. Blest be the tie that blinds!
5. She had no grounds for that action.
6. I hope he finds out in time.
7. Friends are a necessity—not a luxury.
8. The boss made unreasonable demands on me.
9. The ends do not justify the means. Well, that depends.
10. I think he stepped out of bounds on that play.

/sks/

1. She asks every teacher the same question.
2. Who carves those symbols on the desks?
3. He refuses to take any risks at all.
4. Joyce never shirks her tasks.
5. The Rusks are an old, respected family in this community.
6. The flasks are all empty.
7. What makes this desk so rough?
8. I think the elephant tusks are fake.
9. He has several slipped discs in his back.

10. Now Shelley basks in the Florida sun.
11. Do the police have the right to frisk suspects that way?
12. What makes musk so pungent?
13. You have to risk something to get something.
14. These tasks are not menial.
15. It's illegal to wear the masks out on the street.

/sps/

1. My sister is afraid of wasps.
2. Wisps of smoke were visible on the horizon.
3. She grasps everything very quickly.
4. Cleopatra and the asps were bosom pals.
5. She said that malocclusion was the reason she lisps.
6. The hasps are always broken on these doors.
7. I wish I could grasp some of your ideas.
8. The dentist mentioned defective cusps—whatever they are.
9. He told me to make a clear, crisp sound.
10. She tightly clasps every new psychological fad to her tortured psyche.

Two Stops Followed by a Sibilant

To master these consonant clusters, you should remember two things we have told you earlier: (1) when two stop sounds come together, the first is stopped, but not exploded, and then the second is stopped and exploded; and (2) when a stop and a fricative come together (in that order), a firm closure is made for the stop, but the release is made through the opening for the fricative.

If you combine these two principles, you will have no difficulty with these clusters. Be sure that you completely obstruct the outgoing air stream to form the first stop; then, firmly stop the air column with the articulators to form the second stop; and, finally, release the second stop sound at the place of articulation of the sibilant. The /ts/, remember, is a consonant combination, and there is only one release of the air on that combination; the /t/ is released through the /s/ position.

/kts/

Read the following pairs of words, being certain that you distinguish the first from the second by getting a good firm closure for both plosives:

ax	acts
tracks	tracts
packs	pacts
sex	sects
ducks	ducts

1. He tried to get all the facts before making a judgment.
2. The professor's wife corrects all the papers for him.
3. The reformers stood on the corner distributing tracts.
4. My partner deducts his gambling losses on his tax return.
5. The chain restricts my movement considerably.
6. I didn't expect so much attention.
7. Let's hope the judge acts on his case soon.
8. I didn't say "What sex do you know about?"; I said "What sects do you know about?"
9. This course inflicts a lot of pain on the students.
10. I hope she perfects all my papers in this same way.
11. She certainly expects a lot from us.
12. After the representative packs in all the necessary clauses, then the pacts are to be signed.
13. That statement conflicts with your earlier position.
14. The ducts are clogged, and the ducks are dying.
15. She always exacts a high price.
16. She acts as if she doesn't see me.
17. I've got to reject some of these demands.
18. She attracts a lot of admirers.
19. After those willful acts, the ax fell.
20. How can you act so calm in a crisis; these conflicts are unbearable.

/pts/

1. That fiend corrupts everyone with whom he has contact.
2. The orchestra performed excerpts from a number of longer works.
3. The crypts are beneath the church.
4. That clique disrupts every meeting of the fraternity.
5. I'm told that she accepts any invitation she receives.
6. I don't want to be around when she erupts again.
7. He interrupts every sentence his wife starts.
8. He invited them to view the crypts.
9. Everybody's coming except Sam.
10. He's a very inept soldier.
11. She's never slept so long before.
12. They kept searching until they found it.

Sibilant Plus Two Stops

This cluster formation should offer you no difficulty if you have mastered the principle related to two consecutive stops sounds. The usual simplification of these clusters results from omission of the first of the two stops and the combining of the two remaining sounds. In careless speech, then, *masked* becomes *massed* and *clasped* becomes *classed.* Listen to what some of your friends do to the word *asked,* and you will be more careful to articulate all the sounds of these clusters. As in any other consonant combination involving two consecutive stops, the first stop is completely closed but does not explode, and the second both stops and explodes.

/skt/

1. She risked her reputation to come tonight.
2. I asked her a dozen times and always got the same reply.
3. All day at the beach we basked in the sun.
4. We attended every masked ball during Carnival.
5. That tremendous tusked animal came charging at us.
6. He frisked us but found nothing.
7. The performers were whisked away quickly.
8. She said I asked a lot of senseless questions.
9. The farmer disked the field.
10. The masked actor could not see; he risked injury every performance.

/spt/

1. I gasped in wonder at the sight.
2. She thrust her tongue between her teeth when she lisped.
3. He grasped my hand and welcomed me to the United States.
4. In her clenched hand she clasped the dollar bill.
5. Her voice rasped out its angry message.

Three Continuants

Making the articulatory adjustments necessary to produce a cluster made up of three continuants requires flexibility and control, but you should have no difficulty adding the initial continuant if you mastered the production of two consecutive fricatives. The usual distortion of this cluster formation is the omission of the second continuant, so that *health's*, for example, rhymes with *else* and *fifths* rhymes with *if's*.

Three Consecutive Continuants

1. Three fifths of the class were extraordinarily gifted.
2. He had difficulty adding seven twelfths and nine sixteenths.
3. He said those strange chords were ninths and thirteenths.
4. Why does liquor come in fifths?
5. The variation in lengths made sorting easier.
6. Youths that get into trouble are not always delinquents.
7. How one breathes this polluted air and lives is a mystery!
8. The physician advised us to move West for our health's sake.
9. Not prelaw, but prewealth's his major.
10. Her strength's returning, but it has been a slow process.

Vowel Combinations

NONPHONEMIC DIPHTHONGS

Earlier, we defined a diphthong as a blend of two vowels. (See p. 46.) We also distinguished between phonemic and nonphonemic diphthongs. (See pp. 238–239.) The difference, you remember, is that phonemes cannot be broken apart; they are the lowest separate sound unit in a language. If a diphthong functions as a phoneme, its two components cannot be broken apart; they are not recognized (perceived) as separate units pasted temporarily together. Rather, those components have lost their individual identity, and the diphthong itself is heard as a sound unit—an indivisible sound unit. In that sense, phonemic diphthongs resemble affricates. Just as affricates are made up of two component consonant articulations, but are recognized as single sounds, so also phonemic diphthongs are made up of two vowel qualities but are recognized as single vowel sounds (phonemes). On the other hand, nonphonemic diphthongs are diphthongs (blends of two vowels) in which each vowel retains its own individual identity. The two vowels do not function as a single unit (phoneme); they can be pulled apart and combined with other sounds.

Look at (and listen to) the words *ear, air, Ayre, or, oar, your,* and *are.* All of these words contain diphthongs, but they are nonphonemic diphthongs. They are blends of two separate vowel phonemes. *Ear* begins with the vowel /ɪ/ (ĭ) and ends with the little unstressed vowel /ɚ/ (ər). All of these words contain the unstressed vowel /ɚ/ (ər). These vowel blends are very common in American English, and you should get used to producing the combination of vowels.

Here are some practice materials to assist you in work on these nonphonemic diphthongs.

/ɪɚ/ (ĭər)

ear	mere
beer/bier	near
beard	peer
dear	queer
fear	rear
fierce	seer/sear
gear	sheer
hear	steer
cheer	tear
jeer	veer
clear	we're
leer	year

1. Here we go again. How dreary!
2. Speak clearly if you want to appear educated.
3. Others may sneer, but Pam thinks Billy Saltine sincere.
4. Bob has no fear of flying, but we're terrified.
5. Shakespeare wrote some weird plays.
6. The performers staged a fierce war dance with spears.
7. Cheer up! The rest is sheer enjoyment.
8. My dear, you are always in arrears.
9. He merely said he thinks the end is near.
10. The plea seared his conscience, and he tearfully repented—again.

/ɛɚ/ (ĕər)

air	lair
bare	mare
Blair	ne'er
dare	pair
fare/fair	rare
flair	share
hair	snare
chair	spare
care	stare
Claire	wear

1. There is no excuse for such overbearing behavior.
2. What is the air fare to Dallas? I couldn't care less.
3. How do you repair an affair of the heart?
4. Get yourself an affair repairman. But beware of his price.
5. You can't scare me. How dare you try?
6. Mike was not aware that Charlotte was upstairs.
7. It was a daring show, but the dancer barely moved.
8. Don't despair. Someday the government will "promote the general welfare."
9. I want to live where you can dare to be different.
10. Don't stare, but glance at that man standing on the chair.
11. I don't share your views, but I'm prepared to chair the meeting anyway.
12. I don't care if they are scarce; I wouldn't wear them on a bet.

/eɚ/ (āər)

Ayre
Bayer
gayer
grayer
layer

mayor
conveyor

1. I only know what Sayre told me.
2. The lyrics say, "Gayer than laughter are you."
3. I am a little grayer this year than last.
4. I fell onto a conveyor belt.
5. It doesn't matter who the mayor is.
6. I have found a player piano in working condition.
7. Convinced by the commercials, she would only buy Bayer.

/ɔɚ/ (ôər)

or	orb
for	nor
war	ward
quart	horse
order	border
morn	warn
warm	north
lord	cord
dwarf	quarrel

1. The border guards ordered us out of the bus.
2. I look forward to her warm greeting every morning.
3. They had their worst quarrel standing on a corner.
4. I didn't forbid you; I just warned you of the results.
5. Why do nations resort to war?
6. I'm short on cash. Can you put in a quart of gas?
7. I don't even know what quarter horses are.
8. The warden is lord of this manor.
9. The resort is north of the city.
10. After the stormy fight, he showed remorse.

/oɚ/ (ōər)

Most Americans, but not all, would pronounce these words with /oɚ/ (ōər). You may discover that in your idiolect or your dialect, the pronunciation is /ɔɚ/ (ôər).

oar	more
bore	pour
door	roar
fore	sore/soar
gore	shore
whore	tore
core	store
lore	wore

1. The gold is stored at Fort Knox.
2. After the game, I was hoarse and had a sore throat.
3. I have been bored all through this course.
4. Fun? Of course, the matador was gored.
5. The crowd roared when he tore into the opposition.
6. I adore the color, but why would she paint the door green?
7. I've told you before I know where everything is stored.
8. The bartender refuses to pour any more after four drinks.
9. She wore out the record before you came.
10. I can't afford to go into that store again.

/ʊɚ/ (o͝oər)

boor	tour
Coors	your
lure	pure
jury	Europe
moor	endure
poor	ensure
sure	mature
allure	adjure

1. There is no cure for boorishness.
2. He may be poor, but he is rich in assurance.
3. He was a poor choice for the jury.
4. I won't go to Europe on a conducted tour.
5. How can we assure that only mature audiences will see it?
6. You're just expected to endure it.
7. Why do impure substances have such allure?
8. I can't be completely sure, but I think it's secure there.
9. I adjure you: Stay pure!
10. Such fury! I'm sure it must be phony.

/ɑɚ/ (äər)

are	mar
bar	par
darling	part
far	shard
hard	smart
jar	star
char	start
car	tar
card	partner
lard	yard

1. You may not be smart, but you drive a hard bargain.
2. I hate to start going to bars again.
3. Darling, I'll leave the door ajar.
4. I don't want to mar the party, but I hate all forms of cards.
5. Are you sure that lard works better than Crisco?
6. The star of the show took a hard fall right on stage.
7. Don't start. I haven't got a partner!
8. Fill the jar with oil, and the urn with charcoal.
9. Art can't go much farther.
10. He darted into the crowd as the rally started.

NONPHONEMIC TRIPHTHONGS

Triphthongs are simply three vowels blended together. If you take a phonemic diphthong and add another little vowel to it, you have a nonphonemic triphthong. The little vowel /ɚ/ (ər) can be added to all three phonemic diphthongs. Here are practice materials for those three combinations.

/ɑʊɚ/ (ouər)

hour	glower
bower	power
cower	sour
dower	shower
Gower	tower
Howard	devour

1. I'm sure she was glowering at Howard.
2. She said I was a tower of strength in her hour of need.
3. The two spiders' relationship turned sour and she devoured him.
4. Why are you cowering? I have no power over you.
5. Mr. Brower was showered with gifts at his promotion.

/ɑɪɚ/ (iər)

ire	mire
buyer	pyre
dire	pliers
fire	sire
flyer	inspire
hire	desire
cryer	tire
lyre	wire

1. He was hired by the law firm of Muck and Meyer.
2. I have no desire to see another of his tiresome plays.
3. Why was he fired? His complaints raised the boss's ire.

4. You can't fix a tire with pliers!
5. Dimitri tried to inspire me by playing on his lyre. You shouldn't call anything or anyone a liar!

/ɔɪɚ/ (oiər)

Boyer
employer
destroyer

1. Is one who annoys an "annoyer?"
2. I enjoy her Southern accent.
3. He was stationed on a destroyer in the navy.
4. In my judgment, Boyer is the best.
5. My employer will not give me a recommendation.

6
Pronunciation of Words

I N THE preceding chapters, we talked only in terms of improving your production of sounds—either individual sounds or combinations of sounds. We are now ready to give attention to putting those sounds and sound combinations together into meaningful speech. We turn now to the problems of words and thought groups (phrases).

A word is a verbal symbol. When spoken, a word stands for an idea; when uttered by a speaker and heard and understood by a listener, it "means" something. A word can stir up associations (meanings) in the mind of a receiver.

Sounds (phonemes) do not *have* meaning or *represent* meaning or *stir up* meaning; they *affect* meaning. If you substitute one phoneme for another in a word, the change can change what the word is and what the word represents. Replace /i/ (ē) with /e/ (ā) in the word *meat* and the word is changed to *mate*. Spoken alone, however, the sound /i/ (ē) does not mean anything.

Syllables are defined as a sound or group of sounds uttered on one chest pulse. Words are made up of syllables—sounds uttered on these little chest pulses of exhaled air. But syllables, removed from the word in which they appear, do not mean anything either. (Of course some words are only one syllable long, but it is the *word* that conveys the meaning, not the syllable.) Pronounce the word *wonderful*. How many little pulse units is it broken into? Three: *won-der-ful*. Pull out the middle syllable (although we really cannot pronounce an unstressed syllable alone), and see if *der* means anything. Of course it does not. Syllables are not the units that represent ideas. Words are.

From studying Chapter 1, you know that words are constructed of little meaning units called morphemes. The morphemes are the building blocks of which words are made. But morphemes, like syllables, cannot stand alone (unless, of course, the word is made up of only one morpheme). We use /z/ to represent the idea of more than one (plural) and attach that morpheme to words ending in a voiced sound. But the morpheme /z/ uttered by itself would be meaningless to a listener. However, say *words* (/wɜ˞dz/ or *wûrdz*), and a listener will get the idea.

The point is that words are the symbols we use to convey our meanings.

And distortions of words—mispronunciations—may interfere with the process of communication. Mispronunciations may very well present a major barrier to communication between a speaker and a listener. If a sender deviates much from the customary way of pronouncing the word, and the word received differs very much from a listener's expectations of what that word should sound like, misunderstanding may easily take place. A listener may associate a completely different meaning with the word—if you send a pronunciation that differs very much from the norm, the usual pronunciation.

Because the pronunciation of words is so important to effective and efficient communication, we will analyze the two basic elements of word pronunciation.

Elements of Pronunciation

There are two basic elements involved in pronouncing words. Pronunciation, of course, is the way words are uttered. The two component elements are (1) the selection of sounds, and (2) the stress given to the various syllables in the word. You can, then, mispronounce a word in two ways. Either you can use incorrect sounds in the word's formation, or you can put the stress on the wrong syllable or syllables.

SELECTION OF SOUNDS

Because Chapters 2 and 3 dealt with sounds—the customary way to produce them and the common deviations associated with them—this section is, in a sense, a review. We will be focusing on the material in a different way, however, because we will be looking at the entire word. Four types of sound changes affect the pronunciation of a word. Or, put another way, four problems related to selection of sounds result in the mispronunciation of a word: (1) omission of a sound or sounds, (2) addition of a sound or sounds, (3) distortions and substitutions of a sound or sounds, and (4) transposition (reversal) of sounds.

Omissions

Leaving out sounds (remember we are not talking about the letters of the words as they are spelled, but the sounds of the words as they are pronounced) is one of the most common forms of mispronunciation. Just as a reminder, we will look at some of the sounds most in danger of being omitted.

Consonants in the middle of words—especially if there are two consonants together—are certainly in danger. Pronounce this list of words. Do you omit any of the consonants in the middle of the words? Are you tempted to omit any of the consonants?

center
handle
holder
wonder
matter
atlas
Easter
mister
recognize
exactly
headless
after
Mazda
handling
obvious
obfuscation
subvert
softer
draftsman
helper
lumber
pumping
outstanding
outspoken
Southern
heater
alley
arrid
Barret
already
almost
Calder
falter

Well, the list could be endless. In fact, *endless* should have been on the list of tempting words. But a review of Chapters 2 and 3 should remind you of the sounds most in danger of omission; try again the lists provided for you in those chapters, testing for the omission of middle consonants.

Consonants at the ends of words are also in danger of being omitted. Here are just a few examples to remind you of this problem. If you review Chapters 2 and 3, you will find many more examples of such tempters.

last
hand
hold
kept
dreamed
plant
banked
Colt
hurts
words
sagged
act
clasp
kicked
rubbed
sobs
helm
ask
polled

Consonant combinations—both blends and clusters—afford ample opportunity for omissions. At the beginning, in the middle, and at the ends of words, consonant combinations often get cheated by omitted consonants. Pronounce these words aloud to check for possible omissions. A thorough review of Chapter 5 would be useful also.

statistics
sceptical
screaming
structure
smother
special
specific
splutter
sprinkle
pacts
feasts
holds
hands
tenths
fifths
unmasked
tasks
cents

colts
roads
shelves
thrives
swerves
blends
swiftly
abruptly
gifts
concepts
acts
facts
wooden shoes
shouldn't
wasps

Vowels between consonants are often in danger of being omitted—
especially if the consonants can then be combined into a blend, or the
consonants then become abutting consonants (one ending a syllable and
the other beginning the next syllable). Check your own pronunciation
of these words to check for this problem.

support
parade
delicate
relevant
suppose
believe
belong
palacial
bereaved
alimony
satirical

Another common problem related to the omission of vowels is that of
omitting the second of two vowels separated by a hiatus (a tiny pause
to separate consecutive vowels into separate syllables). The omission of
the second vowel makes the distorted word shorter by giving it one syllable less than it deserved. Check your pronunciation of these words, and
listen carefully to be sure you get all the vowels in.

poem
ruin
museum
liable

geography
sociology   (But which vowel is in danger?)
violet
Iowa
intuition
McKuen
Owen
jewel
society
sodium
hilarious
riot
quiet

As we noted earlier in the chapter on sound changes, dissimilation accounts for some omissions. The omitting of a repeated sound (or related sound) is called *haplology*. Haplology usually results in the loss of an entire syllable, so we refer to this kind of omission as "telescoping." If a whole syllable disappears, it seems to slide inside another syllable and disappear like one segment of a telescope pushed inside the next one. If two syllables in a row have the same sound (or a related sound), there is a danger of omitting one of the sounds or of omitting an entire syllable. *Probably* may turn into *probly* and *attitude* into *a-tude* and *constitution* into *constution*. An example of dissimilation without the loss of a syllable would be the pronunciation of the word *library* as *liberry*. Here are some words that may tempt you to omit a sound or even a whole syllable.

probably
institute
constitute
restitution
attitudinal
candidate
Mississippi
catatonic
irrepressible
titillation
fastidious
necessary
necessity
anonymity
immemorial
particularly
similarly

Additions

Just as you can mispronounce a word by omitting sounds, so also you can mispronounce a word by adding sounds. If you review Chapter 2, you will note several sounds that commonly get added to words in which they do not belong. We will not repeat all of those additions here, but we will remind you of a few of the most common ones.

Adding /g/ in words like *singer* and in phrases like *Long Island* is not uncommon. (See pp. 142–145.) Nor is adding /r/ in words like *gnawing* or in phrases like *saw it* very uncommon—at least in greater New York and parts of New England. We encourage you to remove the /g/ from *singer* and the extra /r/ from the "idear of it" and the "lawr of the land." In the South and Midwest, some speakers add /ɚ/ in the words *wash* and *Washington*. This addition is considered nonstandard, and we encourage you to remove the *r*.

Oncet for *once*, *sumpthing* for *something*, *how wit is* for *how it is*, and *I yam* for *I am* are all examples of mispronunciations caused by the addition of sounds.

Spelling leads some people into mispronunciations. As you know, letters in the spelling of a word do not always indicate sounds. A few people, probably trying to be precise, add sounds to words (and thus mispronounce them)—having been led astray by the spelling. Putting an /h/ in *honest*, a /b/ in *subtle*, an /l/ in *calm* and *palm* (and other such words), and /n/ in *kiln* are all examples of such additions.

Almost all of the additions we have mentioned so far have been added consonants. But vowels can get added to words also. Because we are used to having vowels between most consonants of separate syllables, some speakers insert a schwa between the final consonant of one syllable and the initial consonant of the following syllable. In that case, for example, *athlete* becomes *athalete*. Here are some words that present such a problem for some speakers:

athlete
athletics
ably
airplane
amazement
bracelet
burglar
business
capably
evening
lively
lovely
nestling

nimbly
rivalry
tablet
ticklish
toddler
ugly

Some speakers are tempted to insert a schwa between the /l/ and /m/ when the blend /lm/ is final in a word. Check your pronunciation of these words:

elm
helm
film
realm
overwhelm

You may be tempted to insert a schwa between the /o/ (ō) and the /n/ in words ending in /on/ (ōn). You might even be tempted to add /w/ and schwa both between the /o/ and /n/. Check your pronunciation of these words. (For further examples, see p. 215.)

bone
groan
known
shown
stone
won't

Some speakers are wont to pull consonant blends apart and insert schwa between the two consonants. The blends /tr/, /dr/, /br/, /bl/, /pr/, and /pl/ seem to offer the greatest temptations. Pronounce the following list of words. Each contains a consonant blend in which some speakers insert a schwa.

monstrous
foundry
hindrance
laundry
wondrous
brace
umbrella
unbroken
bleed
blight

bloated
prince
unproved
pretty
please
plead
plenty

We have a number of words in the language which end in ĭəs (/ɪəs/).
Devious is one example. Perhaps, by analogy, some speakers mispronounce some words ending in əs (/əs/) by adding ĭ (/ɪ/) or y (/j/). Of
course the *-ious* words come from words that ended in *-y* or whose roots
ended in that sound. A person filled with *envy* would be *envious*. But a
fault that would make one *grieve* would be *grievous*—not *grievious*.
Check your pronunciation of the following words. They all contain /əs/—
not /ɪəs/ (ĭəs) or /jəs/ (yəs).

bulbous
contagious
disastrous
gorgeous
genus
grievous
heinous
membranous
mercurous
mischievous
momentous
outrageous
stupendous
sulfurous

Some of you are bound to be wondering about such words as *contagious,
gorgeous,* and *outrageous.* Why only -əs (/əs/) and no ĭ (/ɪ/)? A review
of the material on sound changes (assimilation) should give you the
answer. In any case, as the words are pronounced today, they do not
contain that ĭ (/ɪ/).

An interesting vowel insertion that does not fit into any of the categories we have discussed is the case of turning the word *heartrending*
into *heartrendering.* Frankly, we can only guess at the origin of this
addition. *Rending* is based on the old word *rend,* which means to tear, to
rip. (The past tense of that verb was *rent,* as in "The veil was rent in
twain." Because we don't use the word *rend* much any more (except in
this clichéd phrase), it probably made little sense to many speakers

who heard (and used) it. *Render* is a verb with several modern meanings. One meaning is "to give," but that meaning makes no sense in this cliché. Another meaning—still familiar to many, if not most, Americans until the last couple of generations—has to do with a process of applying heat to meat so as to extract the fats and oils. It means to melt down. Lard is rendered (extracted, melted out) from the fat of butchered hogs. Perhaps that was the metaphor seen by the people who turned *rending* into *rendering*. If not, there is no explanation we know except that an /ɚ/ (ər) was inserted after the /d/ and before the -*ing* suffix. The addition is considered nonstandard.

Distortions and Substitutions

In Chapters 2 and 3, we discussed the common distortions of all the sounds of the language. There is no point in repeating all that material here. Go back and review the various distortions and substitutions we discussed there. Dentalization of lingua-alveolar consonants, unvoicing of final consonants, raising of the tongue on the /θ/ (th) and /ð/ (*th*) sounds, retraction of /ɔ/ (ô) and /ɑɪ/ (ī), nasalization of vowels and diphthongs, diphthongation, substitution of /ɪ/ (ĭ) for /ɛ/ (ĕ) or /n/ for /ŋ/ (n̂g), and raising the /æ/ (ă) vowel—all of these and many other distortions and substitutions—were discussed at length in Chapters 2 and 3. It should be enough here to remind you that all these distortions and substitutions of sounds result in the mispronunciation of the words involved.

Transposition of Sounds

Reversing sounds is another means of mispronouncing a word. Switching the sounds, of course, turns it into a different word—which may or may not mean something. The word that suffers this indignity most often is probably the word *relevant*. Look at the word, and think of what you say for that word. Is it really *relevant*, or are you tempted to say *revelant?* And what about *irrelevant?* Do you reverse the /l/ and /r/ there? (The scholarly name for sound reversal is *metathesis.*) Another word that is a candidate for most metathesized word is the little word *asked*. Perhaps because the word is so commonly used, it gets twisted around more often than *relevant*. Look at the word *asked*. It has only four sounds: /æ/ (ă), /s/, /k/, and /t/. But many speakers reverse the second and third sounds. Then *asked* becomes *axed*. Indeed, the same speakers may also say *ax* (/æks/) (ăks) for *ask* (/æsk/) (ăsk). When a student says to us, "Don't ax me," we assure him (or her) we have no intention of cutting anyone down with a hatchet, ax, or any other dangerous weapon. Even then the student may not hear the distinction between *ax* and *ask*, because he or she may be so used to the reversal of sounds it sounds right.

Sometimes letters seem to get reversed in the mind and the sounds follow. That would account for turning *perspiration* into *prespiration, hundred* into *hunderd, children* into *childern,* and *pronounce* into *pernounce.*

Turning the word *escape* into *ekscape* is not quite sound reversal because the /k/ reappears in the second syllable—after having switched with the /s/.

SYLLABIC STRESS

The first element of pronunciation we discussed was the selection of sounds to include in the word. You must choose the right sounds and produce them in the conventional way if the word is to be pronounced "correctly." (Of course, "correctness" has to do with acceptability—with what is expected and respected.)

But you can mispronounce a word, even if you have selected all the right sounds to go into it. There is another element in pronunciation that is very important in English. That element is the *stress* we give the different syllables in a word.

Unlike some other languages in which syllables get level or equal stress, American English is characterized by differences in the amount of stress on syllables. It is difficult to define exactly what stress is. It is much easier to tell you how stress is achieved than to tell you precisely what it is. But we will try. Stress is the giving of emphasis or prominence; it is the process of making a sound or group of sounds stand out. All of the syllables in a word do not get equal prominence or attention; those differences are differences in stress.

Although we have talked about stressed syllables and unstressed syllables (and vowels) in earlier chapters, in truth there is no such thing as an *un*stressed syllable. All syllables get *some* stress or attention—or they would not be heard at all. The difference we were calling attention to earlier was a difference of degree: more stressed and less stressed. The so-called unstressed syllables are given less attention and prominence than are the "stressed" syllables.

Indeed, there are three degrees of stress in American English. These various levels of stress have been labeled primary (for the greatest stress), secondary (for less attention than primary but more than tertiary), and tertiary (the lowest or weakest stress of the three). It is the tertiary stress that we have been referring to as unstressed. A one-syllable word will receive, when spoken alone, primary stress. In connected speech, its stress would depend on its meaning, its function in the sentence or phrase, and the syllables around it. A two-syllable word, spoken alone, will probably have one syllable with primary stress and one syllable with tertiary stress. (The exceptions are two-syllable words that have equal primary stress on both syllables; these are called spondee words.) Some words may have enough syllables to contain primary, secondary, and tertiary stress in the one word. Let us examine these three levels of stress in a little more detail.

Most people think of primary stress as an accented syllable. That is a syllable that gets the highest attention we accord syllables. Say the word *stand* out loud. That word received primary stress. It stood alone, so it had to stand out.

Now say out loud the word *standard*. That word has two syllables. The two syllables divide between the /n/ and /d/ in the middle of the word. So we have two syllables: *stan-dard*. Which of the two syllables gets more attention? Which stands out more as you say the word? That is correct: *stan* does. (Note that you used a strong vowel in that syllable, but a weak /ə/ (ər) in the second syllable.) In that two-syllable word, we had the first syllable receiving primary stress and the second syllable receiving tertiary stress.

Now try the word *perform* out loud. Here again is a two-syllable word. Which receives the primary stress this time? Right again. It is the second syllable: *form*. The first syllable contains the little /ə/ (ər) vowel, and the syllable gets tertiary stress. Perhaps you should think of the three levels of stress as a kind of class system. Primary is first-class treatment, secondary is second-class treatment, and poor tertiary gets third-class treatment.

We mentioned that some two-syllable words (and phrases) contain two syllables of equal stress. And we mentioned the word *spondee*. That word comes to us from poetics, the analysis of poetry. If the rhythm has two strong beats in a row, the foot containing those two consecutive strong beats is called a spondee. Try this command out loud: *Stand back*. Which is the syllable that is stressed more? Which is the syllable that is stressed less? Or, which gets primary and which gets tertiary stress in this phrase? The answer probably is that you gave equal stress to both syllables in that phrase. Both are important ideas and of equal importance. Both get primary stress. The rhythm of the phrase *stand back*, therefore, is spondee: equal primary stress. The following words and phrases are also examples of spondee. You should be able to think of other examples.

> bookcase
> ice cream
> handmade
> archfoe
> quite so
> left hand
> toolbox
> strongman

no show
Old Maid
right on!
well done
blackbird
jackknife
get set

So far, we have given examples of words containing primary and tertiary stress, but none containing secondary stress. We are now ready to do that. Such examples will have to contain three or more syllables.

If you pronounce *polka dot,* you will note that it has three syllables: *pō-kə-dät.* You should also note that each of the three syllables gets a different amount of attention paid to it. The first syllable gets primary stress; the second syllable gets tertiary stress; and the third syllable gets secondary stress—more stress than the second syllable, but less than the first. Pronounce it again—just to be sure you hear the difference.

Pronounce the following words. Check to see if you can determine which syllables receive which level of stress.

dictionary
secretary
education
dormitory
institution
president
accident
generally
accuracy

Now, after you have checked on your own pronunciation of these words and determined what level of stress you use on the various syllables in the words, we will give you the customary stress patterns for those words. We will represent the words both in dictionary symbols and in IPA phonetic transcription. In the dictionaries, primary stress is indicated by an accent mark in thick, heavy type *after* the stressed syllable; secondary stress is indicated by a lighter accent mark; tertiary stress is indicated by the absence of a stress (or accent) mark. Hence, the word *avalanche* would be represented this way: *ăv′ə lănch′.* In IPA, the stress marks go *before* the syllable receiving the stress. The mark for primary stress is a short vertical line above the line of symbols; the mark for secondary stress is a short vertical line below the line of symbols; tertiary stress is indicated by the absence of a stress mark of either kind. Hence, the word *avalanche* would be represented this way in IPA: ˈæv ə ˌlæntʃ. Here are the sounds and stress patterns for the nine words.

REGULAR SPELLING	DICTIONARY DIACRITICS	IPA SYMBOLS
dictionary	dĭk′sh̯ə nĕ′rē	ˈdɪk ʃən ˌɛrɪ
secretary	sĕk′rĭ tĕ′rē	ˈsɛk rɪ ˌtɛ rɪ
education	ĕ′jŏŏ kā′sh̯ən	ˌɛd ʒʊ ˈkeɪ ʃən
dormitory	dôr′mə tō′rē	ˈdɔɚ mə ˌto rɪ
institution	ĭn′stĭ tōō′sh̯ən	ˌɪn stɪ ˈtju ʃən
president	prĕz′ə dənt	ˈprɛz ə dənt
accident	ăk′sĭ dənt	ˈæk sɪ dənt
generally	jĕn′ər ə lē	ˈdʒɛn ə rə lɪ
accuracy	ăk′yə rə sē	ˈæk jə rə sɪ

Do these stress patterns match your own? Can you now tell the difference between primary, secondary, and tertiary stress?

Thus far, we have talked about what stress is and noted three different levels of stress on the syllables in our words. But how is stress achieved? What do we *do* to stress a syllable and to make these differences in degree of stress? There are three factors involved in stressing a syllable: (1) increase in loudness, (2) higher pitch, and (3) longer duration. The amount of stress a syllable gets depends, then, on how much volume we give the syllable—how loud we make it; how high the pitch is when we utter the syllable; and how long we make the sounds in the syllable (and, hence, the relative length of the syllable itself).

Check for yourself and see if these three factors are not the cause of stress changes. Read the list of nine words out loud again. *Listen* to the words as you utter them. Can you tell that the syllables with primary stress are louder, higher (in pitch), and longer than the other syllables? Can you tell that the syllables with tertiary stress (third-class status) are the lowest in volume and pitch and the shortest in duration (time)? Can you discern that the syllables with secondary stress are in between on all three factors, or variables? We hope so, because you must be aware of these differences if you are to be able to control them.

Shifts of Stress

Every word uttered has a pattern of stresses, depending on the amount of stress given to the syllables in the word. On some words, the stress pattern can be changed to indicate meaningful differences. Generally, we may shift the stress around in the word for one of four reasons: (1) to underscore the contrast implied in similar words, (2) to indicate, in a two-syllable word, the difference between its use as a noun or adjective and as a verb, (3) to indicate, in words of three or more syllables, the difference between the word's use as a noun or adjective and as a verb, and (4) to underscore the meaning implied in a form word.

1. *Contrast.* We may alter the usual stress pattern of a word if we want

to underline the difference between that word and another word that is very similar. Ordinarily, for example, we stress the second syllable of the words *offense* and *defense*. If, however, we want to stress the difference between the two words, we put the stress on the syllable that makes the difference—the first syllable. That is why crowds at ball games yell "*de*-fense, *de*-fense." Another example: A judge might say, "I said *re-mand*, not *de*mand!" And still another: One student could tell another, "I'm taking *bi*ology, not *ge*ology." The purpose of the changed stress in each instance was to call attention to the contrast built into the two words, to point up the difference between two similar words—indeed, to make that difference the center of attention.

2. *Noun or adjective and verb contrast in words of two syllables.* When we shift the stress to underline the meaning of a word and point out its contrast with a similar word, we do not change the word's meaning. But it is possible to change the meaning of a word by changing the stress pattern. Many two-syllable words receive stress on the first syllable if they are used as nouns or adjectives, but they receive stress on the second syllable if they are being used as verbs. This shift in stress will affect the vowels in the syllables, of course, because the duration (and strength or weakness) of the vowel in the syllable is one means of indicating its relative degree of stress. Let us look at the word *perfect*, for example. If the word is used as an adjective to describe someone or something, the word is stressed on the first syllable. The vowel is the first syllable, then, is /ɝ/ (ûr); the vowel in the second (weakly stressed) syllable is /ɪ/ (ĭ) or [ɨ]. But what happens if the word is used as a verb—if you want to talk about trying to *perfect* something (or someone) that (or who) has a few flaws? Then the stress shifts. The primary stress is put on the second syllable, and, in the process, the vowels are changed. The vowel in the first syllable would then be /ɚ/ (ər); the vowel in the second syllable would be /ɛ/ (ĕ).

We have prepared a list of two-syllable words that illustrate this shift in stress. Read each word aloud twice: once as a noun or adjective and the second time as a verb. Note the shift of stress each time.

absent
abstract
address
annex
blowup
breakdown
castoff
collect
combat
combine

compact
compound
concert
conduct
conflict
conscript
console
consort
construct
content
contest
contract
convert
convict
decrease
defect
desert
detail
digest
discharge
discount
egress
entrance
extract
ferment
frequent
imprint
increase
inset
insult
invert
misprint
misrule
misquote
object
outset
perfect
permit
pervert
present
produce
progress
project
protest

rebel
recess
record
recount
refuse
reject
research
subject
survey
transfer
traverse
upset

3. *Noun or adjective and verb contrast in words of more than two syllables.* There are some words of more than two syllables that also shift stress to indicate the difference between the word used as a noun or adjective or as a verb. These words end in *-ate* or *-ment*. When the word is used as a verb, there is a secondary stress on the final syllable (*-ate* or *-ment*). When the word is used as a noun or adjective, this stress is weakened to tertiary stress. This shift in stress changes the strength and length of the vowel in that final syllable. For verbs, the *-ate* is /et/ (åt) and the *-ment* is /mɛnt/ (mĕnt); for nouns and adjectives, the *-ate* is /ət/ (ət) and the *-ment* is /mənt/ (mənt).

The following list of words illustrates this shift in stress in words of more than two syllables. Read the words aloud, pronouncing each word twice—once as a noun or adjective and once as a verb. Note the shift in stress each time.

advocate
affiliate
aggregate
animate
associate
certificate
conglomerate
congregate
consummate
degenerate
delegate
deliberate
estimate
pontificate
postulate
segregate
complement

compliment
implement
ornament
regiment
supplement

4. *Form words.* In Chapter 4, in the section on vowel gradation, we discussed form words at some length. Form words are those words that are necessary for the form of our sentences, but that do not contribute major ideas (see pp. 263–266.) These words ordinarily get only tertiary stress in connected speech. In the phrase "I will go," for example, the first word-syllable gets secondary stress (because it is an idea word, but not the major idea in the phrase); the second word-syllable (a form word: helping or auxiliary verb) gets tertiary stress (because the meaning of the word is clear and does not need to be stressed); and the third word-syllable gets primary stress (because it is the major idea in the phrase). Try that phrase out loud: "I will go." If you are making a simple statement of the fact, you will not give anything more than tertiary stress to the word *will*. But if you have been contradicted or you have had doubts about going or if you have been forbidden to go, you may want to stress the idea implied in the word *will*: intention, choice, and determination. If the idea is (I had thought I wouldn't, but . . .) I *will* go; or (You say I won't, but . . .) I *will* go; or (You may forbid me to, but . . .) I *will* go; or (There may have been some doubt, but . . .) I *will* go, then the word *will* assumes a special importance. It is now an important idea word, and the importance can be stressed and given its proper prominence by giving primary stress to the word *will*. All form words can be stressed in this way. The only danger is that you may use the wrong strong vowel in the process of restressing the word. The strong form of *the* is not /ðʌ/ (*thŭ*), and the strong form of *a* is not /ʌ/ (ŭ). The stressed forms of these form words are /ði/ (thē) and /eɪ/ (ā). And the strong form of *was* is not /wʌz/ (wŭz), but /wɑz/ (wäz). Again, refer to the material on strong and weak forms on pp. 263–266.

Problems in Pronunciation

We cannot give you hard-and-fast rules for stress patterns in American English. The guidelines are only general. Your ear (and the dictionary's record of current acceptable usage) must be your guide. We can pass on this observation: stress in English tends to be recessive (it tends to go early in the word), and strong and weak stresses seem to alternate in our words and sentences.

Pronounce the word *wonderful*. Listen to the stress pattern in the word. Where is the heaviest stress? That is correct: it is early in the word, on the first syllable. Try the word *elementary* aloud. Where is the primary stress in that word? On the *men,* the third syllable from the end. These examples demonstrate the general statement that stress tends to go early in the words in English. (British English carries this principle much further than American English does. In British English, for example, the words *dictionary* and *secretary* have their primary stress on the first syllable. In American English, of course, we give that first syllable only secondary stress and put the greatest (primary) stress on the next-to-last syllable in the word.) The problem is that, although this generalization about recessive accent is true, we have already looked at many words stressed on the last syllable or near the end of the word. That is the reason we only talked about the *tend*ency; the generalization is certainly not a universal rule to guide your pronunciation.

Robert Frost once said that in English we have two rhythms from which to choose: loose iambic and strict iambic! (Iambic is the meter in which one weakly stressed syllable alternates with a strongly stressed syllable consistently.) He was exaggerating a little, but his point was quite clear: We have a basic rhythm in English based on alternating strong and weak stresses in our syllables. The pattern is not rigid (spondee breaks the pattern, for example), but it is present in our words and sentences. Listen to the words *absolutely, elevator, stationary, satisfactory, legislator,* and *comprehension.* Can you see the regularity of the pattern? Can you detect any exceptions to the alternating of stronger and weaker stresses? Read the following sentence aloud, just as you would say it in conversation: "I hope to go to the movies tonight." Say it again, listening carefully for the pattern of stress in the sentence. How rigid is the pattern of alternating stress? Well, we never said the principle was absolute. That is one of the problems with stress in English; of course, if the stresses were absolutely regular, the rhythm would be very monotonous!

One "problem" that we must face is that some words in the language have more than one acceptable pronunciation. The word *adult,* for example, can be pronounced with the stress on either syllable. The word *abdomen* can be stressed with primary stress on either the first or second syllables. Do you put the primary stress on the *ver* syllable or the *tise* syllable in the word *advertisement?* Either is acceptable; both are commonly heard. Your authors put the primary stress on the first syllable in the words *comparable* and *chastisement,* but many American speakers put the primary stress on the second syllables of those words. One last example is the word *infantile.* What kind of stress do you give the last syllable—secondary with the diphthong /ɑɪ/ (ĭ) in it, or tertiary with the tertiary with the consonant blend /tl/ and no vowel (unless possibly the little schwa)? Both are standard pronunciations of this word. If we gave you a list of the words in American English with more than one acceptable pronunciation, the list would be rather long. Now, that is a problem!

Determining Current Usage

How do you go about deciding on the pronunciation of a word, when you are unsure of its current pronunciation? In the long run, your ears are your best guide. Listen to what educated, cultivated, prominent leaders are saying. They set the styles for acceptable usage (and they also follow the styles). They are a good gauge of what pronunciations to use.

But the most dependable source of information about how to pronounce a word at any given time is a current, reputable dictionary. The dictionary is not a Bible, but it *is* a record of current usage, and carefully, warily used, it is an invaluable aid to deciding how to pronounce a word. There are several good dictionaries available, and you must develop the habit of using yours regularly. Of course, if you are to use a dictionary, you must understand the diacritical marks and the stress-marking system your dictionary uses. Every dictionary has its own system for representing sounds and stress, and you can make intelligent use of your dictionary only if you understand its particular symbol system. Each dictionary fully explains its system and gives key words to guide you on what symbols represent what sounds. Before you look up *any* word, you must study that explanation and master it.

We certainly will not recommend a particular dictionary to you, but we will mention a special dictionary that gives only pronunciations—no meanings of words or histories of words. This pronouncing dictionary is *A Pronouncing Dictionary of American English*, by John S. Kenyon and Thomas A. Knott. The pronunciations are represented in the International Phonetic Alphabet, and regional variations of pronunciation are noted. It is an invaluable aid.

One of the following dictionaries might serve your particular needs. You should look at them all and then decide which (perhaps more than one) would be best for you.

Webster's Third New International Dictionary. Unabridged. Springfield, Mass.: G. & C. Merriam Company, 1971.
This is a huge—even mammoth—but complete dictionary, useful for reference, but hardly portable. It has been criticized for not making a distinction between standard and nonstandard usage.

The Random House Dictionary of the English Language. Unabridged. New York: Random House, Inc., 1967.
Another very large but complete dictionary, this volume is not portable either. However, it is a useful reference book.

The American Heritage Dictionary of the English Language. Boston: American Heritage Publishing Co. and Houghton Mifflin Company, 1969.

This is a highly readable and attractive large dictionary. It clearly labels words with restricted usage, such as those that are slang, vulgar, and nonstandard. We adapted its symbol system slightly for use in this book. Available in paperback.

Webster's New World Dictionary of the American Language. New York: World Publishing Company, 1974.

A portable, although certainly not pocket-sized dictionary, this volume contains labels to guide usage, such as slang, colloquial, and dialect.

Webster's New Collegiate Dictionary. 8th ed. Springfield, Mass.: G. & C. Merriam Company, 1973.

Portable, although not pocket-sized, this volume contains usage labels and distinguishes between "nonstandard" (words disapproved by many but sometimes heard in "reputable contexts") and "substandard" (words not chosen or preferred by the prestige group).

A Pronouncing Dictionary of American English. (Springfield, Mass.: G. & C. Merriam Company, 1953.)

This is a guide to pronunciation only. It contains no definitions or other information usually found in dictionaries. It represents the usage of cultivated, educated Americans of all regions of the country. Regional variations are noted. The pronunciations are transcribed in IPA, not in the usual dictionary diacritics.

Drs. John S. Kenyon and Thomas A. Knott edited this unique and most useful guide to pronunciation.

7
Rhythm and Melody

E VERY language has a music of its own, based on its rhythms and melodies. If you heard a group of people talking in French, Swedish, Chinese, or American English, you would be able to hear the musical differences in the languages being spoken. We call these elements of language *prosodic features*. (The word *prosody* has descended from a Greek word that means "an accompanied song.") Languages have two musical, or prosodic, elements or features: *rhythm* and *melody*.

Rhythm has to do with stressed beats, or pulses, and the patterns of those stressed beats or pulses. Melody has to do with pitches—their levels, their relationships, and the patterns they make as a group of successive pitches. We will discuss each of these prosodic features separately, although they are interrelated.

Rhythm

We have defined rhythm as the pattern created by recurring, stressed beats. In connected speech, these beats occur in three kinds of units: the syllable, the foot, and the phrase. To understand rhythm and the patterns of stresses that create rhythm, we must look at each of these units individually.

SYLLABLE

A syllable is a sound or group of sounds uttered on one chest pulse. That means the syllable is produced on air pushed out by the external chest muscles. The syllable is the basic unit in rhythmic patterns. We discussed syllabic stress in Chapter 6 as an element of word pronunciation. Now, we will look at these variations in stress of syllables as part of a total rhythmic pattern. First, however, we must look at syllables themselves a little more closely.

Syllables, as we noted in Chapter 2, have three component parts: an initiating consonant or consonants, a vowel or diphthong, and a terminating consonant or consonants. The syllable pulse, then, like most movement, consists of two strokes—a beat stroke and a back stroke. The beat stroke starts the pulse, and the back stroke stops the pulse.

Although there can be three component elements in any syllable, a syllable does not necessarily have all three. There are four types of syllables, if we classify them on the basis of their components:

O V O   *Oh*
C V O   *Ho*
O V C   *Oak*
C V C   *Coke*

O stands for nothing; *V* stands for vowel; and *C* stands for consonant (or consonants). Consonants start and stop syllables, and vowels and diphthongs provide the quality (or resonance, sonority, carrying power) of syllables. (The one exception, you should remember, occurs in the case of syllabic consonants, when such consonants as /l/ and /n/ provide the carrying power or resonance of the syllable.)

As we told you in Chapter 6, there are three degrees of stress given to syllables in words spoken alone. (See pp. 306–308.) We labeled these degrees of stress primary (first degree or first class), secondary (second degree or second class), and tertiary (third degree or third class). When words are spoken in connected speech, there is another degree of stress possible. This stress is greater than primary stress, and for lack of a better term we call it superstress. We will discuss this degree of stress in more detail later. There is no consistent symbol system for representing these levels of stress. For our purposes, we will represent the four degrees of stress with these symbols:

tertiary   ˬ
secondary   ʹ
primary   ˏ
super   ×

Syllables are separated from each other by tiny breaks or pauses. These breaks are called *juncture*. Read aloud the following pairs of words and phrases. In each pair, the difference will not be the succession of sounds (the sounds in sequence), but where the syllables are divided by juncture.

white shoes   why choose
a nice house   an ice house
I scream   ice cream
nitrate   night rate
this tile   this style

These junctures, or breaks, of course, affect the rhythm in the flow of speech.

In some languages, stress patterns are almost absolutely regular. In French, for example, stress is put on the syllable at the end of a word or phrase. This regularity makes the rhythmic pattern fairly predictable. In English, on the other hand, the position of stress is quite variable.

That means that almost any syllable has a chance of getting stressed. Let us look at the various patterns of stress used in words in American English. (And remember our symbol system.)

In the list of syllabic stress patterns that follow, we are noting stress in words spoken alone, not in larger units.

NUMBER OF SYLLABLES	STRESS PATTERN	KEY WORD
1-syllable words	′	joke
2-syllable words	′ ˘	stupid
	′ ′	bureau
	′ ′	bookstore
	˘ ′	above
	′ ′	tattoo
3-syllable words	′ ′ ˘	grasshopper
	′ ˘ ˘	syllable
	′ ˘ ′	envelope (noun)
	˘ ′ ˘	awarded
	′ ′ ˘	Titanic
	˘ ′ ′	piano
	˘ ˘ ′	undertake
	′ ˘ ′	afternoon
4-syllable words	′ ˘ ′ ˘	education
	′ ˘ ′ ˘	liberating
	′ ˘ ˘ ˘	charitable
	′ ′ ˘ ˘	insidious
	˘ ′ ˘ ˘	oblivion
	˘ ′ ˘ ′	eradicate
	′ ′ ˘ ′	incarcerate
	˘ ˘ ′ ˘	understanding
5-syllable words	˘ ′ ˘ ˘ ˘	obliterated
	˘ ′ ˘ ′ ˘	uncomfortable
	˘ ′ ˘ ′ ˘	consideration
	′ ˘ ˘ ′ ˘	edification
6-syllable words	˘ ′ ˘ ′ ˘ ˘	dependability
	′ ˘ ′ ˘ ′ ˘	interdigitation
	′ ′ ˘ ′ ˘ ˘	unprovability
	′ ˘ ˘ ′ ˘ ˘	interdependency
	˘ ′ ˘ ˘ ′ ˘	internalization
7-syllable words	′ ˘ ′ ˘ ′ ˘ ˘	constitutionality
	˘ ′ ˘ ˘ ′ ˘ ˘	inseparability
8-syllable words	′ ˘ ′ ˘ ˘ ˘ ′	internationalization

FOOT

The *foot* is a larger unit than the syllable; the foot is made out of syllables. Syllables are produced by little pulses of pressure from the intercostal chest muscles (the short muscles between the ribs). The tiny contraction of these chest muscles pushes out little pulses of air that make up the syllable. The foot is produced by an abdominal pulse (or push). The foot is made up of a single strongly stressed syllable alone or a few syllables grouped around a single strongly stressed syllable. In either case, the foot contains only one strongly stressed syllable. Hence, each foot will contain one strong, rhythmic beat. It is on this strongly stressed syllable that the abdominal muscles give their little extra push.

Feet may be composed of various numbers of syllables. A foot can be only one syllable long: "Nó!" for example. Or a foot can be an entire sentence: "Í will gó." The foot can contain any number of syllables, so long as only one of those syllables receives primary or super stress.

In English, the feet are fairly even and consistent in length. There is almost uniform time between the primary or super stresses. Our language, then, when spoken, has a fairly steady beat, because of the equal time from heavy beat to heavy beat. Say this sentence out loud, and pat your foot on the heavily stressed syllables: "I have *sworn* upon the *al*tar of *God* eternal hos*til*ity against *all* forms of *ty*ranny *over* the *mind* of *man.*" Did you find that the strong beat made by the stressed syllables was pretty regular? Was your foot patting steady?

In feet with many syllables, some syllables must be shortened (spoken more quickly) to keep the feet relatively even in length (to keep the strong beats regular). This shortening and weakening of syllables reduces the stress on these syllables and changes the vowel sounds in them. (See pp. 263–266.) In feet with one syllable or few syllables, the syllables will be lengthened. We stretch out the sounds—especially the vowels and diphthongs. This lengthening increases the stress, and it also serves to keep the feet relatively even in length and to maintain the steadiness of the strong beat.

Pauses at the end of feet can be short or long. This variation in the length of pauses is another means we use to keep the strong beat regular and the feet even in length.

When we stress a syllable, we increase the force, or intensity; raise the pitch; and increase the duration, or length, of the syllable. Stressing syllables is a means of giving some syllables more prominence, or attention, than others. Just as some syllables in a word are more important than others and, therefore, receive more stress, so also some words in a sentence are more important than others. We give these more important words extra prominence or attention through *emphasis*. We stress a syllable, but we emphasize a word in a foot or phrase. Emphasis in feet and phrases is achieved by centering attention on the stressed syllable of the word to be emphasized. These important words usually come at the beginning or end of the foot. This stress on top of stress creates the super degree of stress that we talked about earlier. We need only three degrees of stress for the pronunciation of a word. But we need this new category of stress to describe the effect of emphasis. We move to thought-bearing words when we speak. They are mountaintops of attention surrounded by weak-syllable valleys.

A change in emphasis changes the rhythm. We can illustrate this principle with a simple sentence. The sentence is made up of one phrase, and that one phrase is made up of only one foot. There are four words in the sentence, but shifts in emphasis yield at least five possibilities for various rhythms. Pronounce each of these variations aloud. Listen to what the shifts in emphasis do to the rhythm.

$$\acute{}\ \breve{}\ \acute{}\ \acute{}$$
I will not go.
$$\times\ \breve{}\ \acute{}\ \acute{}$$
I will not go.
$$\acute{}\ \times\ \acute{}\ \acute{}$$
I will not go.
$$\acute{}\ \breve{}\ \times\ \acute{}$$
I will not go.
$$\acute{}\ \breve{}\ \acute{}\ \times$$
I will not go.

Emphasis conveys extra meanings—underscoring the idea built into the word *emphasized*. A speaker shifts emphasis from word to word to communicate his or her intent and feelings. A speaker uses emphasis to point out what is important to him or her.

When you are the speaker, you will need to be able to control these shifts in emphasis and these changes in rhythm to communicate your own intentions and feelings. When you are a listener, you need to understand the implications of these shifts in emphasis and rhythm to be able to interpret the speaker's meaning correctly.

PHRASE

A *phrase* is a thought group, a sense group, a unified idea that can hang together. From the physiological point of view, it is a breath group, uttered on one stream of outgoing breath.

A phrase is made up of feet. It can contain various numbers of feet. A phrase could be only one foot long, such as: "No!" It can also contain many feet. Look at these examples (in which the diagonal line separates the feet of the phrase).

How could I / possibly / do / such a thing?

Will you go / to the theater / tonight?

It's been / such a difficult / year.

What / a big / one!

A sentence may contain more than one phrase. Note these examples (in which double diagonals separate the phrases and single diagonals separate the feet).

That he / is really / guilty // is far / from clear.

// . . . and that government / of the people // by the people //

and for the people // shall not perish / from the earth.

The beat created by the strongly stressed syllables stays relatively steady (regular) throughout the phrase. Read aloud each of the preceding examples, and pat your foot on the strongly stressed beat of each foot. You should find that the beats are separated by about equal time.

Melody

A *melody* is a tune—a succession of pitches that form a pattern. When we speak, we do not utter every syllable on the same tone or pitch; the pitches vary from syllable to syllable and word to word. Because we do not speak in a monotone (all on one pitch), we have *intonation* (a succession of different pitches that creates melody). Our sentences all have a melody to them; some phrases have distinctive melodies also. If you do not use the usual melodies when you speak, you will have a "foreign accent."

The melody patterns of sentences in one language will be different from those of another language. Each language has its own distinctive "tunes" for thought groups and sentences. In fact, those melodic patterns are an important and integral part of the language itself. Although there has not been a great deal of study of the subject yet, our ears tell us also that dialects of the same language vary in intonation patterns from other dialects.

A detailed analysis of intonation (or melody) in American English is outside the scope of this book. But we must give you some basic information about this important element of our language. To do so, we must discuss with you three basic elements of melody: (1) phrase terminals (sometimes called clause terminals), (2) levels of pitch, and (3) intonation contours.

PHRASE TERMINALS

At the ends of phrases and sentences, we indicate extra information about the content of the phrase or sentence through the use of pitch. (This use of pitch to tell the listener how to interpret the information contained in the main message is an excellent example of nonverbal metacommunication. See pp. 339–340.) How we end the phrase or sentence alerts the listener to the speaker's intentions and private meanings. If the pitch slides up at the end of the phrase, the speaker is uncertain, and the statement is incomplete. If the pitch slides down at the end of the phrase, the speaker is certain, and the statement is complete and final. If the pitch is kept level and is sustained at the end of the phrase, the speaker is not finished with his idea; there is more to come. And if the pitch slides up and then back down again—or if the pitch slides down and then back up again—the speaker is expressing irony (saying one thing but meaning another) or is hinting at a double meaning.

There are, then, four possible phrase terminals in English: a rising pitch terminal, which indicates uncertainty or incompleteness; a falling pitch terminal, which indicates certainty, completeness, and finality; a sustained pitch terminal, which indicates nonfinality; and a circumflex pitch terminal, which indicates a double meaning (*double entendre*). To symbolize these four types of terminals, we will use little arrows to indicate the direction of the pitch change: ⟋ for rising; ⟍ for falling; ⟶ for level (or sustained); and ⟍ or ⟍ for circumflex.

Look at these examples:

> (You asked if I were sure.) I know. ⟍   (I am sure.)
> (You falsely said I was sure.) I know? ⟋   (I am not sure at all.)
> I know ⟶ (for who could doubt his word?) he is innocent.
> (You may think something different is true, but . . .) I know. ⟍

Each of these phrase terminals ended the same phrase "I know." And each changed the meaning of the phrase and indicated how the listener should interpret the message. The words in parenthesis were never said; they were implied—by the pitch moves of the terminals.

Try these examples out loud. Listen for the terminals, and note the changes in meaning effected by the terminals.

> (There's no doubt about it:) She's nice.
> (In shock you'd think so:) She's nice?
> (Hold them in suspense for the punch line:)
> She's nice—for a Barnard girl!
> (There's an extra, hidden, and maybe dirty meaning in my words:) She's nice!!!

PITCH LEVELS

If you listen to someone else speak, or if you listen carefully to your own speech patterns, you will discover that you do not say each syllable on exactly the same pitch. The pitch varies from syllable to syllable. (Indeed, as we saw with phrase terminals, it is possible to change the pitch *during* the utterance of the syllable.) Do these pitches matter? Do they change the meaning? Well, some of these pitch changes are very significant to listeners in English, and others are far less important.

Generally, scholars have noted four levels of meaningful difference in pitch. These four levels are not exact frequencies; rather, they are relationships established by each speaker in his or her own voice range. There are four levels of pitches, each higher or lower than the other levels. How high is the highest level? We can't tell you; it depends on a person's voice. How low is the lowest level? The same thing: it is dependent on the range of the speaker's voice. But we can tell you that a speaker, speaking American English, will use four different pitch levels, and the speaker's highest level will be used for the same purposes as other speakers' highest levels. And the speaker's lowest level will be used in the same way as other English speakers' lowest pitch levels. These pitch levels are relative, and it is their relationships that are important, as the listener decodes meaning.

Here are the four levels, with 1 representing the lowest level and 4 representing the highest pitch level. Note the use of each of these levels of pitch:

4	Special Emphasis	4
3	Primary Stress	3
2	Home Base; Normal, Modal Pitch; Weak Stress	2
1	Finality, Certainty	1

Each syllable we utter can be placed in one of these four levels; or, perhaps we should have said, each syllable can be classified into one of these levels. Listen to this short sentence as you say it aloud. Listen to the pitch changes, and decide which category each syllable would fit into:

I hate him!

We classified level 2 as home base, and that is where this phrase would start, because the first syllable does not get heavy stress. (Note that stress and pitch are interdependent.) But how did you say the second word-syllable? Did you just give it emphasis? If so, it went up to level 3. Or did you really punch it, giving special emphasis to the word? Then you probably pushed it up into level 4. And what happened on the final word-syllable? The pitch of this last syllable was lowest of all, was it not? Was it lower even than when you started the sentence (in level 2)? And did the last syllable have a pitch change while you uttered the syllable, with the pitch dropping down from where you started in the beginning of that last syllable? That is the phrase terminal; it is the falling terminal.

Let us graph another simple sentence, looking at the level of each of the syllables (or words—because each word is one-syllable long). Here is the sentence: "I don't want one."

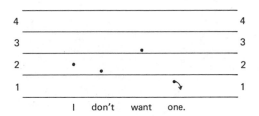

Here, you will note, there is a difference in pitch between the first two words. The second is lower than the first, but it is still within the range of pitch variation recognized as level 2. The third syllable, however, is the syllable that gets primary stress or attention in this phrase, and it shifts gears up to level 3. The final syllable, at the end of the sentence, is in level 1. And it has its little tail on it—the phrase terminal, the falling terminal of finality and certainty.

CONTOURS

We have already moved into the subject of contours. It is almost impossible to discuss pitch levels and not discuss the patterns they make. Pitch levels make no sense alone; they mean something only in terms of a relationship. What matters is the melody (contour) created by a succession of pitches, because melodies—tunes, intonations—mean something. The patterns made by shifting from one pitch level to another, together with phrase terminals, are nonverbal metacommunication that are essential to intelligent message reception.

We cannot list in detail all the possible melodies in the language. Your meaning, your feelings, your intentions, and your emphases will change melody patterns to your own purpose. But we do want to give you some of the most common contours. These patterns will include pitch levels and phrase terminals. Try the sentences out loud to see if your pronunciation of them follows the contour (pitch pattern) given.

1. *Statements of fact and commands.* Statements of simple fact and imperatives (commands) usually follow this contour:

2. *Statements of doubt.* Statements of wonder, amazement, and doubt usually follow this contour:

He's doing that!

3. *Statements with phrases in series.* Sometimes we have a sentence in which we give a series of phrases—a kind of list. Each phrase in the list gets one kind of contour—until the last one. The first pitch pattern indicates that the series is not yet over, and the contour of the last phrase in the series indicates that the series is at an end. Look at these possibilities:

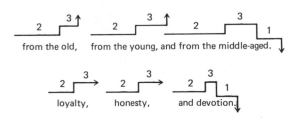

4. *Questions starting with interrogative words.* Some people have the mistaken notion that every question in English has a melody with a high last pitch level and a rising terminal. Of course, this is not so. We have many questions that have a different contour completely. If you ask someone for specific information—questions beginning *what*, *where*, *when*, *why*, or *how*, for example—you will use the same contour we used for statements of fact and for imperatives (commands). Such questions use the 2 3 1 ⬊ intonation pattern (contour).

2 ⌐3¬1

Where is it?⬎

5. *Questions with yes or no answers.* If you ask a question that can be answered with either yes or no, the contour will end with level 3 and a rising terminal. Such questions use the 2 3 ⟋ intonation pattern.

Is he ready?

6. *Maybe this or maybe that questions.* Sometimes we ask questions that offer choices to our listeners. We ask them if they like or dislike one thing or another; or we ask them if they want to do one thing or another; or we ask if they feel one way or another. By choosing a certain melody, we can offer them the chance to accept or reject either or both of the alternatives we offer. (By choosing a different melody, as we will see in a moment, we can try to make them choose *between* the two alternatives we give them.) By using the same contour for both phrases, the 2–3 ⟋ pattern, we express doubt about both choices and leave the listener free to accept either or both of the things we suggest. Read the following sentence out loud, paying attention to the intonation pattern.

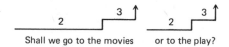

Shall we go to the movies   or to the play?

7. *Either this or that questions.* Here again, we ask a question and give the listener a choice. But this time, by changing the intonation pattern in the second phrase, we indicate that the two choices are the complete choices the listener has. Remember, we do not tell the listener this information verbally; we tell him or her nonverbally—with our pitch levels and phrase terminal: the contour of melody with which the phrase is said. Note the difference when the question is asked using this intonation:

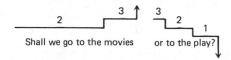

Shall we go to the movies   or to the play?

Articulation Analysis Form

Consonants

Evaluation		Comments
p_____	b_____	
t_____	d_____	
k_____	g_____	
l_____	r_____	
m_____	n_____	
ŋ_____		
f_____	v_____	
θ_____	ð_____	
s_____	z_____	
ʃ_____	ʒ_____	
ʍ_____	w_____	
h_____		
j_____		

Vowels

Evaluation	Comments
i_____	
ɪ_____	
ɛ_____	
æ_____	
ɑ_____	
ɒ_____	
ɔ_____	
ʊ_____	
u_____	
ʌ_____	
ə_____	
ɝ_____	
ɚ_____	

Affricates

tʃ_____
dʒ_____

Diphthongs

eɪ_____
aɪ_____
ɔɪ_____
ou_____
ɑu_____

Specific Articulation Problems

Omissions

Additions

Substitutions and distortions

Transpositions

Consonant combinations

Consonant clusters

Incorrect syllabic stress

Overassimilation

Pedantic precision

Stressed form words

Articulation Bibliography

ARNOLD, G. F. *Stress in English Words.* Amsterdam: North Holland Publishing Company, 1957.

BRONSTEIN, ARTHUR J. *The Pronunciation of American English.* New York: Appleton-Century-Crofts, 1960.

BRONSTEIN, ARTHUR J., and BEATRICE F. JACOBY. *Your Speech and Voice.* New York: Random House, Inc., 1967.

DANCE, FRANK E. X., ed. *Human Communication Theory.* New York: Holt, Rinehart and Winston, Inc., 1967.

DENES, PETER B., and ELLIOT N. PINSON. *The Speech Chain: The Physics and Biology of Spoken Language.* Garden City, N.Y.: Anchor Press, Doubleday & Company, Inc., 1973.

FRANCIS, W. N. *The Structure of American English.* New York: The Ronald Press Company, 1958.

GLEASON, H. A., JR. *An Introduction to Descriptive Linguistics.* rev. ed. New York: Holt, Rinehart and Winston, Inc., 1961.

KENYON, JOHN S., and THOMAS A. KNOTT. *A Pronouncing Dictionary of American English.* Springfield, Mass.: G. & C. Merriam Company, 1953.

MACDONALD, EUGENE T. *Articulation Testing and Treatment: A Sensory-Motor Approach.* Pittsburgh: Stanwix House, 1964.

PEI, MARIO, and FRANK GAYNOR. *Dictionary of Linguistics.* New York: Philosophical Library, 1954.

PIKE, KENNETH L. *The Intonation of American English.* Ann Arbor: University of Michigan Press, 1946.

STETSON, R. H. *Motor Phonetics: A Study of Speech Movements in Action.* Amsterdam: North Holland Publishing Company, 1951.

THOMAS, CHARLES KENNETH. *An Introduction to the Phonetics of American English.* 2nd ed. New York: The Ronald Press Company, 1958.

WINITZ, HARRIS. *Articulatory Acquisition and Behavior.* New York: Appleton-Century-Crofts, 1969.

WISE, CLAUDE MERTON. *Introduction to Phonetics.* Englewood Cliffs, N.J.: Prentice-Hall, Inc., 1957.

II
Voice

Voice Glossary

Abduct: To pull away from the midline; referring to the opening of the vocal folds.

Adduct: To draw toward the midline; referring to the closing of the vocal folds.

Afferent: Refers to nerves that convey sensory impulses from the PNS to the CNS.

Amplitude: Largeness of range; directly related to intensity of sound and to resonance.

Aphonia: Loss of voice due to the failure of vocal fold vibration.

Arytenoids: Pair of triangular shaped cartilages to which the vocal folds are attached; involved with the opening and closing of the vocal folds.

Assimilation nasality: The result of nasal resonance being carried over from the nasal sounds in a word to the neighboring non-nasal sounds within the word.

Auditory feedback: The aural reception and discrimination of your speech as it reaches the ear immediately after speaking.

Aural: Pertaining to your sense of hearing.

Central Nervous System (CNS): The brain and the spinal cord.

Clavicular: A type of breathing involving the use of the clavicles, or collarbones, to raise the rib cage during inhalation.

Denasality: A type of vocal quality that lacks sufficient nasal resonance during speech.

Diaphragm: Dome-shaped muscle that separates the thoracic cavity from the abdominal cavity; involved with respiration.

Duration: Measurement of time consumed between produced sounds and/or the measurement of time consumed between words and phrases.

Efferent: Refers to nerves that convey impulses from the CNS to the muscles (motor activity).

Exhalation: One phase of respiration; air is expelled from the lungs.

Glottis: Opening between the vocal folds.

Gross abdominal muscles: Large muscles in the abdominal cavity used actively during the phase of exhalation.

Hyoid bone: A horseshoe-shaped bone at the top of the thyroid cartilage; the larynx is extended from this bone.

Hypernasality: A type of vocal quality that has excessive nasal resonance during speech.

Hypertension: Having excessive tension.

Hypotension: Having insufficient tension.

Kinesthetic: "Muscle sense"; your perception of how the muscular action of your body "feels."

Labial: Pertaining to the lips.

Laryngeal tone: The sound initiated at the larynx as the vocal folds begin to vibrate in phonation.

Laryngitis: Hoarseness of voice due to inflammation of the vocal folds.

Laryngologist: A certified physician specializing in the study and treatment of the throat, pharynx, larynx, nasal passage, trachea, and bronchial tubes.

Laryngopharynx: Throat area behind the larynx.

Lingual: Pertaining to the tongue.

Loudness: Intensity of sound.

Muscle tonus: Pertaining to adequate muscle tension for effective muscle functioning.

Nasal: Pertaining to the nose.

Nasopharynx: Extension of the throat area behind the larynx.

Negative practice: Involving the practice of the wrong techniques in order to increase your awareness of the correct techniques.

Oropharynx: Extension of the throat area behind the oral cavity.

Overtone: A sound frequency that is in addition to the fundamental tone.

Paralanguage: Extralinguistic features of voice, including vocal range, resonance, and tempo.

Pharynx: Throat area with three sections: laryngopharynx, nasopharynx, and oropharynx.

Phonation: The process of producing vocal tone as a result of breath being vibrated between the vocal folds.

Resonance: Amplification and modification of sound.

Resonators: Three areas for amplifying and modifying the basic laryngeal tone for speech: the laryngeal cavity, oral cavity, and nasal cavity.

Respiration: A process involving breathing for life sustenance and for speech.

Soft palate: Attached to the hard palate; separates the oral cavity from the nasal cavity; involved with production of nasal versus oral sounds.

Support of tone: Involves the use of the gross abdominal muscles as the breath stream is emitted during phonation.

Tactile: Pertaining to the sense of touch.

Thorax: The upper part of the torso of the body; houses the lungs.

Thyroid cartilage: "Adam's apple"—large cartilage of the larynx.

Trachea: The windpipe.

Velum: The soft palate.

Viscera: The soft organs of the body in the abdominal cavity.

Vocal folds: Known as vocal bands; vocal cords; ligaments that produce "voice" when set into vibration.

Voice: Sound produced when vocal folds are set into vibration; added dimensions include resonance, loudness, and pitch.

8
Basic Principles

"Y OUR voice is you,"[1] stated in today's street-wise argot would probably translate as, "You sound like you are, man. Dependin' on how
good ya' got it together." In this chapter we will introduce the student to
"getting it all together"—vocally. We will focus on all of those aspects
of you and your voice that are involved in acquiring the kind of voice
production you want and need. You will learn how to use your voice so
you won't abuse it, and you will develop a voice with the most resonance
possible, with meaningful pitch variation, with enough volume, with controlled rate, and with interesting variety.

Historically, the term *voice* can be traced back as far as approximately
500 B.C.—the time of Pericles, the Greek orator. This was the beginning
of the era when the famous Five Canons of Rhetoric were being discussed, analyzed, and applied. These canons (principles) included (1)
inventio (content); (2) dispositio (argumentation); (3) elocutio (style);
(4) memoria (memorization); and (5) pronunciatio (delivery, voice,
articulation, and gesture).[2] Aristotle (who was born in 384 B.C.) declared
that "the art of delivery has to do with voice."[3] Over 2,000 years later, in
his book, *The Voice of Neurosis*, Paul J. Moses wrote, "Voice is the prime
expression of the individual."[4]

Since the early 1920s when the communication field (then called the
speech field) first became a recognized discipline, emphases and approaches have shifted appreciably regarding the speech (the message),
the speaker (the encoder), and the listener (the decoder).

---

[1] Dominic Barbara, *Your Speech Reveals Your Personality* (New York: Charles C
Thomas, Publisher, 1957), p. 40.

[2] Eleanor M. DiMichael, *A Study of the Treatment of Pronunciatio by the Ancients*, Master's thesis, Louisiana State University, 1945.

[3] Aristotle, *Rhetoric.* Translated by Lane Cooper. (New York: Appleton-Century-
Crofts, 1932), 3.1., 1404a, p. 37.

[4] Paul J. Moses, M.D., *The Voice of Neurosis* (New York: Grune & Stratton, Inc.,
1954), p. 1.

VERBAL COMMUNICATION

1920—Emphasis on the content of the speech. Particular attention paid to the central idea, validity of support material, and reasoning. Some reference to clarity of speech (articulation) and adequate volume.

1930—Emphasis on the speaker. Standards of speech were being researched and a more effective use of voice was being encouraged due to a growing interest in oral reading.

1940—The audience became central. Strong attention was given to audience analysis and adaptation to that audience. The speaker delivered a speech adapted (or tailored) to the type of audience and the occasion. The speaker studied the audience in advance, prepared to capture and move the audience, and monitored the audience's reactions while speaking. The interaction became "interpersonal."

INTERPERSONAL COMMUNICATION

1950—Influenced by the fields of psychology and psycholinguistics, inroads were made into what was happening "inside" of the speaker as he communicated the message.

INTRAPERSONAL COMMUNICATION

1960—"Sensitivity" awareness added a fourth dimension to the communication process—nonverbal communication. Kinesics and proxemics became familiar words, even though they had been written about as early as the 1940s.

NONVERBAL COMMUNICATION

It is important to note that these emphases, or shifts, were not isolated, disconnected, or clear-cut. Rather, they were gradual, overlapping, fused and interrelated.

Today, the name of the game is *communication,* on all levels: intra-/interpersonal and verbal/-nonverbal. These terms have been explained in Chapter 1. In the following chapters on voice, a "communication" approach will be used in teaching you how to more effectively "let your voice be you." You will be asked to consider your voice production verbally, nonverbally (yes!), intrapersonally, and interpersonally. In order to achieve these goals, we will follow these procedures:

1. An assessment will be made. (What *is* the problem?)
2. An evaluation of the assessment will be discussed. (How severe and/or involved is the voice problem?)
3. A treatment plan will be proposed. (What will be the skills or alternatives of therapy services?)
4. Treatment services will be applied.

Sometimes—perhaps often—we will use clinical procedures and methods to reach our goals. These procedures and methods are appropriate and useful in obtaining specific behavioral objectives. But the real goal is not isolated objectives or skills. The real goal is *you:* you learning to use your voice effectively for all of the many varied social situations of your life.

Perhaps you are (or plan to be) an actor, classroom teacher, lawyer, salesman, an involved member of the community, or someone else whose speaking voice is essential to his or her work. Perhaps you are plagued with any one of the countless voice problems or voice pathologies. Or perhaps you do not fit into any of these categories. No matter! In order to communicate with other human beings, the effective use of voice can be an asset. For all of you, then, this section focuses on something very important to you: you and your effective use of voice.

Preparation for Voice Improvement

UNDERSTANDING YOUR VOICE

Your voice is the result of many coordinated processes working together efficiently. It is a complicated operation. Of course everyone uses the same organs of the body to produce voice. Air is exhaled from the lungs and then is vibrated in the larynx, transforming it into vocal tone. That basic tone is then modified and amplified in the cavities of the larynx, throat, mouth, and nose. Your respiratory process (breathing process) and the vibratory process (the process of vibrating the vocal folds in the larynx) work together to produce sound (phonation); the modification and amplification of that basic sound in the chambers of the larynx, throat, mouth, and nose produce resonance. We use them as resonating chambers to build up the basic sound. These three processes working together (respiration, phonation, and resonation) result in your basic voice quality (characteristic and distinctive sound—the sound of "you").

All voices are not alike—even though we all use the same kinds of organs to produce vocal sound. Indeed, as we have said, your voice is disinctively *yours*. Your listeners (receivers) recognize you by your voice, identify your voice with you, and receive messages about you from your voice. And you (the message-sender, the speaker) manipulate your voice to transmit your ideas, intentions, attitudes, and feelings. You use your voice not only to transmit your words (verbal communication) but also your emotions (through nonverbal communication).

Although everyone does use the same kinds of organs to produce normal voice, we know that there are almost infinite varieties of voices. Other factors account for those variations in voices. Heredity, environment, emotionality, paralanguage, and skill all play a role in influencing your voice and making you sound like you.

Heredity plays an important part in influencing what your voice sounds like. We all use the same *kinds* of organs to produce voice, but we use different organs. Each of us has a body that is different from anyone else's. It is the body that heredity gave us, so one reason you sound like you do is your choice of ancestors! Heredity can determine the structure, size, and even possibly the physiology of the larynx (how we *use* the body we have—how the body *functions*). A reference to the Kennedy family might illustrate the point. A Kennedy "sounds like a Kennedy." Even the layman on the street can make this identification.

Environment is an important factor influencing your voice. You tend to sound like those people around you. Your family, friends, school, local community, and the part of the country from which you come all help shape your voice. Speech is caught rather than taught; we learn to speak by interpersonal contact and imitation. And we will imitate the voices of the people with whom we have interpersonal communication—especially in our formative years. The voices that surround us (our environment) are a powerful influence on our speaking voices.

The factors of *personality and emotionality* should not be minimized here. We call these the psychological factors. Your psychological make-up affects your voice, and your emotional states "color" your voice. Psychologists are involved with the behavior of human beings and with the relationship between personality and behavior. The vocal patterns you use to communicate are vocal *behavior*. Voice patterns and voice production, therefore, are necessarily involved with you as a person. What kind of person you are and how you feel at the moment are going to help determine the voice you have and use.

Paralanguage is closely related to the factor we have just discussed. *Para* means "extra" or "beside" in Greek; paralanguage, then, involves elements of the spoken message that are beside, or in addition to, the words of the message (the language). It might be helpful to define one other term, *metacommunication.*

Meta (from the Greek, meaning "next to" or "along with") implies that there is a message communicated in addition to the main message. Metacommunication can be either verbal or nonverbal; the added message tells the receiver how to interpret the original message, the principal message. If a mother says, "Don't you touch that vase! I'm not kidding this time. Don't touch it!", the main message to the child is "Don't touch the vase!" The metacommunication added (*verbally*, in very plain *words*) tells the child to interpret the message as meaning business. Paralanguage (also called paralinguistic features) is a subdivision of metacommunication. Paralanguage tells the listener how to interpret the main *word* message, but paralanguage is always *non*verbal. Paralanguage is not only in addition to the *main* message (making it metacommunication); it is in addition to the *word* message. There are two elements of paralanguage that any student of human speech communication will note: the audible (what the listener hears) and the visible (what the listener sees). The audible element of paralanguage is produced by the *voice* of the speaker; the visible element is produced by the *body* of the speaker. The receiver takes in the first element with his or her ears, and the second with his or her eyes.

In this book we are concerned with the *vocal* aspects of paralanguage—those aspects of the use of voice that convey meaning, apart from the words spoken. "It's not what you're saying that offends me, but how you're saying it,"[5] succinctly hints at what paralinguistic features are all about. We convey meaning with our voices (without words) when we sigh, scream, grunt, groan, giggle, and make other nonword sounds. We also convey meaning with pitch changes (making our voices higher or lower), rate changes (making our voices go faster or slower), volume changes (speaking louder or softer), quality changes (changing the "sound" of our voice), and articulation-pattern changes (changing how we make speech sounds). These paralanguage meaning markers affect our voices and the way we sound to other people in interpersonal communication. Paralinguistic factors can also be indicators of one's ability to cope with intra-/interpersonal communication. Do you consistently heave "sighs" accompanied by a ripple movement of the lips as you communicate a message? Billy did. Billy, a white male, six years old, was a referral to one of these writers. The diagnosis of the otolaryngologist was bilateral nodules and spastic movement of the vocal folds. At the initial assessment interview, Billy communicated the following: (1) constant downcast eyes during all of the conversation; (2) repetitious sighs accompanied by a ripple movement of the lips; and (3) inability to find the words to answer questions ("I don't know" accompanied by a raised, tense shrug of his little shoulders). Seemingly, Billy was giving off a number of vocal and nonvocal, and verbal cues. An educated guess would suggest that Billy was a very shy, insecure, up-tight, and frustrated six-year-old boy whose voice had finally yelled "help!"

The final factor influencing these basic variations in voice quality is skill. Individuals vary in the degree of their control over the speech mechanism, and this variance in control produces perceptible differences in vocal output. You were born into your environment with your own degree of speech proficiency, but any native skill can be developed and extended. Under conditions that encourage the growing child to function productively in all areas—physically, intellectually, and emotionally—his speech proficiency should also progress. Far too frequently,

---

[5] Abne Eisenberg, *Living Communication* (N.J.: Prentice-Hall, Inc., Englewood Cliffs, 1975), p. 134.

skill in this area is not encouraged at early ages and is even hampered. Previously we mentioned that you learned to speak and use your voice as a result of a combination of factors. Consider some possible situations. If a young child develops a lisp (and the reasons for this articulatory defect are highly complex) and the parents think "It's sweet," or perhaps are even unable to recognize the articulation problem, then the child's skill in speaking is hindered. If the vocabulary level in a child's home or in his or her community is of a low level, then the child's chances for learning to use a meaningful vocabulary can be hampered. More seriously, if a child grows up in a home where the attitude is "Speak when spoken to," or "Speak only when you have something important to say," then the child can develop serious psychological handicaps that can influence his communication pattern. One of these handicaps could be an ineffective use of voice. Proficiency in voice production cannot be treated as if it were an entity outside of oneself. Remember, "your voice is you."

DEVELOPING SELF-AWARENESS

In the following pages a very personal part of you will be considered: your voice. This voice is as distinctly yours as your religious beliefs, your political loyalties, and your fingerprints. Because "your voice is you," any change, any improvement, is going to involve more than mechanics. Your voice reflects you in your many moods, your thinking, and your behavior patterns—all of those factors that add up to form your personality. In these pages you will be given the knowledge and the skills necessary for good voice production. Then you will be told how to use this "good" voice production. However, much of the value of all of this knowledge will be lost if you do not develop, as quickly as possible, self-awareness. This awareness refers specifically to your fluctuating physical conditions, your emotional states, and the day-by-day progress in your voice-improvement program. For instance, you will soon become aware that on days when you are fatigued your voice practice will be less effective. The very fact that you have less physical energy to expend is reason enough not to be able to practice. However, physical fatigue also affects your mental state, so the problem is compounded. Mentally you are in no mood to work, and physically you are unable to work. Tired muscles do not respond easily to physical stimulation, and if the muscles are *forced* to function, the result could be increased muscular tension. This hypertension would certainly not produce the kind of voice response you want. You will discover also that on days when you have experienced an emotional upset, voice practice might be practically worthless. The fact that your emotions affect your physical condition, your powers of concentration, and your attitudes contributes to a highly complicated picture of why you are unable to practice when you are tense, anxious, or worried. If you are emotionally upset, your body reacts—your breathing is affected, muscles become tense, and coordinated muscular action is hampered. Concentration during this period is almost impossible because your thoughts are on your worries. Your attitude toward the practice session will either be "I couldn't care less" or "I'm going to acquire this skill—or else." In this highly charged atmosphere, either attitude could obviously interfere seriously with productive practice.

On the brighter side, however, you will become sensitive to days that are potentially good for voice work. These days can be discovered only on a highly individual basis. For some of you it will mean days when you are physically well and emotionally at ease. For others, it will mean days when attitudes are optimistic. Whatever the conditions, you can encourage profitable vocal practice on days when the vocal mechanism is functioning well (for example, no colds, hoarseness, or allergy irritations) and when mental concerns are minimal. Remember, such days do not always just "happen." More often than not they must be encouraged to happen.

We have referred frequently in this book to the psychological involvements in the speech process. At this point we would like to assure you that not all changes in attitude and in application are spontaneous or deliberate. You may be a person who feels very hostile in the initial stages of the improvement program. Do not force yourself to reconsider or to reevaluate your feelings or position immediately. Let knowledge, time, and experience help you on the way to self-acceptance.

DEVELOPING AUDITORY DISCRIMINATION

There are several basic requirements for a voice improvement program. These three are absolutely necessary:
1. An awareness and a knowledge of the voice problem itself.
2. A willingness to change or improve your present voice.
3. A resolute attitude toward a planned practice program.

Usually a person is made aware of a voice problem after an examination by an otolaryngologist or a qualified speech therapist. Sometimes a person becomes aware of his voice problem because of physical discomfort, or because of remarks made by friends, or simply because he has heard a recording or taping of his voice. What is important is for you to learn to recognize the *exact* sound of your voice. You should try to develop as quickly as possible *acuity of auditory feedback*—the ability to hear your own voice accurately. This is really another form of self-awareness. You must become aware of your present method of producing voice and of the changes in your voice production as you try new vocal techniques. Before you can improve your voice you must learn to *listen*. Remember, your voice will improve in direct proportion to how much you are aware of your voice problem. Become "voice," or "sound," conscious.

How well are you able to analyze the sound of voices at this early stage? Experiment with the following suggestions:

1. Face a corner wall of a carpeted room. Cupping a hand behind each ear, pull the ears slightly forward and begin to speak into the corner. The voice that reaches your ears will be fairly close to your voice as other people hear it. Become acquainted with it.
2. Have a "new listening experience" the next time you listen to your favorite disc jockey or television program. Can you *put into words* the descriptions of the voices you are hearing?

Let us take a close look at some of the factors that will specifically aid you in controlling and monitoring your own voice production. The Central Nervous System (CNS) coordinates and directs the speech act. The CNS functions like a computer. The more information you feed into a computer, the more precise and inclusive will be the information returned. The CNS acts in approximately the same manner. The more stimuli fed into it, the more precise and inclusive will be its control over the nerve stimulation and muscle action involved in the speech act. The CNS reacts to visual, tactile, kinesthetic, and aural stimulation. This means that for maximum control and awareness of your use of voice, you must be able to (1) *see* what you are doing; (2) *feel* what you are doing by using touch; (3) *sense* what you are doing by feeling "inside"; and (4) *hear* what you are doing. Musicians and athletes know this kind of awareness and control.

As you practice the suggested voice exercises in this book look at yourself in a mirror (visual) and note how the articulators are moving. Are they active? Is the lower jaw too rigid? Are the back teeth clenched? Using your hand, spread the thumb and middle finger to cover the lower jaw area. Feel (tactile) the muscular action of the jaws and the muscular action under the lower jaw bones. Is this area hypertense? Is it too lax? Along with the visual and tactile approach, take advantage of the kinesthetic (muscle) sensations you experience as you practice. As you feel the muscular action tactually, close your eyes and try to perceive that muscular action. Can you recognize *how it feels?* Now you are ready to encourage the aural (hearing) sense.

Momentarily pause and try the following suggestions to help you check on *how well you hear your own voice:*

1. Think for a moment: Does your voice sound like the voice of anyone in your home? An indication of this would be the fact that you are frequently mistaken on the telephone for another member of your family. If this happens to you, then be assured that your voice has some aspects of the other person's voice quality. Listen to the voice of this person. Do you like the quality? If so, why? If not, why not?
2. Record your own voice. Deliberately use it in different emotional

settings—anger, pleasure, surprise. What differences in the sound of your voice do you hear? What accounts for the vocal differences— the sound of your voice, the words you are saying, or a combination of both?

Auditory discrimination will develop in a very specific way. In the initial stages of improvement you will be able to discriminate to a degree. You might become discouraged because you feel that you cannot discriminate aurally at all. The best advice is to be patient, because in due time you will become sensitive to sound discrimination. You will first be able to recognize deviations of speech in your friends, classmates, and parents— in anyone except yourself. You will so sharpen your discriminatory ability in this respect that your former favorite announcer or TV personality will begin to annoy you with his communication faults. The next stage of progress will be applied to you directly. You will begin to hear yourself *after* you have made the error in articulation or after you have started to produce voice incorrectly—all too late because the sounds have been produced. This is the most frustrating stage of all. The next stage of development is the most encouraging. As you start to speak you will have begun to change (as a result of continued practice) the involved muscular action enough so that you are able to *initiate* the pattern correctly. Then you will be well on the way to permanent speech improvement. At this point do not be concerned about criteria in the use of your senses. You will be advised about these as you are introduced to the new vocal skills.

DEVELOPING NEW VOCAL SKILLS: PRACTICE SESSIONS

Basically, voice improvement involves retraining muscle action, but you must not force this action. Rather, you must firmly encourage the desired muscular response. It should be obvious that this kind of practice must not be continued for any long span of time. Muscles used in a new or different manner tend to get tired, and long periods of practice can cause varied reactions. One of these reactions is related to aural fatigue. When you undertake your new voice improvement program, your aural feedback will be unreliable. As you practice, you will be able to detect some changes in the quality of your voice, but the ability to discriminate will be short-lived. As you attempt a new skill, aurally and kinesthetically, you will be aware of differences, but if the muscles tire and revert back to their old pattern of movement (tired muscles tend to do exactly this), you probably won't notice that the voice produced has your "old" quality. Short periods of practice help to avoid this danger. In the beginning work about five minutes at a time, but plan on frequent periods of practice. Short, but repeated, periods of work are highly beneficial. Two minutes out of every waking hour is ideal. Plan on *daily* practice, because skipping days between sessions only retards your progress. Also, be inventive about your time to practice. Do not rely on an allotted "hour" for voice improvement skills, because this time seldom materializes. Rather, make use of odd periods during the day. Practice in your car while driving to work or driving to school; practice as you walk across campus; and practice as you dress in the morning or before you retire (if you are not too fatigued). It is better to plan for a specific time to try a new skill, but the reinforcing of that skill can be done during odd periods of the day. Whatever your approach, it is important for you to *progress* in your voice improvement. Do not allow irregular practice periods to be responsible for spasmodic progress. Relearning and retraining can be the beginnings of boredom and dissatisfaction. Be assured that if you follow these instructions regarding your practice sessions, you *will* improve. Your progress will approximately go through the following stages:

1. As your self-awareness develops, you will first become sensitive to the voices of *other* people (family, friends, and so on).
2. In the second stage of growth, you will hear yourself *after* you have spoken and used the incorrect or ineffective voice. This is the most frustrating stage of all because the sound is out, it is over with and you *know* it wasn't correct.
3. The third stage, that gratifying stage, is when you initiate correctly and are able to control and sustain your "new" voice.

In the voice section we will follow this order for your acquisition of knowledge and skills:

1. Achievement of basic skills:
   a. Adequate muscle tonus (relaxation).
   b. Sufficient breath and control of that breath for voice production (respiration).
   c. Amplification/modification of the outgoing breath stream as it is resonated in the involved cavities (resonance).
   d. Adequate laryngeal vocal fold tension where needed (phonation).
2. Application of these basic skills to:
   a. Quality of voice.
   b. Volume.
   c. Pitch.
   d. Rate.
3. Development of refined vocal skills

Remember, all of this knowledge and these skills will be developed within the framework of your intra/-interpersonal communication pattern and the verbal/-nonverbal use of your voice.

In the foreword we referred to the limitations of this text as a guide to articulation and voice improvement. The orientation here is not toward pathology. For example, there will be only a passing reference to some of the articulatory process problems, such as neurological disorders and spasmodic dysphonia. However, there will be a more intensive treatment of the vibratory process problems (nodules—polyps resulting in hoarseness and huskiness). Respiratory support problems related to vibratory problems will be treated in depth, such as raspiness, stridency, throatiness, hyponasality, hypernasality, thinness, and breathiness. This is a speech improvement book whose focus is on your present habitual communication pattern and how to help you manipulate that pattern for more effective communication. You will be given all of the necessary information to help you to acquire the needed skills. Such knowledge will not only give you a rationale for improvement, but this knowledge will also provide you with a firm basis for following procedures. In addition this knowledge can be supportive and reassuring. You will more quickly "stop holding the hand of your teacher," and you will develop a point of reference for improvement.

Voice Production: The Processes Involved

THE RELAXATION PROCESS

Before we give you the necessary information and instructions regarding the assessment and management of your specific voice problem, serious consideration must first be given to your acquiring *adequate muscle tonus*. Today's world can be demanding, fast-paced, impersonal, taxing, and enervating. People react to these "vibrations" with varying kinds of behavior. When pressures become too great, many people become "hyper"—anxious and overtense. Others withdraw and cease, or refuse, to function. No matter what the symptoms are, what does matter is that these forms of behavior are anxiety-based. Hypertension becomes a way of life, a habitual experience. Usually a personal price is paid physically, physiologically, and/or psychologically. For many, the price is a voice problem. Why the voice? An educated guess suggests that the voice of the individual is his weak spot—the spot that nature uses to signal for help. At this point what is *not* needed is to be told, "Relax. If you would just relax you would feel better." The implication of that useless advice is that hypertension can be turned off like a faucet. That is just not so. You need to *experience* relaxation as opposed to experiencing hypertension.

In producing voice, muscle tension (adequate muscle tonus) is basic. What is *not* needed is hypertension (muscles that are too tense) or even hypotension (muscles that are too relaxed). The muscles involved in voice production must be *ready* so that you can effectively manipulate vocal quality, volume, pitch, and rate. In order to raise your own level of awareness of your habitual muscle tonus, a number of check exercises are suggested here. How are you functioning muscularly? Let's see.

Exercises for Relaxation

ADEQUATE MUSCLE TONUS

Good posture, or proper alignment, is essential. Check yours. Most of us hold ourselves incorrectly, causing and maintaining unnecessary tension in the body. Few of us are able to stand freely and easily, with an open stance and proper tonus.

1. In front of a full-length mirror, stand with your feet parallel and close together (avoid a V position). Close your eyes and shift your weight on your feet. Lean to the front, the side, and the back, letting your balance shift over your toes and inside and outside of your feet and your heels. Now find the point at which your weight is evenly balanced on both feet. Notice *how* you feel. Could you stand comfortably for a long time? How are you holding your shoulders? Are you aware of any pains in your lower back? Get a sense of being securely "grounded." Then, continue up your body, checking to see if your knees are straight. Turn and look at yourself sideways in the mirror. Place one hand on your abdomen and one on your lower back. With the hand on the lower back, press down hard, tilting and tucking the pelvis under; lift the hand on the abdomen up slightly. Experiment with that movement. Repeat it. Use your hands to help your tactile feedback; close your eyes while repeating the movement to encourage the kinesthetic sense. The mirror will further the visual feedback. Most of us sink into the pelvis and have excess curvature in the lower back. This provides poor vocal support and creates much of the lower back problems Americans experience today.

2. Release your hand. Now check in the mirror to see if your back is straight. Think of elongating the back rather than arching it in military fashion. If your arm is hanging down, you should be able to see your back behind it—if not, you are arching the back too much. Many of us lean back when we are standing. This must be corrected. Again, use the mirror as your guide.

3. Now turn and face front. Look in the mirror. Lift your shoulders way up and then drop or press them down. Think of someone holding you by a hair at the back of the top of your head so your neck is lengthened. You may need to tuck in your chin slightly and bring your head back over your body. So many of us "lead" the body with our head, tense up our shoulders, and shorten the neck. This creates vocal tension, headaches, and neck pains.

4. Finally, go back over your body, beginning at the feet and continuing upward. Have a sense of being securely balanced and of lightness. When you properly align the body standing is effortless. The body feels as if it were floating. Don't get discouraged. It is possible to correct your

posture and enjoy its affects on over-all energy, a sense of well-being, and good vocal production.

FULL BODY RELAXATION

The following exercises should be done *in sequence*.

1. Lie down on a carpeted floor or on a mat—*on your back*. Place your arms about six inches away from your body, with the palms of your hands turned up.

 a. Roll your *head* gently from side to side, bringing each ear to the carpet. After each roll of your head, roll it to the center position.

 b. Raise your right *arm* about six inches off of the floor and then just let it *drop* back on to the floor. Repeat this movement with your left *arm*.

 c. Raise your right *leg* a few inches off of the floor and then let it drop back on to the floor. Repeat this movement with the left *leg*.

 d. Raise your shoulders up off the floor, leaving your head on the floor, and then release the shoulders back on to the floor.

 e. Lift your *hips* a few inches above the floor and then release them.

 f. Tense all of your facial muscles, making as small a face as possible, and then relax the face.

 g. Finally, check your body to see if you need to make any adjustments to be comfortable and then lie perfectly still for a few minutes more. *Enjoy!*

2. Stand with your feet about twenty-four inches apart, toes slightly turned out. Drop your head to your chest. Imagine your head is a heavy lead ball and s-l-o-w-l-y let it pull your upper torso forward toward the floor, bending at the waist. Continue falling forward, bending at the waist and allowing your arms and hands to hang loose until your fingertips reach knee level. This should take you about fifteen seconds. When your fingertips reach your knees, drop to the floor, knees bent, and hang loose and limp. Keep your arms swinging and relaxed, your head bent and "bouncey," and your neck relaxed. Now, straighten your knees and then come up slowly to a standing position with an "unrolling" motion upward, vertebra by vertebra.

THE THROAT, NECK, AND JAW AREAS

1. Stand with feet about twenty-four inches apart. Drop your head to your chest and then begin a circular motion from right to left involving your head and shoulders. Start with the head on your chest and aim for your right shoulder, then back of your neck, your left shoulder, and then back to your chest. It is important that you don't just move your head, but that you involve your shoulders and upper chest. Move the entire upper portion of your body in the circular motion.

2. Sit comfortably with your back as straight as possible. Keep the body erect (but relaxed) and still from the shoulders down. Inhale gently as you drop your chin to your chest. Exhale as you slowly let your head drop back. Repeat this four times. Then, inhale as you let your left ear come to the left shoulder. The face should be forward and the shoulders level. Feel the stretch in the opposite side of the neck. Then exhale, moving the right ear straight over to the right shoulder. Repeat this four times. Next, inhale while turning to look over your right shoulder. Be sure that the rest of your body is still and your back is straight. Exhale to the right. Repeat this activity four times.

3. This exercise (a massage) is designed to relax the shoulder muscles across the upper part of your back. The relaxed muscles will, in turn, help to relax the neck and throat muscles that must have *only* adequate muscle tonus for effective voice production. Your chest cavity, shoulders, and neck must *not be hypertense.*

Work with a partner. Stand "Indian file," both facing in the same direction. Partner A places his hands on partner B's upper back area on the muscles (trapezius) extending across the back from shoulder to shoulder (*not* at the shoulder blade level). Begin to gently squeeze each side, first alternately and then simultaneously. Partner A should then raise his elbows high and "play the piano" with his fingers in this area. During this massage session, partner B should think "Relax!" He should keep his shoulder area as pliable as possible so that partner A can work efficiently. Exchange roles and repeat the massage action.

4. To help you understand and feel more accurately how muscular actions differ, try the following exercise. Begin with good posture. Place one hand on your chest over the sternum (breastbone), while your other hand hangs relaxed at your side. Tighten all of your muscles, particularly those from the waist up, by deliberately pulling back and raising your shoulders, biting down on your teeth so that all of your neck and facial muscles are also tightened. This should be done with your eyes open, preferably looking into a mirror (visual stimulation). Now close your eyes and try to experience and feel what happens next. Slowly begin to progressively relax your hand on the sternum, the upper chest cavity, and shoulders (dropping them to a comfortable position). Continue on to the neck area and then the jaw area. Ending with your head bent, chin dropped to your chest, and your shoulders and chest cavity "collapsed" inward. Closing your eyes heightens the kinesthetic sense.

Now that you have worked on body relaxation in general and on the relaxation of those areas specifically involved with voice production in particular, the point must be made that these forms of relaxation, *in themselves,* might contribute very little to your voice improvement program. "A sound mind and a sound body" translated into voice production terms might become "A relaxed mind and a relaxed body." Relaxation can be an art when it is a *process* that you *consciously* create. All that it requires is a willingness and an attentiveness to *process* rather than *product*. Do not *take on* general body relaxation without being aware of its intricate involvement with your *total* functioning. Take a closer look at yourself.

1. Am I presently feeling physically well? If not, why not? If not, then an assessment by a competent physician is crucial.
2. How am I functioning psychologically? Am I overanxious? Am I overreacting to pressures? How am I interrelating with my family, friends, and associates?
3. How am I living with myself? Am I happy or unhappy professionally, socially, and personally?
4. Do I like myself? If not, why not?

THE INNERVATION PROCESS

Speech is bodily actions made audible, and these actions don't just happen! Our bodies act as we tell them to act. There is a complicated system of message sending and message receiving inside our bodies and we call that inside-the-body communication intrapersonal communication. We send messages from the brain to parts of our bodies, ordering those parts into action. We get messages back from the brain, informing us of the nature and progress of that action. Part of that incoming information comes from inside your body and part of it comes from the world outside your skin.

Innervation is the name given to the process of stimulating activity in the body by the nerves. The word *innervate* (coming from *in + nerve + ate*) is the verb, meaning "to stimulate activity by nerves," and innervator is the noun. The innervators are the nervous systems that do the stimulating (intrapersonal message carrying) inside our bodies.

The Central Nervous System (CNS) is specifically involved in the speech act. Its role is one of direction and coordination. Specific nerve stimulation to the larynx is the laryngeal branch of the tenth cranial nerve. A consideration of the *reflex arc* will possibly add another dimension to your understanding of the *innervation process*. The human nervous system can be divided into the Peripheral and the Central Nervous Systems. The PNS is both sensory and motor, depending on its specific function at the time. The sensory neurons of the PNS are concerned with the transmission of impulses initiated by an *external* stimulus that can be either visual, tactile, or auditory—or all three combined. The motor fibers of the PNS are responsible for getting nerve impulses to areas of the body where they stimulate muscle action. The CNS directs and coordinates all of this activity.

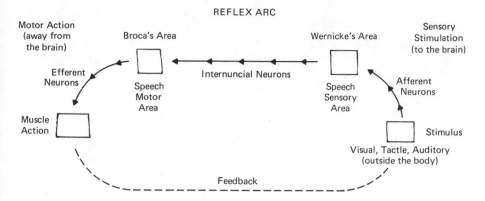

The PNS receives the stimuli (from outside of the body); afferent neurons carry the sensory sensations to the speech sensory area (Wernicke's area) where they are received, decoded, and acted on; afferent neurons continue to carry the stimuli to the speech motor area (internuncial neurons involved); and the sensory stimuli arrive at the speech motor area (Broca's area) where they are carried away from the brain by the efferent neurons to become a motor activity. Muscular action is initiated and verbal speech takes place. We must tell you that this is a simplified version of the complex and intricate process by which speech is produced. For example, it is said that in order to produce one syllable, forty pairs of muscles are called into play.

Now, what does all of this have to do with your voice improvement program? In order to change any muscle action, the progessions indicated on the reflex arc are approximately followed. Let us zero in on a change of muscle action as it is related to voice production. You see Jim coming toward you (visual stimulation) with outstretched hand (tactile stimulation) and he says, "How are you?" (auditory stimulation). The PNS and CNS coordinate to decode, interpret, and formulate your reply. Monitored nerve to muscle stimulation results in the reply, "I'm fine." Your reply becomes auditory feedback (stimulus) to your PNS and the process starts all over again. Only this second time around, as a result of your intensified effort, increased awareness, and skill, changes in your muscle action can occur. You could repeat your reply, "Yes, I'm really fine," reinforcing that "new" voice on which you have been working. In short, constant repetition becomes reinforcement, which is a crucial ingredient in acquiring the skills necessary for encouraging the habitual use of your new vocal you. Over the years these writers have been barraged with, "I'm fifty years old. Can I really change?" Or, "Billy is only six. Can he really learn to use his voice differently?" Our immediate reply is always, "Yes, you *can* learn to produce voice differently, or we're in the wrong profession."

THE RESPIRATION PROCESS

Perhaps the process most vital to the production of human speech is respiration. The entire process has two phases: inhalation and exhalation. The purposes of respiration are twofold: (1) you breathe for your very existence, and (2) you breathe for the production of speech. In breathing for life, the combined phases take anywhere from three to five seconds and are about *equal in length*. This means that the amount of air taken in by the lungs when you inhale is about equal to the amount of air expelled when you exhale. Also, the phase of inhalation, which brings fresh oxygen to your body, is an active phase, whereas exhalation, which expels the waste products from your body, is passive. Actually, exhalation is nothing more than relaxation following the contraction of the necessary muscles in inhalation. The entire *process is involuntary* and is controlled by the brain stem, which is the core of the brain, essentially an extension of the spinal cord (through which all nerve impulses are channeled)—specifically, the medulla. Proof of the involuntary nature of this act can be found in the incident of the infant who holds his breath in anger while the nervous parents stand by helplessly. Their fears are groundless because the infant can voluntarily control the breathing process only for a limited time. As soon as there is enough accumulation of carbon dioxide in his blood stream, the infant will black out, and immediately the involuntary breathing pattern will resume.

In addition to the respiratory process (for life) being involuntary and the phases of inhalation and exhalation being about equal in length, the process has a third distinctive feature. The *breath is smooth flowing*, generally speaking. The smooth flow of air is interrupted only when the speaker engages in physical exertion or becomes emotionally involved (anger, fear, or joy).

This is not so with breathing for speech. The *control is voluntary* (the cerebrum, or cerebral cortex, is the control center for this voluntary action) and is entirely in the hands of the speaker. The phases of inhalation and exhalation *are not equal in length*, but vary according to the physical and/or semantic demands of the speaker. No one is more aware of this fact than the actor, newscaster, or comedian—in fact, any person experienced in speaking to an audience. Judging how to control the outgoing breath stream sometimes determines the difference between a forcefully delivered line or a laid egg. Grabbing for needed breath at an inopportune moment could interfere with the perfect punch line. An illustration: you begin an important line of dialogue. In the middle of the line you realize that you are running out of breath, so you stop to take the needed breath. What about your listeners? You have forced them to continue your thought in spite of the interruption. This "interruption," no matter how small or insignificant, can be a deterent to a forceful delivery. Carry your listeners along! Don't force them to become distracted from your goal by poor breath control.

Breathing for speech, as previously noted, has three distinct features: 1) the control is voluntary; 2) the phases of inhalation and exhalation are not equal in length; and 3) the flow of air is smooth but erratic. The various patterns of syllabic stress in word pronunciation interfer. In American English there are a number of such stress patterns: primary, secondary, tertiary, and weak. Syllabic stress gives our speech pulsations that are varied and irregular (See Chap. 6, p. 306). Couple these pulsations with semantic involvement (the emotional content of word meaning) and the situation is compounded. The erratic outward flow of breath challenges the speaker even more. For example, you are speaking. As you express your ideas (no matter the situation), your flow of breath is influenced by your feelings at the moment of utterance and by your phrasing (grouping of words to express complete ideas). If you are angry, your voice will probably be used more forcefully, with a jerky rhythm that demands more breath. If you are in a relaxed mood, the flow of breath might be as smooth flowing as it is in breathing for life sustenance. In any event, the point for you to remember is that you, the speaker, determine how your breath is to be controlled and used—and it can be controlled!

Effective Breathing for Voice Production

Because breath vibrated in the larynx is the basis for voice production, ineffective breathing habits, or inadequate breath control, can be partially responsible for almost all voice quality defects—functional or organic. It is important in your voice improvement program to check very carefully for *efficient* respiration. The process itself is a complicated one, with places for many pitfalls. There are various types of breathing patterns: the clavicular, the thoracic, and the thoracic-abdominal (or central breathing). Because we believe that the thoracic-abdominal method is best suited to speech needs, it will be discussed first.

The torso of the body is divided into two cavities: (1) the thoracic (chest) cavity, which extends from the clavicles to the waistline, and (2) the abdominal cavity which extends from the waist to the pelvic area. These two cavities are separated at the midriff by the diaphragm, a dome-shaped muscle attached to the edges of the lower ribs. (In a relaxed position it looks like an open umbrella, opening upward toward the thoracic area and forming the floor of this cavity.) The thorax, or chest, is composed of the rib cage, which is made up of the sternum (breastbone), twelve pairs of ribs, and the spinal column. The lungs are housed in this cavity. All of the ribs are attached to the backbone, but the attachments in the front vary, thus forming a structure capable of considerable movement. The last two pairs of ribs are floating ribs, the next four pairs are attached to each other by cartilage, and the upper six pairs of ribs are joined to the sternum. This arrangement of the musculature makes possible three movements of the thoracic cavity that are important in inhalation: (1) a slightly upward and forward movement, (2) a back-to-front expansion, and (3) a side-to-side expansion. A fourth action is an elongation of this cavity as a result of the downward movement of the diaphragm during the phase of inhalation.

Your individual respiration process was started at the birth cry, and this life process is concerned with an involuntary rhythmic pattern of contraction and relaxation of the thorax. Because of this contracting and relaxing movement, a partial vacuum is created in the thoracic cavity in the lung area, resulting in an imbalance of air pressure between the air pressure inside the cavity and that outside the body. This has to be rectified for survival, so nature allows air to rush in through the nasal and oral cavities, serving two purposes: oxidation of the bloodstream, and equalizing the air pressure. The air enters the oral and nasal cavities, passes through the trachea (windpipe), enters the bronchial tubes and the bronchioles, and fills the alveoli (or air sacs), which comprise the lungs. The lungs themselves do not move, but the expansion action of the rib cage allows room for the air sacs of the lungs to fill with air. As this action takes place we have the concomitant contraction of the diaphragm, forcing this muscle into a flattened position and, thereby, elongating the thoracic cavity. The diaphragm is a very important muscle in respiration because its involuntary action in inhalation necessarily involves the action of the muscles of the abdominal cavity for effective breath control. As the diaphragm contracts, the viscera (soft organs) are pushed gently downward, causing the abdominal wall to protrude slightly. Immediately, the opposite muscular action takes place, and exhalation begins. The abdominal muscles contract, pushing the viscera upward as the diaphragm assumes an open umbrella position. This action of the diaphragm allows the muscles of the rib cage to return to their relaxed position. Meanwhile, the air is forced out of the lungs and passes through the trachea and between the vocal folds.

Now you are ready to check your own respiration pattern.

1. Lie on a flat surface (preferably the floor), place a light book or magazine on the diaphragm, and *relax*. Do not think about your breathing pattern; just close your eyes and do nothing. After a few minutes, take note of the gentle rising and falling motion of the book. Apply your knowledge of what you read here in the previous paragraphs. As you take a breath, the book will rise. As you exhale, the book will be lowered. Notice the related coordinated movements of the thoracic and abdominal cavities.

2. Now stand up. Check your posture. See that you are as relaxed as you were in the position on the floor. Keep the shoulders straight, but

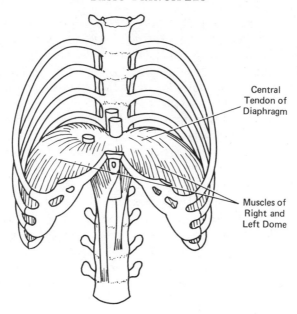

FIGURE 8–1. *Anterior view of the diaphragm.*

comfortable, and do not hump over at the waist, because this interferes with the effective functioning of the diaphragm. Straighten your knees. Place your hands on your chest and breathe quietly. Does this cavity function with a rising and falling motion? It should do so. Now place your hands over the abdominal wall, with light pressure of the fingertips on the broad bands of muscle that make up the front wall of the abdomen. Again, breathe quietly. Is there a protrusion of this area in inhalation? Is there an inward motion on exhalation? If so, you are breathing efficiently.

Control and Use of the Respiratory Process

Some further information may be helpful in understanding respiration. In breathing for speech, central breathing is considered the most efficient because it uses the gross abdominal muscles in exhalation. These muscles are most effective in controlling the outgoing air stream so that it can be emitted smoothly and evenly. This kind of breath emission is necessary for a firm, well-produced voice. The breath must not be allowed to gush out. Neither must tension be allowed to develop in the thoracic cavity by pushing on the thoracic muscles in exhalation, and, most important, no hypertension must develop in the pharyngeal area in an effort to emit the breath. The breath must be controlled by a strong, steady push by the gross abdominal muscles. This technique is known as support of tone. Specifically, this skill involves *the use of the muscles of the abdominal cavity to exert a controlled muscular pressure in order to support a steady stream of breath between the vocal folds.* To further clarify the technique:

On inhalation: thoracic muscles tense, diaphragm tense, abdominal muscles relaxed.

On exhalation: abdominal muscles tense, diaphragm relaxed, thoracic muscles relaxed.

Try the following exercises to help you recognize the various types of muscular action that can be present in exhalation.

1. Place one hand on each side of the chest area, with your fingertips almost touching at the line of the sternum. Inhale a large amount of air and then gently push with your hands on the chest cavity as you exhale. Feel the muscular action in this area as the air is expelled from the lungs. You should feel a collapsing of the muscles.

2. Now place one hand on each side of the midriff, with your fingertips meeting at the front. (You are now directly over the diaphragm). Inhale again, but this time deliberately push in on the muscles in this area as you exhale. You are now using the diaphragmatic muscle in exhalation.

3. Effective central breathing demands even more muscular control than the preceding exercises. You are now ready to feel the action of the gross abdominal muscles in effective exhalation. Place one hand on each side of the abdominal cavity, fingertips almost touching. (This is the location of the viscera, the soft organs). You recall from your reading in this chapter that on the phase of inhalation, the muscles in this area tend to push out. So, as you breathe, this time on exhalation, concentrate on pushing in or on tensing the gross abdominal muscles. With this kind of muscular action, as the vocal folds vibrate, the breath will be released in a steady, firm stream. The end result should be a strong, firm basic laryngeal tone.

If in speaking the occasion demands a lot of breath for a lengthy sentence or a strong breath to express a vivid emotion, the extra breath need not come from more breath being taken in on inhalation, but rather should be the result of controlling breath in exhalation. If you feel that you must take in more breath on inhalation, remember that it is not acquired by gasping with an *inward* movement or a pulling *in* of the abdominal cavity as you inhale. A clavicular breather is often guilty of this kind of incorrect muscular action.

In clavicular breathing the clavicles (collarbones) are used to help raise the thoracic cavity on inhalation, so that instead of the *correct expansion* action outward there is a limited *lifting* action of this cavity. The result is unsatisfactory because the lungs can be only partially filled with air. Hypertension in the thoracic muscles limits the expansion of this cavity, thereby limiting the amount of air to be inhaled. More serious is the effect such inhalation has on the larynx. In an effort to raise the thorax by using the clavicles, the extrinsic muscles of the larynx are also placed under strain. This results in hypertension of these muscles, and the voice quality is directly affected. Usually the quality is *breathy, thin,* and sometimes *strident,* the latter depending on the amount of resonator hypertension. The pitch of the voice is necessarily adversely affected. On exhalation, clavicular breathing is also undependable. Because there is a shallow intake of breath, the speaker either has to rely on added strain in the thoracic or pharyngeal areas to sustain the voice or he must resort to quick intakes of air as he phonates. This gasping for breath is distracting to his listeners and certainly interferes with meaningful phrasing in his speaking.

You may now be aware that you do not consistently utilize diaphragmatic action when you speak. (Remember that you do so automatically in breathing for life sustenance.) If this is so, then you must *acquire* this skill and make it habitual. Central breathing (thoracic-abdominal) is an asset to good voice production. Margaret Greene, in her book, *The Voice and Its Disorders* (the "Bible" of many voice therapists) says: "The paramount importance of correct breathing in speech and song cannot be overestimated. Permanent improvement in the voice cannot possibly be achieved without improvement in respiration. . . . After relaxation has been established, the first step in teaching is always by far the most difficult; this is the development of the diaphragmatic intercostal method in place of the upper thoracic habit already in existence, and it is very necessary that much attention is spent on this stage before beginning exercises for increase of inspiration and control of expiration."[6]

If you are not sure of the exact muscular feel (kinesthetic) of central breathing, then review pp. 355–356 of this text. One further point to help you to clarify your thinking about central breathing before you begin the exercises: you might recall that previously we talked about how your body is divided into two cavities (see p. 353) and we also spoke about the importance of the action of the diaphragm during breathing for both life and speech. We want to stress here the point that in central breathing, which directly involves the thoracic and abdominal muscles and the diaphragm, *you will not actually feel the movement of the diaphragm during respiration.* What you will feel is the movement of the outer wall of your midriff section, along with the movement of the abdominal muscles.

[6] Margaret Greene, *The Voice and Its Disorders.* 3rd ed. (New York: Pitman Publishing Corporation, 1972), p. 92.

Now you are ready to continue with the following exercises, which should help you to develop more control over the outgoing breath stream as you speak. When you practice, make use of all possible sensory help: visual, tactile, aural, and kinesthetic.

1. Good posture—(nonverbal communication). See p. 347.
2. Self-awareness of adequate muscle tonus and avoidance of hypertension in the pharyngeal area (nonverbal/-intrapersonal communication see pp. 347–349).
3. A steady, even flow of breath on exhalation (see p. 359).

Exercises for Control of the Respiratory Process

1. Standing with feet firmly on the floor, knees straight, hands placed over the abdominal cavity, take a deep breath. Count from one to six as you exhale. Begin the count at the *peak of inhalation*. Do not allow any breath to escape before you say the number 1. Concentrate on expelling all of your breath by the time you reach the last number. Do this exercise on one intake of breath. During this practice take note of the movement of the gross abdominal muscles. There should be a gentle muscular action *inward* as you exhale.

2. Repeat exercise 1, trying for different ranges of breath control.
a. Count from one to twelve.
b. Count from one to six.
c. Count from one to ten, and so on.

This exercise is designed to make you aware tactually and kinesthetically of the fact that *you* are in control of your breath emission as you speak. At this stage of voice improvement, do not let the phase of exhalation *just happen*. Be deliberate in your control.

3. The following paragraph is composed of sentences that grow progressively in length. Using the same approach as in exercises 1 and 2, read the sentences in the paragraph with an intake of breath on the first word of the sentence and plan complete exhalation at the period. You might find that the amount of intake of air will have to be varied slightly as the sentence becomes longer. However, the important technique will be to control the emission of breath.

Begin now. Notice your posture. Stand with straight knees. During practice aim for central breathing. Do you know the meaning of this? Inhale with an open, relaxed oral cavity and unclenched back teeth. Begin to speak at the peak of inhalation with no escape of air before you phonate. During exhalation, attempt to control the breath stream so that you will have enough breath to complete the sentences. It is important that you feel a push from your gross abdominal muscles as you try to control the outgoing breath stream. This muscular control is important in effective voice production because this control will help you to maintain a firm, steady stream of breath during phonation.

Exercises for Effective Use of the Breath Stream

At the beginning of this section on the respirators the point was made that perhaps the process most vital to the production of human speech is respiration. You were encouraged to develop effective breathing habits and then you were taught how to control the outgoing breath stream. There is a third skill that, in our opinion, is not to be minimized (in fact, it is to be emphasized): having a *free-flowing emission of breath out of the larynx into the specific resonating cavity and then out of the mouth.* So many times the student masters the first two techniques (effective respiration and control) and then stops short of alleviating the voice problem by not completing the cycle of breath *emission.* Throaty, raspy, and strident voices particularly benefit from emphasis on this skill. (See pages 383–388.) Try the following exercises:

1. Hold the palm of your hand about four inches away from your mouth. Place your other hand over the diaphragm area. With an open, relaxed oral cavity and the tongue low and forward in the mouth (do *not* retract the tongue), let the breath be emitted on the palm of the hand as you say "ha." Do *not* vocalize. Do *not say* the word. Take a breath and just let the breath flow out as you form the mouth and lips for "ha." Watch that you do not say "huh." *Open* your mouth for a good /a/ (/ɑ/) sound: /ha/. Do this exercise with your eyes open and then repeat it with your eyes closed (kinesthetic stimulus). Get the feel of *free-flowing breath out of the mouth.* Now transfer this feel to speech. Try exercise number 2.

2. Hold the palm of your hand about four inches away from your mouth. Place your other hand over the diaphragm area. Count from one to ten, taking a breath for the individual numbers. On each count gently push the air stream out of the oral cavity and against the palm of your hand. There will be, of course, more breath emission on some numbers than on others because of the nature of the sounds produced (Plosives will have more breath emission than nasals). As you are doing this exercise, attempt to feel muscular action in the abdominal cavity. If the voice begins to sound too breathy, try for more oral resonance by allowing the breath (sounds) to resonate a little longer in the oral cavity. Work for a "round" feeling in the mouth. Keep in mind a relaxed pharyngeal cavity and put the tension on the gross abdominal muscles.

3. Now try phrases and sentences. Let your practice material be pragmatic and meaningful. Don't run to the nearest textbook for material. Use your daily patter. All of us have it. What's yours?

    a. Good morning!

    b. What's for breakfast? Lunch? Dinner?

    c. I'll be home at six tonight.

    d. Is your term paper finished?

To review the preceding material, consider these essential points:

1. Learn to use diaphragmatic action in breathing for speech.
2. Learn to increase and control the outgoing breath stream by first increasing intercostal expansion.
3. Learn to emit breath from the mouth rather than hold it back in the pharyngeal area. Many people speak as if they are walking backward or away from people (interpersonal communication?). Rather, work on acquiring a "forward" feel. Think "up and out."

THE VIBRATORY PROCESS

Your voice is initially produced in the larynx, which is commonly referred to as the Adam's apple. Its anatomy and physiology are determined by heredity and environment. For example, your skeletal framework can include a smaller- or larger-than-average-sized larynx. Also, the length of the vocal folds can vary, measuring anywhere from seven-eighths of an inch to one and one-fourth inches in length. Notably, the female vocal folds are shorter in length, thus accounting for the generally higher pitch of the female voice. The larynx, about the size of a walnut, rests on top of the trachea (windpipe) and is made up of nine cartilages bound together by ligaments and membranous tissue. There is one bone in the larynx, the hyoid bone from which the larynx is suspended. The bone is to the larynx what the basketball hoop is to the net extending from it. The hyoid bone is at the top of the larynx and from this bone extends the cartilaginous framework.

For our purpose it is relatively unimportant for you to know the names and location of all of the parts of the larynx. Only those parts of the larynx will be discussed that will contribute to your knowledge of its physiology and the parts that have a direct bearing on your manipulation of this organ. You should become acquainted with the following parts of the larynx (see Figure 8–2):

1. Hyoid bone: The larynx is suspended from this bone.
2. Thyroid cartilage: This cartilage forms the contour of the larynx; the vocal folds are attached to the center of the front, inside wall of this cartilage.
3. Cricoid cartilage: This cartilage forms the last section of the larynx, directly attached to trachea.
4. Arytenoid cartilages: These are a pair of pyramid-shaped cartilages to which the vocal folds are attached at the rear of the larynx.
5. Vocal folds: These are a vibrating body that produces basic laryngeal tone as breath is emitted between them.
6. Glottis: This is an opening between the vocal folds.

The vocal folds are housed within the larynx and are attached at its front just under the notch of the thyroid cartilage, the larger of the two cartilages. The folds stretch across the larynx and are attached at the

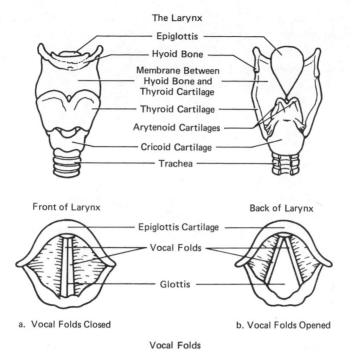

The Larynx

Epiglottis

Hyoid Bone

Membrane Between
Hyoid Bone and
Thyroid Cartilage

Thyroid Cartilage

Arytenoid Cartilages

Cricoid Cartilage

Trachea

Front of Larynx　　　　　　　　　　　　　　Back of Larynx

Epiglottis Cartilage

Vocal Folds

Glottis

a. Vocal Folds Closed　　　　　　　　　b. Vocal Folds Opened

Vocal Folds

FIGURE 8–2. *Front and rear views of the principal cartilages of the larynx and diagrammatic representation of the vocal folds showing attachments to cartilages of the larynx.*

rear to two small pyramid-shaped cartilages, the arytenoids. The opening between the folds is called the glottis, through which passes the exhaled breath stream as it is emitted from the trachea. The vocal folds open and close with a rhythmic motion that is the result of two forces: inner-vation by the laryngeal nerve and air pressure. The most widely accepted theory of the abduction of the vocal folds is the myoelastic-aerodynamic theory.[7] This theory relates the movement of the muscles of the larynx (myo-muscle: elastic-movement) to the force of the exhaled air (aero-air: dynamic-force). This theory postulates that when the air pressure (exhaled breath stream) beneath the vocal folds equals the muscular pressure that holds the folds together, the folds are forced open. Along with this movement there is innervation by the tenth cranial nerve, the vagus nerve. The laryngeal branch of this nerve specifically innervates the vocal process. The vibration of the folds gives your voice its funda-mental vocal tone, or basic laryngeal tone. This laryngeal tone is in-fluenced by the physical structure of your larynx and is established by

[7] Vanden Berg, J., "Myoelastic-aerodynamic Theory of Voice Production," *Journal of Speech and Hearing Research*, 1, 227–243, (1958).

two actions: (1) by the vibration of the outgoing breath stream, and (2) by the amount of tension within the muscles of the larynx and within the vocal folds themselves. The basic process of producing voice is termed phonation from the Greek word φωνη, meaning "a sound."

Biologically, the main functions of the larynx are to prevent food from entering the trachea and to protect the lungs. The vocal folds act also as a valve during any form of physical exertion, by preventing the expulsion of air from out of the lungs. In speech the larynx acts as the organ of voice production. It has previously been stated in this text that the process of phonation involves the emission of breath between the vocal folds, breath that is then set into vibration by the movement of the folds, resonated in the three resonating cavities, and emitted as sounds by the movement of the articulators.

The *extrinsic* muscles of the larynx aid in its positioning. These muscles connect the larynx to the hyoid bone and to other parts of the pharynx, and they are also concerned in part with the movement of the larynx in swallowing and coughing. These muscles are of importance in voice production only if you have hypertension in the pharynx or in the musculature of the jaws, tension that affects the larynx proper. The result can be an unnaturally high-pitched level or an obvious strain in your voice quality. Place your fingertips on the larynx and then swallow. Take close note of the fact that the larynx is not a tense organ, but that it does become tense—that is, *adequately tense* (muscle tonus)—when you swallow.

The *intrinsic* muscles of the larynx have as their main function the opening and closing of the vocal folds. These may be limited to the general categories of the *abductors*, which open the vocal folds, the *adductors*, which close the folds; the *tensors*, which stretch and elongate the folds, and the *relaxors*, which relax and shorten the folds. These muscles have their origin and insertion within the larynx itself. The opening and closing of the vocal folds are controlled by a slight rocking motion of the thyroid cartilage, by movements of the arytenoid cartilages, and by pairs of antagonistic muscles connected to and from the thyroid cartilage, the cricoid cartilage, and the arytenoids.

Even though the muscles mentioned here act involuntarily—in that you cannot control them individually and directly—knowing their involvement in phonation can be most helpful. You can experience kinesthetically and tactually the changes in movements of the larynx as it functions, and this awareness should increase your control over the larynx. The real test of control demonstrates itself in terms of the results you get as you try to manipulate the muscles of the larynx.

The vocal folds are the vibrating body in the production of voice. During respiration for life they are slightly abducted at the midline, allowing the air to escape from the trachea. During a deliberate gasp

THE MUSCULATURE OF THE LARYNX IN THE PRODUCTION OF VOICE

Organs and Muscles	Movement	Purpose
Thyroid cartilage is connected in front to the cricoid cartilage.	Slight rocking back and forth	Affects opening and closing of folds
Cricoid cartilage forms the posterior wall of the larynx.		
Base of the arytenoid cartilage joins with the cricoid cartilage, to form a joint.	Pivoting motion; gentle rocking back and forth; sliding together and apart	Directly involved with the adduction and abduction of the vocal folds
Adductor and abductor muscles		Shorten, lengthen, tense, and relax vocal folds

or quick intake of breath, the folds are held wide apart. In a whisper they are closed at the anterior portion and held apart at the posterior portion. The latter is important for you to know, for you might think that you are saving your voice by whispering if you are suffering from laryngitis. *When you whisper the vocal folds are in a strained position.* Do not whisper if you are suffering from a cold or have some other physical irritation. Rather, speak *softly* so that the folds can vibrate evenly at the midline. In phonation for speech this is their normal position.

As we grow physically, we develop gross and refined muscle action and control for example, the one-year-old infant learns to walk (gross muscle action and control). When asked to, the four-year-old youngster can walk on a straight line (refined muscle action and control). The gross muscle actions involved in playing basketball become refined muscle actions when a player attempts to throw the basketball into the basket. If you are going to productively utilize the vibratory process in your voice improvement program, then you must aim for refined action and control of the laryngeal muscles.

The vibratory process is under your direct control—to a certain degree. For example, you can learn to increase or decrease muscle tension in the laryngeal-pharyngeal areas. Similarly, you can learn to manipulate the adduction of the vocal folds to attain a harder attack or a softer attack.

a

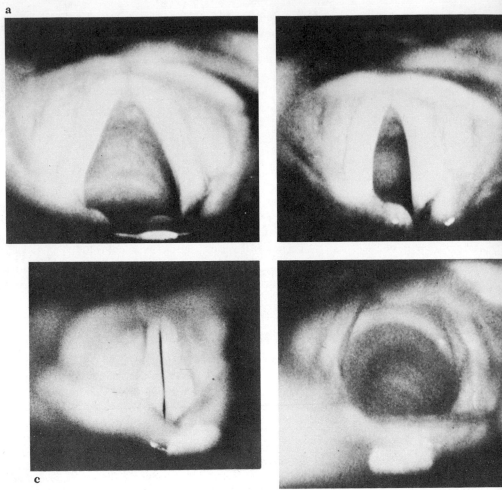

c

FIGURE 8–3. *Position of vocal folds* (a) *on quick intake of breath;* (b) *during whispering;* (c) *during phonation; and* (d) *during a hard cough.* (Courtesy of Bell Laboratories.)

What makes all of these skills so difficult for you to acquire is influenced by the fact that you cannot see what is happening *inside* of the larynx. Nor can your teacher or speech therapist point to a particular muscle in the laryngeal area and say, "Move *that* muscle." A case in point is the difficulty experienced very often by the parents of a child who has developed vocal nodules to get the child to practice the new vocal techniques necessary to alleviate the pathology. The nodules cannot be seen by the parents or the child (the otolaryngologist says that they exist) and, to compound the frustrations of all involved, the child seems

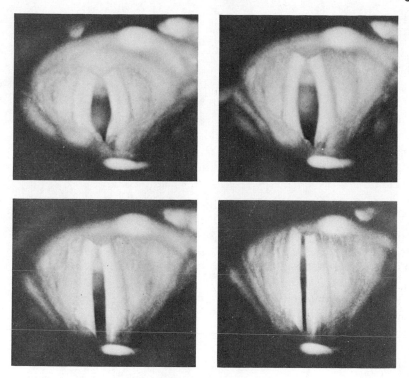

FIGURE 8–4. *Open and closed positions of the human vocal cords at 124, 174, 248, and 330 cycles.* (Courtesy of Bell Laboratories.)

"normal" in every respect. He or she walks, eats, plays, *and* has a voice. However, the parents have been told that there is a serious medical problem with the larynx. To demand practice periods to alleviate something that cannot be seen can be frustrating to both parents and child. We fervently wish that vocal nodules developed on the *outside* of the throat where they could be *seen*. What time and anguish would be saved!

The vibratory process demands refined muscle control if you want to use your voice effectively. Refined muscular control is essential in maintaining adequate muscle tonus in the pharyngeal-laryngeal areas. In your voice improvement program, if you are going to make the most of the vibratory process, you must acquire:

1. Over-all body relaxation (See p. 348.)
2. Relaxation of the specific muscles in the pharyngeal and laryngeal areas (See pp. 348, 349.)
3. Adequate muscle tonus in the pharyngeal and laryngeal areas. (See pp. 347–349.)
4. Central breathing and control of exhalation. (See pp. 355–356.)
5. Controlled breath emission. (See p. 359.)

6. Effective adduction and abduction of the vocal folds during phonation.

We will not describe exercises for the control of refined muscle action
of the vibratory process at this time. Rather, the various exercises and
techniques will be found in the following sections where they will be
applied to the specific voice problems under consideration.

There is one last point to be made before you begin your voice improvement program. We said earlier in this chapter that the anatomy
and physiology of your speech mechanism are largely determined by
heredity and environment. Information about the anatomy of the speech
mechanism (specifically the larynx) has just been covered to help you in
your voice improvement program. Physiologically speaking, we tend to
take on the skills of those around us. Olympic stars tend to have children
who either become another generation of Olympic stars or at least are
above average in the particular sport skill. True, an early introduction
to a particular skill is a factor (the child of an Olympic swimmer learns
to swim before he or she learns to walk), but, nevertheless, how our
environment influences our physiology (how we function) cannot be
minimized.

THE RESONATION PROCESS

Resonance can be defined as the amplification and modification of
sound. Resonance of voice simply means the development and reinforcement of the basic laryngeal tone as it leaves the larynx. This tone is
originally a rather weak one and needs to be amplified. The amplification
takes place in three cavities: the laryngopharynx (larynx–throat), oropharynx (mouth–throat), and nasopharynx (nose–throat). All three
kinds of vocal resonance are necessary for good voice production.
Pharyngeal and oral resonance help to increase the mellow, rich tones
of your voice. Nasal resonance, apart from being needed in the production of the nasal consonants of American English, is necessary to give
your voice quality-needed brightness.

The resonance system is so structured that what affects one resonance
area necessary affects, to some extent, the other two areas. If you are
working on developing good oral resonance, which demands an open,
enlarged oral cavity, with the lower jaws relaxed and the back teeth
unclenched, the physical structure of the mouth itself will force the soft
palate up against the back pharyngeal wall during this practice. This
kind of movement of the velum often closes off the nasal passages and
eliminates nasal resonance. This might be the very physical action you
want if you are working on eliminating nasality or assimilation nasality
(see Chapter 10, p. 392). Therefore, you must be aware that concentration on improving one kind of resonance will noticeably improve the
resonance process in general. However, for a clearer understanding of

resonance in voice production, we will consider the three kinds separately.

The physics of sound tells us that the shape and size of the resonator, the size of its opening to the outer air, and the surface texture of the resonator are all influencing factors in determining the quality and amount of resonance produced. Because the size and shape of your nasal, oral, and pharyngeal cavities can be manipulated, and because the size of the openings of these cavities can be varied, the fundamental tone of your voice can be reinforced. Generally speaking, the larger the resonating cavity, the lower the frequencies produced. An illustration of this might be the comparison of three musical instruments: the violin, the cello, and the bass fiddle. Notice how the "sound" (frequencies) get *lower* as the *size* of the instrument (resonator) gets larger. Similarly, within limits, the larger the opening of the resonating cavity to the outer air, the higher will be the frequencies produced. By keeping these basic sound-production principles in mind, you can encourage a more mellow, more vibrant, and a fuller voice by using your resonators effectively. Concentrate on enlarging the resonating cavities and working for increased lip and jaw movements.

Another factor to keep in mind is that of the influence of surface texture on vocal resonance. Tension in the resonating cavities encourages a rigid surface texture and a rigid surface texture minimizes a mellow vocal quality. Relaxation of these cavities is necessary and desirable. Sounds reverberated off hard surfaces do not benefit from the cushion effect of soft surfaces, where the unpleasant overtones are dampened.

Kinds of Resonance

We previously explained that the pharynx (throat) can be conveniently divided into three areas—the laryngopharynx, the oropharynx, and the nasopharynx. You probably recall that the term *pharynx* applies to that area behind the larynx, continues upward behind the oral cavity, and extends still further upward behind the nasal cavity (see Figure 8–5). This entire pharyngeal area, including the back wall of the throat, is all intricately involved with resonance. Familiarize yourself with the various kinds of resonance because your voice improvement program could very well depend a great deal on your knowledge and understanding of resonance balance.

Laryngopharyngeal Resonance

Laryngopharyngeal resonance takes place the moment the fundamental tone of your voice is produced. At the onset of the vibration of the vocal folds during voice production, this fundamental tone is immediately amplified or modified in the laryngopharyngeal area. It is of extreme importance that the muscles in these two areas are neither too tense nor

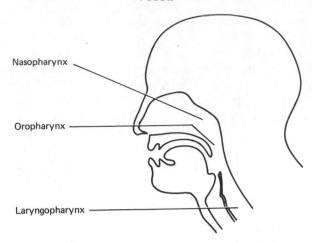

Nasopharynx

Oropharynx

Laryngopharynx

FIGURE 8–5. *The principal resonators.*

too lax during voice production, but rather that they should have just enough muscle tonus to encourage the amplification or modification of the fundamental tone of your voice.

Oral Resonance

Oral resonance is involved with the amplification or modification of your voice in your mouth. Because the oral cavity is more easily manipulated than the laryngeal or nasal areas, your voice improvement program must rely heavily on the manipulation of this cavity. Because effective oral resonance depends on how effectively the oral cavity is used, you should concentrate on control in this area. We would like to minimize your frustrations at this point. You are probably saying to yourself right now, "This is *another* skill I have to acquire?" Yes! As a result of your work in the beginning chapters of this text, you acquired correctness and clarity of articulation. In the process you became aware of the necessity of moving your articulators. The term *oral activity* is used to designate this skill. You found that the tongue tip was capable of reaching up and touching the alveolar ridge for the /t/, /d/, /n/, and /l/ sounds of American English. In the production of the /aɪ/ (ī) and /aʊ/ (ou), you discovered that the tongue and lip positions had to be modified if these sounds were to be made without deviations. You also found that many sounds were produced with more accuracy and clarity when you opened the oral cavity and worked for a relaxed lower jaw and opened back teeth. You discovered that a tight jaw was to be avoided. Whether you were aware of it or not at the time, you were developing a very important aspect of good voice quality, oral resonance.

Oral resonance is so basic to voice production that it can be said to be a necessary component of every characteristic of voice (volume, pitch, and rate). On the other hand, lack of adequate oral resonance contributes to many defective qualities of voice (throatiness, stridency, raspiness, thinness, and nasality).

Nasal Resonance

Nasal resonance is a necessary component of good voice quality. Breath vibrated by the vocal folds and resonated in the nasal cavity contributes a brightness, or brilliance, to the human voice. Proof of this can be found when one has a cold and nasal resonance is either minimized or restricted entirely. The result is a muffled, dull vocal quality—actually, a quality that can interfere with intelligibility of speech. Because the cold has irritated the membranous tissue in the nasal cavity, you are unable to breathe through your nose and, therefore, are unable to resonate in this cavity. This lack of nasal resonance specifically causes the distortion or substitution of the /m/ (m), /n/ (n), and /ŋ/ (ŋ) sounds. These three sounds depend on nasal resonance for their production. Therefore, the phrase *Good morning* can become *Good bordig*. From your study of sound production and placement, the substitutions in this phrase should be obvious: /b/ (b) as a bilabial plosive sound replaces the bilabial nasal /m/ (m), the lingua-alveolar plosive /d/ replaces the lingua-alveolar nasal /n/ (n), and the linguavelar plosive /g/ (g), replaces the linguavelar nasal /ŋ/ (n).

From your work in articulation and from concentrating on developing oral resonance, you must now be conscious of the involvement of the soft palate in the production of both articulated sounds and good voice. You must now be able to recognize the deliberate movement of this part of the oral cavity as you produce nasal sounds and as you try to achieve an "open" oral cavity for improved oral resonance in your voice. At this point take a minute to reinforce the kinesthetic sensation.

1. Using a mirror as a visual aid, open your mouth wide, trying for an open throat, and inhale a large amount of air. Gasp *inwardly*, with a prolonged intake of breath. You will experience a "drafty" sensation inside the mouth and you will see the velum move upward and then immediately relax with a downward motion. Repeat this several times, slowly with your eyes closed.

2. Now quicken the pace. Using the mirror again with the same physical positioning of the mouth and throat, pant hard on an *intake* of breath, repeating rapidly. The velum will move vigorously. You can be assured of this action by the quick, jerky movements of the uvula, which terminates the soft palate.

3. To reinforce the visual and kinesthetic sensations in the movement of the soft palate, try the following: Use the mirror to note the opening and closing of the nasopharyngeal area as you pronounce

a prolonged /ŋ/ sound followed by a prolonged, relaxed /a/ sound.
/ŋ/ (ŋ)—/a/ (a)—/ŋ/ (ŋ)—/a/ (a)—. *Repeat.*
Note how the velum lowers on the /ŋ/ (ŋ) sound and perceptibly raises on the /a/ (a) sound. Repeat this with closed eyes.

THE ARTICULATION PROCESS

Previously in this book, the term *articulation* was defined as the process by which the outgoing air stream is divided up into distinguishable speech sounds (see pp. 20, 21). *Do* you distinguish your sounds as you speak? Perhaps you're the well-recognized "mumbler," who speaks through clenched back teeth and tight jaws and who runs his sounds into and over one another. Commonly known as "sloppy speech," this kind of articulation is technically called overassimilation (see pp. 256, 257). Or perhaps you *overdistinguish* your sounds as you speak. Then you're the well-recognized pedantic (precise) speaker who explodes each sound and/or word with a clarity and precision that is nothing short of painful to the ears of your listeners. Perhaps you have neither of these extreme symbolic kinds of articulation patterns. Perhaps you are just the average "Mr." or "Ms." who is interested in improving his articulation, or voice, in interpersonal communication. In any case, as one who is intent on speech improvement, you cannot ignore your articulation.

Your ability to use your articulators with precision and accuracy affects not only the sounds you speak but also your voice production. As teachers of speech, these writers are constantly and consistently amazed at what happens to the *voices* of our students in our *articulation* classes. Why? If you will reread the material on the resonation process in this chapter, you will understand this phenomenon more clearly. Additional information concerning voice problems that involve resonance balance can be found in Chapter 9. For the present, be assured that all of the skills you have mastered as a result of your work in the articulation section of this book have more than amply prepared you for developing a better voice.

9
Quality

Hello, Betty? This is Mary calling." Betty and Mary are old friends and have had occasion to speak with each other many times. Betty did not need Mary to identify herself on the telephone. From the *sound* of her voice (sometimes referred to as *timbre*), Mary recognized that *Betty* and not *Jean* was on the other end of the line. This general, over-all, personal, identifying sound of your voice is termed vocal *quality.*

There are, as we have already noted, four elements of voice: quality, loudness, pitch, and rate. These characteristics of voice can be changed or varied. Loudness, you remember, has to do with variations of loud and soft; pitch has to do with variations of high and low; rate has to do with variations of fast and slow. Quality? We have a lot of adjectives to describe all of the possible deviations—mellow, pleasant, harsh, hoarse, husky-breathy, nasal, and thin—to name a few.

It is more difficult to define the voice characteristic *quality* than it is to define the other three voice characteristics. Quality is a plastic term. To help you better understand its meaning, consider the "sound" difference between two musical instruments—a trumpet and a violin. Let's try an experiment, but first close your eyes. A specific note will be played on the trumpet first and then repeated on the violin. Assuming that the note played was played with the same amount of loudness and held for the same amount of time, would you recognize a difference in sound between the trumpet and violin? Of course you would. That difference in sound is known as *quality*—that distinctive characteristic sound made by the sound producer.

Why did these two instruments sound so different? Basically because the instruments of sound production (trumpet and violin) are constructed of different materials and also because they have different kinds of resonating chambers. *Your* voice quality is *different* from anyone else's because *you are constructed differently!* Your voice is different because your resonators are different.

Vocal quality cannot be discussed in simplistic terms because it is affected by many factors. Your anatomy (your body structure); your physiology (how your body functions); and your emotionality (involving both your basic personality and your varying emotional states) all

371

can influence your vocal quality. Cultural, ethnic, and socioeconomic levels can also influence your vocal quality. A report by the Medical Tribune World Service (*Medical Tribune,* Aug. 1971) on a study of children with voice disorders documented the following findings. The Jewish Hospital of St. Louis, Missouri, and the St. Louis County Special School District sponsored a large-scale screening of schoolchildren for voice disorders. The findings indicated that the two most common abberations (arytenoiditis and bilateral nodules) were related to socioeconomic levels and emotional stability. Arytenoiditis (irritation of the arytenoid cartilages) was common in children from the areas considered to be *depressed.* Bilateral nodules (a growth on each fold edge) were found in children from *middle-* and *upper-middle-class environments.*

Vocal quality is not only affected by the four processes involved in speech production (respiration pattern, phonation habits, balance of vocal resonance, and articulation), it is also affected by the other characteristics of voice (volume, rate of speaking, and pitch).

How many times have you heard someone say, "He has such a pleasant voice. He should be on radio or TV"? What is a "pleasant sound" to one person is not necessarily a pleasant sound to another. Was Marilyn Monroe's voice sexy? Do you find Howard Cosell's voice grating and irritating? However you may rate them, their voice qualities can certainly be described as *distinctive.* Quality is in the ear of the listener, just as beauty is in the eye of the beholder.

Guidelines for Improved Voice Quality

There are no "standards" of voice quality. Rather, your voice quality is a reflection of you and is highly individual and personal. To try to explain when your voice quality is healthy or when it is unhealthy is about as dangerous (and as unscientific) as opening the proverbial can of worms! Interpretations can be as varied as the professionals making the diagnoses. The M.D., the ear, nose, and throat doctor, or the speech pathologist would have great fun reaching a mutually acceptable definition.

In this section on quality, we prefer treating those problems of quality *which are problems* and then guiding you on to a voice improvement program that makes the most out of the attributes of your basic voice quality.

We would first like to take a closer look at what your voice quality communicates about you *to you* and then what it communicates about you *to your listeners.* What your voice quality communicates to you is *intrapersonal* communication; what your voice quality communicates to your listeners is *interpersonal communication.* Your own perception of your voice production might raise the following questions:

1. What am I experiencing visually, tactually and kinesthetically as I produce voice?
2. What am I hearing as I produce voice?

As you produce voice, ask yourself, How do my body and my throat look (visual) as I produce voice? Is my body tense? Are the muscles in my throat bulging, indicating physical strain? If I place my hands on my throat as I speak, does this area feel too tense (tactile)? What am I *experiencing inside* my body as I produce voice? How does it feel *inside my head* (kinesthesia) as I produce voice? What am I *hearing* (aural) as I produce voice? Information about your voice quality is coming back to your brain both from inside and outside your body. Your monitoring of how it *feels* comes back through inside-the-body routes. Your monitoring of how it *sounds* comes back both inside and outside, through your ears. Review the diagram on p. 351 to see how the reflex arc works. If you use this information from your monitoring system to adapt and change the outgoing production of voice, the information is called *feedback* (incoming information that affects the outgoing message production). So try to be aware of the information you are collecting about your voice as you speak.

Just as your voice quality can convey messages to you, the speaker, it also conveys messages to your listeners. These are the important interpersonal communication questions here: What message is my listener getting from the quality of my voice? What is my voice saying about me —me as a person and me as the speaker of the message? What is my voice quality saying about my physical state, my emotional state, my attitudes toward the listener and toward the subject about which I am talking? And what does my voice do to clarify, support, or confirm the verbal message I am trying to transmit?

There is no question about whether your listener will get messages from the quality of your voice. The only question is whether those messages are the ones you intend the listener to get and—more importantly—whether you are *aware of the kinds of messages your listener is receiving*.

Problems of Voice Quality

In this chapter we will examine those vocal qualities that sound unpleasant. We will also indicate those deviant qualities that might be the result of vocal pathology or that, if used constantly, might provoke pathology. Specifically, the following deviant qualities will be considered: husky-breathy, hoarse, raspy (glottal fry), harsh, strident, thin, throaty, and hypo/hypernasal. It is important to note that the term *normal* in voice quality can cover a wide spectrum. For instance, cases of hoarseness found in the screaming child or in the fatigued schoolteacher might be considered *abnormal* (and in need of voice therapy), whereas the chronic hoarseness of the drill sergeant or of the street vendor might very well fall within the bounds of *normalcy*. We repeat, there is no "standard" of voice quality. You will be helped to achieve the best possible quality *you are capable of producing*.

We will treat each specific deviant quality (problem related to voice quality) in the following way:

1. We will assess the acoustic symptom. (What is the *sound* of your voice?)
2. We will examine the underlying physiology causing the disorder. (*Why* does your voice sound as it does?)
3. We will establish goals to work toward. (How *should* your voice be produced?)
4. We will suggest specific skills needed to achieve your goals. (What should you be doing in order to achieve effective voice production?)
5. We will provide exercises designed to help you develop the skills you need. (What exercises or techniques will develop the needed skills?)

The approaches to treatment could include any one or all of the following:

1. Medical (medicine, psychotherapy, and supportive therapy).
2. Surgical (removal of nodules, polyps, tonsils, and so on).
3. Voice therapy (specific techniques of voice production).
4. Voice management (vocal rest, restricted use of voice).

Hoarse Quality

The hoarse voice sounds rough and somewhat breathy. It has a gravel sound as if it has been strained. This type of voice deviation can be medically, physiologically, or psychologically based. It can be (and most often is) involved with all three. The person with this kind of problem is usually a compulsive talker; is high-strung, with an inability to relax or rest; and has very poor vocal habits. Frequently this person is totally unaware of how this voice "happened." Therapy must be multidimensional. An intrapersonal and nonverbal approach is essential, initially. The person should be made aware of (1) the excesses in his or her life style (usually led at a frenetic pace) and (2) nonverbal vocal habits (visible tension in the strap muscles of the neck, tight jaw, and tension in the upper thoracic cavity). Once inroads are made into the intrapersonal (sometimes there is psychological overlay) and nonverbal aspects of the problem, voice therapy on a *verbal* (vocal) level can begin.

ACOUSTIC ELEMENTS

1. Breathy, raspy, and strained sound.
2. Minimized volume.

3. Narrow pitch range: low.
4. Pitch breaks and/or periodic aphonia.

UNDERLYING PHYSIOLOGY

1. Possible medical problem (cold, allergies, and so on).
2. Possible pathology: vocal nodules, polyps, contact ulcers, or paralysis of one vocal fold.
3. Vocal abuse (excessive yelling or talking).
4. Edema of the vocal folds.
5. Incomplete closure of the vocal folds.
6. Hypertension of the intrinsic laryngeal muscles.
7. Hyperpharyngeal tension (throat area).

GOALS

1. Elimination of all medical problems. An examination by an otolaryngologist is crucial if the hoarseness is chronic.
2. Relaxation of the neck and throat muscles; acquisition of adequate muscle tonus.
3. Complete gentle adduction of the vocal folds on phonation.
4. Elimination of any spastic movement of the vocal folds during phonation.
5. Central breathing for support of tone.
6. Central breathing to reduce hyperpharyngeal tension.

SKILLS

1. Vocal rest (where prescribed by the physician or voice therapist).
2. Acquire gentle adduction of the vocal folds. See pp. 374–378.
3. Develop *habitual* central breathing so that any excessive tension is placed in the diaphragmatic-abdominal areas rather than in the neck and throat areas. See pp. 355, 356.
4. Work for adequate muscle tonus. See pp. 347–349.
5. Work for a firm, steady stream of breath on exhalation in order to minimize or eliminate spastic movement of the vocal folds. See pp. 355, 356.
6. Develop adequate *oral* resonance. See p. 368.
7. Emit the breath stream *out* of the mouth. See p. 359.

Exercises for Gentle Adduction of the Vocal Folds

Keep in mind that a hoarse or rough voice is an abused voice. A gentle approach to adduction of the vocal folds is not only desirable but necessary.

1. *Chewing.* This is an old and tried method that still produces fine results. Looking into a mirror (visual stimulation to the CNS), begin to

chew with *open* lips. (Your mother would disagree. Be impolite!). Get the feeling of relaxed jaws, tongue, throat, and larynx. Let the tongue r-o-l-l around in the mouth as you chew. *Really feel as if you are chewing a piece of food.* Watch your respiration. Take a breath (hand on the diaphragm). When you reach the peak of inhalation, begin to chew as you emit the breath. Do this exercise at least five times, taking a breath each time. Now you are ready for the next step.

2. *Humming.* With one hand on the diaphragm (tactile sensation), take a breath. When you reach the peak of inhalation, begin humming on the sound /n/. *Note:* we do *not* recommend the sound of /m/ because on the production of the sound /m/ the lips are closed (bilabial nasal sound). We want the breath free to escape *out of the mouth.* Take any pitch. Try to start in midrange. Hum gently and softly. Move from high to low or low to high. No matter. Hum on each pitch for about ten seconds, taking a breath on *each* pitch change. Do *not* hum with a great deal of intensity (loudness). Do not allow the hum to fade away. Try to keep the hum consistent in volume and firmness. Watch that the hum does not acquire a vibrato. If the sound begins to vibrate excessively, concentrate on pushing from your midriff (the diaphragm area). Continue this exercise with your eyes open. Repeat it with your eyes closed (kinesthetic sensation). Try to experience a feeling in the laryngeal area of *firmness.* This firmness is the gentle adduction of the vocal folds.

3. *Humming and Chewing Methods Combined.* Begin the chewing motion (see exercise 1 here), looking into the mirror. Notice all of the nonverbal aspects. With one hand on the diaphragm, take a breath. When you reach the peak of inhalation, begin to hum on /n/ *as you continue the chewing action.* Yes, it's difficult. It's very much like patting your head and rubbing your stomach simultaneously. Aim to coordinate the humming, chewing, and controlled respiration. Notice the *sound* of your voice. It should sound clear (no strain), firm (no vibrato), and more resonant and should even have more volume (which is really *not* volume, but more phonation). Each time you practice this exercise, do it in its complete form.

a. Begin the *chewing* motion. Continue chewing until all of your face, neck, and laryngeal muscles feel tension-free.

b. Take a breath (hand on the diaphragm).

c. When you reach the peak of inhalation, begin to hum on /n/.

d. *Combine* the humming and chewing action for about ten seconds. Remember, the tip of your tongue will *not* be on the alveolar ridge for the sound /n/ as it is usually because your tongue will be rolling around in your mouth during the chewing action. You must *think* /n/ as you hum.

e. Take another breath each time you repeat this exercise.

f. Do this exercise looking at yourself in the mirror (visual stimulation to the CNS).

g. Repeat this exercise with closed eyes (kinesthetic stimulation to the CNS).

4. *Squeezing action.* Stand tall with your feet slightly apart. Place your hands and arms across your chest, your left hand gripping your upper right arm and your right hand gripping your upper left arm. Slowly squeeze your crossed arms and hands simultaneously with a good amount of pressure so that your chest cavity is noticeably tightened. Keep your chin level (do not look down) during this exercise and try to "feel" the tightening in the laryngeal area. Your vocal folds are being made to close! Repeat the squeezing action rhythmically five or six times with your eyes open. Alternate with your eyes closed to increase the kinesthetic stimulation to the CNS.

5. *Squeezing and Humming Methods Combined.* Begin the squeezing action and hold it as you feel the vocal folds tighten.

a. Take a breath and at the peak of inhalation begin to hum on any note for about five seconds.

b. Continue to hum as you exhale your breath, maintaining the squeezed position of the chest.

c. Do this exercise with your eyes closed (kinesthetic stimulation to the CNS).

6. *Push ups.* Feeling in top shape today? Try the following modified version of a push up. Lie on the floor with your face turned to one side, your legs together, your hands placed next to your shoulders with your fingers pointed forward and your palms down. Push up off the floor until your arms are fully extended and your torso is supported by your hands and knees. Your back should be straight. Take a breath and gently exhale the breath as you lower your torso to the floor. Relax! Repeat this action three or four times. By this time you must know and realize that the "pushing" action up off the floor closed your vocal folds.

If you really feel in top shape repeat the exercise with the following version. As you push up off the floor until your arms are fully extended, support your raised torso *by your toes only.* Your back should be straight. Take a breath and gently exhale the breath as you lower your torso to the floor.

7. *Push ups and Humming Methods Combined.*

a. Start the push up and reach the position of fully extended arms.

b. While in that position, take a breath and at the peak of inhalation begin to hum (on any note) for four or five seconds.

c. Stop the hum and exhale as you lower your torso to the floor.

d. Do not continue this exercise for any length of time if you feel strain or fatigue.

8. *Pushing*. Stand tall in a doorframe with the palms of your hands flat against each side of the frame. Push firmly against each side of the door frame. Notice how the abdominal muscles, the diaphragm area and the chest cavity all tighten. Hold the pushing position from three to five seconds (this action forces the vocal folds to gently close). Release the pressure and relax! Now add the following:

   a. Push against each side of the door frame.
   b. Take a breath (be sure of central breathing) and at the peak of inhalation begin to hum on any note. Continue humming for three to five seconds.
   c. Continue to hum as you exhale your breath.
   d. Repeat this exercise three to five times, alternating with eyes open (visual stimulation to the CNS) and then with your eyes closed (kinesthetic stimulation to the CNS).

9. *Lifting*. Become a furniture mover for this exercise! Find a piece of furniture in your home that you can lift *at one corner*. The furniture must be of such weight that you are forced to use muscular effort to raise the one corner. Don't overtax yourself.

   a. Lift the corner of the piece of furniture about one inch off of the floor (vocal folds are forced to close).
   b. While in this position, take a breath and at the peak of inhalation begin to hum on any note. Continue the humming for about three to five seconds.
   c. Stop humming and begin to lower the piece of furniture as you exhale the breath stream.

It is one thing to be able to do these isolated exercises, but it is the conviction of these writers that *you must get into speech* as quickly as possible. You must *transfer* your knowledge and skill in the foregoing exercises to your everyday use of voice.

Now you should be ready to try words and loaded sentences. Using the sounds /n/ and /m/ as catalysts to gently adduct the vocal folds, attempt to continue the clarity and firmness of vocal quality throughout the words and sentences found in the articulation section of this book.

Use the material on the following pages:

   1. /m/ words, p. 124.
   2. /m/ words, p. 126.
   3. /m/ phrases, p. 127.
   4. /m/ phrases, p. 128.
   5. /m/ phrases, p. 129.
   6. /m/ phrases, words, sentences, pp. 129, 130.
   7. /n/ words, p. 132.
   8. /n/ words in pairs, p. 131.
   9. /n/ words and phrases, pp. 134, 135.

10. /n/ words and sentences, pp. 136, 137.
    (Stop at sentence No. 25).
Now try the following sentences:
  1. The mean man met his match on the rim of the mountain.
  2. Much money is manipulated on the stock exchange.
  3. Semantics is a science which analyzes the emotional content of the words we use in conversation morning, noon and night.
  4. The minister in his sermon to the congregation screamed many warnings concerning sin and damnation.
  5. John needed consultation in order to manage his finances more efficiently.
  6. Politicians tend to spend much of their time making promises, promises and more promises.
  7. Nan needed more money than she counted on for her expedition.
  8. I find that I cannot count up to 999 without becoming confused.
  9. "The rain in Spain is falling on the plains," is a line from a song long to be remembered by the many fans and enemies of Professor Higgins.
  10. "Taxation without representation" had much meaning for our ancestors during the American Revolution.

The next step in skill acquisition is the daily use of your new clear and firm voice in conversation. Make a list of ten words, phrases, and sentences that you use daily. All of us have a daily patter. For example:

  1. What *time* will you be *home* for *dinner?*
  2. Good *morning, Mary.* (Assuming Mary is your secretary!).
  3. How *long* will you be *gone* for *lunch?*

Begin by practicing *in isolation* the words in the sentences that contain an /n/ or /m/ sound. Then work on the entire sentence, attempting to transfer the clarity and firmness of your voice throughout the entire sentence.

Breathy/Husky Quality

This deviant vocal quality (asthenic or weak voice) is the "sexy" sounding voice. It lacks sound (vocalization) and volume. It is deliberately acquired by some. Movie, TV, and radio personalities frequently find it desirable to develop this quality for an effect. It is too bad that they are not aware that their efforts to be vocally sexy could result in vocal pathology (nodules, polyps, or thickened vocal folds). This voice is sometimes associated with a "personality" type that has a poor personal image, feelings of inadequacy, and the inability to assert the self. When the breathy voice becomes overrelaxed, it acquires a *husky* quality. The pitch range lowers. Intrapersonal awareness is crucial to the verbal (vocal) therapy of the breathy/husky voice.

ACOUSTIC ELEMENTS

1. Vocal folds are not adducted during phonation (the voice sounds as if there were an /h/ between sounds and/or words).
2. Severe voice fading.
3. Limited volume; inability to make the voice "carry."
4. Pitch range: low.

UNDERLYING PHYSIOLOGY

1. *Hypo*tension of the laryngeal muscles.
2. Inefficient use of the outgoing breath stream during phonation (usually a clavicular breather).
3. Use of pharyngeal muscles and extrinsic laryngeal muscles to increase volume.

GOALS

1. Acquire adduction of the vocal folds on phonation.
2. Develop efficient use of effective, habitual respiration habits.
3. Be aware of a "push" or tension, on the diaphragmatic-abdominal muscles during exhalation.
4. Intrapersonally and kinesthetically be aware of resonating the voice in the oral cavity. Avoid excessive pharyngeal resonance.

SKILLS

1. Work for a "hard" attack on initial phonation. See pp. 380–382.
2. Central breathing. See pp. 355, 356.
3. Control of outgoing breath stream. See p. 356.
4. Develop *oral* resonance. See p. 368.

Exercises for Acquiring a Hard Adduction of the Vocal Folds

1. *Bouncing Technique.* Stand comfortably away from a wall, perhaps two to three feet away. Fall against the wall with your hands extended and the palms flat on the wall at about eye level. Keep your elbows flexed (*not* extended, but straight within the body line), and keep your heels off of the floor. You should have the feeling that if the wall were suddenly removed, you would fall flat on your face. In this leaning position, gently bounce up and down on the wall, keeping your hands *on* the wall. Try to feel a gentle tightening in the larynx. That tightening

is the adduction of the vocal folds. Close your eyes to add kinesthetic feedback. You are now encouraging vocal fold adduction so necessary for a firm, clear tone during phonation.

Now "bounce" off of the wall until you are back *on your heels,* standing in an upright position. Repeat this technique a number of times.

2. *Pushing* and *Phonation.* Start exercise 1. When you reach the leaning position, take a breath (*be sure* you are using central breathing) and at the peak of inhalation begin to *hum* on /n/. Continue humming on /n/ until all of your breath is exhaled. You are to be in a leaning position during all of this exercise, with your heels off of the floor. We ask you to hum on /n/ and *not* on /m/ because we do not want your lips closed. This exercise will encourage adduction of the vocal folds *and* a firming up of the vocal fold edges.

3. *Bouncing, Phonation, and Speech.* Note that all of the exercises to develop adduction of the vocal folds are meaningless *unless* you can *transfer* the tactile and kinesthetic sensations of phonation to speech. If you have mastered the preceding exercises, you are ready for vocal fold adduction *in speech.* Try the following:

a. Assume the leaning position on the wall. Instead of *humming* after you take a breath, say the number one *as you bounce off of the wall.* You have adducted the folds by pushing on the wall. Maintain that physical sensation in the larynx by bouncing off of the wall and saying a *word— one.* Lean again. Bounce off of the wall and say "one" and then "two," on one breath exhalation.

b. Now here is a challenge. Do the exercise a, but add a skill. Bounce off of the wall as you say "one." When you are back on your heels, *repeat* "one." Does it sound the same as when you gave your vocal folds the impetus of the pushing? It should!

4. *Squeezing action.* Stand tall with your feet slightly apart. Place your hands and arms across your chest, your left hand gripping your upper right arm and your right hand gripping your upper left arm. Slowly squeeze your crossed arms and hands simultaneously with a good amount of pressure so that your chest cavity is noticeably tightened. Keep your chin level (do not look down) during this exercise and try to "feel" the tightening in the laryngeal area. Hold the squeezed position for one or two seconds. Release the arms and hands with a "jerk" and try to be aware of the vocal folds being forced to close with a hard attack and then being forced to open with a "jerk." Notice how the breath is released out of your mouth with almost a pop sound?

Now add speech. As you release your arms and hands with a jerk, say the number 1. Try to take advantage of the firm closure of the vocal folds on the squeezing action and use the closure to get phonation on speech. Add additional numbers always keeping in mind smooth emission of breath as you say the numbers.

5. *Pushing action; Bouncing action.* Stand tall in a doorframe with the palms of your hands flat against each side of the frame. Push firmly against each side of the door frame. Notice how the abdominal muscles, the diaphragm area and the chest cavity all tighten. Hold the pushing position from three to five seconds (this action forces the vocal folds to close). Release the pressure and relax! Repeat a number of times. Now try the following variations:

a. Push firmly against each side of the door frame, *bounce* off of each side of the frame and end in a tall standing position.

b. Do this rhythmically four or five times.

c. Add speech. As you bounce off of the door frame say numbers, one; one, two; one, two, three and so on. Take a breath on each new set of numbers. Remember, try to have the additional numbers sound as firm as the number 1. even though you no longer are relying on the pressure of your hands on the door frame.

d. After you have mastered firmness of tone on the numbers, try short phrases which you use everyday.

Now you are ready for *transference.* Because you cannot go around for the rest of your life humming and counting numbers, the next logical step is to transfer all of your acquired skills to conversational speech. We urge you to write out a list of responses or phrases you use daily. For example, "What time will you be home for dinner?" "Good morning." "I won't be home until late tonight." Now try these phrases while you "bounce off of the wall" or when you are "back on your heels," keeping in mind all of the time:

1. Good posture, p. 347.
2. General relaxation coupled with adequate muscle tonus, p. 348.
3. Central breathing, pp. 355, 356.
4. Controlled breathing, p. 358.
5. Breath emission, p. 359.
6. Adequate laryngeal tension, pp. 365, 366.

Previously, we alluded to an oral communication approach to voice improvement (See p. 336). In this section we are going to ask those of you with husky/breathy voices to rely heavily on the nonverbal and intrapersonal aspects of voice communication. More often than not, the husky/breathy voice is involved with pathology—that is, after an examination by an otolaryngologist, the medical findings disclose one or more of the following: vocal nodules, polyps, thickened vocal folds, spastic movement of the folds and/or failure of the folds to adduct at midline during phonation. There is, more frequently than not, some indication of a psychological overlay. Specifically, the person with this kind of voice production is usually a verbally aggressive person with "standards up on the ceiling." In our experience the person with this kind of voice problem has usually developed very *poor vocal habits*. In addition, the person usually has to be *forced* to review his or her own attitude about the *sound* of the voice. Seldom do any of these people seek help because of the *sound* of the voices; usually it is for a medical problem (severe hoarseness or laryngitis). In order to make *you* more aware of the *hyperpharyngeal* and hypolaryngeal tensions that are intricately involved with the husky/breathy voice, we are going to ask you to become very aware of nonverbal and intrapersonal aspects as you try the following exercises.

Exercises for Minimizing Hyperpharyngeal Tension

1. Review the exercises for general body relaxation and acquisition of muscle tonus. See pp. 347, 348.
2. Review the exercises for the throat and neck. See pp. 348–349.
3. Review the exercises for free-flowing breath emission. See p. 359.
4. Stand in front of a mirror. *Take note of your nonverbal communication during the following exercise.* Place one hand on your diaphragm and the other hand about three inches away from your mouth. As you say the following groups of numbers keep in mind: (a) putting *tension* in the diaphragm area; (b) opening the oral cavity (open your *back* jaws); (c) emitting a steady stream of breath out of the oral cavity and (d) having no excessive muscle action in the throat area. No muscles should *show* during phonation. Utilize controlled breathing.

   1, 1–2, 1–2–3, 1–2–3–4, 1–2–3–4–5

5. Repeat the preceding exercise with your *eyes closed*. You are involving the kinesthetic sensations, which are a part of your intrapersonal communication.

Throaty Quality

"Your voice sounds so heavy and so thick. Do you have a sore throat?" The acoustic elements of heaviness and thickness are the main marks of the deviant voice quality of *throatiness*. Sometimes this quality of voice is spearheaded by a medical problem such as enlarged tonsils and/or adenoids. Once the medical problem is removed, help in voice improvement is still needed because you usually take on a voice production pattern directly related to the medical problem (this is also true of organically based articulation problems). After the medical problem has been removed, you tend to talk with a thick and throaty voice. You have to learn to use your vocal musculature differently.

At other times throatiness is the direct result of faulty voice production involving, principally, the position of your tongue. Because the hyoid bone of the larynx (see Figure 8–2) is suspended from the back of the tongue, the resonance of your voice is acoustically affected. The position of your tongue directly affects laryngeal resonance because as your tongue is retracted, it "sits on the hyoid bone" and limits the muscular action of the laryngeal muscles. The throaty voice sounds as if the tongue were "getting in the way" and the result is a voice that lacks clarity and brightness. The throaty voice usually has a low pitch range and is very frequently accompanied by a heavy or an indistinct articulation pattern. Voice improvement for this deviant vocal quality should rely heavily on the inherent mobility of the tongue. Not only is the tongue known to be the most important articulator, but it is capable of perceptibly changing the size of the oral and pharyngeal cavities. The shape and the position of the tongue are constantly being changed by the intrinsic muscles (shape) and the extrinsic muscles (position).

ACOUSTIC ELEMENTS

1. Heavy, thick, and muffled; lacking brilliance and brightness.
2. Pitch range restricted (low) and lacking variation.
3. Articulation pattern: heavy and periodically overassimilated.
4. Usually lacks adequate and varied volume.

UNDERLYING PHYSIOLOGY

1. Possible medical problem.
2. Tongue pulled back (retracted) in oral cavity; hypertension in the tongue.
3. Limited oropharyngeal and nasopharyngeal resonance due to changes in the position and the shape of the tongue.
4. Restricted movement of the laryngeal musculature.
5. Soft palate movement limited or hindered by the humping of the middle or back of the tongue on the front and medial phonemes.

GOALS

1. Assessment, evaluation, and removal of all existing medical problems by an otolaryngologist.
2. Proper positioning and shaping of the tongue on all phoneme production.
3. Adequate tongue tension during the production of all phonemes.
4. Increased lingual and labial movement while speaking.
5. Effective use of the outgoing breath stream during the production of all phonemes.

SKILLS

1. Alleviation of the retracted tongue while producing the various phonemes. Look in the mirror (visual stimulation). Is your tongue tip away from the back of your lower front teeth while you are speaking? We hope not. If it is, then check the articulation section of this book for the proper placement of your tongue on all front and medial vowels. (See pp. 183–204).

2. Increased labial (lip) and lingual (tongue) movement while speaking. Stress the phonemes /t/, /d/, /n/, /l/ to help you increase the agility of the tip of your tongue (see pp. 62–128). Stress all of the bilabial consonants to increase your labial (lip) movement (see pp. 55–61).

3. Development of adequate muscle tension of the tongue on all vowel production. Take particular note of the difference between the tense and lax vowels of American English.

4. Increased oral and nasal resonance. Dwell on acquiring an open oral cavity with unclenched back teeth. This emphasis away from excessive laryngopharyngeal resonance to increased oropharyngeal and nasopharyngeal resonance will add more brilliance and brightness to your voice. Particularly work on the nasal sounds (see pp. 122–146) and on all of the back vowels and diphthongs (see pp. 204–254).

5. Increased effort to get the outgoing breath stream (breath emission) *out of the mouth*. Think and talk "forward."

Thin Quality

Have you ever been told, "You sound like a little girl/boy," or "You sound so much younger than you look," or "You sound so young, you must not have had much experience. Sorry, you just are not suited for this job." A voice that unconsciously conveys the quality of a "little girl" or "little boy" (not quite so common) can be a real detriment to one's self-image; to meaningful interpersonal relations; to personal fulfillment; and even to employment.

Of all of the deviant voice qualities, this particular quality, more frequently than not, has a psychological overlay (we're now referring to problems of serious thinness). It suggests a mild, meek, and dependent (perhaps even weak) personality. A childlike voice is expected from a child but not from an adult. In addition to voice improvement help, the person with the thin voice may find that supportive therapy with a qualified psychologist is not only needed but necessary. However, we hasten to add that innumerable times, in our experience, voice work alone has brought about the desired vocal change. The individual became *aware of his vocal* and *personal inadequacies* and subsequently made the necessary life-style adjustments *and* developed vocal quality that was a true reflection of his new adult personality.

ACOUSTIC ELEMENTS

1. Immature, childlike sounds (sometimes even whiney).
2. Narrow pitch range: usually high.
3. Severe voice fading at ends of sentences and phrases.
4. Escape of puffs of air out of the oral cavity during phonation.
5. Usually lacks adequate volume.

UNDERLYING PHYSIOLOGY

1. Inadequate oral resonance; high position of tongue.
2. Lack of lingual and labial movement; tight jaw.
3. Usually clavicular breathing; failure to develop support of tone.
4. Moderate hypertension in the laryngeal area.

GOALS

1. Relaxation of the upper thoracic area, neck, and throat.
2. Diaphragmatic (central) breathing.
3. Increased oral resonance.
4. Adequate volume.
5. Personality development.

SKILLS

1. Over-all body relaxation and specific relaxation in the neck and throat areas (see pp. 348, 349).
2. Acquire effective diaphragmatic breathing (see pp. 355, 356).
3. Learn to *sustain the breath until the end of the sentence.* Use the appropriate abdominal muscle support. Do *not* use the laryngeal muscles (see pp. 358, 409, 410).
4. Stress practice in back vowel production (see pp. 204–254) because work in this area *opens* your back teeth, enlarges the size of the oral cavity, and results in an increase of the lower overtones. The result is a more *mature*, resonant (not thin) quality.
5. Volume will *seemingly* be increased when your voice becomes more resonant. However, you must learn how to increase volume *muscularly* without involving the pharyngeal muscles (see pp. 401, 402).

Harsh and Strident Qualities

The harsh voice and the strident voice have much in common. Even though the acoustic elements differ somewhat, the underlying physiology is very similar. Because of this similarity, these two deviant vocal qualities will be considered together but with differentiating treatment services and skills clearly defined.

Harsh quality is usually associated with the aggressive, sometimes abrasive, male personality. It has a low pitch. Strident quality, on the other hand, is seldom found in the male but is usually associated with the female personality. It has a high pitch. However, nervousness, experienced by either sex, can be responsible for strident tones. It is interesting to note that *both* of these voice qualities are associated with personalities that tend to be energetic, excitable, and aggressive. None of these traits is necessarily negative or objectionable within itself.

ACOUSTIC ELEMENTS

Harsh Voice:
1. Strained, raspy sound.
2. Narrow pitch range: low.
3. Hyperpharyngeal resonance.

Strident Voice:
1. Metallic, sharp sound.
2. Narrow pitch range: high.
3. Excessive high-frequency overtones.

UNDERLYING PHYSIOLOGY

(Applicable to Both)
1. Hyperlaryngeal tension.
2. Hyperpharyngeal tension.
3. Resonance imbalance.
4. Overly loud.

(Harsh Voice)
5. Increased action (intensity) at the edges of the vocal folds (the vocal folds tend to "bang together.")
6. Ineffective use of outgoing breath stream.

(Strident Voice)
7. The constrictor muscles of the back pharyngeal wall are extremely tense (a metallic quality is the result).

GOALS

(Applicable to Both)
1. Reduce hyperlaryngeal tension.
2. Reduce hyperpharyngeal tension.
3. Increase oral resonance.
4. Decrease "overenergizing" (amplitude) in voice production.

(Harsh Voice)
5. Develop a soft attack (adduction) of the vocal folds.
6. Acquire control of respiration; do not use reserve breath for phonation.

| (Strident Voice) | 7. Relax the nasopharyngeal, oropharyngeal, and laryngopharyngeal cavities. |

SKILLS

(Applicable to Both)	1. Relaxation of neck and throat muscles (see pp. 348, 349).
	2. Acquisition of "open oral cavity and un-clenched back teeth." Work on back vowels and diphthongs (see pp. 204–254).
	3. Reduction of "energy" during phonation; reduction of compulsiveness in communicating ideas and feeling. Learn to take it easy. Relax! Cool it!
(Harsh Voice)	4. Work for a gentle adduction of the vocal folds without hypertension of the tensor and adductor muscles (see pp. 374–378).
	5. Develop control of the outgoing breath stream on exhalation; keep the breath going; do not continue to phonate as you squeeze out the last ounce of breath (see pp. 356, 358, 359).
(Strident Voice)	6. Work for adequate muscle tonus in the nasopharynx, oropharynx, and laryngopharynx. Relax! Your pitch range will lower noticeably.

Raspy and/or Glottal Fry

There have been innumerable references throughout this section to the fact that voice is the result of the vibration of the vocal folds as breath (under pressure) is released from the lungs and vibrated between the vocal folds. The air seemingly escapes in strong "puffs." Periodically these puffs of air get *caught* in the glottis during phonation so that the resulting sound is one of "meat frying in a pan." The technical term is *glottal fry*. Formally, this term was used interchangeably with raspy or gravelly. No matter the confusion in terminology—this kind of voice production abuses the vocal folds. It *feels* and *sounds unpleasant*. It usually never lasts long and is confined to the ends of phrases and sentences. It is very unusual to have it continue throughout vocal production. As the speaker nears the completion of the phrase or sentence, the voice tends to "drop back" and "fry" at the glottis.

ACOUSTIC ELEMENTS

1. Severe raspy or gravelly sound.
2. Narrow pitch range: low.
3. Erratic drop in amplitude at ends of words, phrases, and sentences.

UNDERLYING PHYSIOLOGY

1. Hyperlaryngeal tension (the edges of the vocal folds become extremely hypertense).
2. Hyperpharyngeal tension.
3. Ineffective control of exhalation phase of respiration.
4. Sporadic lack of support of tone during phonation.

GOALS

1. Reduction of tension in the laryngeal and pharyngeal area.
2. Acquisition of habitual central breathing; control of breath during exhalation.
3. Development of support of tone at the ends of phrases and sentences.
4. Awareness of the voice dropping back in the throat after exhalation has been completed.

SKILLS

1. Acquire relaxation of the muscles in the neck and throat area (see pp. 348, 349).
2. Make central breathing a habit so that exhaled breath can be used efficiently (see pp. 355, 356).
3. Emphasize the emission of breath *out of the oral cavity during phonation.* Think "up and out." Feel as if you have no *throat, only* a diaphragm and an oral cavity.
4. Attempt to keep the breath flowing *out* of the oral cavity as you near the end of a phrase or sentence. Be aware that this technique does *not* interfere with dropping your pitch. Do *not* try to phonate at the end of exhalation and squeeze out the final sounds. You can successfully *drop pitch* and simultaneously continue the flow of breath out of the oral cavity.
5. Practice steps 3 and 4 with one hand about three to four inches away from your mouth. Experience the emission of breath out of the oral cavity tactually and kinesthetically (repeat steps 3 and 4 with your eyes closed).

Glottal Shock

Up to this point, all of the deviant voice qualities assessed have been according to: (1) acoustic elements, (2) evaluation (underlying physiology and degree of severity), and (3) treatment services (goals and skills). Treatment services (particularly the skills to be acquired) were not only multiple but involved. Glottal shock can be explained more simply. This is a *specific* vocal deviation, limited to the initial release of breath as it is vibrated between the vocal folds. It is also involved with *duration* (see p. 421).

In glottal shock the vocal folds become hypertense and "explode" the initial release of breath. There is almost a "pop" sound. This kind of hypertense movement usually occurs on initial vowels in words, particularly on the back vowels and diphthongs: /a/ (ä); /aɪ/ (ī); /au/ (ou); /eɪ/ (ā). What is so wrong about this kind of initial vocal fold movement? Well, it gets you off to a bad start. *Initially* your voice is produced with hypertension. You must then *manipulate* and try to attain vocal fold vibration, which is produced with laryngeal muscles having *adequate muscle tonus.*

If glottal shock is your problem (and this *can* be a *serious* problem for actors, radio and TV personalities, and teachers—all of whom need a voice that is reliable), master the following skills:

SOME DO'S

1. Acquire a smooth release of breath out of the glottis as you begin to phonate. (See the following exercises.)
2. Be *tactually* and *kinesthetically* aware of the hypertense action at the glottis on the initiation of phonation. Place one of your fingers on the larynx while you deliberately exaggerate the glottal shock sound.
3. Keep vocal intensity (loudness) down until you acquire smooth breath emission on initial vowels.

SOME DON'TS

1. Do not rely on your *ear* for the correction of this problem. It is difficult for an untrained ear to hear this sound (at the initial stages of awareness).
2. Do not use glottal shock as a means of emphasis (hitting particular words hard) as you communicate meaning. There are other devices (pausing, pitch changes) that are not inherently injurious to the vocal mechanism. (This advice is only for those of you with glottal shock problems.)

Exercises for the Correction of Glottal Shock

1. Avoid a sudden explosive movement of the vocal folds on initial vowels by stressing a relaxed adduction (closing) of the folds. Producing the sound /h/ accomplishes this for you. With open, relaxed jaws, say a prolonged /h/ sound. Look at yourself in the mirror (visual stimulation). Check to see if your neck and jaws are relaxed during the production of /h/. Repeat /h/ several times. Close your

eyes for increased kinesthetic sensation and repeat the sound /h/.

2. Now move to the trouble sounds, the vowels. See pp. 85–88 for lists of words beginning with the /h/ sound. As you say the word, *prolong* the initial /h/ sound and then *complete* the word. Check all the muscle action in the neck and jaws. Were you able to g-l-i-d-e easily from the /h/ sound into the following sounds? If so, then try the accompanying word, which does *not* begin initially with /h/. Concentrate on emitting the breath easily (avoid a sudden explosive action). For example, howl–owl. A word of caution. Don't overchallenge yourself. Try the exercise *sentences* only when you feel you have acquired an effective adduction of the vocal folds on initial vowels.

3. Perhaps you are now ready for conversational speech.

In order to help you progress more quickly from the clinical setting of practicing loaded material to a habitual conversational setting, we have found that the vehicles of extemporaneous speaking and impromptu speaking are very effective. No, we are not referring to forms of *public speaking*. We are talking about the *concepts* of extemporaneous and impromptu speaking. *Extemporaneous* implies "thinking through your content" (not *writing* it down) and then delivering it. *Impromptu* implies an *immediate* reply without "thinking through." You might recognize the latter form when you recall the last time you were asked an unexpected question in class and had to reply immediately. Perhaps, at one time, you were asked to "say a few words," unexpectedly, at a dinner where you thought you were just an invited guest. The point is, you must *transfer* your newly acquired vocal skills to everyday conversational speech. Practicing the following exercises with deliberation and care will help you.

Exercises for Transference

1. *Extemporaneous Speaking*

   Think through a short incident, six to eight sentences in length. The incident might be about your vacation or an incident at a party, for example. Tape the incident applying all of the skills you acquired related to your particular voice problem. Concentrate on *how* you are producing and using your voice. On tape, repeat the incident a few times. Compare vocal quality.

2. *Impromptu Speaking*

   Decide on a topic. Start the tape recorder and begin to speak without any preliminary thought about the particulars involved in the incident. Do not attempt anything lengthy. Start with three or four sentences of impromptu speech. An impromptu subject might concern your plans for the remainder of the day:

> After I complete my recordings, I'm going to eat lunch and then go shopping. Later on in the afternoon I'll take a short nap.

Do not *repeat* the incident for a second recording because then you are then no longer involved with impromptu speaking. Use a different topic for each recording. After two or three recordings, play the tapes back and analyze the results. Consider:

  a. The quality of your voice.

  b. All of the skills that contribute to your effective quality and/or lack of skills that are interfering with it. For example, effective control of the exhalation phase of respiration; balanced resonance; and so on.

3. *Combination of Extemporaneous and Impromptu*

This exercise is better carried out with two people—teacher and student or two students. The student with the voice problem prepares an incident (an extemporaneous one—see exercise 1). When the tape recorder is turned on the student should begin speaking. At some arbitrary interval, the second person should interrupt the speaker with an unexpected, but pertinent, question on the material being delivered. The first student then has to shift gears to answer the question *impromptu*. The student then continues with the incident (extemporaneous) being interrupted with as many *impromptu* interruptions as are meaningful.

Hypernasality/Hyponasality/Assimilation Nasality

Nasality refers to the negative aspect of nasal resonance and falls into two categories, *hypernasality* and *hyponasality*. Hypernasality refers to excessive nasal resonance in the voice (talking through your nose) and hyponasality, or denasality, refers to insufficient nasal resonance. A third term, *assimilation nasality,* also belongs to this group of resonance deviations, even though it is limited to specific sound relationships that will be explored on p. 393. All three resonance problems are directly related to the action or inaction of the soft palate and its interaction with the oral cavity.

In producing effective nasal resonance the soft palate moves downward, allowing the exhaled breath to be resonated in the nasal cavity. Nasal resonance is basic to the production of the three nasal sounds of /m/ /n/ /ŋ/ (See pp. 369–370.) Hypernasality is the result of the soft palate being lowered during the production of most or all of the sounds during speech (on nasal and non-nasal sounds alike), with no appreciable soft palate action taking place to close off the opening to the nasopharyngeal cavity (see Figure 9–1). As a result of this inactivity of the soft palate, the entire articulation-voice pattern is colored with excessive nasal resonance.

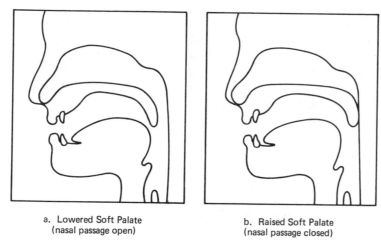

a. Lowered Soft Palate
(nasal passage open)

b. Raised Soft Palate
(nasal passage closed)

FIGURE 9–1. *Hypernasality and hyponasality.*

It has long been a point of contention as to the exact amount of movement and involvement of the velum during the production of nasal sounds. Studies by G. O. Russell, published in 1931, and a study by J. S. Calnan, published in 1953, support the findings that the velum moves much less than was generally believed for most of the vowels, nasals, and plosives. However, present opinions support the theory that the *relationship* of the nasopharynx to the movement of the oropharynx during the phonation of the nasal sounds *is vital.* Exercises to examine and develop this relationship can be found on p. 395. Conversely, if the soft palate remains elevated while you are speaking, thus closing off the nasopharyngeal cavity so that even the nasal sounds do not have the necessary nasal resonance, the vocal quality becomes hyponasal or denasal.

Hyponasality occurs when the soft palate is raised and held up against the back pharyngeal wall during the production of most or all of nasal and non-nasal sounds during speech. Seemingly, the soft palate gets "stuck" in a fixed position against the back pharyngeal wall and the resulting voice quality lacks brilliance and brightness. Your voice sounds as if you have a cold in your head. In our discussion of resonance (see pp. 369, 370), you will recall that when there is hyponasality the phrase "Good morning" can become "Good bordig." The bilabial nasal /m/ becomes the bilabial plosive /b/; the lingua-alveolar /n/ becomes the lingua-alveolar plosive /d/ and the nasal, velar-pharyngeal /ŋ/ becomes the velar-pharyngeal /g/.

Assimilation nasality involves nasal resonance on sounds that do *not* require nasal resonance for their production. The word *assimilation* comes to us from the Latin *ad similare,* meaning to "take into," "to affect." In assimilation nasality a word containing a nasal sound is completely nasalized. Instead of only the *nasal* sounds having nasal resonance, the nasal sounds "affect" the neighboring non-nasal sounds so that these non-nasal sounds are nasalized. The solution is found in the movement of the soft palate. It must be made to function productively—that is, the muscular action of the soft palate must be so controlled that it moves downward for all nasal sounds, allowing for nasal resonance. It should then move upward and back against the pharyngeal wall for all of the other non-nasal sounds.

There is a special resonance problem called nasal twang. It is characterized by hypernasality compounded by hypertension in the constrictor muscles along the back pharyngeal wall. In addition to excessive nasal resonance, the voice quality has a pinched, tight sound—a "twang."

Because hypernasality and hyponasality are the result of faulty action of the velum compounded by poor interaction with the movements of the oral cavity, these two deviant voice qualities will be considered together, with differentiating treatment services indicated.

ACOUSTIC ELEMENTS

Hypernasality
1. Excessive nasal resonance throughout voice production (on all sounds).
2. Minimized oral resonance.
3. Monotonous pitch.

Hyponasality
1. Inadequate nasal resonance on nasal sounds; voice lacks brilliance and brightness.
2. Minimized oral resonance.
3. Monotonous pitch.

UNDERLYING PHYSIOLOGY

(Applicable to Both)
1. Limited action of the soft palate.
2. Minimized interaction of the nasopharynx with the oropharynx.
3. Restricted movement of the lips and tongue.
4. Hypertension in the pharyngeal areas.
5. Possible clavicular breathing.

GOALS

(Applicable to Both)
1. Effective use of the soft palate on nasal and non-nasal sounds.
2. Increased oral resonance.
3. More action of the lips and tongue during articulation.

4. Relaxation of the pharyngeal muscles.
5. Habitual central breathing.

SKILLS

(Applicable to Both)   1. Stress relaxation of the neck and throat areas (see pp. 348, 349).
2. Acquire habitual central breathing. See pp. 355, 356.
3. Increase interaction between the oropharynx and nasopharynx by stressing open back jaws.
4. Develop labial and lingual movement by stressing bilabial sounds (p. 55) and all back vowels and diphthongs (pp. 204–254).

Hypernasality

1. Attain closure of the nasopharynx by (a) swallowing (experience this kinesthetically); (b) yawning (experience this kinesthetically).
2. Stress back vowels and diphthongs in practice. Concentrate on emitting the breath *out of the oral cavity* (see p. 359).

Hyponasality

1. Using a tactual and kinesthetic approach, reinforce your awareness of nasal resonance in the nasal cavity. Place your thumb and forefinger over the bridge of your nose (lightly) and say a prolonged /n/ sound and then change your tongue position for a prolonged /a/ sound. Note the vibration in the nose on the /n/ sound. There should be no vibration in the nose on the /a/ sound.
2. The following sentences may be used for both hypernasality and hyponasality by stressing the appropriate sentences. If you have hypernasal resonance, use the sentences in pairs. Listen carefully as you practice the sentences with the nasal sounds in them. Feel vibration in the nose *only* on the words with the nasal sounds. During practice, try prolonging the vowels to increase the needed oral resonance. The sentences without nasal sounds in them should sound very similar to the sentences that have nasal sounds. If you have hyponasality, spend more time on the sentences with nasal sounds in them—prolonging the nasals for increased nasal resonance.

Exercises

1. The five players asked for a rest period.
2. The nine men on the team demanded a new decision from the umpire.
3. Her favorite period of the day is right after breakfast.
4. Can you imagine having only candy for lunch?

5. Wait for Bill to go with us to the beach.
6. Lying on the sand under the burning sun can be dangerous to one's complexion.
7. As he galloped up the hill, the ahtlete realized that he was about to loose the race.
8. The challenger met his match on the rim of the mountain.
9. No doubt, practically all people try to better their lives.
10. Most men want to improve their miserable living conditions.
11. "Pay as you go" could be a good rule to follow.
12. Money and investments are dangerously manipulated in the stock market.
13. Styles today are triggered by the variety of textiles available.
14. Much of the material was woven in mediocre manufacturing mills.
15. Ideas are like pearls—precious!
16. Can't you find a more meaningful slogan for the advertisement?
17. I could eat food all through the day but my head resists the urge.
18. Nuts are one of my favorite snacks.

Assimilation Nasality

For the improvement of assimilation nasality try the following pairs of words. Stress the *vowel* before the nasal sound and then make a real effort to have nasal resonance *only on the nasal sounds*. The *vowels* in the pairs of words should have the *same amount of oral resonance*.

at	an
abbey	Aunty
attitude	amplitude
cat	can
it	in
lit	linen
settle	sentinel
cow	now
sow	sound
I	nine

For an extra challenge put the pairs of words into sentences:

1. *At* the World's Fair I noticed *an* attitude of friendliness among the visitors.
2. Westminster *Abbey* will never be the same after *Aunty* Mame's visit last summer.

3. The *cat* ate her dinner out of the tin *can.*
4. I put *it in* the small container on the counter.
5. Only one candle was *lit* on the table which was covered with the pink *linen* tablecloth.
6. Did you *settle* the argument with the *sentinel* about his rounds?
7. *How now* brown cow?
8. The "oink" of the *sow sounded* angry as she called her little pigs to meal time.
9. *I* find that I cannot count up to *nine* hundred and ninety-*nine* without losing count.

Nasal Twang

1. Because this quality deviation is basically a hypernasality problem compounded by hyperpharyngeal tension, refer to all of the material pertinent to the elimination of hypernasality. (See pp. 392–395.)
2. Take note, in particular, the section *Underlying Physiology.* (See p. 394.)
3. Read very carefully the section on *Goals* (See p. 394.)
4. In the section on *skills,* stress:
   a. Relaxation of the neck and throat areas. (See pp. 348, 349.)
   b. Open oral cavity and unclenched back teeth. Develop oral resonance. (See p. 368.)
   c. Auditory discrimination. (See pp. 342–344.)

If anyone of the forms of deviant nasal resonance is your particular voice problem (hypernasality, hyponasality, assimilation nasality, or nasal twang), we suggest that you carefully read the rest of this chapter. We would like to remind you that there is

1. A general type of nasality which can be heard throughout your entire speech pattern.
2. Assimilation nasality which occurs when the nasal sound(s) within a word affect the neighboring non-nasal sounds.
3. Nasality which occurs on certain vowels (see pp. 200–205).
4. Nasal emission on certain consonants (see pp. 58–62).
5. Nasality which is increased by hypertension in the constrictor muscles of the pharynx (nasal twang).

Whatever your nasal resonance problem, keep in mind the following:

1. *Effective movement of the soft palate.* Contrast the movement of the tongue and soft palate on the /a/ and /n/ sounds. See pp. 395, 396.

2. *Negative practice.* Practice all of the vowel and diphthongs with exaggerated oral resonance and then deliberately nasalize them. Compare the difference in both *feel* and *sound.*

3. *Relaxation.* Work on relaxing the oropharynx and the nasopharynx. See pp. 348–349.

4. *Auditory discrimination.* Tape yourself frequently! Analyze, evaluate and compare the tapings. See pp. 342–344.

10
Loudness

DO PEOPLE ever ask you to repeat what you have said because they did not hear you the first time? And do some frank souls say, "Speak up. I can't hear you. Talk louder!"? Or, on the other hand, do people ever say to you, "You needn't shout. I'm not deaf, you know."? Either way, these are illustrations of the problem of *loudness*.

On initial assessment, loudness (or intensity of sound) is seemingly one-dimensional. It would appear that all you have to do is to "talk louder," or "talk softer." That is just not so. A closer look at what is involved when we adjust our "loudness" will reveal that loudness is multidimensional.

When you speak, obviously you must be heard by your listener(s) or the communication process never gets off the ground. *Your loudness must meet the needs of the listener.* Many times it only meets the speaker's needs. For example, if you had the occasion to address a group of one hundred people, your loudness of voice would be noticeably different than if you were engaged in a conversation at a small party. This seems obvious. But, have you ever had the experience of being involved in a heated discussion with only *one* person and had the *conversational* loudness become so loud that the words being said were blotted out by the shouting? Or, have you ever been placed in the position of having to ask a favor of someone and have that person say, "What are you asking? I can't hear you." An analysis of these real-life scenes tells us that apparently many things are involved with loudness.

What do we mean by "volume" or "loudness"? Well, intensity of the sound produced is *part* of the answer. Intensity can be measured. How loud is the siren or the train noise? Measure the decibels! But when we talk about loudness with regard to a person's voice, we are talking not about measurements of decibels exactly, but rather about how loud did it *sound?* We are talking about perceptions! And how loud somebody's voice sounds to you (or how loud any sound seems to you, for that matter) depends on a number of factors, not just the amount of intensity at the source of the sound.

How loud your voice sounds to your listener (interpersonal communication) and how loud your voice sounds to you (intra-personal communication) is determined by the following factors:

1. *Amplitude of vocal fold vibration.* (How must the vocal folds be controlled physically?)
2. *Physical distance* and *spatial relationship.* (How does distance and your relationship to that distance affect your control of vocal fold vibration?)
3. *Psychological distance.* (How do your feelings about your audience affect your control of loudness?)
4. *The emotional state of the speaker.* (How do your feelings about *you*, the speaker, affect your control of loudness?)
5. *The speaker's reaction to ambient noise.* (How do surrounding noises affect your control of loudness?)
6. *Semantics.* (How does the *emotional* content of the words you are saying affect your loudness?)
7. *Syllabic stress.* (How does the amount of stress on the syllables within a word affect your loudness?)

AMPLITUDE OF VOCAL FOLD VIBRATION

In order to make your voice *louder* or *softer*, these physical actions must take place: (1) the force of breath pressure beneath the vocal folds must be increased (for increased loudness) or decreased (for decreased loudness); and (2) the vocal folds must retain a maximum of elasticity during either process. If you are a clavicular breather, change!! This type of breathing does not provide adequate breath for loudness control. Also, you don't benefit from this kind of tension in the upper chest area or in the throat-laryngeal areas. Be very sure that all vocal hypertension is at the midriff area (the diaphragm is structured to take this kind of punishment) and *do* involve the abdominal muscles during central breathing.

It is crucial that you grasp the importance of the activity and involvement of the vocal folds as you control loudness. We said that the vocal folds must be *elastic*—that is, capable of many kinds of movements during this process. As far back as 1948, von Leden and Moore made us aware of laryngeal vibrations.[1] Their findings confirmed that (1) the glottis *opens more slowly* for increased loudness but *closes more quickly* for increased loudness; and (2) the glottis *remains closed longer* for increased loudness. Wouldn't all of this imply a great deal of elasticity on the part of the vocal folds during increased (or decreased) intensity?

[1] R. Timcke, H. von Leden, and P. Moore, "Laryngeal Vibrations: Measurement of the Glottal Wave," Part II, *American Medical Association Archives of Otolaryngology,* **68**:11–19 (July 1958).

How do you assure vocal fold elasticity? *Don't tense the larynx!* In voice production it is very difficult to follow the dictum, *"don't tense up!"* What we prefer to suggest is, *"put the tension some other place"*—preferably in the diaphragm area. One of these writers had the following experience. During a voice therapy class at a leading university, the professor at the opening class greeted us with, "Kick off your shoes." Now, all of us had been warned that this fellow was somewhat of a "kook," but this was going too far! However, we dutifully kicked off our shoes. His next instruction came: "Imagine you are at the beach." (All of us wished, at that moment, that we *were* there.) His voice barked out again, "Now close your eyes and with your toes push into the sand." And then he screamed, *"In this class that is where you are going to push for voice production."* Our "kooky" professor wasn't really so "kooky" after all. He was not content with putting the tension in voice production even at the diaphragm area. He wanted to make very sure that we were not hypertensing the laryngeal muscles. He was aiming at our *feet* for support of tone.

We have just taken a general look at the amplitude of vocal fold vibration. All of the material applies to *both* the voice that is not loud enough and to the voice that is too loud.

Exercises

1. *Central breathing.* It is crucial for you to check for effective respiration habits. Make sure that you are breathing efficiently and that your *energy* for voice production is initiated at your midriff (the diaphragm area). Further check to see that vocal tone is supported by the use of the abdominal muscles. See pp. 355, 356.
2. *Laryngeal tension.* Hypertension in the larynx during voice production limits adequate loudness by restricting the movement of your vocal folds. See pp. 347–349.

PHYSICAL DISTANCE AND SPATIAL RELATIONSHIP

By physical distance we mean the number of inches, feet, yards, or rooms by which you are separated from the person(s) with whom you are communicating. This "distance" can present a problem—physical and/or psychological. Let's talk about the physical problem first (the psychological problem will be treated later). No matter what kind of loudness problem you have (too loud or too soft), you must take steps to adjust and manipulate your loudness if you want to communicate effectively. To be able to efficiently and effectively project your voice can be a real asset to all of you—teachers, businessmen, actors, whomever. But, take note, this must be done *without vocal strain.*

Exercises

1. *Central breathing.* Be sure you are using (as tension spots) the diaphragm and the gross abdominal muscles during exhalation (see pp. 355, 356).

2. *Laryngeal tension.* Do not use the laryngeal muscles to push the exhaled breath between the vocal folds. Keep the laryngeal area *very* relaxed. If you tense up in this area your pitch will go up. The voice will then become high pitched and strained. See pp. 347–349.

3. *Breath emission* is very necessary as insurance against developing hyperpharyngeal tension on increased loudness. Hold the palm of your hand about four inches away from your mouth. Place your other hand over the diaphragm. Count from one to ten, taking a breath for the individual numbers. On each count gently push the air stream out of the oral cavity and against the palm of your hand. There will be, of course, more breath emission on some numbers than on others because of the nature of the sounds produced (plosives will have more breath emission than nasals). As you are doing this exercise, attempt to feel muscular action in the abdominal cavity. If the voice begins to sound too breathy, try for more oral resonance by allowing the breath to resonate a little longer in the oral cavity. Work for a "round" feeling in your mouth. Keep in mind a relaxed pharyngeal cavity and put the tension in the diaphragm area.

4. *Increased loudness.* Using the number one exercise as a basis, repeat the position of holding the palm of your hand about four inches away from your mouth. Place your other hand over the *abdominal cavity.* Say the number one three times.

   a. The first time use a *conversational* volume (imagine that the the person is standing next to you).

   b. The second time use a *slight* increase in volume (imagine that the person is standing about ten feet away from you). *Important: Be sure to feel a definite push on the gross abdominal muscles as you increase the volume.* If you are doing this exercise correctly you will have *no change in pitch.* Should your pitch rise, this means that you are needlessly involving and tightening the pharyngeal and laryngeal muscles to increase the intensity.

   c. The third time use a decided increase in volume (imagine that the person is across the room). This setting should be a "natural" for teachers. Make that disruptive student in the back of the room *hear you without undue vocal strain.*

5. *Transferring increased loudness to everyday speech.* Using phrases you say daily, repeat exercise 4. For example:

"Sit down, Billy." (Bill is standing next to you.)

"Sit down, Billy." (Billy is in the middle of the classroom).

"Sit down, Billy." (That aggravating child is tormenting a fellow classmate in the back of the room.)

We opened this chapter by referring to an occasion when you might have been told, "Speak up. I can't hear you. Talk louder." Perhaps you have never been told this, but perhaps you have been made aware that *not all* of what you said was heard by your listener. Your listener remarked that the first part of what you said was heard and understood but that the last part was not. The loudness problem is called *voice fading*. As you speak, you tend to begin with adequate loudness but then your voice fades off and becomes almost inaudible.

For a better understanding of this problem read all of the material on physical distance and spatial relationship (see pp. 401–403). Then consult p. 409, which deals specifically with voice fading.

SPATIAL RELATIONSHIPS, PSYCHOLOGICAL DISTANCE, AND EMOTIONALITY

Up to this point we have considered the *physical skills* involved in increasing or decreasing loudness. We have concentrated on the control of the amplitude of vocal fold vibration through the use of efficient respiration habits and through the manipulation and use of the oral cavity (breath emission).

In the opening of this chapter, we referred to the fact that loudness is also involved with spatial relationships, psychological distance, and the emotional state of the speaker. Loudness is multidimensional. We would like to discuss these three dimensions together because they are so inextricably entwined. Psychological overlay is not to be minimized in your control of loudness. How we control the loudness of our voices as we speak can say a good deal about our intrapersonal and interpersonal communication. Consider the following:

1. How do you feel about standing close to people as you communicate? Do you feel more comfortable speaking to them at a distance?
2. If you are forced to stand near people when you speak, do you *overproject?* Why? Do you *underproject?* Why?
3. If you underproject, is the reason that you *really* don't want your audience to *hear* what you have to say? Consider that if they *hear* you, they can react; they are then free to judge you; they can be critical.
4. If you *overproject,* is the reason that you feel you can *control* your audience by your shouting? Does this give you a sense of power?
5. Have you found that your feelings about your subject matter and your feelings about your audience affect your loudness *at the very*

moment of utterance? Have you found that far too often your personal feelings about your content colors your communication?

Emotionality plays a vital role in our human relations and in our vocal management. In any kind of setting where you are personally involved and where you know that you have strong feelings about the matter under discussion, controlling your vocal quality, volume, pitch, and rate can be troublesome. Your emotions can take over and, unless you are vocally disciplined, communication can break down. Your listeners can become so overwhelmed by *how* you are communicating that *what* you are saying loses not only its meaning but also its impact.

However, there is no doubt that at times we are better able to express our ideas objectively and to control our voices accordingly. In this whole multidimensional setting, the role our individual personality plays is not to be minimized. It is basic not only to our *ability* to communicate but also to our *willingness* to communicate. Some of us give more freely of ourselves than others in an interpersonal communication situation. Some of us tend to hold back, seemingly threatened. Our basic behavior pattern is the key to the way we function. Many times during a voice improvement or voice therapy program, supportive psychological therapy is not only desirable, but is necessary. Not being able to clearly *face up to yourself* can be the missing ingredient in a successful voice improvement program. Try it! You may like it!

AMBIENT NOISE

In our daily living, our minds and ears survive surrounding (ambient) noises that engulf them. Much of the time we are impervious to these intruders, out of habit. We either turn them off or tune them out. At other times these noises can cause us real concern and even worry. A crowded party, with its accompanying ambient noise, can be a real worry to a person with a neuralsensory hearing loss. The ambient noises tend to blot out or distort the sounds the person *wants* to hear—the conversation of his *immediate* group. Ask entertainers how much they enjoy doing a dinner show with its aggravating rattle of knives, forks, and tinkling glass. When *you* are worried or concerned about ambient noises, do you "talk over" the noise? Do you out shout it? Do you ignore it?

A college student we knew found a solution to handling ambient noises. From childhood on he had led a never-ending battle to be heard at the family dinner table over the chatter of his five older sisters. This student appeared in one of our voice classes because he was told that he would not be accepted for candidacy as a student teacher on the elementary level unless he could learn to "talk louder." He dutifully attended every voice class, learned ever theory of effective voice production, and was even able to acquire the necessary skills for increased loudness, but he was failing the course. He seemingly could not *transfer* his knowledge and skills to conversational speech. Finally the story unfolded. Over the years he had learned that to get attention from his sisters, either at the table or wherever, he had to get very quiet and then *softly* state what he wanted or had to say and—miracles—his mother and sisters would stop chatting and *listen* to him. His vocal conditioning over the years was so successful that he almost wrecked his professional career.

How do *you* handle ambient noise? Do you tend to increase your loudness? Do you tend to decrease your loudness? Whatever your approach, you must minimize vocal strain in the process. For those of you who shout over any noise around you, reread pp. 408, 409. Acquire the needed skills for increasing loudness so that you minimize vocal strain that can go into vocal abuse, which in turn can result in vocal pathology.

Do you tend to decrease your volume when you are threatened aurally by surrounding noise? Perhaps a particular kind of hearing loss forces you to talk with less volume. Whatever your reason for decreasing your vocal output, your task is to learn how to decrease volume without allowing your voice to drop back in your throat. Usually the vocal quality that results is either raspy, husky, or throaty. The following section on the too loud talker will give you some ideas on how to decrease vocal volume without vocal strain.

Up to this point, we have concentrated on *increasing* the loudness of your voice. The area of *ambient* (surrounding) noises introduces another dimension to loudness—*too much loudness*. Has anyone ever asked you, "Why do you shout all of the time?" Are you one of those people who finds, while dining in an intimate restaudant, that you have to deliberately talk softer than you usually do or otherwise you have adjoining tables commenting on your conversation?

Too loud talkers, let's talk about you. Usually your profile describes you as a person with energy, vitality, and a love of life. You tend to let the world know that you are there! May we suggest a re-evaluation of you (intrapersonal) and your communication pattern (interpersonal). Too much voice; too much personality and too much of *you* can be defeating. Too much of a good thing is not always desirable. Back off! Take a close look at the following exercises. The suggestions may help you to develop a significantly more effective use of your voice in interpersonal communication.

Exercises

1. *Central breathing.* Make sure you are using effective central breathing during phonation. See pp. 355, 356.
2. *Laryngeal tension.* Check signs for hyperlaryngeal tension during

voice production. Do you strap muscles in your neck puff out while you are speaking? If so, reread the information on hypertension in the laryngeal and pharyngeal areas during phonation. See pp. 348, 349.

3. *Breath emission.* This is your trouble spot! While speaking, you tend to *over-energize* (you use too much physical energy during voice production). Take it easy! Don't allow your breath to *explode* out of your mouth while speaking. Use your oral cavity as your main resonator, not your throat. See p. 359.

4. *Variation of loudness.* Strive to vary your volume in terms of the emphasis you wish to give to the sentences and words you are using. Not every word you utter is equally important. Be selective. Read the section in this chapter on *Semantics.* See pp. 406, 407.

5. *Adaptation of loudness.* When you use your voice, become more sensitive to physical distance, spatial relationship, and your own personal involvement with the message you are trying to communicate. Learn to accommodate your volume to the occasion and to your listeners. Refer to the section in this chapter on semantics and then try the following exercises for adaptation of loudness.

Read the following sentences in two ways: 1) as if you were in an intimate situation; and 2) as if you were involved with a larger group of people. Keep in mind variation and adaptation of loudness.

1. I am delighted to be with you this evening.
2. This is, indeed, a sad occasion.
3. Tonight is a night for celebration.
4. My fellow conspirators!
5. This is your responsibility.
6. Let by-gones be by-gones.
7. What are you willing to do about this?
8. I'm hoping to settle this case out of court.
9. I couldn't care less.
10. You shouldn't have done that!
11. How did it happen?
12. For your health's sake, you should stop smoking.
13. I feel so disillusioned.
14. Would you be willing to support this cause?
15. I don't agree with you at all.

SEMANTICS

The study of word *meanings* (including their emotional content) is called semantics. Semantics plays a vital role in communication, in general, and in loudness, in particular. Your choice and use of words can affect not only the meaning of the context but can be directly involved with you, personally. Why do you choose certain words to express your thoughts and feelings? Do you seldom (or never) use "four-letter" words when you are upset or angry? Do you often (or constantly) sprinkle your conversation with the latest "in" vocabulary? Perhaps you're the "cultured" type who always uses the most correct grammar, the most imaginative vocabulary, and the most precise articulation.

How is the conveying of your message affected at the moment of utterance by your personal feelings? Have you ever cried while telling of a happy experience? Anger can be shown by yelling words, or by saying them softly and coldly through clenched jaws and teeth. Whether you are engaged in conversation, reading aloud, or delivering a speech, semantic implications can be emphasized in a number of ways, one of which is to vary your loudness. Other ways include changing your pitch, varying your rate, and using a pause. These techniques of emphasis will be discussed in more detail in subsequent chapters.

To make you more aware of how semantics and loudness can affect each other, try the following exercise. The sentence below has five words in it. Each time the sentence is repeated, a different word within the sentence is emphasized by using more force (loudness). Notice how the meaning changes when the emphasis changes.

I don't fell well today. (Not you, *I*)
I *don't* feel well today. (Opposite of I *do*)
I don't *feel* well today. (Physical discomfort)
I don't feel *well* today. (I'm ill)
I don't fell well *today*. (Yesterday I did feel well)

The following sentences would certainly not be said with the same degree of loudness:

"Isn't it a bright morning?"
"My mother is very ill."

Obviously semantics, emphasis, and loudness are interrelated. They certainly complement each other.

We are now ready to consider a final area—syllabic stress—and its involvement with loudness. In the articulation section of this book, you were informed about syllabic stress in American English (see p. 306). Primary, secondary, tertiary, and weak stress involve levels of force or loudness on certain syllables in words. The dictionary gives us this information. However, stress on particular syllables can also affect meaning. Many nouns are changed to verbs by changing stress:

'record (n.)   re'cord (v.)
'address (n.)   ad'dress (v)

In this section we are interested in what happens to meaning when stress (involving loudness) is given to ordinarily unstressed words. Notice the change in meaning in the following two sentences:

1. This is the /ðə/ (thə) book related to the assignment. (Implication: There could be other books.)
2. This is *the* /ði/ (thē) book related to the assignment. (Implication: This is the *only* book related to the assignment.)

People trained (or just plain interested) in oral reading and public speakers make frequent use of the technique of stressing (by force-loudness) a particular syllable in a key word. Politicians are masters of this device of emphasis.

Problems of Volume or Loudness

We said earlier in this chapter that a speaker should achieve "enough" or "adequate" or "appropriate" volume when speaking. The trick is to avoid getting too much or getting too little; the goal is to regulate your vocal volume (or loudness) so that it is just right! There are three problems to be faced: (1) too little volume or the too soft voice; (2) voice fading; and (3) too much volume or the too loud voice. Perhaps one of these problems plagues you.

We will treat each of these problems related to volume (or loudness) in the following way:

1. We will note the acoustic symptoms. (How does your voice sound?)
2. We will examine the causes of the problem. (Why do you have this problem with vocal loudness?)
3. We will establish goals to work toward. (How should your voice be produced to achieve adequate volume?)
4. We will suggest specific skills needed to achieve your goals. (What should you do in order to achieve effective voice production?)
5. We will provide exercises designed to help you develop the skills you need. (What exercises or techniques will develop the needed skills?)

THE "TOO SOFT" VOICE (INADEQUATE LOUDNESS)

Acoustic Elements

1. Minimal audibility.
2. Periodic breathiness.
3. Voice fading.

Underlying Physiology

1. Poor respiration habits.
2. Poor support of tone.
3. Minimal subglottal pressure.
4. Minimal use of the oral cavity as resonator.

Goals

1. Adequate loudness.
2. Central breathing.
3. Support of tone.
4. Balance of resonance.
5. Increased use of physical energy.
6. *Willingness* to communicate (personal involvement with material).

Skills

1. Habitual central breathing. See pp. 355, 356.
2. Use of support of tone to sustain loudness. See pp. 355, 356, 410.
3. Increased physical energy. See pp. 401, 402.
4. Increased oral resonance. See p. 368.
5. Increased involvement with semantics and emotionality of content. See pp. 406, 407.

VOICE FADING

Acoustic Elements

1. Minimal audibility at the ends of sentences and phrases.
2. Breathiness at the ends of sentences and phrases.
3. Lower pitch at the ends of sentences and phrases.

Underlying Physiology

1. Poor respiration habits.
2. Poor support of tone.
3. Minimal use of oral cavity as resonator.

Goals

1. Central breathing.
2. Support of tone through effective respiration.
3. Increased use of physical energy.
4. Increased oral resonance.

Skills

1. Habitual central breathing. See pp. 355, 356.
2. Use of support of tone to sustain loudness. See pp. 355, 356, 410.

3. Increased physical energy. See pp. 401, 402.
4. Increased oral resonance. See p. 368.

Try the following additional exercises for developing *support of tone* through speech.

1. Stand tall with your hand on the diaphragm area. Take a breath and begin counting: one; one, two; one, two, three, and so on. Take a breath on each new group of numbers. Concentrate on having the *last* number you say sound *identical* in loudness as the first number. Keep the breath going!
2. Using the same techniques as recommended in the Number One exercise above, add speech. Use your daily "patter."
   a. Hello, Professor Allen!
   b. I'll be home for dinner.
   c. Are you free to go to the dance with me tonight?

Remember to keep the breath going until the end of the sentence. Don't fade off. Use the abdominal muscles to help you to support the tone. Keep your loudness level up!

THE "TOO LOUD" VOICE (EXCESSIVE LOUDNESS)

Acoustic Elements

1. Excessive loudness (too loud).
2. Harsh, raspy, or throaty vocal quality.
3. Minimal pitch range: too high or too low.
4. Minimal pitch variation.

Underlying Physiology

1. Hyperpharyngeal/hyperlaryngeal tension.
2. Excessive push of breath on exhalation.
3. Hyperpharyngeal resonance.
4. Minimal oral resonance.

Goals

1. Whole-body relaxation.
2. Central breathing.
3. Balanced resonance.
4. Decreased physical energy during phonation.
5. Reduced personal envolement with material by watching emotionality.

Skills

1. Whole-body relaxation. See p. 348.
2. Relaxation of neck and throat areas. See pp. 348–349.

3. Habitual central breathing. See pp. 355, 356.
4. Increased oral resonance. See p. 368.
5. Semantic involvement. See pp. 406, 407.
6. Specific skills. See pp. 402, 403.

Before we conclude our discussion of loudness, we would like to state a few *do* and *don't* suggestions for those of you with loudness problems.

1. Be aware of the relationship of vocal hygiene to loudness. On days when your throat feels raw and sore, or when you are suffering with laryngitis or pharyngitis, *be kind to your voice!* Don't overuse it. Don't abuse it. Keep talking to a minimum. Forget about developing or controlling loudness. However, *do not whisper!* Even though this point was made earlier in the voice section of this book (see p. 363), it bears repeating. When you whisper, your vocal folds are held in a strained, widely abducted position (see Figure 8–3), so you are doing your voice no favor by whispering. The best treatment, if you must speak, is to speak *softly*, allowing the vocal folds to vibrate gently. If necessary, use an amplifying system as a temporary measure.
2. Familiarize yourself with amplifying systems.
   a. *The stand-up microphone* (sometimes attached to the lectern) limits your ability to move around and can limit interpersonal communication.
   b. *The lavalier microphone* (attached to a chain or cord around your neck) allows you greater freedom of body and hand movement.
3. Aim for two skills in loudness: variation and adaptation.

11
Pitch

P ITCH refers to the highness or lowness of a sound and to all of the degrees of highness or lowness you hear in the human voice. Your own voice has pitch, a basic pitch that is dramatically influenced by your inherited laryngeal structure (anatomy) and how you use this structure (physiology). For example, a child's larynx is smaller than the larynx of an adult, which basically accounts for the childlike vocal quality you've come to recognize and expect. Also, the vocal folds of the female larynx are generally shorter in length (seven-eighths of an inch to one inch in length) than the vocal folds of the male (one inch to one and one-fourth inches). The result is the higher pitch range found in the female voice as opposed to the lower pitch range of the male. For acoustic confirmation, look at the strings of a piano (a baby grand makes it easier). You will see that the strings of the piano that give us the low notes are longer and have more flexibility than the strings that produce the high notes.

Your voice has a pitch range within which it operates. You can change pitch from syllable to syllable and from word to word as you speak. You can even change pitch during a syllable. It is the pattern of pitches that make up the melody of our speech when we talk (see pp. 322–327).

Factors Related to Variations in Pitch

The pitch of your voice and your ability to change pitch depend on many factors, some simple and others very involved. Simply stated, your voice changes pitch with the increase or decrease of the number of vibrations per minute of the vocal folds. However, the length, thickness, and flexibility of the vocal folds significantly affect the frequency of vibration. For example, if you lengthen the folds by tensing them, you get a faster vibration, which results in a higher pitch. We also know that vocal pitch and intensity are so interrelated that it is impossible to isolate one from the other. There is a marked interplay between vocal fold tension and subglottal pressure. It is apparent that there is a direct relationship between

1. Frequency of vocal fold vibration.
2. Tension of vocal fold vibration.
3. Length and thickness of the vocal folds.
4. Intensity—subglottal pressure.

Reread Chapter 8 of this book for a physiological and acoustical explanation of how these factors influence the pitch of your voice.

In addition to the four physiological and acoustical factors related to pitch that we have already mentioned, there are five other factors that are also related to pitch changes.

1. Medical condition of the speaker.
2. Personality and temperament of the speaker.
3. Emotional state of the speaker.
4. Melody and syllabic stress.
5. Semantics and vocal color.

If you consider all of these factors together, a fairly involved picture emerges, possibly even more involved than that of loudness. There are nine different factors related to pitch variation. Obviously, pitch and its variation is not a simple matter.

Before you begin to work on your pitch and pitch variation, it is advisable for you to recheck your basic voice production. Using your voice effectively allows you maximum flexibility of vocal fold vibration and minimizes laryngeal-pharyngeal hypertension. Review the following skills:

1. Relaxation of the laryngeal muscles (see pp. 348–349).
2. Efficient respiration (see pp. 355–356).
3. Controlled respiration (see p. 358).
4. Breath emission (see p. 359).

Changes in the pitch of your voice depend on many factors, most of which are very complex. *Take note of all of them.*

Factors That Influence the Pitch of Your Voice

MEDICAL CONDITION OF THE SPEAKER—PHYSICAL ASPECTS

It is not only conceivable, but entirely possible, that your pitch problem is medically based. Infrequently (but definitely possible) the endocrine system is involved. Many kinds of voices can be affected—for example, the adolescent voice during puberty and the female voice during menopause. If you have a serious problem with pitch, a medical assessment is a must. Two cases of an endocrine involvement remain in our memory: a male student with a high-pitched voice (the male student weighed around 250 pounds!) and a fifty-year-old female who could not remember ever having been addressed as Ms. on the telephone—the usual reaction on the other end of the line was "Mr." Both had endocrine involvements and both had developed some very bad vocal habits.

On the *physical* (acoustical) side, amplitude of vocal fold vibration and tension of the vocal folds are two factors related to pitch. These areas were discussed in Chapter 10 (see pp. 400, 401), but a quick review might be beneficial at this time. With increased amplitude and increased tension of the vocal folds, the pitch of your voice will go up. The *physics of sound* tells us that *any* vibrating body (guitar string or piano string) when tightened causes pitch to rise. Your vocal folds react in the same physical way. In some cases the higher pitch is not only desirable but *necessary* (in contact ulcers, a vocal pathology, for example). In other cases the rise in pitch (or lowering of pitch) is indicative of vocal strain.

PERSONALITY AND TEMPERAMENT OF THE SPEAKER

By now you must be convinced that these writers are addicted to psychological interpretations of communication problems. We may seem to be because we keep stressing the involvement of your personality and temperament with the characteristics of voice: (1) quality; (2) loudness; (3) pitch; and (4) rate.

Yes, your personality and temperament *are* involved with the pitch of your voice. Go back and read what we said about *loudness problems* and their psychological overlay. Because pitch is so directly involved with loudness *physically,* pitch cannot help being involved with loudness psychologically. The anxious, high-strung personality is usually experiencing hypertension. This kind of hypertension more often than not transfers itself to the physical "self." The body tension which results (precipitated by the mental tension) usually affects that part of the persons's physical self which is his Achille's heel, his physical or psychological weak spot. Some people develop an ulcer. Some people have a heart attack. Many times the voice is affected. With the increased body tension, the vocal folds tighten and U-U-U-P goes the pitch of the person's voice. Turn the coin over. Some anxieties reveal themselves by withdrawal symptoms. Those affected seem to crawl inside themselves, exhibiting little or no outward emotions. The voice is held back in the throat and becomes raspy, breathy, or husky. People with these kinds of deviant vocal qualities sound as if they are "walking backwards," pulling the voice back with them. The breath gets stuck back in the throat, there is minimal breath emission on phonation, and a poor vocal quality is the result. Their pitch becomes lowered and usually lacks range.

EMOTIONAL STATE OF THE SPEAKER

At this point we ask you to review the material in Chapter 10 dealing with spatial relationships, psychological distance, and emotionality (see pp. 403, 404). All of this material applies directly to your pitch control. In addition, how your emotional state affects your pitch range *at the very moment of* utterance cannot be underestimated.

In a given situation your feelings (your emotional state) show themselves vocally in different ways. When angry, some people scream, sending their pitch sky high; other people withdraw, taking their pitch down with them. In all such emotional settings, your pitch will react accordingly. However, if you are vocally disciplined, if you are aware of the techniques used to effectively control and vary your pitch, and if you are able to apply these known techniques, then no matter the emotional setting, you will be better equipped to communicate effectively.

MELODY AND SYLLABIC STRESS

The term *melody* is used to indicate pitch changes as you speak. These changes are made up of inflections: a rising inflection ↗, a falling inflection ↘, and the circumflex ⤳, which is a combination within a word or phrase of the rising and falling inflections. For a more detailed explanation of this area see pp. 322–327 in the articulation section.

Your own melody pattern is influenced by

1. The semantic implication of the words you are saying.
2. Your emotional interpretation of the words you are saying.
3. Your emotional reaction to the words you are saying.
4. Syllabic stress.

All of these influences are an integral part of what is commonly known as vocal color. The term might seem vague, but the skills involved are very concrete. Vocal color is the "happening" when your voice takes on the mood and meaning (semantics) of the words you are saying. For example, consider the following two phrases:

Isn't it a lovely day!
I feel very fatigued.

The wording of the two sentences strongly suggests a different meaning, and particularly a different mood. The first sentence ("Isn't it a lovely day!") suggests a brightness of vocal quality and a "light" voice, in contrast with the second sentence ("I feel very fatigued"), which suggests a heavy mood, lacking in spirit and energy. In order to communicate effectively the meaning of the two sentences, there should be a marked difference in use of voice. However, vocal color can be acquired

1. If your voice is effectively produced so that there is no hypertension in the larynx.
2. If you are breathing efficiently because breath control is necessary for the effective expression of ideas.

3. If there is adequate resonance balance of the basic laryngeal tone. Voices with limited resonance cannot easily acquire vocal color.
4. If there is effective pitch variation.
5. If there is a psychological willingness on your part to express the emotional content of the words you are saying.

We do not mean to suggest that everyone become a dynamo in order to develop vocal color, but it will help if you try to react emotionally to what is happening to you. A deliberate attempt to react psychologically will stimulate vocal color in your voice.

Before you attempt vocal variety, let's see if you can deliberately (mechanically) move your pitch up and down. Our approach to this skill is *tactile* and *kinesthetic* rather than *aural*. You will learn to listen later.

Exercises:

1. Place your fingertips on your larynx and swallow. You will feel slight tension. *Become acquainted with this muscle action.* Using

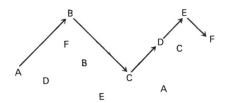

the alphabet, say each letter on a different pitch. What pitch you use is unimportant. Say one letter high, the next letter lower, the second letter a little lower than the first, and so on. The point is to *deliberately* vary the pitch of your voice. *Feel* the difference in muscle action in the larynx as you vary your pitch. Do this exercise with your eyes open and then with your eyes closed (kinesthesia). Try *listening* for the changes in pitch. You might benefit from using the piano keyboard as a guide. Say the letters of the alphabet on the different notes, changing the notes indiscriminately. A word of caution: as you practice this exercise keep in mind open oral cavity and relaxed jaws in order to minimize hyperlaryngeal tension. Concentrate on central breathing.

2. Use the following phrases in the same way as in the Number One exercise, only this time say *each word in the phrase on a different pitch*.
   a. Come here.
   b. Hello, there!

c. Sit down.
d. Where's the fire?
e. I feel fine.
f. She's a beauty!
g. Its time for dinner.
h. My head really hurts.
i. Hurry up. Your're late!

How did you succeed? Were you able to move your pitch around? If not, keep trying. Use the piano keyboard (the white keys) as a help in making you more aware of your pitch changes. The tape recorder can become your best friend. Tape your pitch improvement sessions. Play back the tape. Listen closely and carefully as you analyze and evaluate your performance. Have a friend listen with you. It's a help. Don't fall into the trap of thinking, "I'm tone deaf. I'll never be able to learn to vary the pitch of my voice." We assure you that very few people are diagnosed as tone deaf. It can happen and it does happen, but let your otolaryngologist (ENT) decide this for you.

You are now ready to add vocal color to your pitch variation. At this point you might want to review the material on pp. 415, 416, which deals with vocal color, before you proceed to the next section.

Exercises for Acquiring Vocal Color and Pitch Variation

1. Review the exercises in this chapter on pp. 416, 417 for a mechanical approach to pitch variation.
2. Try the following sentences, keeping in mind the *meaning* of the words and the *mood* created by the meaning.
   a. Hello! (Call out cheerfully to a friend across the room. Concentrate on correct projection and attempt a rising inflection.)
   b. How are you feeling today? (Express *concern*. Try a circumflex pitch pattern.)
   c. Don't you dare make an accusation! (Express quiet anger. Intentionally try a precise diction with a monotonous tone of rising inflection.)
   d. Consider the word *goodbye*. Say it with the following meanings: leaving a party of friends at a social gathering; parting in anger; leaving a child with whom you've been playing; and anticipating a long departure from a friend.
3. Challenge your self a little more by moving on to prose. Choose some material that you will enjoy reading, preferably a paragraph that has either colorful language or emotional content. Don't read the box scores of the players of your favorite team!
   a. Examine the material closely for meaning and then decide on the idea(s) and words that you want to emphasize.

    b. Decide on *how* you are going to emphasize them. Are you going to use changes in loudness, pitch, or rate for this? Perhaps you are going to use all three?

4. Move on to extemporaneous speaking. Think through an incident you want to talk about. Plan the incident in your head only. Do not write it out. Turn on your tape recorder and tell the incident to your tape recorder. Play back the tape. Is your voice beginning to have more pitch changes? If not, repeat the incident. This time make a real effort to move your voice up and down and around.

5. Perhaps you are now ready for conversational speech. Invite a friend to help you in this exercise. Don't decide what the two of you are going to talk about beforehand. Turn on the tape recorder and begin talking—about anything. This is easier if the subject matter is of interest to both of you. Talk for about three minutes. Listen to the replay both critically and analytically.

Most books on voice include one or more paragraphs on optimum pitch and/or modal pitch. Because this book is not pathologically based, we prefer not to go into this area in depth. However, we want to make some mention of the pitch level at which your voice seemingly functions with the least amount of effort. If you want to find your level of "least effort," try this. Hum up and down the scale. Concentrate on finding a midpoint—that point at which you experience little or no muscle tension in the larynx. When you feel you have reached this comfortable place, hum *down* the scale until you reach a point of *discomfort*. Hum back up the scale approximately five notes. Your optimum pitch can usually be determined within this five note range. If necessary, use a piano. Use the white keys in the middle of the piano and hum each note as you play, going up one at a time and down one at a time. The general idea is to speak within this range or, more specifically, to use this five-note range as a *basic pitch range for your everyday use of voice*. Note that your *modal pitch* is that range of pitch that you use *most*. It may or may not be your optimum pitch.

We prefer *not* to recommend this mechanical way of finding your optimum pitch. It is arbitrary and artificial. Our suggestion to you is to work on achieving an over-all effective voice production and then to use this as a firm foundation for encouraging a wide pitch range and variation within that range.

The vibratory process is not simple and perhaps this is the basis for the philosophy of these writers concerning the area of pitch. *Deliberate manipulation of pitch is to be avoided* unless extreme conditions demand it. Our school of thought postulates that *voice* (like water) *will seek its own level when effectively produced*. We suggest that stress be placed on (1) an over-all attempt to make the vibratory process work efficiently and (2) a serious, concentrated effort to relate the person to his own voice, physically and psychologically. Understand that we *do* urge pitch manipulation with certain pathologically based voice problems (hysterical aphonia and contact ulcers, for example). However, for most voice improvement cases, pitch manipulation is needless, less than effective, and can even be dangerous. A case in point is a young lady with a serious case of huskiness and voice fading who registered in one of our voice classes. Our assessment included a third element: narrow pitch range (low). She was startled. Her immediate reply was, "I can't believe it! My voice low-pitched? All of my life I've been told about my high, squeaky voice." Further questioning revealed the following facts. During a recent course in oral reading, the instructor kept hammering away at her to "Do something about that high-pitched voice." The student took it upon herself to talk at a lower pitch and with less volume. The result was a tortured sounding breathy, husky, low-pitched voice. An otolaryngological examination revealed the beginnings of pathology (pinhead nodules on both vocal folds).

How do you know if you, or someone else has *effective* use of pitch? How do you know if you, or someone else has *ineffective* use of pitch? Let's take a look at the indicators.

1. *If the pitch of your voice is effective it should*
   a. Be appropriate for your sex and for your age.
   b. Have pitch range.
   c. Be efficiently reinforced by loudness.
   d. Be involved with melody and vocal color.
   e. Have pitch variations related to the meaning of what is being said (semantics).
2. *If the pitch of your voice is ineffective it can be the result of*
   a. Malfunction of the endocrine (glandular) system of the body.
   b. Poor use and control of your laryngeal musculature and poor control of loudness.
   c. Lack of psychological involvement.
   d. Your emotional state at the very moment of utterance.
   e. Lack of vocal color and vocal variety.

If you are plagued with any of the following deviant voice qualities, take note of the possible related pitch problems:

1. Hoarse (usually low pitched; occasional pitch breaks).
2. Breathy/husky (low pitch; limited range).
3. Thin (high pitch; limited range).
4. Harsh (low pitch; limited range).
5. Strident (high pitch; limited range).

At this point we would like to spell out pitch problems:

1. Voices that have a pitch that is too high.
2. Voices that have a pitch that is too low.
3. Voices that have a minimal range of pitch.
4. Voices that lack pitch variation.

All of these points have been analyzed and evaluated in this chapter. For a review of the discussion and for the appropriate exercises, take note of the indicated pages.

1. *Voices with a pitch that is too high.*
    a. Assess the medical situation (see pp. 413, 414).
    b. Evaluate your present physical condition (see p. 349).
    c. Recheck your over-all habits of effective voice production (see pp. 346–348; 355–359; 366–370).
    d. Watch emotionality!
    e. Acquire vocal variation and vocal color (see pp. 417, 418).
2. *Voices with a pitch that is too low.*
    a. Assess the medical situation (see pp. 413, 414).
    b. Evaluate your present physical condition (see p. 349).
    c. Recheck your over-all habits of effective voice production (see pp. 346–348; 355–359; 366–370).
    d. Watch emotionality. Try to be a little more outgoing! Let go!
    e. Acquire vocal variation and vocal color (see pp. 417, 418).
3. *Voices with a minimal range of pitch.*
    a. Assess your physical condition. How's your energy?
    b. Recheck your over-all habits of effective voice production. This is *crucial!* (See pp. 346–348; 355–359; 366–370.)
    c. Become emotionally involved with your material (see pp. 416, 417).
4. *Voices that lack pitch variation.*
    a. Assess your physical condition. How's your energy?
    b. Recheck your over-all habits of effective voice production (see pp. 346–348; 355–359; 366–370).
    c. Become emotionally involved with your material (see pp. 416, 417).
    d. Take particular note of semantic involvement (see pp. 406, 407).

12
Rate

THE ELEMENT of rate in speaking is not thought to be an integral part of voice production by many speech "experts." This conclusion is supported by evidence to be found in voice and articulation textbooks. Many of them give little, if any, attention to vocal rate. We feel that rate *does* play a role. We feel that your rate can affect (1) vocal resonance by either helping to amplify or modify it; (2) your intelligibility, in how clear or unclear you sound to your listeners; and (3) your interpersonal relations, in that rate of speech helps to form a "picture" of you for your listeners. These points will be clarified subsequently.

The term *rate* refers to the number of words you speak per minute. Documented studies show that the so-called normal, or conversational, rate of speech is anywhere from 120–140 words per minute. Your rate when reading aloud is slightly faster, with an average of between 150–170 words per minute. The term *duration* supplies more information about rate in speech. Duration can be defined as the measurement of time consumed between produced sounds and/or the measurement of time consumed between words and phrases. Your rate of speaking coupled with your pattern of duration forms the basis for your individual *rate profile.*

Skill in rate control and variation, like skill in pitch and volume, *can be acquired* and you can learn to use these skills meaningfully. But, first we have to decide what your needs are. Perhaps you rate of speech is fine. Then again, perhaps it is not. In this chapter you will learn how to

1. *Assess your rate profile.* (How many words do you speak per minute?)
2. *Evaluate your rate profile.* (Is this assessed rate too fast? Too slow?)
3. *Set goals.* (When do I *increase* rate? When do I *decrease* rate?)
4. *Exercise.* (What do I *do* to achieve my goals?)

Before we take a close look at you and your rate profile, we feel that it is very important for you to consider those factors that *influence* your rate.

Factors That Influence Your Rate of Speech

We have frequently commented on the fact that it is the differences between your anatomy and physiology and those of others that make your problems in speech highly individual. Your rate of speech is another mark of your individuality. Your inherited anatomy and your ability to develop gross and refined motor skills are basically involved. For example, some of you move more quickly than others; and some of you have better muscle coordination. Your rate of speech is a result of such factors.

A fast rate of speaking is found most frequently in the energetic, quick-moving person. The unusual case is to find a mild-mannered, taciturn speaker with an excessive rate. Your rate and duration of speaking seem to be related to your over-all physiology and to your intellectual quickness or slowness. Heredity, early environmental stimulation, conditioning, and even the type of education to which you were exposed all helped to develop your intellectual powers and have also played a substantial role in affecting the *pace* of your thinking. Have you ever played the game of charades and been unable to decipher the cues (which are usually given at a rapid-fire pace) in time to give an answer? Still more frustrating, did you have the experience of *understanding* the given cues and not being able to formulate the answer as quickly as the person next to you simply because he or she spoke faster than you? Obviously, the trick to playing charades successfully is not dependent on IQ.

We want to make the point, rather strongly, that none of these ways of functioning has the element of "right" or "wrong." It is not necessarily better to be able to move more quickly than the next person; nor is it necessarily advantageous to be able to think more spontaneously than your friend. *You are you and you must be you.* But be aware that because your rate of speech is so much a part of your mental and physical pace, it is sometimes difficult to change a rate pattern. Many times (as with loudness) you have to change a little bit of you in the process.

Everyone has a phsyical and an intellectual pace at which he moves more comfortably or uncomfortably. In the same way everyone has an individual emotional pace inextricably interwoven with the physical and intellectual. His *rate of emotional reaction* also affects rate of speaking. He may be capable of feeling as deeply as his friends, but due to the complexities of his nature, he may not be inclined to demonstrate the emotion as quickly—either verbally or nonverbally.

From all we have discussed so far, it is fairly obvious to assume that *your rate profile is not the result of any single factor.* Rate is multidimensional. It is deeply involved with your physical, intellectual, and psychological, self.

1. *The physical*
   a. Basic physiology.
   b. Gross and refined muscle control.
   c. Respiration.
   d. Physical state of the speaker.
2. *The intellectual*
   a. Mental quickness.
   b. Understanding of the content.
   c. Semantics.
3. *The psychological*
   a. Personality.
   b. Emotional state of the speaker.

PHYSICAL ASPECTS

Basic Physiology

This area refers back to how you basically function. Do you move quickly? Slowly? It does not matter as there are no standards. But realize that your basic speed of muscle movement affects your rate profile. If you tend to move quickly, your rate of speech will be related, or if you move slowly, your rate of speech will probably be slower than average. Whatever your pattern of muscle action, be prepared to deal with con-comitant rate patterns and problems.

Gross and Refined Muscle Coordination

A number of factors are involved here: (1) age; (2) physical prowess; and (3) ability to control muscle action. When dealing with any kind of communication problem (voice, articulation, rhythm), it is important to remember that man speaks almost spontaneously. You are asked a question and zooo-oo-m-m-m! The answer is formulated and expressed. There are fewer times when we deliberate over a verbal response. In view of the immediacy of speech response, rate problems are usually very difficult to control. We speak—the reply is given. Who has had *time* to think about rate? *There are a few controls.* For instance, usually age slows down the rate of speaking. As we grow older, our body func-tions assume a slower tempo. Speech is no exception. Notice the vocal quality of an older person. The laryngeal muscles start to lose their flexibility and the voice begins to sound raspy, or even squeaky. The rate also changes. It slows down.

Your physical prowess and your ability to control muscle movement (physiology) are also involved with your rate. We turn to sports for an example here. If all baseball players functioned physiologically in the same way, then all baseball players would be Willie Mays! If all pianists functioned alike physiologically (and, of course, had the same fine sense of interpretation), then all pianists could be an Arthur Rubenstein! However, take heart! You have other means of control. Begin by developing a high level of awareness of your rate pattern. You will find some exercises for acquiring this facility at the end of this chapter. You could also benefit from reviewing the material on "Raising Your Level of Awareness" in Chapter 8, p. 341.

Respiration

On the surface you might question the importance of respiration to rate control and manipulation. Studies support the following findings. The average time of expiration in *quiet breathing* approximately equals the time of inspiration. The ratio is 1:1. The average ratio of expiration to inspiration in *speaking* is 5:1—*five times* as much as in quiet breathing. In actual speaking situations, the ratio may rise as high as 10:1. This suggests that the way we control our exhalation could basically affect our rate of speaking. Those of us who have worked with stutterers or cerebral palsied or dysarthric patients are well aware of the relationship of respiration to rate.

When your respiration is affected by physical activity you will notice that your rate of speech is also affected. For example, after a game of tennis (or any other physical activity), your rate of speech is usually slowed down as you "spurt out" the words in your attempt to grab for breath. *Poor posture* can also affect your rate of speech. From your study of respiration (see pp. 347, 348) you have been made to realize the importance of using your posture to advantage. Not enough breath or poor control can result in (1) slow rate or (2) fast rate with a "staccato" sound as you grab for more breath.

Physical State of the Speaker

How well you are feeling and how much energy you have play an important role in your voice production, in general, and in your rate, in particular. Many pages ago in this book in the section on "Practice Sessions," we referred to the fact that on days when you are feeling well your voice production will reflect this physical state. Try to take note of what happens to your rate on days when you are ill or on those days following an illness. Even the fast talker slows down.

Diet is also very important. Don't be a perpetual "quick snack" eater. Snacks don't make for sustained energy, which is crucial to good health. Make no mistake about it, good health is basic to *good voice production and rate control.*

INTELLECTUAL ASPECTS

Mental Quickness—Understanding Content

Just "naturally" some people seem to be able to think faster and react faster (intellectually and/or emotionally) to a given situation. Earlier in this chapter we talked about the fact that this "pace of reaction" was the result of many things: your heredity, your environment, your personality, and even the kind of education you had. Reference to the game of charades (see p. 422) was our way of showing you how your physical, intellectual, and emotional pace are not necessarily linked to your IQ.

The slow, deliberate thinker usually has a slower rate of speech than the person who thinks and reacts more quickly. An understanding of what is being asked or said at the moment (the content) plays a vital role in this process of reaction and rate of speech. People need more (or less) time to mull over the ideas and/or words presented to them. They answer either with deliberation or spontaneity—slowly or quickly. "You needn't fly at me! I only asked you a simple question and you haven't answered me yet!" Does that sound familiar?

Phrasing for Rate Control

The meaning and emotional content of words (semantics) coupled with the two factors just discussed (mental quickness and understanding of content) complete our picture of the intellectual factors that influence your rate. Words have meanings and the meanings are understood (or misunderstood) and accepted (or rejected) by your listener. Have you ever had someone say to you, "Oh, but I didn't *mean* that. You misunderstood." Your reply, "No, I didn't misunderstand you. You *said* . . . ." If the discussion becomes heated, your rate of speech will undoubtedly be affected in direct proportion. Either your rate will increase and you will begin to speak shotgun fashion (words coming out a mile a minute), or your rate will decrease (depending on your personality) and you will begin to "bite out your words" through clenched teeth. Even your loudness will be affected.

Phrasing is another area directly linked to rate of speech. By a phrase we mean a group of words that presents a *complete idea*. Phrases are *not* determined by commas. We have often asked students, "Why did you pause at that point?" Their reply has been, "Because there's a comma." No! Consider the following sentence: *I have a blue, yellow, white, red, and green blouse.* There is no reason to pause after each comma. The commas are for grammatical purposes and for the eye. Take a look at the following.

> After I finish eating dinner, I'm going to the movies.
> 1. After I/ finish eating dinner I'm/going/to the movies.
> 2. After I finish eating dinner/ I'm going to the movies.

Version 2 would certainly be considered more meaningful phrasing. You might even say the sentence *without* a pause. Many speakers either over-phrase (pause too frequently) or underphrase (continue too long before a pause). Either pattern understandably affects your rate of speech. *Overphrasing slows down your rate* and *underphrasing speeds up your rate.*

Stress and Rate Control

You probably learned about the technique of *emphasis* from your oral reading or public speaking classes. Stress is a form of emphasis, and it involves using greater "force" on words, phrases, and even on complete sentences. However, in your attempt to use greater (or less) force neces-sarily you become involved with rate of speech. Greater force generally demands a slower rate; less force usually allows for a faster rate. We would like to repeat an exercise here, only *this* time try to *be aware* of how force is affected by rate. Try the following:

> *I* don't feel well today. (Not you, I)
> I *don't* feel well today. (Opposite of I *do*)
> I don't *feel* well today. (Physical discomfort)
> I don't feel *well* today. (I'm ill.)
> I don't feel well *today*. (Yesterday I was well.)

PSYCHOLOGICAL ASPECTS

Emotional State of the Speaker—Personality

It is practically impossible to separate the kind of *personality* you are from how you react emotionally in a given situation, so the two areas of personality and the emotional state of the speaker will be considered together with reference to rate control. Your personality determines how you will *behave* in an emotional setting. *Intellectually* you can manipulate your behavior, but it is difficult to control your *initial* emo-tional reaction. For example, you have just received what you consider to be an unfair grade from a teacher. Your initial reaction is one of *fury* ("I'm going to tell that teacher off!"), but intellectually you know that you will be far better off if you *calmly* discuss the grade with the teacher.

Whatever kind of personality you think you are (outgoing, with-drawn, introspective, reactionary, and so on) so goes your ability to interrelate. Your rate of speech is deeply involved with this interrelation-ship. Rate is an integral part of you as a person—as a personality. If you feel strongly about a situation, your rate of speech will be related not only to your feelings about that situation but also to *how you express those feelings—verbally*. Remember the shotgun delivery of speech ver-sus the slow, through-the-teeth rate of speech?

If you feel that you are on the extreme ends of the continuum of fast versus slow rate of speech, then take the time to consider the following sections so that you will acquire the necessary skill for *effective rate control.*

YOUR RATE PROFILE

Assessment

In order to judge if your rate of speaking is too fast or too slow for effective communication, a determination must first be made of the *number of words you speak per minute,* known as *wpm.* Then an evaluation of your rate can be intelligently made, goals set, and exercises recommended.

Start with *read* material. In the beginning of this chapter we said that in reading an average wpm was anywhere from 150–170. Usually your wpm for conversational speech is a little slower. Try the following:

1. Select a passage you can comfortably handle in terms of content and vocabulary. *Don't* read the box scores from yesterday's baseball games or chemistry formulas.
2. Set up your equipment: a clock with a second hand, a quiet room, and your material. It is helpful to record your reading for an auditory reaction to your rate profile. You are now ready to begin, but first, take a deep breath and *relax.*
3. Read your selection aloud at a comfortable speed for *one* minute. Repeat the reading *at least twice more.* Three times in all. You will now have *three* minutes of the *same* passage to evaluate.
4. Determine the *total* number of words you read during the *three* readings over a three-minute period. Divide the total number of words by *three* (the number of minutes). This will give you your average wpm.
5. For an estimate of your *conversational* speech (and this is a little more difficult to do), record a conversation with a friend for two or three minutes. Try to determine the number of words spoken during the alloted time period. Again, divide the total number of words by the total number of minutes and you will arrive at an average wpm. Now this total won't be *exactly* accurate because the conversational situation was somewhat structured and not entirely spontaneous. However, the recording will give you an approximation of wpm for conversational speech.

Evaluation

How did you do? Did you read much faster than the average wpm? Did you read much slower than the average wpm? Perhaps you were right on target. Or perhaps your reading wpm was slower than the average wpm and your conversational wpm was faster than the average wpm. Do you think that you have a problem? Whatever the outcome, before you judge yourself too harshly and decide that your rate problems are so unsurmountable that they barely deserve your consideration (much less your effort), remember that the numbers we quoted for wpm were *average*. Who is to say what is *average for you?*

Goals

Don't set any goals either for your wpm for reading or your wpm for conversation until you go back and reread "Factors that Influence Your Rate of Speech" (see p. 422). Remember that speech is highly individual. However, your goals should include (1) speech that is *intelligible* and (2) meaningful rate variation.

Exercises for the "Too Fast" Speaker

1. Use a tape recorder for this exercise. Write out two or three sentences or phrases that you use daily. Record this material as you would ordinarily say it. Repeat it, only this second time, *deliberately slow down your rate by saying the number one between each word of the material.* Let the number one represent one second between each of the words.

   I (one) am (one) going (one) out (one) to (one) lunch (one).
   The object is to take you to the extreme, slow end of the rate continuum; to slow you down as much as is physically possible; and to raise your level of awareness regarding the *differences* in the rate of speaking.

2. Repeat exercise 1, but this time do *not* say the number one between each word. However, do try to slow down a little, or at least try to *change* your pattern of rate. Try to get a *feel* about a difference in your rate of speaking—no matter what the difference. What we are attempting to do here is to *break through your old habitual pattern of rate.*

3. Turn to pp. 395–396. As you say the prescribed words and sentences, s-t-r-e-t-c-h the vowel sounds. Resonate them in the oral cavity. This demands more time, so this will help to *slow you down.* Your too-fast rate of speech will be affected by the prolongation of vowel sounds.

4. Take a closer look at your phrasing. Do you *underphrase?* Do you tend to go on and on before pausing either for meaning or for a breath? *Stop!* Review the communication situation: (a) note your audience; (b) the occasion, and (c) the emotional setting. Do

these factors tell you that a more relaxed, slower rate is the more appropriate?

5. Does everything sound alike in your speech? Do you stress every-thing? Does every idea sound equally important? Back off! Re-assess your stresses.

Exercises for the "Too Slow" Speaker

1. Use a tape recorder for this exercise. Write out two or three sen-tences or phrases that you use daily. Record this material as you would ordinarily say it. Repeat it, only this second time *deliber-ately speed up your rate*. Use the second hand on the clock. *Make yourself "beat the clock!"* If the sentence originally took you *six* seconds to say, repeat it in *three* seconds. The object is to take you to the extreme, fast end of the rate continuum; to speed you up as much as is physically possible; and to raise your level of aware-ness regarding the *differences* in the rate of speaking.

2. Turn to pp. 395–396. As you say the prescribed words and sen-tences, *do not prolong the vowels*. Rather, attempt to run the words and sentences together. Really *overassimilate*. Don't worry about your speech sounding a little sloppy. What we are trying to do here is to make you aware of the *differences* in rate of speaking and to help you to *break through* your old habitual pattern of rate through assimilation techniques.

3. Take a closer look at your *phrasing*. Do you overphrase? Do you tend to pause too frequently for either meaning or a breath? Re-view respiration (see pp. 353–354). Perhaps you are a clavicular breather. Perhaps you keep running out of breath and this slows you down.

4. Does everything sound alike in your speech? Do you emphasize the important words? Are there no high points in your delivery? Check your health. Check your energy. Check your interpersonal involve-ment. Reassess!

Summary

Before we conclude this section on voice, we would like to stress that your writers are not of the *Don't* school of voice improvement:

1. *Don't* scream or yell.
2. *Don't* use your voice too much.
3. *Don't* talk on the telephone.
4. *Don't* attend parties where there is a lot of ambient noise.

5. *Don't* go into smoke-filled rooms.
6. *Don't. Don't. Don't.*

We not only suggest, but we *urge* those of you with voice problems to *learn to use your voices effectively.* We do have our *Don'ts* concerning your voice improvement program and we hope these have been clearly stated throughout this section. We half-facetiously say that if people did not use their voices, there would be no voice problems.

A Final Word!

The mental twister "Which is more important, *what* is said or *how* it is said?" can be of real significance at this stage in your speech improvement program. We firmly believe that *what* is said is of paramount importance (in terms of the content of the message, the reasoning, the evidence submitted, and the ethical, personal, and psychological elements involved), but we also firmly believe that what is said can be more effective *if it is said with more meaning.* A parapharase of the adage "You cannot appreciate what you do not know" might appear as "You cannot meaningfully communicate what you do not understand." The skills involved with vocal quality, loudness, pitch, and rate must be concerned with this *understanding* and with *willingness* on your part to become personally involved with your speech.

We have stressed many times that in any speech improvement program, improvement begins on a highly mechanistic, or clinical, level. Then begins the hard work of transference, at which time you must work through loaded material, oral reading (the printed page), extemporaneous speaking, and finally spontaneous speech. It *can* and *will* happen!

Voice Analysis Form

(Terms defined according to this book)

Evaluations   *Comments*

Vocal quality

Laryngeal function

Breathy_____

Husky_____

Strident_____

Raspy_____

Throaty_____

Harsh_____

Adequate_____

Resonance

Thin_____

Hypernasal_____

Hyponasal_____

Assimilation nasality_____

Balanced_____

Pitch

Too-high range_____

Too-low range_____

Pitch patterns_____

Monotonous_____

Adequate_____

Other_____

Volume

Inadequate projection_____

Overprojection_____

Voice fading_____

Lack of meaningful variation_____

Adequate_____

Other_____

Rate

Too rapid_____

Too slow_____

Lack of meaningful variation_____

Adequate_____

Other_____

Laryngological Examination Form

Organization Heading

_____

_____

_____

_____

(date)

To the Laryngologist:
examination of

_____

(name)

_____

(address)

_____

(age)   (tele.)

as part of a speech re-education program. The speech examination
revealed:

_____

Thank you for your cooperation.

_____

Speech Therapist

Nasal Examination

Are the nasal passages normal in size and shape? _____

Are there any deviations or obstructions in the nasal passage? _____

Is there any congestion in the nasal passage or sinuses? _____

Where? _____

Is there a postnasal drip? _____

To what extent has the postnasal drip influenced other areas? _____

_____

Larnyngological Examination

Is the palate unusually high or narrow? _____

Is the uvula normal in size and shape? _____

Are the sensory motor abilities of the soft palate normal? _____

Is the epiglottis abnormally long? _____

Are any of the areas of the pharynx inflamed? _____

Are the vocal cords normally developed? _____

Are the vocal cords abnormally thick? _____

Is there complete closure of the vocal cords or arytenoids? _____

Are there nodes on the vocal cords? _____

Is there mucous on the vocal cords? _____

Are the vocal cords inflamed? _____

Recommendation for treatment: _____

Prognosis: _____

Would corrective speech work be harmful at this time? _____
If so, how long should work be postponed? _____
Have you communicated your findings to the patient or the parent? ____
Comments: _____

_____

_____

(examiner)

Voice Bibliography

BOONE, DANIEL. *The Voice and Voice Therapy*. Englewood Cliffs, N.J.: Prentice-Hall, Inc., 1971.

BRODNITZ, FRIEDRICH. *Vocal Rehabilitation*. 3rd ed. Rochester, Minn.: American Academy of Ophthalogy and Otolaryngology, 1965.

EISENSON, JON. *Voice and Diction*. 3rd ed. New York: Macmillan Publishing Co., Inc., 1974.

FAIRBANKS, GRANT. *Voice and Articulation Drillbook*. 2nd ed. New York: Van Nostrand Reinhold Company, 1953.

FISHER, HILDA. *Improving Voice and Articulation*. 2nd ed. Boston: Houghton Mifflin Company, 1975.

GREENE, MARGARET. *The Voice and Its Disorders*. 3rd ed. New York: Pitman Publishing Corporation, 1972.

MOORE, PAUL C. *Organic Voice Disorders*. Foundations of Speech Pathology Series. Englewood Cliffs, N.J.: Prentice-Hall, Inc., 1971.

MOSES, PAUL J., M.D. *The Voice of Neurosis*. New York: Grune & Stratton, Inc., 1954.

MURPHY, ALBERT T. *Functional Voice Disorders*. Foundations of Speech Pathology Series. Englewood Cliffs, N.J.: Prentice-Hall, Inc., 1964.

RUSSELL, G. O. *Speech and Voice*. New York: Macmillan Publishing Co., Inc., 1931.

TRAVIS, LEE EDWARD. (ed.) *Handbook of Speech Pathology and Audiology*. Englewood Cliffs, N.J.: Appleton-Century Crofts, 1971.

WILSON, KENNETH D. *Voice Problems of Children*. Baltimore: The Williams & Wilkins Company, 1972.

Related Reading

ARISTOTLE. *Rhetoric*. Trans. by Lane Cooper. Englewood Cliffs, N.J.: Appleton-Century-Crofts, 1932.

BARBARA, DOMINIC. *Your Speech Reveals Your Personality*. Springfield, Ill.: Charles C. Thomas, 1957.

CALNAN, J. S. "Movements of the Soft Palate." *British Journal of Plastic Surgery*, 5 (1953) 286.

DENES, P. B., and E. N. PINSON. *The Speech Chain: The Physics and Biology of Spoken Language*. Whippany, N.J.: Bell Telephone Laboratories, 1963.

DiMICHAEL, ELEANOR M. "A Study of the Treatment of Pronunciatio by the Ancients." Master's M.A. thesis, Louisiana State University, 1945.

EISENBERG, ABNE M. *Living Communication*. Englewood Cliffs, N.J.: Prentice-Hall, Inc., 1975.

GRAY, GILES WILKESON, and CLAUDE MERTON WISE. *The Bases of Speech*. 3rd ed. New York: Harper & Row, Publishers, 1959.

GREENE, MARGARET. *Disorders of Voice*, The Bobbs-Merrill Studies in Communicative Disorders, Harvey Halpern (Ed.). Indianapolis: Bobbs-Merrill Company, Inc., 1971.

HARRISON, RANDALL P. *Beyond Words*. Englewood Cliffs, N.J.: Prentice-Hall, Inc., 1974.

JACOBSON, E. *Progressive Relaxation*. 2nd ed. Chicago: University of Chicago Press, 1951.

MOORE, PAUL C., and H. VON LEDEN. "Dynamic Variations of the Vibratory Pattern in the Normal Larynx." *Fola Phoniatrica*, 10 (1958).

NEGUS, V. E. *Comparative Anatomy and Physiology of the Larynx*. New York: Hafner Press, 1962.

NEGUS, V. E. *The Biology of Respiration*. Baltimore: The Williams & Wilkins Company, 1965.

TIMCKE, R., H. VON LEDEN, and PAUL MOORE. "Laryngeal Vibrations: Measurement of the Glottal Wave." *American Medical Association Archives of Otolaryngology*, 68 (July 1958).

Voice: Films

Board of Education, New York, N.Y., *Bureau for Speech Improvement,* John E. Lent, Director. "Voice Therapy," filmstrip and cassette; in three parts: (1) classification and diagnosis; (2) basic therapy techniques; and (3) specific therapy techniques. Prepared for teachers on the elementary school level.

PAUL C. MOORE and H. VON LEDEN, the film, "The Larynx and Voice: The Function of the Normal Larynx," 1957.

PAUL C. MOORE and H. VON LEDEN, the film, "The Larynx and Voice: Physiology of the Larynx Under Daily Stress." Laryngeal Research Laboratory, William and Harriet Gould Foundation, Northwestern University, Chicago, Illinois, 1961.

Index

Boldfaced numbers refer to definitions or main entries; italics to illustrations.